Acting with the Voice

THE ART OF RECORDING BOOKS

Acting with the Voice

THE ART OF RECORDING BOOKS

ROBERT BLUMENFELD

LIMELIGHT EDITIONS • NEW YORK

First Limelight Edition April 2004

Published in the United States by
Proscenium Publishers, Inc., New York

Interior design by Rachel Reiss

Manufactured in the United States of America

LIBRARY OF CONGRESS CATALOGING-IN-PUBLICATION DATA

Blumenfeld, Robert.
Acting with the voice: the art of recording books / [edited by]
Robert Blumenfeld.-- 1st limelight ed.
p. cm.
Includes bibliographical references.
ISBN 0-87910-301-9 (pbk.)
1. Acting. 2. Voice culture. 3. Audiobooks. I. Title.

PN2071.S65B58 2004
792.02'8--dc22

2004002788

For my dear brothers, Richard H. Blumenfeld and Donald S. Blumenfeld-Jones, with love and my warmest thanks for their encouragement and support.

Contents

List of Illustrative Texts and Practice Exercises

Acknowledgments

My parents, Max David Blumenfeld (1911–1994) and Ruth Blumenfeld, encouraged my interests in literature and in languages. This book would never have been written without their love and support, for which I am always deeply grateful. My father, a chemist and bacteriologist, was not only gifted intellectually, but was a true humanitarian, who won several awards for his volunteer services to the community in Princeton, NJ. Many thanks for their unfailing love and support to my sister-in-law Corbeau Blumenfeld-Jones, and to my nephew and niece Benjamin and Rebecca Blumenfeld-Jones. My extended family has always been supportive as well, especially my mother's sister, whom we all miss, the sweet and brilliant Bertha Friedman (1913–2001); my mother's brother Seymour Korn; my dear, wonderful aunt, his wife Shirley Korn (1919–2004); and my cousins Rita and Bill Korn, and I thank them all. I owe a very special thanks to Mr. David Rapkin for much helpful information on and insights into the business of book recording. Many thanks to my friend, that excellent actor, Mr. John Guerrasio, for a great deal of helpful information from London, where, among many other activities, he has recorded books. I give special thanks to the erudite Anthony Henderson, who not only hired me to do my first Talking Book (a biography of Napoleon for young adults) at the American Foundation for the Blind, but whose extraordinary breadth and depth of knowledge, linguistic and otherwise, has been incredibly helpful over the years to me and everyone else at the AFB. To Antonio Harrison, Manager of the Talking Book Studios, one of the gentlest, kindest, most thoughtful and levelheaded, not to say the most tireless, of men, I also owe very special thanks for his unfailing support. I acknowledge the contributions of and give thanks for their thorough, indefatigable work to the monitors/sound engineers of Talking Books, and I especially want to thank the always helpful Bruce Kitovich for interesting and informative discussions on book recording; and expert in old-time radio, and in the difficulties of the English language, Derek Tague, for helpful suggestions and for information about the vagaries of English pronunciation. Great thanks as well to my fellow readers L. J. Ganser, Richard Davidson, Steven Crossley (for helpful information about the book recording business in England), and to Gordon Gould, for the information they have supplied; and special thanks to my fellow reader Peter Johnson, who is also a copyright lawyer, for very helpful legal and literary advice. I thank Ed Bosch, former Talking Books monitor, and Iris Robinson, Talking Books subscriber, for helpful discussions; and Ann Burdick, Executive Assistant/House Counsel with AFTRA, for information about union contracts and procedures. Very special thanks to my friends Tom Smith for permission to use two poems from *Waiting on Pentecost* (Delhi, NY: Birch Brook Press, 1999); Stephanie Cowell for permission to use excerpts from her novels *The Physician of London: A Novel* (New York: W. W. Norton, 1995) and *The Players: A Novel of the Young Shakespeare* (New York: W. W. Norton, 1997); and Russell O'Neal Clay for permission to use a poem from *From Ghost Through Bone to Man: New and Selected Poems 1994–1996* (New York: West End Poetry Press, 1996). Many thanks to copy editor Nina Maynard for all her help, and to graphic designer Rachel Reiss, who has done such a beautiful job of designing this book. And, finally, heartfelt gratitude to my always warmly supportive friend and publisher, the knowledgeable, erudite Mel Zerman, his very kind associate, Jenna Young, and friendly, helpful assistant, Dane Williams.

FOREWORD

The Art and the Business of Recording Books

Why go into the book recording business as an actor? The short, obvious answer is that it expands the possibilities for work. It is another way to earn at least part of your living. To all the usual areas of employment for the professional actor—film, television, stage, and radio and television commercials—you may add book recording.

Recording books is a skill, a craft and an art. And recording books professionally is work that can only be done by actors. Who but an actor, or an author who can also act (there are authors who record their own books), can breathe life into a text? Don't we spend our working lives creating characters, clothing them fully, and portraying them in all their psychological complexity? The same instincts, the same skills, the same mastery, are prerequisites for playing characters vocally, for acting with the voice. You bring your art, your training, your education, your mind, and your heart to your individual interpretation of a text. The chapters on general reading technique and on reading fiction, plays, poetry and nonfiction are devoted to technical skills, to how to interpret texts, and read them aloud. And when you record a book you get to play a lot of characters. You don't even have to look the part. You will have the pleasure of playing roles for which you may be the wrong physical type, and in which as a consequence you would never be cast in a film or stage adaptation. This enjoyable experience expands your abilities and your range enormously.

The skills you need to acquire and the craft of recording are described in Chapter Three: Microphone and General Recording Techniques. These techniques are of paramount importance, because, although you will be sitting as motionless as possible in a recording studio with headphones on and in front of a microphone, you still have to use all your vocal acting skills to give the impression of action taking place.

There is a huge market for recorded books on cassette tape and on CD. People listen at home and in their cars to classic and contemporary fiction and nonfiction read by professional actors, and in the noncommercial sector there is a large amount of both volunteer and paid recording done for the blind by various private and public organizations. For example, every year the Talking Books department of the American Foundation for the Blind in New York City and similar organizations such as the American Printing House for the Blind in Louisville, KY and Talking Books Denver (all three under the auspices of the National Library Service [NLS]), make hundreds of recordings, which are available, along with the special cassette player required for listening to them, by free subscription to blind readers and others with disabilities.

Should you wish to volunteer your services, you will find many organizations, such as the Lighthouse for the Blind and the Jewish Braille Institute, that would be very happy to use them. Some volunteers are professional actors, who give their time for charitable purposes. It is a good idea for any actor wishing to record books professionally to volunteer, both to gain experience and to build up a resume. You may also, perhaps, be able to obtain some or parts of your recordings, which could form the basis of a demo tape or CD; see page 4 for more on the subject of demos.

If you want to pursue commercial book recording, don't be misled: This is a very tough field to get into, and it will take a lot of determination, hard work and perseverance. You will find full scope, however, for your imagination and your creativity, when you get a good book to record. And do get into the habit of saying "when," and not "if."

A few words about the illustrative practice exercise texts I have chosen: First of all, I have picked them for variety, so that you have lots of different kinds of things to practice.

They are taken mostly from eighteenth-, nineteenth- and early twentieth-century authors, and are often more difficult to read aloud than some contemporary fiction, but they sound wonderful when they are read aloud, because they are so dramatic and so beautifully written. Indeed, almost all great writing, classic or contemporary, sounds marvelous when read aloud, and it is easier to read great writing aloud than it is to read bad writing. I feel that if you can master reading these classic texts, certain contemporary texts you may be asked to record will be easier, particularly the pulp fiction and nonfiction. These excerpts from classic writings show a feeling for language and a breadth of vocabulary, which are almost gone from a great deal of contemporary writing, and completely gone from pulp.

Unfortunately, much contemporary fiction and nonfiction comes under the heading of pulp, for the mass market, and is rather lackluster, ephemeral and shallow. Nevertheless, there are many wonderful mid- to late-twentieth-century and twenty-first century British and American writers, and wonderful authors from all cultures and of all nationalities, whose works have been splendidly translated into English. Such extraordinary authors as Martin and Kingsley Amis, Nadine Gordimer, John le Carré, Isaac Bashevis Singer, Simon Winchester, Alain de Botton, Stephanie Cowell, Mark Kurlansky, P. D. James, Naguib Mahfouz, Michel Tournier, Amin Maalouf, Bernard Malamud, Saul Bellow, P. G. Wodehouse, Evelyn Waugh, F. Scott Fitzgerald, Ernest Hemingway, and William Faulkner developed their own individual styles of writing, tell the most engrossing, riveting stories, and have a marvelous feeling for language. Very much worth reading, too, are such great works as the admirable books of the Proust scholar, expert and biographer William Carter, and of biographer Graham Robb, whose superb lives of Victor Hugo, Honoré de Balzac and Arthur Rimbaud are absolutely fascinating. There are not a few authors whom one could add to the list of excellent contemporary writers of nonfiction.

It is a very good idea to listen to commercially available recordings, in order to have some notion of both the nature and quality of the recordings and the kinds of voices and readings producers want. Many commercial book recordings are of abridged versions, edited by the production houses and/or publishers who release them, but there are also a considerable number of unabridged recordings available, such as those of classic works of fiction by Naxos AudioBooks. Listen, as well, to the Caedmon recordings of well-known actors reading stories and poems—Basil Rathbone reading Edgar Allan Poe, to take one example; and of authors such as Lorraine Hansberry, Dylan Thomas and Robert Frost reading their own work. And be sure to listen to Ruth Draper's monologues: they are superb examples of how to record material so that it comes vividly alive visually as well as aurally. Some recordings are done by stars or by the authors of the books themselves, but most recordings are made by less well-known working actors, and they, too, can be absolutely riveting when done by a master craftsperson.

Knowledge of literature, a love for books and for language, and a passion for telling stories, are essential. But then, if you didn't have these attributes you would probably not be interested in getting into this kind of work. My own love of books dates from my earliest years. My parents read to me and to my two brothers from the time we were very small children. The first book I can remember is a Golden Book entitled *Peter and the Wolf*, which I loved. I can still recall its first words: "Way up north in Russia..." Apparently I memorized it, and I am told that when I was three I used to recite it, turning the pages at the right places, as I had seen my father or mother do. I went on to tell stories at school assemblies when I was still in elementary school. From there to recording books was but a short leap of about forty-four years. I have been recording Talking Books for the American Foundation for the Blind, and learning endlessly from the books I record, for about eighteen years now, and I have done more than 280 of them.

During those forty-four years I became an actor, first in college and then professionally. Since I also had an ability to imitate and analyze accents and an academic background in languages, with degrees in French language and literature, it was equally natural that I become a dialect coach. Acting and a facility with accents and languages have proved most useful in recording books, both fiction and nonfiction.

Each book recording experience is unique, in a sense, because each requires one to learn the art of book recording all over again, just as each role an actor plays involves learning to act all over again, in that it requires learning an entirely new set of responses. But the techniques, methods and craft involved in interpreting a role and recording, and the approach to interpretation, remain the same.

I hope this book will help actors and volunteers develop the techniques necessary for practicing the art of reading aloud. And I hope, too, that the process of learning and of performing will be enjoyable and inspiring. I wish you all the best!

HOW TO USE THIS BOOK

A Note About the Phonetic Symbols and the Illustrative Texts

Throughout the book I have transcribed various pronunciations phonetically. The system I have used seemed to me logical for English speakers: For instance, for the Greek mythological name Thyestes, I have used the transcription "thigh ESS teez." Stressed syllables are always in capital letters. A colon [:] after a vowel indicates that the vowel is long; for example "a:" indicates the sound of "a" in the word *father*. The only International Phonetic Alphabet (IPA) symbol I have used consistently throughout is the one for the schwa [ə], which is the weak vowel heard in the word "the" when it occurs before a consonant. The symbol "æ" stands for the sound of "a" in *that*. The symbol "é" is used in French transcriptions to indicate the pronunciation of a closed "e" vowel, the exact sound of which does not exist in English. The symbol "e" stands for the vowel in *met;* I have sometimes used the digraph "eh" to indicate that sound. I have sometimes used "eye" to stand for the diphthong in "I" [IPA symbol "ai"]. The italicized letters *"M"* or *"N"* mean that the preceding vowel is nasalized. The digraph "oh" stands for the long diphthong in the word *home*. Everything else should be self-explanatory.

You will find illustrative texts in Chapters One, Two, and Five through Nine, which are meant as practice exercises, some short, some quite long. They each are followed by a section called Notes, Comments, and Hints, which gives you information on the books from which the texts are taken, as well as background material which may help you in interpreting the texts and in putting them into a historical, literary and social context, and pointers on how to prepare and read them. I encourage you to find your own individual way of reading the texts. The background material is meant to show you the kind of research you have to do when preparing texts, and the hints are intended to show you the sort of decisions you have to make about your performance, whether consciously and calculatingly, or unconsciously and spontaneously. Spontaneity, which is organic and arises directly out of the situation and the moment, as it does in a stage play or a film, may yield some very happy results. The longer exercises are intended to help you develop skill in sustaining a narrative, as well as in creating and sustaining characters, and in playing actions vocally; so try to read them all the way through without stopping.

To practice the texts, I suggest that you record them and then listen to yourself. Sit quite still, as you would in a recording studio, with the text resting comfortably in front of you. You must develop the discipline of acting only with your voice. If you are recording a work of fiction, even though you will feel the emotions of a character in your body, and have the impulse to do something physical, you are obliged to remain still.

When you listen to the playback, listen especially to hear if you have done what you set out to do. Be self-critical, but not self-deprecating. Record the texts as many times as you need to in order to train yourself to be able to do what you plan to do when preparing the text.

INTRODUCTION

Getting Started in the Book Recording Business

There are three categories of people who record books for commercial release: authors who record their own books, celebrities, and working actors. The latter usually have to audition, although, partly on the basis of previous recordings they have done for a particular director or publishing house, they may be asked to do a book without having auditioned. Some publishing houses have their own in-house recording studios and directors. Others use independent contractors to direct recordings, and rent studio space. Some companies do a combination of the two.

If you are serious about recording books commercially, you should become a member of the American Federation of Television and Radio Artists (AFTRA), the union that covers book-recording artists in the US, and regulates both minimum payment scales and working conditions. Membership involves paying an initiation fee and annual dues, but the benefits are enormous, because your employer not only pays you to record the book, but also pays a percentage based on your earnings into the union's Health and Retirement Fund. After a certain number of years as a union member you will be vested for a pension, which you can either collect early, beginning at age 55, or when you turn 65.

If you earn a stipulated amount per annum, you qualify for health insurance at a minimum premium, for yourself and your dependants. The costs of providing free insurance proved prohibitive, hence the institution of a premium for union members earning that specified amount (which has changed over the years). Nevertheless, if you collect a pension beginning at age 65, you will, as things stand currently, receive free health insurance. If you chose to collect your pension early, you would have to pay for insurance, until you reach 65. Contact the union for further information at (212) 532-0800 in New York or (323) 634-8100 in Los Angeles, or go to their web site: www.aftra.org.

Although the book-recording business in the US is not as yet completely unionized, in a large center of the industry, such as New York, the major publishing houses and recorded book companies do use union actors pretty much exclusively, on a book-by-book or project-to-project basis. They are not signatories to AFTRA's aptly named "National Code of Fair Practice for Sound Recordings," because there is no such thing as a general signatory to the code, as there is, say, between Actors' Equity Association and producers' organizations for Broadway and Off-Broadway contracts, but the contracts producers sign with union actors for individual recordings are union contracts that are regulated by the code.

Some public service organizations, such as the American Foundation for the Blind, record books under collective bargaining agreements made with the union; these organizations also contribute to the union's Health and Retirement Fund. And, of course, there are organizations that use volunteers and therefore require no contracts.

What You Need to Get Started

You may possibly find some listings or information about book-recording jobs in *Backstage* and *Show Business*, the excellent theatrical trade papers published in New York, and for information on theater and show business generally you can go to their web sites, and that of *Variety*, the trade paper published in California. All the unions have their own web sites as well, and they are a mine of useful information.

Before you begin to look for work and for an agent who might submit you for jobs, you need an up-to-date resume and a demo CD. The usual actors' headshots are not required in the book-recording business.

The Resume

Your actor's resume can be used when you apply for book-recording jobs, but it is not nearly as important as a good demo CD or tape. This is especially true

ROBERT BLUMENFELD

Phone: Agent:
E-mail: AFTRA/SAG/AEA Voice: Baritone

BOOK RECORDING

Eighteen years with Talking Books at the American Foundation for the Blind, more than 280 books recorded

A SAMPLE LIST (Complete list and Actor's Resume available on request)

Fiction

The Complete Sherlock Holmes (Sir Arthur Conan Doyle; 4 novels; 56 short stories)
The Stories of Bernard Malamud (Bernard Malamud)
The Count of Monte Cristo (Alexandre Dumas' great epic)
The Hunchback of Notre Dame (Victor Hugo's classic novel)
The Portable Chekhov (stories, letters, essays, plays)
Beach Music (Pat Conroy)
Palace of Desire (Naguib Mahfouz)
Cousin Bette; Old Goriot (2 novels by Honoré de Balzac)
The Master and Margarita (Mikhail Bulgakov)
The Isaac Leib Peretz Reader

Nonfiction

Same-Sex Unions in Premodern Europe (John Boswell) (knowledge of the phonetic systems of 23 languages required)
The Norton Book of Travel (excerpts from travel literature through the ages)
The Drowned and the Saved (Primo Levi)
The Classical Greeks (Michael Grant)
Oxford History of the French Revolution (William Doyle)
A Year in Provence (Peter Mayle)
The Complete Essays of Montaigne (trans. Donald M. Frame)
Balzac (Graham Robb)
Hitler's Willing Executioners (Daniel Jonah Goldhagen)
Cromwell The Lord Protector (Antonia Fraser)
Lives of the Great Composers (Harold Schoenberg)
The Joys of Yiddish (Leo Rosten)
The Crusades Through Arab Eyes (Amin Maalouf)

EDUCATION, SPECIAL AWARDS, SKILLS

1999 Alexander Scourby Talking Book Narrator of the Year in the Fiction category
1997 Canadian National Institute for the Blind Torgi Award, Talking Book of the Year Fiction Award for Pat Conroy's *Beach Music*

Speech: Liz Smith **Acting:** Uta Hagen, Alice Spivak, Bill Hickey

B.A., Rutgers University; M.A., Columbia University (French Language and Literature); Ph.D. courses, Rutgers University (Comparative Literature)

LANGUAGES: FLUENT French, German, Italian; some Russian, Spanish, Yiddish

NUMEROUS DIALECTS, including British Isles and Commonwealth, Europe, North America, Africa, Asia

AUTHOR: *Accents: A Manual for Actors* (Limelight, 1998; Revised and Expanded Edition, 2002)

for someone starting out, because a resume geared to book recording can only be compiled when you have had some experience in the field. A resume should be no more than one page long. You will notice how this sample book-recording resume of my own differs from the general actor's resume with which you are familiar.

The Demo Tape or CD

A demo (demonstration) tape or CD should be between three and five minutes in length. It should demonstrate all your skills in segments of no more than twenty to thirty seconds each: narration, dialogue, accents, character voices. Because it should be professional, you may have to rent a sound studio and hire a sound engineer. Expect to spend at least several hundred dollars for the recording session and for having copies of the tapes or CDs made. There are any number of sound studios that also have their own sound engineers who will work with you. Look in the Yellow Pages for listings and shop around for the best deal.

Once you have done a certain amount of recording, request copies of your recordings from producers, before they are even released commercially, and compile a new demo tape with excerpts from your professional work. This is a more impressive demonstration of your skills and talents, and should supersede the specially prepared studio recording that you need to get started.

Directors will usually accept demo tapes or CDs from any source, whether agents' submissions, or directly from an actor. If you send a demo directly, enclose a covering letter explaining whether the tape is sent entirely on your own initiative, or by invitation from a publisher (if the director himself has requested the demo he or she will hardly need such a reminder, but write a cordial letter anyway), or on the advice or recommendation of a third party.

Getting an Agent

Although it is not always strictly necessary in the book-recording business, as it is in commercials and for Broadway productions, it is a good idea to have an agent who can receive information on recording projects, and then submit you for them.

As the cover of the widely available *Ross Reports: USA Talent Directory*, a

Back Stage/Back Stage West publication, released monthly, informs us, it is "A Nationwide Guide to Agents and Casting Directors," and contains complete updated listings of talent and voice-over agents, as well as information on many other areas of show business. For further information contact them at 770 Broadway, New York, NY 10003; telephone (646) 654-5730.

Many agents listed do not want actors either to call them or drop by their offices, but most will accept resumes and demo tapes or CDs by mail. You may follow up the mailing with a phone call several days after you have sent it, to make sure it has arrived. You will usually speak only to the agent's secretary. Be very professional and courteous in your approach. It is perhaps unnecessary to say this, but being aggressive or belligerent in any way will only earn you the opprobrium of the agent, who will then not want to work with you.

One of the best ways to get an agent is through a personal recommendation by one of the agent's clients or through a professional friend or acquaintance, who should usually be a director or a producer. A fellow performer who is signed or freelances regularly with an agent might be asked for a recommendation. However, it is a very chancy thing for one performer to recommend another, since it reflects on the professionalism of the person giving the recommendation. Never ask anyone to recommend you unless the person knows your work. Similarly, if you are asked to give a recommendation, never do so unless you know that person's work. Ask to hear the demo if you are unfamiliar with your colleague's skills.

You must bear in mind that most agents won't even want to see you unless you are a member of one of the performing arts unions: Actors' Equity Association (AEA), Screen Actors Guild (SAG), or AFTRA. If you want to do voice-overs and radio commercials as well as books, you simply must be a union member. And if you don't want to do voice-overs as well as books, an agent will probably not want to represent you. After all, they are in business, and to stay in business they need to make money, which they get in the form of commissions. And your chances of an agent sending you for a job are lower if you do not have the experience to be in a union. Most important, talent agents are franchised by the unions, and generally have to deal with union members; although there may be room for non-union actors, from the agent's point of view you are a long shot, and perhaps one not worth taking. It is up to you to convince the agent that you are worth his or her taking you on as a client, whether signed or on a freelance basis.

Technically, the agent is working for you, not you for them, but in practice it often feels the other way around. Don't be intimidated by agents. And don't be discouraged by what I have said. If you really want to do this work, pursue it, and do not be dissuaded.

The Casting Process

Casting is a complex process. There are often several people who make the final casting decision, or there may be only one: Some best-selling authors, for instance, have a clause in their contracts with their publishers giving the author the right to make a final casting decision. In practice, however, authors often prefer to leave the casting decision to someone in the publishing house. Usually a director, whether independent and hired for the particular project, or in-house, makes the decision in concert with the publishing executive in charge of the book-recording program or department. The process involves marketing, as well as artistic, considerations. It is important from the producer's and director's point of view to have a reader who is appropriate in the mind of the listening public to the particular kind of material being recorded, even in the case of celebrities. For instance, John le Carré is highly adept at reading his own material, which he does very dramatically, and one associates him with his readings, so that one would scarcely want to hear anyone else. "If the publisher says, 'Get me Bruce Willis, or Paul Newman,' the director is more than happy to comply with the request," to quote David Rapkin, a noted independent producer/director who has directed recorded books for Random House Audio Publishing, HighBridge Audio, and Putnam Berkeley Audio.

There are three types of auditions in the commercial book recording business, and much depends on who is making the final casting decision:

1. The most common type is when a working actor, who has been given "sides" (selected pages) to prepare, arrives in a waiting area, called the green room, and signs in for the audition. The actor will be called into the studio to record the pages in the order of signing in. He or she may have been submitted by an agent, or have been asked by a director or publisher to audition.

2. Less common is a request by the director for a demo tape or CD, which an actor has been asked to submit either on her or his own, or through the actor's agent. This is the actor's own general demo, and may have nothing specific to do with the material to be recorded. The director will be listening to it for voice quality, and assessing the actor's delivery of the material.

3. An actor's agent receives sides from the book to be recorded. The actor, often called the "talent" by people who do the casting, records them on tape at the agent's office in a small recording studio, or at home, if condi-

tions are professional enough to permit that. The agent then sends the tape to the director or to the appropriate person at the publishing company. If the author of the book to be recorded has the final casting decision, the demo tape will be passed on to the author, unless the writer prefers to leave the decision to the publishing house.

Auditions: What a Director Expects

Rule Number One: Be on time for your audition. In fact, be early, so that you can relax and go over the material. One of the worst things you can do to yourself, aside from being late, is to rush in at the last minute flushed and out of breath. Being late or running in on time, but unprepared, are both highly unprofessional. First impressions count, and if you are perceived immediately as unprofessional, you had better do the best reading in the world, or forget being cast.

If you are auditioning for a commercial book-recording house you will hopefully receive the text well ahead of time, at least some days in advance of your audition. This will give you ample time to prepare it. Feel free to write useful notes in the margins of the text. Underline words you wish to stress and make any other marks that are meaningful to you, such as up or down arrows to indicate inflection or intonation.

If you have dialogue to read, you will want to make such phrases as "she said" or "he said" parenthetical by lowering the pitch of your voice slightly when you say them. Any character voices you do should be as simple as possible, and by all means do an accent, if one is required, to demonstrate this valuable skill. The person auditioning you is looking for fluency and fluidity, ease of reading, and a sense of style, as well as a feeling that you are talking to someone rather than pontificating, declaiming, reciting or orating.

Even when casting celebrities, directors look for someone with a set of skills that are suitable for the particular project. For a book about the Middle East, the director will want someone who can pronounce the Arabic and Hebrew names and phrases that are inevitable in such a book in an authentic fashion. For a work of fiction with characters requiring work with accents, the director wants to make sure that the actor can do them. If there are foreign words and phrases, can the actor handle them?

To summarize: The director or casting person looks for two things: 1) professionalism, that is, courteous, professional, businesslike behavior at the casting session; and 2) a professional reading, that is, one which flows smoothly and shows that the actor is capable of flexibility, variety and expressiveness.

The Recording Session: What a Director Expects

Once you are cast you will be given the material to be recorded, either directly, or through your agent. Schedules will be arranged. A director expects, first of all, that you will be on time, or even early, for the recording session, and that you will be rested and in good vocal shape. All of this is very important because, whether the studio has been rented for a particular recording or is one belonging to the publishing company, time means money spent.

You will have studied and prepared the material as thoroughly as possible. You will have had to do most of your rehearsing at home, on your own unpaid time. Before the recording session actually begins, the director will answer any questions you have as to both the material and the way the recording session is to be conducted. See Chapter Three: Microphone and General Recording Techniques for more on this subject, and for information on how the recording session works and on how directors and actors work together.

Publishers of Recorded Books in the USA

For a complete list of audiobook publishers you can go to the Audio Publishers Association web site: www.audiopub.org, which is useful for general information about the book-recording industry.

R. K. Bowker publishes the annually updated *Words on Cassette,* one of the major reference works for the book-recording business; in it you can find lists of all the publishers and distributors of audio material, as well as lists of available recorded books, and much more besides. Visit their useful and informative web site at www.bowker.com/bowkerWeb/. You may order the book directly from them.

Filled with reviews of new releases, *AudioFile Magazine* is a major organ of the industry, and a major source of information. It is available on line, by subscription, and in stores. AudioFile also publishes an annual *Audiobook Reference Guide,* which lists publishers, distributors, producers, manufacturers and talent; each of these categories can be accessed on their web site: www.audiofilemagazine.com, which covers a wide range of information about the industry.

Listed below are some of the major publishers of recorded books in the United States. You can contact them to find out their requirements: whether they audition actors who contact them, and/or listen to demo CDs and tapes, which they might accept by mail from individual actors, or whether they work only through agents; and any other information you wish. I have not listed the names of personnel, such as casting directors, since they tend to change.

Audio Renaissance
175 Fifth Avenue
New York, NY 10010
Phone: (212) 674-5151; Fax: (917) 534-0989
E-mail: audio@hbpub.com
Web address: No listing

Bantam Doubleday Dell Audio Publishing
1540 Broadway, 15th Floor
New York, NY 10036
Phone: (212) 792-9489; Fax: (212) 782-9600
Web address: www.randomhouse.com/audio

BBC Audiobooks America
PO Box 1450
Hampton, NH 03843-1450
Phone: (603) 926-8744
E-mail: customerservice@bbcaudiobooksamerica.com
Web address: www.bbcaudiobooksamerica.com

Blackstone Audio
PO Box 969
Ashland, OR 97520
Phone: (541) 482-9239; Fax: (541) 482-9294
E-mail: black@blackstoneaudio.com
Web address: www.blackstoneaudio.com

Brilliance Audio
1704 Eaton Drive
PO Box 887
Grand Haven, MI 49417
Phone: (616) 846-5256; Fax: (616) 846-0630
E-mail: sales@brillianceaudio.com
Web address: www.brillianceaudio.com

HarperCollins Publishers
10 East 53rd Street
New York, NY 10022
Phone: (212) 207-6805; Fax: (212) 6978
Web address: www.harperaudio.com

HighBridge Audio
1000 Westgate Drive
St. Paul, MN 55114
Phone (General Business): (800) 755-8532; Fax: (651) 659-4495
E-mail: highbridgeaudio@rivertrade.com
Web address: www.highbridgeaudio.com

Naxos AudioBooks
Note: Classic fiction is one of their specialties.
Cambridge House, Suite 7
Williamsville, TN 14221
Phone: (716) 634-3215; Fax: (716) 634-3051
E-mail: inquiries@naxosusa.com
Web address: www.naxosaudiobooks.com

New Millennium Entertainment
301 North Canon Drive, Suite 214
Beverly Hills, CA 90210
Phone: (310) 273-7722; Fax: (310) 273-7755
Web address: No listing

Penguin Audiobooks
375 Hudson Street, 4th Floor
New York, NY 10014
Phone: (212) 366-2000; Fax: (212) 366-2643
E-mail: info@audiobooks.org
Web address: www.penguinputnam.com

Putnam Berkeley Audio
375 Hudson Street, 4th Floor
New York, NY 10014
Phone: (212) 366-2000; Fax: (212) 366-2643
E-mail: info@audiobooks.org
Web address: www.penguinputnam.com

Random House Audio Publishing
1540 Broadway, 15th Floor
New York, NY 10036
Phone: (212) 782-9000; Fax: (212) 782-9484
E-mail: audio@randomhouse.com
Web address: www.randomhouse.com

Recorded Books, Inc.
270 Skipjack Road
Prince Frederick, MD 20678
Phone (General Business): (800) 638-1304;
Fax: (410) 535-5499
E-mail: recordedbooks@recordedbooks.com
Web address: www.recordedbooks.com

Simon and Schuster Audio
1230 Avenue of the Americas
New York, NY 10020
Phone: (212) 698-2353; Fax (212) 698-7664
E-mail: ListenUp@simonandschuster.com
Web address: www.simonsaysaudio.com/

Time Warner AudioBooks
1271 Avenue of the Americas, 11th Floor
New York, NY 10020
Phone (General Business): (212) 522-7334; Fax: (212) 588-7944
Web address: www.twbookmark.com/audiobooks/

Book Recording in the UK and Canada

In the United Kingdom the situation is somewhat different from that in the US; recently British Equity, which covers all areas of employment for actors, has been trying to unionize the extensive book-recording business there. The Royal National Institute for the Blind (RNIB) uses readers on a volunteer basis, or for minimal pay and without an agreement with the union. Many actors read for the RNIB for charitable reasons, and to stay in practice. If you are interested you can learn more about the situation for blind listeners to recorded books in the UK at the RNIB's web site: www.rnib.org.uk/.

There are a great many book-recording companies in Britain, many of them located in the West Midlands. Three of the major companies are:

Chivers Audio Books
Web address: www.chivers.co.uk/

Chivers Audio Books has its headquarters in Australia. Their web address is http://www.southernscene.com.au. You can e-mail them at info@southernscene.com.au.

Isis Publishing, Ltd.
7 Centremead
Osney Mead
Oxford OX2 0ES
Web address: www.isis-publishing.co.uk/;
E-mail: sales@isis-publishing.co.uk;

Longman Publishing
E-mail: enquiries@talkingbooks.org

A generally useful web site with links to all kinds of other informative sites is "Top of the Top Links" at www.talentroom.com/2003/rzlinkssM.html. The UK's premier weekly theatrical newspaper is *The Stage*, web address: www.thestage.co.uk/. British Equity also has its own web site: www.equity.org.uk.

I have been reliably informed about a practice, albeit quite rare, in the UK that we in the US find extraordinary, not to say incredibly abusive and unconscionable: If some of the smaller, less well-off companies, which use the services of local (union) actors, decide not to release a book, apparently they don't pay the actors for all their time and hard work. Only if the book is released commercially do the actors receive their money. This exploitative practice does exist, and it is something for actors to watch out for. Always make sure you have a written contract, with the appropriate agreements in it securing your rights.

It is possible that an actor's work may be found unsatisfactory, and the actor may be fired partway through a recording. Any producer in the US or the UK or Canada would have the right to do that, and would follow the proper procedures involved. However, in the US, if a reader had finished a recording, which was then found unsatisfactory and which the company refused to release, and perhaps even had to record again with another actor, the actor who was fired would still be paid, as he or she would be even for work completed partway through the recording.

If the British actor is required to travel from London to the West Midlands, or elsewhere, many companies pay travel and per diem expenses, usually for a bed-and-breakfast establishment, but smaller companies often do not reimburse such expenses, which can amount to quite a bit. The workweek can also be incredibly long, with some companies working actors from nine to five for five days a week, until the book is finished. And the pay is apparently not very good even by UK standards, which are generally lower than in the US. As I said earlier, there is a way to try to avoid these situations: Always get provisions in writing for specified working conditions, pay for travel, and for per diem expenses.

British Equity is trying to redress all of these abuses, but unfortunately many actors who have been victimized are simply afraid to speak up, because they don't want to be known as troublemakers, and because they feel they will lose work if they do. The union is working towards establishing a set amount of hours for a workday, with proper breaks, and guaranteed minimum wage scales, as well as a system of residual payments, such as the one that exists for commercials.

There are a lot of American books recorded in the UK—bestsellers, westerns, and mystery novels are very popular—including American classics by such authors as Mark Twain. As in all areas dealing with voice, including commercials, voice-overs and film dubbing—and the same thing is true in the US—many of the same people are used over and over, so that some become "regulars." Whereas in the US the publishers usually hire editors especially for the purpose of making abridgments, in the UK some readers earn extra money by abridging the books they are going to record, and the company then approves the abridgement. As in the US, celebrities, such as the versatile Prunella Scales, her husband Timothy West, their son Samuel West, Felicity Kendal, and Penelope Keith, often record books, generally British material.

The casting processes in the UK are very much the same as those described above for the United States. What you need to get started, notably a demo CD, is also much the same, but actors in the UK often use not a simple book-recording demo, but a demo CD with a combination of commercials and narrations. If the material to be recorded is specific, or unusual, then the actor is generally asked to audition, although ordinarily the actor would simply have to submit a demo. When there are auditions, actors are usually asked for a more extended casting session than in the US. The business is slightly less formal than it is in the US, so there is normally no signing-in process for a casting session, as there is in America. Also, contracts may sometimes be signed weeks after a job is done, which is strictly illegal in the US, where, under union contractual rules, the contract must be signed before work starts, often in the studio on the day of the first recording session. Again, British Equity is trying to correct this abuse.

Many actors in the UK look for and find voice work (except voice-overs), on their own. In the areas of radio drama, audio books, language tapes, film dubbing and animation, an agent is often not needed or used, although this is not the case in commercial voice-overs, where an agent is needed. The union sets the rates and they are not negotiable, except in areas, such as book recording, which are not yet unionized. On the other hand, if an actor were offered a long-term job in, for example, a radio serial, or a starring voice role in a major animated feature, he or she would probably have an agent negotiate the contract. And there are always exceptions: Some actors do all their work through agents.

Canada imports a great many American recordings, as you might expect, but it does have a book-recording industry. Procedures for getting work are much the same as in the UK and the US. The following web sites should give you all the information you need on the Canadian audiobook industry:

Association of Canadian Publishers: www.publishers.ca/Research.html

Acqwebs: www.acqweb.library.vanderbilt.edu/acqweb/pubr/audio.html

Awesome Audiobooks: www.awesomeaudiobooks.com

Book and Periodical Council: www.freedomtoread/ca/bpc

Canadian National Institute for the Blind: www.cnib.ca/

Canadian Publishers' Council: www.pubcouncil/home.html

CanBooks: www.meabt.com/canbooks

CHAPTER 1

The Voice

The Nature and Care of the Voice

The first requirement, the first necessary attribute, for a book-recording career is a pleasant, interesting, and even distinctively sonorous voice that can be listened to for long periods of time. Vocal training is a great asset for a volunteer at one of the charitable organizations, and an absolute necessity if you wish to record books professionally. Placing the voice correctly, controlling the breath, and supporting the voice correctly not only allows the voice to sound its best, but also prevents all kinds of vocal problems. Not breathing correctly and not placing and supporting the voice correctly can result in a sore throat, injury, or conditions such as pharyngitis or laryngitis. Having the vocal stamina to be able to record for hours at a time is also of paramount importance, and correct vocal technique is the only way to ensure that. The ability to vary the voice is also extremely important, and this book will tell you a good deal about how to develop the ability to read with expression and variety.

In fiction the use of character voices can be desirable. A word of caution in this regard is in order: How much you vary your voice depends partly on how many characters you have to portray, and how good your memory of them is. If there are a great many characters in a book, you may prefer to change your voice only slightly and play the characters' attitudes, actions, and attributes (male or female, old or young, weak or strong, authoritarian or submissive, etc.), which will automatically change the voice anyway. If necessary, a director will be able to help you decide just how much to vary your voice. See Chapter Six, Recording Fiction, for more advice on playing characters vocally.

Another word of caution: If you are a man reading the role of a woman, do not attempt (unless the situation is similar to the one in the film *Some Like It Hot* [1959], where Tony Curtis and Jack Lemmon both had to disguise themselves as women, in full drag and with voices to match) to imitate a woman's voice. Just play the attitudes and actions of the character, using, perhaps, a slightly breathy voice (depending on the character) and the higher end of your range. Similarly, if you are a woman recording a male role, use the lower end of your range, and play the character's actions and attitudes, but do not try to imitate the male voice.

Take care of your voice. Avoid tiring it out. Don't shout, unless you really have to, and don't whisper too much; both are fatiguing for the voice. Smoking anything is, as the doctors say, contra-indicated. Aside from the well-known fact that smoking is a general health hazard, it irritates and plays havoc with the vocal cords. Nevertheless, there are ill-advised readers and recording artists who smoke. Alcohol, with its dehydrating effect, is similarly deleterious, although a nice glass of wine with dinner and the occasional cocktail cannot harm anyone in normal health. Unlike smoking, which should not be indulged in at all, alcohol can certainly be partaken of occasionally.

People who earn a living with their voice often use throat lozenges, cough drops, hard candies and pastilles. I, myself, only use such things if I am really feeling poorly. For a sore throat, that old-fashioned palliative, tea with honey and lemon, is efficacious. Plain hot water with lemon is also good; the lemon's astringency helps to eliminate extra phlegm. Milk and dairy products are usually not good for the voice just before a recording session, because they can create phlegm and coat the throat.

Some Advice About Vocal Technique

First of all, study vocal technique.* Take classes. In major cities there are any number of studios where classes in vocal technique are offered, and there are many private voice coaches with whom you can study. Buy the trade papers, *Backstage* and *Show Business* in the US, or *The Stage* in the UK, and look at the advertisements. Shop around. Find the right vocal coach for you: someone who is not intimidating, and knows how to teach in an encouraging manner, someone with whom you have a rapport.

---

* Note: See the Bibliography, and Chapter Two: Diction and Pronunciation, for information about books on vocal technique.

The elements of vocal technique include correct "placement" of the voice, so as to bring out its greatest resonance; diaphragmatic support for the voice; correct, sustained and sustainable breathing technique; and the fluid use of a voice trained to be variable and flexible, so that it is in the service of the character being played and is used to express what the character desires to express, without conscious, calculated effect. Vocal effects have, first of all, to be organic, and to arise from the actor's work in rehearsal in creating the character.

On the other hand, calculated vocal effects can be most useful, and even necessary on occasion. Consider the following example from Sir Arthur Conan Doyle's "The Adventure of the Dying Detective." Dr. Watson describes the feverish Holmes's croaking voice during a terrible bout of sickness, and tells us that Holmes has refused his help, even forbidding him to approach his sickbed:

> "You are not angry?" he asked, gasping for breath.
>
> Poor devil, how could I be angry when I saw him lying in such a plight before me?
>
> "It's for your own sake, Watson," he croaked.

A bit later on we have this exchange:

> "You mean well, Watson," said the sick man with something between a sob and a groan. "Shall I demonstrate your own ignorance? What do you know, pray, of Tapanuli fever? What do you know of the black Formosa corruption?"
>
> "I have never heard of either."
>
> "There are many problems of disease, many strange pathological possibilities, in the East, Watson." He paused after each sentence to collect his failing strength. "I have learned so much during some recent researches which have a medico-criminal aspect. It was in the course of them that I contracted this complaint. You can do nothing."
>
> "Possibly not. But I happen to know that Dr. Ainstree, the greatest living authority upon tropical disease, is now in London. All remonstrance is useless, Holmes, I am going this instant to fetch him." I turned resolutely to the door.
>
> Never have I had such a shock! In an instant, with a tiger-spring, the dying man had intercepted me. I heard the sharp snap of a twisted key. The next moment he had staggered back to his bed, exhausted and panting after his one tremendous outflame of energy.
>
> "You won't take the key from me by force, Watson. I've got you, my friend. Here you are, and here you will stay until I will other-

> wise. But I'll humour you." (All this in little gasps, with terrible struggles for breath between.) "You've only my own good at heart. Of course I know that very well. You shall have your way, but give me time to get my strength. Not now, Watson, not now. It's four o'-clock. At six you can go."

NOTES, COMMENTS AND HINTS

This is a thrilling, suspenseful story, which I can recommend for general practice, because it provides the opportunity to play several distinctive characters. According to William S. Baring-Gould in *The Annotated Sherlock Holmes* (Clarkson N. Potter, Inc., 1967) both the names for the tropical diseases Holmes mentions are names for one disease, also called "tsutsugamushi fever" (pronounced "tsoo tsoo ga: mə shee," with a fairly even stress, as is usual in Japanese, and a very weak schwa in the penultimate syllable) and "scrub typhus." Dr. Ainstree is not mentioned in Baring-Gould's notes, so I assume he is fictitious.

The two brief excerpts are full of perfect clues as to how to read the dialogue, for which you have to go back and forth between Watson's normal voice and Holmes's hoarse croak. This is good practice, because in fiction you have to go back and forth between characters all the time.

It is quite clear from Conan Doyle's evocative descriptions that the vocal effects required to record this story must be calculated to some extent (for example, "He paused after each sentence..." and "little gasps, with terrible struggles for breath between"), or the listener will hear a description that does not match the character's voice.

Holmes's natural voice is much changed by his illness. Above all, the quality of the sick man's voice itself must be calculated, rather than the reading of the lines. Using sense memory, pretend you have a sore throat or laryngitis and a high fever, which make it very difficult to breathe and to speak, and even harder to leap out of bed and stop Watson from leaving the room, and then read Holmes's dialogue. Alternatively, simply begin by experimenting with a voice on the high end of your range, and with a hoarse voice; see the section "How to Change Your Voice," on page 25. When you have found the altered voice, allow yourself to be as spontaneous and as organic as you can in your delivery of the lines, while following Conan Doyle's "stage directions."

It was great fun to for me to record this story. In developing Holmes's intermittently breaking voice, with its occasional coughs and sputters and gasps, I used the first method described in the previous paragraph, and the voice came very easily to me. Recording it placed a bit of a strain on the vocal cords, however, so I stopped to take a drink of water periodically.

Finding Your Voice

You need the best, that is, the most resonant, warm and pleasant voice possible, and at the same time you want to avoid sounding artificial or theatrical. Your voice should sound natural and real. And if you wish to sustain a recording over several hours, you must have the voice to do it with.

Here is a simple exercise for "finding" your voice, that is, your optimum voice:

> Stand up in a good relaxed posture. Breathe in deeply, and emit the sound "a:" (that open, back vowel in the word *father*). Gently go up and down the scale on that note. Don't force anything, that is, don't tense the muscles or strain for any kind of effect. Don't tighten the vocal cords or hold the abdominal muscles. Just proceed with as little muscular effort as you can. Find out how high and how low you can go comfortably. Find the middle range where you are most comfortable. That is your best voice. You never want to go too low or too high, except for the purpose of creating a specific effect or doing a character voice.

Placing the Voice

Once you have found your voice you must begin to place it correctly. The previous exercise should have begun to give you a sense of placement, because your optimum voice will have been automatically placed where it should be for best effect.

The voice should be placed in the "masque," which is the sounding board or resonator of the living instrument we call the vocal apparatus. This means that the stream of air being expelled through the vocal cords during speech should go up towards the front of the face and be directed towards the "masque," which is the area centered behind the nose. This directing of the air is an image, rather than an actual physical phenomenon, since all parts of the vocal apparatus are really in play and help to resonate and are used as needed to articulate different sounds. But both the image and the physicality are very important, for two reasons:

1. The resulting sound is the voice at its most resonant; you should feel the bones of that part of the face, and of the cheeks, vibrate; and

2. The vocal cords themselves will be relaxed, because you will be concentrating not on the physical sensation you experience there, but rather on the area where you feel the bones vibrate; in other words, your attention will be away from the vocal cords. Ideally, the vocal cords should not be tense, or contracted, with the triple consequence that a) you will be able to sustain the voice over a long recording session without the fatigue which would result from ignoring this advice; b) you will be able to be flexible and to vary the voice, which you could not do with tense vocal cords; and c) you will not get a sore throat.

When you have correctly placed the voice, you should by no means experience the voice as nasal or as guttural, nor should it have an artificial sound, nor one that sounds too controlled.

Here is an exercise to help you place the voice correctly:

> Select any text you like. When you have found your best voice, as described above, remain standing and begin by humming on the consonant "m." In the voice you have found, say, "am, I'm, ohm, ahm, ihm," dwelling on the "m" sound. You should feel the bones in the masque vibrate. Still dwelling on "m," begin reciting the text you have chosen. Do not worry for now about the meaning of the words or about how effective your reading might be. This exercise is purely for placement.

Once you are sure of placing the voice correctly, make it a habit to do so when reading aloud. Then, most importantly, forget it. The habit you have formed should simply be there, and you should never have to think about it again. You can now concentrate on bringing a text to life and on telling a story.

The placement of the voice in the masque is not like the placement for singing, although it is akin to it. But in singing up and down the scale, the voice has to be in exactly the same place for all the notes. If you have ever heard opera singers speaking dialogue, you know that they often sound quite unreal, false, artificial and put on, because they never vary the placement of their voices. Even though they vary their intonation patterns, and speak their lines on more than one note, they speak every word in the same place in the masque, as if they are singing.

Although the basic center of voice placement is indeed in the masque, the voice should be fluid, going sometimes into the center, sometimes to the bottom of, and sometimes to the top of the masque. At times it will go down into the throat or even slightly above or below the masque, particularly for character work. All of these placements should be habitual, so that you can simply use your voice without thinking about its placement, because thinking about it might interfere with an effective, lively reading.

Supporting the Voice

Once you have found your voice and learned to place it, you must learn to support the voice from the diaphragm, as if you were on stage, but without using the diaphragm to project the voice. Proper support for the voice is attained by a combination of the movement of the ribs in and out; the diaphragm (which is the muscle attached to the ribs below the lungs) supports the movement and the lower muscles of the abdominal cavity are brought relatively less into play.

To find this support, stand comfortably, feet slightly apart, and breathe in and out while being very aware of the activity of all the muscles. They will lower themselves as you breathe in. As you expel the air from the lungs, you cause the abdominal muscles to rise. Try to concentrate on the action of the diaphragmatic muscle. Repeat this exercise until you are conscious of the action of the diaphragm and feel you can control it. Use the diaphragm, rather than the lower abdominal muscles, to help support the voice.

Do these additional exercises all in the same session, one after the other in the order listed, to help you with supporting the voice properly:

1. Stretch up with your arms raised. Bend down with your arms lowered. Stretch from side to side. As you do so, feel the action of the muscles.

2. Stand quite still and place the tips of your fingers just below the line of the ribs, where the diaphragm is. Begin breathing gently, and feel the movement of the muscles. You will feel all of the muscles of the abdominal cavity move. Now, slowly breathe in and, with your fingers, feel the movement of the diaphragm as you breathe out gently on the prolonged sound of "hah." Do the same thing again, but this time, make the sound "hah" a bit shorter. Repeat the exercise and do a series of short "hah" sounds.

3. Continue standing, but now remove your fingers from the diaphragm and breathe in and then out, saying "hah" as you breathe out, and placing "hah" in the masque, as you have learned to do in the exercises in the previous section. You should be able to feel that the lower muscles of the abdominal cavity are moving less strongly than before,

and that the diaphragm is moving more strongly. Do not force the diaphragm to move, or do anything forceful with your voice.

4. Repeat the second exercise, gradually adding a little force to the expelling of air as you say "hah" once again.

5. Now recite a line of the text you have chosen previously, forcefully, but not too forcefully. You don't want to injure yourself.

6. Having done that, still standing, place the voice correctly and, using the diaphragmatic muscle, read your text. You should be conscious of the projection of the voice.

7. Sit down and repeat the exercise until you feel comfortable with the combination of correct placement of the voice and the diaphragmatic support, which should become a habit you can forget about, just as you can the habit of placing the voice correctly.

When recording books you cannot project the voice the way you would on a stage, but you still need to support the voice, in order to avoid injury. Correct placement and correct support will take your concentration off the muscles of the vocal cords, and free them up, which is exactly what you need to do.

Breathing and Breath Control

Good breathing technique is essential for good voice production, and for sustaining the voice over a long recording session. Breathing is something we all do naturally, but strength and breath control and correct breathing technique can be acquired. You must breathe through your nose, and not through your mouth, or you will never be able to develop the breath control required for recording books.

Breath control is important for phrasing, for controlling phrasing and for sustaining tone, as the following exercise will show you. With phrasing comes good pacing, and fluency in the reading. By "phrasing" we mean how one speaks a phrase—a group of words that naturally belong together; a phrase can be one word, two words, or an entire clause of a sentence. When considering the phrasing of a text, you sometimes have to ask yourself, "Am I going to sustain long phrases on one breath? Or am I going to break up the phrase in order to have it make sense? For an example of specific phrasing demands look again at the excerpt from "The Adventure of the Dying Detective" on page 17. Phrasing is often an unconscious natural phenomenon arising organically from the nature of the text. With good breath control, phrasing that is natural will be easy, and you should not have to calculate it except in particularly difficult cases.

"Pacing" means the tempo at which one reads, and a tempo that is either too slow or too fast will be difficult to listen to. The ability to sustain a tempo is partly dependent on breath control. Pacing and tempo themselves are dependent on the nature of the text.

Here is an exercise to help you develop breath control:

> Take a deep breath. Then on one breath say the first line of William Shakespeare's Sonnet XXX, which you will find on page 288, then stop, even if you feel you can go on. Take another deep breath, and say the first two lines on one breath without stopping. Stop and take another deep breath, then say three lines on one breath without stopping. Continue in this way, adding lines, until you find the natural limit of how many you can say on one breath. Repeat this exercise periodically, and after some time you will have developed more control than you imagine.

You can use any of the illustrative texts, prose or poetry, fiction or nonfiction, for the same exercise. I recommend Mr. Jingle's dialogue from *The Posthumous Papers of the Pickwick Club*, which you will find on page 119, for this exercise, as well as for developing variety and flexibility.

Developing Variety and Flexibility

Variety results from varying pitch and tempo, as well as from doing different voices when necessary. The nature of the text you are recording will determine variety of rhythm. Flexibility means being able to switch back and forth at will between pitches, or between different character voices, without having to think about it. Character voices, like the accents with which people speak, should be habitual, so that conscious turning on or off of the voice is unnecessary.

The exercises at the end of this chapter and in Chapter Two are meant to help you develop flexibility, among other things.

Here are some exercises to help develop variety as well:

1. Standing comfortably, feet slightly apart, place the voice correctly, as you have learned to do, on the sound of "em," dwelling on the "m." Now say "mah," and as you say it take your voice smoothly

(legato, if this were singing) first from low to high on this note, then from high to low, which will be close to singing it. Make a conscious effort not to sing, but to speak. Repeat this as many times as you wish, varying the pitches on which you begin and end, until you can do this exercise with ease.

2. Repeat the beginning of the first exercise, standing and saying "em" then "mah." Now, beginning on a low pitch, make a staccato leap to a higher pitch. Reverse the exercise: Begin on a high pitch and make a staccato leap to a low pitch. Do this varying the pitches over the entire range of your voice, until you can do this exercise comfortably.

3. Take any text you choose and, without necessarily trying to have it make the sense it should have, practice it as in the first two exercises, purely for vocal effect. Try reading it with a staccato rhythm, then with legato phrasing. Read on alternately high and low pitches, varying the pitches from low to high, then from high to low.

4. Now read the text aloud giving it the sense it should have. You should find that you have automatically added variety to your reading. Record yourself, and then listen to your recording. Notice how much variety you have been able to put into your reading. Repeat this exercise, varying your reading as you think necessary, based on what you have learned from critiquing your recording.

Paralinguistics: How to Do Different Voices

Paralinguistics is a field of study apart from linguistics, but related to it. It deals with extra-linguistic phenomena, such as the rhythm or tempo of an individual's speech, the quality of his or her voice, whispering, creakiness, hoarseness, high and low voices (timbre), shrillness, the way in which emotions are expressed, expressive vocal sounds such as cries, sobs and shouts which communicate but are not words—all phenomena which exist apart from an actual language, with its grammar, vocabulary, and phonetic inventory of vowels, semi-vowels and consonants.

The paralinguistic tools and techniques described here are meant to be an adjunct to the craft that the actor brings to the art of acting, and to book recording in particular. They are also useful in such jobs for actors as television voice-overs, characters in animation, film narration, and radio commercials, where calculating one's vocal effects can be extremely important.

Even those paralinguistic phenomena that do not relate directly to the communicative aspects of language can communicate information. For example, a hoarse voice may indicate that a person is sick; a phenomenon that may be very useful in recording the voice of such a character in a work of fiction. Put another way, paralinguistics deals with what people actually communicate by using the voice, apart from using language. Actors can use these phenomena to great advantage in recreating behavior; and actors who are recording books can use them in recreating behavior vocally, whatever the method or approach of the actor. They come under the heading of external techniques, but there is no reason why they cannot be incorporated in an organic way into the creation of a character.

How to Change Your Voice

In order to change your voice so that you can do a character voice, you must consider several things, all of which involve manipulating the muscles inside the mouth and directing the flow of air:

1. Placement: nasal, throaty, etc. The first technique to use is imagistic or imaginative: Imagine that the voice is placed where you wish it to be, and feel the placement simply by concentrating on the physical sensation your imagination has produced.

2. Direction of the air: This is related to step one. You must direct the air coming up through the vocal cords to a particular area: Down into the chest; up into the area behind the eyes (for a nasal voice), etc.

3. Tightening or loosening of the vocal cord muscles at the top: Tighten them at the top for higher voices, and lower down at the bottom for lower voices.

Changing the voice involves changing its natural pitch and its natural placement. By now you will have found your voice, and placed it correctly in the masque; you know its range and where its middle is. You can branch out from that center and experiment with high and low pitches and their different placements, and this is the beginning of doing character voices. When you are learning it, such placement for character voices demands some concentration on the muscles of the vocal cords, which is exactly what you want to avoid in your general placement of the voice for most narrative purposes.

Here are some exercises that will enable you to begin developing different voices, if you do not already have the ability to do so. (Of course, many actors simply do different voices naturally and unconsciously, just as some people are naturally good at doing impressions or imitations of well-known people, or of their own friends and acquaintances.) Once again, the placement of the voice for character purposes should become a habit, so that you don't have to think about it. You will thus avoid undue strain on the vocal cords, although there will be some strain in any case. Therefore, while doing the following exercises keep a glass of water handy to help you keep the vocal cords thoroughly moist, as you would in a recording session.

1. **To Create a Whisper:** Stand up straight, open the mouth and say "Hah" as loudly as you can, voicing the vowel. Now repeat the exercise without voicing the vowel, which will give you a loud, but *whispered* sound. Repeat this as often as you like while feeling where you are directing the flow of air, until you can really feel it. Now add some voice to the whisper, and you will have what is called a "stage whisper," which can also be useful in recording dialogue in a suspenseful situation, for instance. A real whisper, in fact, will not record very well.

2. **To Create a "Creaky" Voice:** On the sound "Hah" direct the stream of air so that you feel it going through the top of the vibrating vocal cords. This will begin to give you the high notes of your range, and is the beginning of a "creaky" voice, useful for certain characters. Tighten the vocal cord muscles at the top, so that you have the feeling of holding them. Now direct the stream of air through the tightened vocal cords so that you really feel it through the top of the vibrating vocal cords. You can now begin to play around or experiment with the resulting rough, raspy, creaky voice. Take a line of text and use it for practice.

3. **To Create a "Gruff" or "Hoarse" Voice:** On the sound "Hah" direct the stream of air so that you feel it going through the bottom of the vibrating vocal cords. This will begin to give you the low notes of your range, and is the beginning of a "gruff" voice, useful for certain characters. Tighten the vocal cord muscles at the bottom, so that you have the feeling of holding them. Now direct the stream of air through the tightened vocal cords so that you really feel it through the bottom of the vibrating vocal cords. You can now begin to play around or experiment with the resulting voice. Take a line of text and use it for practice.

4. **To Create High "Older" or "Sick" Voices:** On a high pitch start "whining" on the syllable "ah." Go up and down the scale, almost as if you were imitating the cliché of a ghost. At a comfortable pitch stop and repeat any phrase of text. You should find your voice beginning to quaver slightly, and this trembling effect can be useful in playing certain characters, although you will generally want to avoid the usual sorts of clichés indulged in for the portrayal of feeble or ill people. You don't want to *imitate* them; you want to *be like* them, in order to play them organically "as if" you really were feeble or sick.

Vocal Exercises

Rhythm and tempo, also known as pace, are a major part of the following exercises, which are also good for diction practice. Begin by repeating them at a medium tempo, neither too slow nor too fast; in other words, at a comfortable tempo that feels right to you, and is neither rushed nor artificially slowed. Then do the exercises faster, and afterwards slow them down considerably.

Use these exercises to vary pitch patterns, no matter what the tempo. Go from high to low, and from low to high, on the different phrases. Repeat pitch patterns or vary them, as you wish. Be spontaneous.

Repeat each exercise at least ten times:

1. Never, oh, never, the fatal endeavor, the ties that they sever, the fatal endeavor, the true tried tricycle, the true tried tricycle, the true tried tricycle.

2. Were it far or near or nearer and nearer.

3. The incredible edible sheddable beddable blinking twinking nodding prodding pointed icicle Popsicle appeared out of nowhere to me.

4. How could you? How would you? How did you? How might you? How may you? How can you? How dare you? How fare you?

5. Other than that or this or these or those, might one not speak of a bright red rose?

6. Questionable and quick and quite, quite, quite clean the quiet crawling crazy crabby cricket creeps unseen.

7. Lilacs like lavender bloom like flowers lining the lordly lake luxuriously. Let lambs low lovingly in lonely lovely lees, while lads and lasses live to love and laugh.

8. Take any text you choose, a short poem for instance, and recite it all on one note. Then recite it again a half tone up, then a tone higher, and so forth. Then recite it on successively lower tones. Lastly, recite the text as you would ordinarily wish to do. This exercise is meant to help broaden your vocal range, and to make you comfortable with different pitches. This level of comfort and the ability to use different pitches should become habitual, so that you don't have to think about which pitches to use, but will have them automatically at your command.

CHAPTER 2

Diction and Pronunciation

Good diction, by which we mean clear vowels and well-articulated consonants resulting in easily intelligible pronunciation, is a requirement of paramount importance for book recording. Another requirement is a standard accent (which always varies somewhat from speaker to speaker): General American or Canadian, if you are North American; or British Received Pronunciation (British RP), if you are British. If you have an accent other than those, which you can learn, you may get work that deals with your particular background. But, generally speaking, when you record books in the U.S., Canada or the U.K., you will usually be required to reserve regional variations (Cockney, Texas, etc.) and other world standard accents of English (Australian, Singaporean, etc.) for characters, including first-person narrators, in works of fiction. For example, if you are recording Robert Louis Stevenson's *Kidnapped*, in which David Balfour, the first-person narrator, is a Lowland Scot, you might use a slight, beautiful, easy to listen to Standard Scottish English (SSE) accent.

All languages are spoken with a particular pattern of pronunciation, which we call an accent. Bear in mind that when it comes to accents of English it is difficult to lay down hard and fast rules, and English has many words with more than one pronunciation. Nevertheless, you must be aware of what the standard sounds of the language are. By standard sounds we mean those perceived or observed as being used by the majority of speakers. For instance, in the Midwestern accents of the USA, there is usually no distinction made among the words *Mary*, *marry* and *merry*: All three are pronounced with the very short diphthong "ɛə" [IPA symbol] in *Mary*. But for the majority of speakers of both General American and British RP the three words each have distinct vowel sounds: *Mary* has either the open vowel or the very short diphthong heard in both General American and British RP *air* [IPA symbols ɛ or ɛə]; *marry* has the same vowel as in General American and British RP *cat* [æ]; *merry* has the same vowel as in General American and British RP *met* [e].

To help train yourself in these accents, listen to recordings or films made by the many British, Canadian and American actors and authors with superb diction: Martyn Green, in Gilbert and Sullivan recordings from the late 1940s and early 1950s; the entire Redgrave family; Robert Donat; John Gielgud; Alec Guinness; Wendy Hiller; Alexander Scourby in numerous recordings; Laurence Olivier; Maggie Smith; Edith Evans; Richard Kiley; Edna St. Vincent Millay, in recordings of her poetry; Langston Hughes reading his poetry; Walter Pidgeon; William Powell; Ruth Draper in her monodramas; and scores more. Listen as well to the rich sonorous voice and marvelous diction of Welsh poet Dylan Thomas in his many recordings.

Some Definitions and Some Notes on Language

Note: In this section, in addition to the general discussion of language, and some comparisons between General American and British RP pronunciations, you will find sounds useful in doing various other accents, which may be required in some character's dialogue. See the section "Using Accents" on page 239 in Chapter Six.

The sounds of the English language are divided into the following categories for ease of discussion, but in fact the divisions are not always clear-cut. Is a semi-vowel a consonant or a vowel? If one can prolong the sound of certain consonants, such as "R," what becomes of the definition of a vowel?

Vowel: A single voiced sound made by passing air through the vibrating vocal cords and then through the vocal cavity without the flow of air being stopped. The shape of the vocal cavity changes with each vowel; the tongue is higher or lower; the vocal cavity more open or more closed; and the lips are relaxed or protruded or retracted, rounded or unrounded. The stream of air is directed up and either primarily to the back or middle or front of the palate (the "sounding board" of the mouth); this is called the *focal point*, or the *point of resonance*. Hence we refer to back and front vowels, which can be open or closed, rounded or unrounded. The vowel "a:" in *father*, for example, is an open, back, unrounded vowel. Other vowels are pronounced by lowering the soft palate at the back of the mouth and allowing some air to flow through the nasal cavity just above it, as when articulating the consonants "m" or "n"; these vowels are called nasal vowels.

There is a great confusion on the part of English speakers as to what constitutes a vowel. We are all taught that of the twenty-six letters of the alphabet used in English, five are vowels: A, E, I, O, and U. The names of the vowels in English are all actually diphthongs—one letter stands for two sounds—and as a consequence we mistakenly think of those diphthongs (two sounds) as vowels (one sound).

Semi-Vowel: A vowel during the pronunciation of which the flow of air is beginning to be stopped by the action of tongue or lips and therefore has almost a consonantal quality. Semi-vowels are also sometimes called "semi-consonants"; the terms can be used interchangeably. The two semi-vowels in English are "w," during which the lips are beginning to close and are slightly rounded, in *well*; and "y," during which the sides of the tongue move up towards the roof of the mouth touching it very lightly, in *yes*. Both "y" and "w" combine with many vowels to form diphthongs: ya, ye, yi, yo, yu, wa, we, wi, wo, wu, etc.

Diphthong: Two vowels, or a vowel and a semi-vowel, spoken on one breath, one of the vowels being stressed. The unstressed half of the diphthong is always very short. An example is "I," from "a:" (you may think of this vowel as being spelled "ah"), in *father* and "ee" in *meet*; "a:" is stressed. In the case of diphthongs formed from a semi-vowel and a vowel, the vowel is always stressed: the diphthong "u" as in the word *you* (semi-vowel "y," vowel "oo" as in *boot*) is an example. A diphthong occurs when the jaw relaxes slightly immediately after the pronunciation of a vowel and while sound is still issuing from the vocal cords. The tongue "glides" to a different position. In British diphthongs the glide is greater than it is in American diphthongs.

Triphthong: A sound in which three vowel sounds are uttered on one breath. The sounds so combined form one syllable. There are four triphthongs in English: "a:eeə" and "o:ooə" and "æooə" and "oowə." Some examples: *briar* ("bra:eeə" or "bra: eeər" in General American), *dire, hire, liar, lyre; lower* ("lo:ooə"); *bower* ("bæooə"), *flower, hour, our; newer* ("noowə" or "nyoowə" or "noowər" or "nyoowər"). If you slow these words down you will distinctly hear the three sounds.

Consonant: A sound in which the flow of air is impeded or hindered by the action of tongue, lips or teeth. There are two versions of certain consonants: voiced, in which there is sound from the vibrating vocal cords, and voiceless (or unvoiced), in which there is not. The pairs are, voiced and voiceless respectively: "b" and "p"; "d" and "t"; "dg" (dzh) and "ch" (tsh); "v" and "f"; "g" and "k"; "z" and "s"; "zh" and "sh"; voiced "th" (as in *the*), and voiceless "th" (as in *thing*). To differentiate further, there are actually other versions of these same consonants, including initial aspirated (that is, with a little inaudible puff of breath as the consonant is uttered), as well as middle and final unaspirated versions, and in some cases a more heavily aspirated one; the final unaspirated version is often referred to nontechnically as the "softest." One letter is used in spelling to indicate what is actually a range of sounds. For example, the slightly aspirated "t" at the beginning of a word is actually a different sound from the "t" in the middle of a word, different yet again from the sound at the end of a word: tip, matter, pit. In the more heavily aspirated tapped version of "t" sometimes heard in the middle of a word like *matter* the tongue hardly touches the gum ridge and more air is forced through the vocal cavity. The tapped "d" (that is, a "d" with the tongue not creating the usual pressure against the upper gum ridge, but rather lightly touching or tapping it), is sometimes heard as a substitute for a voiced "th" in some native and foreign accents in words like *other, these, them, those, the*; and sometimes in the middle of words like *whatever*, which, in some accents (a Dublin accent, for example), you might hear as a tapped "t." A similarly tapped "t" is sometimes heard at the end of or in the middle of such words as *matter* and *get* in some American, British, Irish, Australian and New Zealand accents.

Two very important consonants are "l" and "r." The British "l" is usually pronounced with the tongue more forward than is the American "l," and feels as if it is in the front of the mouth, and it is articulated with slightly more pressure than is the American "l," which feels more as if it is in the middle of the mouth. The variations in the sounds of "l" are useful in doing the accents sometimes required in recording a character's dialogue.

In all "l" sounds, which are lateral voiced consonants (there is an unvoiced "l" in Welsh), the blade (the little area just behind the tip) of the tongue is raised and the tongue is slightly grooved; the tip and the blade of the tongue touch an area of the gum ridge near the upper front teeth and slightly block the opening behind the gum ridge into the hard palate; the back of the tongue is low; and air is allowed to pass around the slightly retracted sides of the tongue, hence the term "lateral.". In the articulation of the American "l" the contact of the tongue and the gum ridge is light, and "l" resonates in the same place as the vowel "e" as in the word *met*. But in the formation of one typical Russian "l," the tongue is tensed, and its tip is pressed against the back of the upper front teeth. It resonates where the back vowel "o" does. Another Russian "l," described as "dark," is "palatalized"; that is, the tongue is raised to touch the back of the mouth, and forms the semi-vowel "y" just after the "l" when pronounced before "i" (as in *bit*), or "e" (as in *met*), and resonates where "e" does, so *let* is pronounced "lyet," (*lyet* is Russian for "flight"), but is also heard in a Russian accent in English. Very different is the French "l," which resonates where the vowel "o" in *work* does. During the pronunciation of "l" the tongue is raised slightly as its tip lightly touches the upper gum ridge where it curves into the upper palate.

Rhotic sounds (from the name of the Greek letter *rho*) are the voiced consonants spelled with the letter "r." In English there are two basic versions of "r," each of which has minor variations:

1. The retroflex "r," pronounced with the tip of the tongue beginning to curve upward, so that the bottom of the tongue is towards the roof of the mouth;

2. The tapped or trilled "r," described below.

In General American English (except in regional variations, such as some Southern accents where post-vocalic "r" is dropped; or in Midwestern American accents, where post-vocalic "r" is heavily pronounced), "r" is generally lightly pronounced after a vowel. General American English is therefore described as "rhotic." Even if "r" is not pronounced it still often influences the vowel that precedes it, because the tongue is beginning to curl upwards as if to articulate an "r," thus giving an impression of the letter "r," and we speak of "r-influenced" vowels. In British RP post-vocalic "r" ("r" after a vowel) is silent, unless it is linked to a word or syllable following it beginning with a vowel. British RP is therefore described as "non-rhotic." The sound associated with this letter in another language is often carried into English in a foreign accent.

To pronounce a trilled "r" (with one or more taps or flaps) heard sometimes in old-fashioned British RP between two vowels, as in the word *very*, as well as in many other languages, including Arabic, Spanish, Italian, Swedish, Finnish, Basque, Portuguese, Polish, Russian and Czech, begin by saying a tapped "d," then the word *very* with a "d," instead of an "r." Draw the tip of your tongue back a very little bit and drop the tongue slightly until you have the impression of saying "r." Do not curl the bottom of your tongue towards the roof of the mouth. The tip of the tongue should be just at the opening of the palate in back of the gum ridge. Alternatively, you may begin a trilled "r" by saying *hurrah* and shortening the vowel in the first syllable until it is entirely eliminated, leaving you with a very breathy sound: "hr." Continue tapping the tip of the tongue lightly against the opening of the palate, hardly touching it at all. You can then eliminate the "h."

To pronounce the guttural or uvular "r" heard in various versions in French, German, Yiddish, Dutch, Danish, Norwegian and Hebrew, first lower the tip of the tongue so it touches the back of the lower front teeth, then raise the back of the tongue so the uvula vibrates against it, as in gargling, or as in articulating its voiceless version, the "kh" sound heard in Scottish *loch* or German *Ach!*

Voiced and unvoiced, or voiceless, "th," which are dental consonant sounds pronounced with the tip of the tongue touching the back of the upper front teeth, do not exist in most other languages. The following pairs of substitutions (voiced and voiceless as in *this* and *thing*) are often heard in accents stemming from languages that have no "th" sounds: "z" and "s" (French, Northern German, etc.); "d" and "t" (Canadian French, Austrian German, Italian, etc.); "v" and "f" (Russian, as well as in a London Cockney accent). A tapped "d" is often heard as a substitute for voiced "th" between two vowels in German, Dutch, Yiddish accents, Czech, Russian, Polish and other accents.

A Guide to the Correct Pronunciations of General American and of British RP

There are two standard English accents and dialects (a dialect is a version of a language with its particular grammar and vocabulary and accent; a so-called standard version of a language is thus a dialect) that people learning the language are taught:

1. General American, sometimes called Network English, although there is no longer any reason to call it that, since the standards of pronunciation on television and radio in the U.S. vary so tremendously, and one hears so many regional accents;

2. Standard British RP (Received Pronunciation; as in the phrase "received in the best social circles"), sometimes called BBC English, a term preferred by some linguists. I use the term British RP in this book.

Most Americans speak standard rhotic General American without regionalisms, as much as there can be a standard in a country with so many widely used accents. Standard Canadian English and General American English accents are nearly identical. Some of the greatest Hollywood film actors, with the clearest diction, have been of Canadian origin, a fact that many Americans don't know. Among them are Hume Cronyn, Walter Pidgeon, Raymond Massey, Brendan Fraser, and William Powell.

British RP is the group of English accents associated generally with the upper socioeconomic classes. It is heard, with variations, not only at such schools as Eton and Harrow, and at Oxford and Cambridge Universities, but in the law courts, in government circles generally, and on stage and screen. The upper-class British accent is changing, probably under the influence of the London Cockney accents, so that some sounds, such as glottal stops on "t" sounds at the end of or in the middle of such words as *bit* and *bottle*, are heard that never used to exist in these accents. This contemporary accent has been named Thames Estuary English. Increasingly, in both America and Britain, provincial or regional accents are heard in the media and in theaters and cinemas.

For more information I recommend the following books:

An excellent book on American speech is Edith Skinner's *Speak with Distinction* (Applause Theatre Book Publishers, 1990). She discusses the accent called General American, and also describes what she calls Good Speech, also known as Eastern Standard or Theater Standard, by which she means a clearly articulated, non-rhotic accent, very pleasant to the ear. It is close to the old-fashioned upper-class speech of the 1930s, exemplified by President Franklin D. Roosevelt, or Walter Hampden, Gary Merrill and Hugh Marlowe in the film *All About Eve* (1950). Most Americans, however, do not speak Theater Standard.

For British RP, and for vocal technique in general, J. Clifford Turner's *Voice and Diction for the Stage* (Fifth Edition, edited by Malcolm Morrison, A & C Black, 2000) is terrific, for American as well as for British actors. It is, as that fine actor Alan Bates says on the back cover, "... a great book on voice ... a classic."

For general vocal technique Arthur Lessac's *The Use and Training of the Human Voice* (DBS Publications, 1967) is excellent, with exercises for breathing, posture and general physical conditioning, and a unique approach to the voice as a musical instrument.

All three books provide many practice exercises, and J. Clifford Turner's book has helpful daily routines.

A good guide to General American pronunciations is the second edition of the *Random House Unabridged Dictionary* of 1993, which includes pronunciations once considered nonstandard or even unacceptable, but now considered acceptable. The 1927 edition of *Webster's New International Dictionary* is a supremely useful reference for all kinds of obscure words, mythological names and scientific nomenclature. For the pronunciation of British RP refer to the *Oxford English Dictionary*. The compelling story of how it was conceived and put together is told in Simon Winchester's books *The Professor and the Madman* (HarperCollins Publishers, 1998) and *The Meaning of Everything* (Oxford University Press, 2003).

Daniel Jones's *Cambridge Pronouncing Dictionary*, edited by Peter Roach, James Hartman and Jane Setter (16th edition, Cambridge University Press, 2003) with comparative pronunciations for British RP (they prefer the term BBC English), and General American (they prefer the term Network English) is an important book. So is the phoneticist and dialectician J. C. Wells's *Longman Pronouncing Dictionary* (Pearson ESL, 2000), especially for information on contemporary developments in British pronunciation. (I take issue with both dictionaries on several points, and on many of the pronunciations they consider standard for General American.) A thorough book, which compares British and American English, is Norman W. Schur's *British RP A to Zed*, revised by Eugene Ehrlich (Checkmark Books, 2001).

Positions of the Vocal Apparatus

As compared to their position when speaking British RP, the position of the lips in General American is generally a bit farther back and the jaw a bit slacker. The language "feels" (as an image) as though it is spoken in the middle of the mouth. British RP "feels" much more forward in the mouth, at the point where the tongue stops to form the consonants "t" and "d." That *point of articulation* is very slightly forward of the American point of articulation for "t" and "d." This means that in articulating a British "t" or "d" the tip of the tongue is more forward and the tongue itself raised slightly above the position it assumes in articulating an American "t" or "d." For British RP the *major point of resonance* is slightly in front of the General American major point of resonance; that is, the stream of air passing across the vibrating vocal cords is directed towards the front of the mouth, where the palate acts as a sounding board.

The lips are held slightly more together and both the lips and the tongue are slightly more forward in British RP than they are in General American. It is at the point where the tongue touches the opening into the palate to form the sound of "d" (the point of articulation of the "d") that the general resonance of British RP lies; in General American that point of resonance is just where the tip of the tongue leaves a space to form the consonant "r."

In English there are only four consonants whose place of articulation is near the back of the mouth: "g," "ng," "k," and "h." British consonants differ slightly from their American counterparts in having generally a more forward place or point of articulation. The vocal cavity is usually more closed during speech in British RP than it is in General American English.

Practice for British RP by repeating *da da da do do do hello hello hello* several times until you get the feeling you can direct the stream of air forward to that point in the mouth, so the language skips and plays about.

Practice for General American by repeating *rah rah rah raw raw raw row row row* several times in a row. You should feel the middle of the palate, the sounding-board, vibrate as the stream of air is directed forward and then impeded and directed back again towards the middle of the mouth.

Phonetics

Aside from those mentioned above, there are some other very important differences in consonants and vowels between the two accents. There are also many differences in the pronunciation of individual words, many details of which will be found in this section. Americans say *necessary* as "NE sə SE ree," *egotist* as "EE gə tist" and *garage* as "gə RA:ZH," and the British say "NE sə sree" or "NE sə sə ree," "EH gə tist" and "GÆ rədg" or "GÆ ridg," for example.

Consonants

Another difference between consonants in British RP and consonants in General American consists in the quality, or hardness, of the sounds, stemming from the general position of the vocal apparatus as it is held during speech. The "hard" quality comes from the fact that in British RP the tongue is pressed slightly more hardly during the articulation of a consonant, such as "t" or "d," than it is in General American. In British RP when articulating the consonant "b" the lips are pressed together a bit more firmly and for a slightly longer time than in a General American "b."

L: "L" is a very important consonant for both General American and British RP, because it is articulated differently in either accent, with a more forward point of articulation in British RP than in General American. There are a number of versions of this consonant.

As stated above, the consonant "l" is a voiced lateral; "lateral" because the sides of the tongue are slightly raised to allow the passage of air out of both sides, as the tip of the tongue presses against the alveola, or gum ridge, behind the upper front teeth. In British RP the pressure of the tip of the tongue is firmer, harder and lasts longer than it does in a General American "l." Also, in British RP both the center and the blade of the tongue come closer to the roof of the mouth, without touching it, than they do in General American.

In General American to articulate an initial "l," as in the word *like*, the tongue is slightly relaxed and its tip touches the gum ridge lightly. In a British RP initial "l" the tongue is raised slightly more than in an American initial "l"; at the same time the tip and blade of the tongue are pressed slightly more against the upper gum ridge just forward of where it curves up to form the cavity below the palate. In all positions the British use a dark "l" with the tongue slightly thickened toward the palate, and the position of the tongue also conditions how the vowels surrounding the "l" sound. This positioning is a key to how the accent should generally "feel" in the mouth, indicating the place in the mouth where the stream of air is generally directed to resonate.

R: The consonant "r" is a voiced, retroflex, post-alveolar fricative continuant. It is "voiced" because the vocal cords vibrate when it is pronounced, and it is a "continuant" because the sound can be continued as long as you have breath. The word "fricative" refers to a consonant which is articulated with friction when the parts of the vocal apparatus used to articulate it almost make contact, but do not quite touch. "Post-alveolar" means articulated slightly behind the alveola, which is the area just behind the upper front teeth, immediately before the bone begins to curve up towards the palate. The consonant is "retroflex," because the tongue is beginning to curve up with its bottom towards the roof of the mouth.

Hint for British RP: Think of post-vocalic "r" before another consonant as a silent letter, like the "b" in *lamb* or the "gh" in *daughter*.

At the beginning of a word the sound of "r" is the same in both General American and British RP pronunciations.

In British RP, but not in General American, at the beginning of a syllable in the middle of a word between two vowels the "r" is often, but by no means always, given one tap or trill.

In British RP, as in many non-rhotic accents, there is an "intrusive r." Words like *drawing* become "drawRing" and phrases like *Diana and I* become "Diana Rand I" (where the "r" is really linked to the "a" in *and*).

In British RP, as in many non-rhotic accents, there is also a "linking r," where an "r" at the end of a word is linked to a vowel at the beginning of the following word, as in the phrase *my brother and I*.

Hints for character work: A few members of the upper classes sometimes drop "r" in the middle of a word, so that *very* is pronounced either "ve" or "vay," as in *very true*: "vay true." Also, there can be trouble pronouncing "r" and it is sounded almost like "w," but with the tongue curled up slightly as if to make an "r," but without the tongue's reaching its correct position, because the upper front teeth touch the inside of the lower lip slightly, as of to form a "v."

Vowels

The schwa [IPA symbol "ə"]: This symbol represents the sound spelled with an "e" in *the* before a consonant, and is often heard in British RP in unstressed syllables. This is a very relaxed mid vowel, spoken with the jaw lowered, and the tongue low in the mouth. The stream of air is directed to resonate against the middle of the upper palate. The schwa is often substituted for a longer vowel. This substitution shortens the syllable, eliminating the vowel almost entirely. It is much more widely used in British RP than in General American English.

The use of the schwa is perhaps one of the most important phonetic keys to the British RP accent, and the one least easily assimilated by North Americans learning it. The frequent use of the schwa makes the language sound a bit swallowed up on occasion, and, depending on the speaker, one sometimes has the impression of hearing nothing but consonants, even when the articulation is very strong.

a: The broad, open-throated "a:" is the sound of the "a" in *father*. The lips are relaxed, the mouth wide open, and the stream of air directed to resonate slightly forward of the back of the throat. This vowel is the most open one in the English language. The version of "a:" used in British RP is the most open vowel in any accent of English, and occurs uniquely in the British RP accent, being widely used in British RP in words in which General American English uses the "a" ("æ") in *that*. Practice this sound using the following partial list:

advantage, after, words beginning and ending with after: afternoon, afterwards, hereafter, etc., answer, ask, aunt, banana, basket, bastard, bath, blast, branch, brass, broadcast, calf, can't, cask, casket, cast, caste, castle, chance, chancellor, chant, clasp, class, words beginning with class: classmate, classroom, classy, etc., command, countermand, daft, dance, demand, disaster, downcast, draft, enchant, entrance (verb), example, fast, fasten, gala, ghastly, glass, graft, grant, words ending in -graph: telegraph, etc. (But note that the word graphic is pronounced "græ′ fik"; words ending in "-graphic" are pronounced "græ′ fik"; graphite is pronounced "græ′ fIt"; words ending in "-graphical" such as *geographical* are pronounced "-græ′ fi kel"), grasp, grass, half, lance, last, lather, laugh, lithograph, mask, mast, master, nasty, outcast, paragraph ("æ" in first syllable, "a:" in last syllable: pæ′ rə gra:f), pass, Passover, past, pastor, pastoral, path, perchance, phonograph, photograph, plant, plaster, prance, raft, rascal, rasp, raspberry (ra:z′ bree), rather, reprimand, salve, sample, shaft, shan't, slander, slant, staff, stanch, surpass, task, tomato (Note: The "ay" sound in "potato" is as it is in General American), trance, transcript, transport and other words beginning with the prefix "trans-," vast, waft, wrath.

Note: The "a" in fancy, gas, mass, and glacier (in British RP *glacier* sounds like "glassier" with the final "r" silent; but note that *glacial* is pronounced "glay′ shel") sound like the "æ" in *that*.

æ: The sound, spelled with the letter "a" in both British RP and General American *bat, cat, hat* and *that*; and used in the list above in General American.

This vowel is a front vowel, that is, the stream of air is directed to resonate near the front of the mouth. The vowel is slightly closed, because, literally, the mouth is slightly closed. The tip of the tongue is very low, and the soft palate, at the back of the mouth, slightly raised. The tongue itself is almost flat. The vowel should sound free, without the tension with which some speakers articulate it, because they tense the mouth muscles slightly. Some speakers of British RP diphthongize the vowel slightly, that is, the tongue slides or glides slightly during the articulation of a word like *that*, which then sounds something like "thæət." The final "t" in such a pronunciation is sometimes tapped, in that the tongue does not firmly touch the upper gum ridge, but allows some air to pass through. You can sometimes exaggerate this sound for satiric effect, or simply as a characteristic for a character's voice.

aw: The "aw" in *bought, awful, law, talk,* and *water* never sounds in General American like "a:" in *father*: Pronouncing it that way is a US Middle Western and Western regionalism. This vowel is slightly longer in British RP than in General American. The lips are slightly rounded and the jaw relaxed, with the back of the tongue slightly arched when pronouncing this back vowel. Direct the stream of air to resonate against the back of the upper palate.

e [sometimes spelled "eh" in this book for phonetic purposes]**:** The short front vowel in *bet, get, head, met* is much the same in both British RP and General American. It is spoken with the stream of air directed to resonate against the front of the upper palate, and with the front of the tongue slightly raised.

ee [(i:) ;often spelled "i" as in *machine*]**:** The long front vowel in *meet* is much the same in British RP as in General American. The back of the tongue is arched and the stream of air directed to resonate against the front of the upper palate. In British RP the word *been* is usually pronounced to rhyme with *bean*, and not, as in General American, with *bin*. In British RP "-es" word endings are usually not pronounced with a schwa but with the sound "eez" ("i:z"). In General American they often rhyme with the word *is*.

i: The short front vowel in *bit, busy, mister, pit, tip, trip,* and *will* is much the same in both British RP and General American. It is spoken with the jaw relaxed, the tongue arched and the stream of air directed to resonate against the front of the upper palate.

o: The short, back, rounded vowel "o" in words like *conversation, hot, not, got, model, problem,* etc. sounds almost like the "a:" in *father* in General American, but like a very short "aw" in *law* in British RP. To pronounce it the jaw should be open rather wide, the tongue relaxed with its tip behind the lower front teeth, its back low, and the lips slightly rounded. The stream of air is directed to resonate at the back of the upper palate.

ö: The sound heard in the words *heard, attorney, bird, first, hurt, sir, work,* and *learn* is a closed mid vowel. It is slightly more closed and longer in British RP than in General American. The tongue is relaxed but slightly arched, the jaw opened, but not very much, and the lips protruded slightly for the British RP sound, but in a more neutral position for the sound heard in General American. The stream of air is directed to resonate towards the middle of the upper palate.

oo: This spelling stands for two sounds: the short back vowel "oo" in *book,* also spelled with a "u" as in *put,* and the long back vowel "oo" in *boot.* To pronounce the short "oo" sound the jaw is slightly open and the lips rounded. For the long "oo" sound the lips are protruded and rounded, and the tongue is arched. The stream of air is directed to resonate against the back of the upper palate. The word *room* is generally pronounced with the sound heard in *book* in British RP, and with the sound heard in *boot* in General American. Otherwise the sounds are much the same in both accents.

u: In General American the vowel "u" in *up, above, but, cup, love,* never sounds like the "a:" in *father,* as it so often does in British RP. This sound, which does not occur in many other languages, is a mid vowel, with the stream of air directed to resonate against the middle of the upper palate. The jaw is wide open, the tongue relaxed and low, and the lips unrounded.

Diphthongs and Triphthongs

Note: As mentioned on page 31 the four triphthongs of English are "a:eeə" as in briar; "o:ooə" as in lower; "a:ooə" as in hour; and "oowə" as newer. For information on the four triphthongs, and on the diphthongs formed with the semi-vowels "y" and "w" see the same section, "Some Definitions and Some Notes on Language," page 31.

ay ["ay" as in *say;* often spelled "a" as in *take*]**:** The diphthong in *late* and *say* is much the same in British RP and General American. In British RP this sound is often but not always shortened in words ending with *day,* so *Monday* becomes MONdee, *holiday* HOLidee, etc., but *weekday* and *workday* retain the full long "ay."

I [as in *I* or *eye;* IPA symbol "ai"]**:** This diphthong, heard in *I, fight, might,* and *right,* combines the broad "a:" discussed above with the "ee" in *meet;* the "a:" is stressed. In British RP the full long diphthong is used in "-ile" word endings, as in *hostile, facile, missile, mobile, projectile, servile,* etc. In General American the "-ile" ending is a schwa in most words. In British RP the "ee" half of the diphthong is dropped in some words when they are unstressed, such as *I'm,* for example, which becomes "a:m" or even "əm."

oh [as in *oh;* often spelled "o" as in *home*]**:** The long diphthong "o" heard in such words as *know* and *own* in General American English is a combination of the short vowel "o" and the sound of "oo" in *boot*: o'oo. In British RP it is a combination of the schwa "ə" and "oo": ə'oo. Elongate the lips for the British sound. (Note: The first part of the diphthong is sometimes incorrectly thought of as being like "e" in *met*). In British RP the first syllable is stressed when the following words are nouns, the last when they are verbs, and the long diphthong is used in the nouns *process* (PROH səs; plural: PROH sə seez) and *progress* (PROH grəs), where General American gives an even stress on both syllables when these words are nouns, and stresses the last syllable when they are verbs, and uses the "a:" in *father*: PRA: SES; PRA: GRES.

ow or **ou** [the spelling "ou" is used in this book in phonetic transcriptions]**:** In British RP the diphthong in *how, house* combines the "a:" in *father* and the "oo" in *boot;* the "a:" is stressed. The General American diphthong combines the "æ" in *that* with the "oo" in *boot.*

u [as in *you*]**:** The long sound in *duke* and *tune* is a diphthong combining the semi-vowel "y" with the "oo" in *boot.* In British RP and often in General American the full diphthong is almost always pronounced in *duke, tune, flute, lure, lute, institution, constitution, delusion, illusion, lunatic, Tuesday, newspaper,* etc. When the semi-vowel "y" is inserted after a consonant, that consonant is *palatalized.* Any consonant (or vowel) can be palatalized. Palatalization of this diphthong is much more widespread in British RP than in General American. To drop the "y" is satirical in the British upper classes—*dook,* etc.—and an affectation of the 1920s and 1930s. There are some words in which a simple consonant is pronounced without adulteration before "oo"; for example the "d" in *graduate* does not sound like the "dge" in *edge,* nor the "x" in *sexual* like "ksh": GRÆ dyoo ayt'; SEKS yoo əl (in General American: "SEK shoo əl").

Stress Patterns (Rhythm)

In English every word has its particular stress, which does not vary. If the stress changes, the meaning changes. *FREquent* means "often"; *freQUENT* means "to go someplace or to be someplace often," a distinction frequently forgotten nowadays. Other examples: *IMport* (noun) and *imPORT* (verb); *in-SULT* (verb) and *INsult* (noun); *PROgress* (noun) and *proGRESS* (verb). (Some rare words, such as *besant* [an ancient coin] and *prolix* [unnecessarily wordy] can be stressed on either syllable without changing their meaning; so can some less rare words such as *detail*.) The most important stressed syllable, from the speaker's point of view, is called the "nuclear tone," because it is the "nucleus" of the sentence, and is usually spoken on a longer, stronger and often higher pitch. The schwaed vowels in British RP in the unstressed syllables, for example, lead the speaker to his or her emphasis as quickly as he or she wishes, without necessarily rushing to make a point, and give the sentence a characteristic British rhythm. The nuclear tones are spoken with their vowels more lengthened; and the nuclear tones are more stressed in British RP than in General American. In a General American rhythm, vowels in unstressed syllables are given a fuller value; they literally take more time to utter.

In British RP many words are stressed differently than they are in General American. Such words as *secondary, territory, ordinary* and *extraordinary* lose the secondary stress they have in General American on the "-or" or "-ar" syllables, and are pronounced in British RP either with a schwa, or can even disappear entirely: "SEK ən də ree" or "SEK ən dree," "TE rə tə ree" or "TE rə tree," etc. Note also that the "r" may be trilled when it is between two vowels. Words ending in "-ization" are often pronounced with the diphthong "I" instead of the schwa one might expect: *civilization* (SI və lI ZAY shən); *organization* (AW gə nI ZAY shən), and so forth. The ending "-ess" in such words as *princess, countess,* and *stewardess* (but not *actress*) is often stressed in British RP, and almost never in General American. Among other words pronounced differently in British RP from General American are: *believe* (bleev, occasionally); *cigarette* (sig ə RET; as opposed to General American stress, which is on the first syllable); *corollary* (kə RA: lə ree, as opposed to American KA: rə le ree); *dictate* (as a verb pronounced "dik TAYT"; as a noun it is pronounced "DIK tayt," where Americans use this second pronunciation for both the verb and the noun), *disciplinary* (dis i PLi nə ree); *discriminatory* (dis kri mi NAY tə ree); *fashionable* (FÆSH nə bl); *February,* often pronounced even by newscasters on American television as "FEB yoo er ee," is pronounced occasionally in Britain as "FEB ree"; *frontier* (FRUN ti: ə); *government* (GUV mənt); *library* (occasionally LI bree); *literary* ("Li tə rə ree" or "Li trə ree" or "Li tree," but not like General American "Li tə RE ree"); *literature* (Li trə chə); *mandatory* ("mæn DAY tə ree," as opposed to General American "MÆN də taw ree," although the latter is also heard in British RP as "MÆN də tree); *manufacture* (MÆ nə FÆK tyə; MÆ nə FÆK tshə, as opposed to American "MÆN y<u>oo</u> FÆK tshər"); *national* (NÆSH nəl); *ordinary* ("AW dn ree" or "AW də nə ree," with or without a trilled "r," as opposed to General American "AWR din EH ree"); *perhaps* (præps; phæps; pə HÆPS); *police* (plees); *premature* (PREH mə TYOO ə, as opposed to American "PREE mə TSHOOR"); *temporary* (TEM pree; TEM prə ree; TEM pə rə ree), General American "TEM pə REH ree." For British proper names consult the *BBC Pronouncing Dictionary of British Names.*

Pitch (Intonation, Music)

In English and in Indo-European languages generally, all stressed and important syllables, meaning whichever syllables the speaker wishes to emphasize, are spoken on a differentiated pitch, often a high pitch, sometimes on a much lower pitch, and with more muscular force than is used in unstressed syllables. Such stressed syllables are therefore louder than unstressed syllables; the vowel in them may be longer as well. All unstressed and unimportant syllables are usually spoken on a lower pitch. Stressed syllables may also be spoken on more than one pitch, with a rising or falling tone. Because of the prevalence of diphthongs in English it is easy to use falling and rising tones; one half of the diphthong is at one end of the rise or fall and the other half is at the other end.

At the end of a simple declarative sentence the pitch is usually lowered slightly.

At the end of a question the pitch rises, but this pattern may change in certain circumstances. If the word "are" is stressed in "How are you?" it is also often spoken on an upper pitch and "you" on a lower one, for example.

An imperative, or a command, is usually spoken with a falling tone.

Emotional utterances, such as expletives, may add several pitches to the pattern.

There generally are four or five pitches in a typical sentence, or utterance, in General American English. There are possibly a few more tones or pitches in a typical British RP sentence. One of the features of other native accents is that they have their own typical intonation patterns.

Some Sounds to Avoid

Be very careful to eliminate the following nonstandard sounds from your pronunciation, unless you need them for a character's dialogue. If you don't get rid of these sounds, they may interfere with your getting a recording job.

1. Sibilant or whistling "s." To avoid this phenomenon, come quickly off the "s" as soon as it is pronounced.

2. Glottal stops at the ends of words ending with "t," such as *what, bit, put;* or in the middle of a word such as *bottle, battle* or *matter*. A glottal stop is increasingly heard at the ends of words in the contemporary upper-class accent known as Thames Estuary English, but is not usual in Thames Estuary English in the case of the "t" sound occurring in the middle of the word. Final and middle glottal stops are heard in various British provincial and American regional accents.

3. Typical Southern USA substitution of "i" for "e" (pen for pin, etc.), also heard in some Irish and Scottish accents.

4. Flat Midwestern USA "a" (black; that)

5. Midwestern USA substitution of "ah" for "aw" in such words as "law," "talk," etc.

6. The provincial British substitution in some accents of the "oo" heard in *book* for the standard "u" in such words as *but, love, above,* and *much.*

Some Difficulties of English: Some Things to Look Out For

Look out for the variable sounds associated with the combination of letters "ough": *cough* (awf); *doughty* (ou); *laugh* (General American "æf"; British RP "a:f"); *rough* (uf); *thorough* (General American "oh"; British RP "ə"); *through* (oo).

Always look up nautical terms, such as *forecastle,* pronounced "FOHK səl, or, sl" and *boatswain,* pronounced "BOH sən."

Many abbreviations are pronounced as acronyms, such as the American WAC (Women's Army Corps), often spelled "Wac," for a woman who is a member, pronounced "wæk." Many abbreviations have the letters pronounced, such as the British RAF, Royal Air Force. Always look up abbreviations, unless you are absolutely sure about their pronunciations. For literary abbreviations, find out the director's or the company's requirements, if any. Should you pronounce the letters of "i. e." (the abbreviation for Latin *id est,* which means "that is"), say the Latin words, or say the English words? Some Latin abbreviations, like "ibid." (for Latin *ibidem,* meaning "in the previously mentioned place," whether a book, a chapter, or other source), are pronounced as written; "ibid." is said with two short "i" sounds, and the first syllable stressed: i' bid.

Be careful about regional variations in place names. A geographical dictionary will list some. For others you either have to know them, or call a local telephone operator for advice. *Houston*, for example, is the name of a city in Texas, and of a street in New York. In Texas it is pronounced, like the man for which it was named, "HYOO stən"; in New York it is "HOU stən" Street. The New Jersey city of Newark is pronounced "NYOO ərk," and the Delaware city of Newark is pronounced "NYOO a:rk." Then there are Galveston, Texas, and Galveston, Indiana. In Texas the name of the city is pronounced "GAL vi stən"; in Indiana it is "gal VES tən." In North Carolina and in South Carolina there are two cities named Beaufort, but in North Carolina the name is pronounced "BOH fərt" and in South Carolina it is "BYOO fərt." Always look up names of American towns named after foreign cities, such as Cairo (pronounced KAY roh), Illinois, or Lima (pronounced "LI mə), Ohio; the Peruvian city is pronounced "LEE ma:." In France, by the way, there are two towns with identically spelled names twenty miles apart in the Pyrenees: Salies-du-Salat. But the name of one is pronounced sounding the final "s" in *Salies* and the final "t" in *Salat*, and the name of the other is pronounced with the final "s" and the final "t" silent ("sa: lees dü sa: LA:T" and "sa: lee dü sa: LA:").

There are some words that are quite similar to each other, and therefore easily confused. Two examples: antimony (an ti MOH nee), the name of a chemical element, and antinomy (an TIN ə mee), meaning "a contradiction in terms"; ordnance (AWRD nənts), meaning "artillery," and ordinance (AWRD i nənts), meaning "a decree."

Be sure to look up any obscure words beginning with the orthographic combination "ch," because they can be problematic. In most words "ch" is pronounced "tsh," but in words of Greek and other origins it is pronounced "k": Chalcedon, chalcedony, Chaldean, character, charisma, psychology, psychiatry, etc. In words of French origin (and in the name of the Russian opera singer Chaliapin) it is pronounced "sh": Chamonix, champagne, chiffon, etc. In the word "yacht" "ch" is silent. In some cases "ch" is pronounced like "kh," as in Scottish "loch" or Hebrew/Yiddish "Chasidic" or "Chanukah," although the more usual pronunciations are "Hasidic" or "Hanukah."

You will come across quite a few words, often of Greek origin, in which the initial letter is silent, such as Ctesiphon (a ruined city in Iraq), mnemonic, psalm, pseudo, psychology, ptarmigan, pterodactyl, Ptolemy, etc.

Some Words With Two Pronunciations

There are many words with more than one pronunciation, such as *Himalayas*, *Kenya*, *pianist*, *kilometer*, *either*, *neither*, *status*, *data*, etc. The word *precedence* is pronounced either "PRE si dents, or, sə dənts " or "pri, or, prə SEED ənts," although its meaning doesn't change. However, the first pronunciation is usual when referring simply to the act of going before, while the second is more customary when referring to protocol or to prerogatives, that is, to the right of someone to precede someone else, as in "The prince takes precedence over the duke." You should follow the director's or company's requirements, if any, for those words.

Other words have two pronunciations, each of which changes the meaning of the word. See the section above on Stress on page 42. When the stress in a word changes, the meaning changes: Usually if the final syllable of such a word is stressed, it is a verb; if the first syllable, a noun. Here are just a few examples of a different kind:

aged: Pronounced "AYDGD" it means "old with regard to a thing," such as cheese or wine, or when talking of someone's age: aged twenty. Pronounced "AY dgid" it means "being old," with regard to a person: an aged man.

axes: Pronounced "AK siz" it is the plural of *ax*. Pronounced "AK seez" it is the plural of *axis*.

buffet: Pronounced "BU fit" it means a blow (noun) or to give someone a blow, whether it is a person or the wind (verb). Pronounced "boo FAY" in both General American and British RP it means a banquet table or sideboard. In British RP it also means a railway station or railway car snack bar, when it is sometimes pronounced "BU fee." When it means sideboard or banquet table the pronunciation "BU fit" is sometimes used in the UK in both British RP and provincial accents.

Carnegie: Pronounced "ka:r NEG ee," this is the name of the Scottish-American millionaire and philanthropist. When one talks about New York City's Carnegie Deli or Carnegie Hall, even though they are both named for him, the first syllable is stressed: KA:R nig ee. Go figure!

depot: In General American, when the first syllable is pronounced "dee," the word means a train station; when it is pronounced "deh" it means a military or other storehouse. In British RP the second pronunciation is used for all meanings.

gymnasium: Pronounced "dgim NAY zee əm," the word means "a place where one exercises"; pronounced "gim NA: zee əm" it means a European secondary school.

learned: Pronounced "lö:nd" in British RP, or "lö:rnd" in General American it is the past participle of the verb *learn;* pronounced "LÖ: nid" or "LÖ:R nid" it is an adjective meaning someone who is educated or erudite.

lower: Pronounced "LOH ər," it means "farther down" (adjective), or "to cause something to descend" (verb); pronounced "LOU ər" (with the "ou" of the word *out*), it means "to descend" (verb), as in Shakespeare's *Richard the Third,* Act I, Scene 1: "... and all the clouds that lower'd upon our house."

patent: "PÆ tnt," the usual General American pronunciation, is a noun meaning "the rights granted by a government to an inventor," "the document granting those rights," "a document showing aristocratic status (patents of nobility)," or "a kind of leather"; and an adjective meaning "obvious." "PAY tnt" is the usual British RP pronunciation for all meanings, as in "PAY tnt leather shoes." The pronunciation "PAY tnt" is heard, although more rarely, in General American when the word means "obvious."

placer: When pronounced "PLAY sər" it means either someone who puts something in its place, or an animal or person among the winners of a contest. Pronounced "PLÆ sər" the word means either a deposit of some precious mineral, such as gold, in gravel, or the site of "placer mining," in which a placer deposit is washed to separate out the precious mineral.

primer: Pronounced "PRI mər" [I = eye] it means, among other things, a coat of paint; if the first syllable is pronounced "pri" (as in the word "prim"), it means an elementary schoolbook. British RP uses the first pronunciation for both meanings.

process: As a noun, this word is pronounced "PRA: ses" (General American), or "PROH ses, or, səs" (British RP). As a verb, meaning to go forward in a procession, it is pronounced "proh, or, prə SES."

routed: Pronounced "ROU tid" it means defeated. Pronounced "ROO tid" it means sent to its destination.

second: As a verb, pronounced "si KA:ND," the word is a military term in both the US and the UK, meaning to post an officer temporarily to another assignment. In the UK this pronunciation also has the broader meaning of being sent from one job to another, or from one branch to another, as the employee of a company. As a noun, meaning a unit of time or a place in the order of things, the word is pronounced "SEK ənd." With the same pronunciation when it is a verb, it means to support someone or something, as in the phrase "I second that."

secretive: This adjective is pronounced either "SEE krə tiv" or "sə KREE tiv," and means the same thing either way: reluctant to disclose secrets; reserved, withdrawn, private. But if you are talking of bodily secretions, only the second pronunciation is correct.

slough: This word has several pronunciations: 1) "slou" (with the "ou" in the word *out*) for a swampy place or a hole full of muck, or a condition of despair, as in John Bunyan's *Pilgrim's Progress*: the "Slough of Despond"; 2) "sloo" for a reedy pool; 3) "sluf" for an outer layer of skin, a discard in a game of cards, or anything shed or cast off, as in the phrase *to slough off*.

Comparative Pronunciations for British RP and General American

1. Words ending in *–ory, -ary, -ery* are pronounced with a full vowel in the penultimate syllable in General American and with a schwa in British RP.

2. Words ending in "-es": In British RP these endings are usually pronounced with the sound "eez" or with a lengthened "i:," and not with a schwa. In General American they often rhyme with the word *is*.

3. In British RP the full long diphthong is used in "-ile" word endings, as in *facile, missile, mobile, projectile, servile,* etc. In General American the "-ile" ending is a schwa in most words.

4. Words ending in *–ization* are pronounced with a long diphthong "I" in the antepenultimate syllable in British RP; with a schwa in General American.

5. The words *dictate, frustrate,* and *narrate,* among others, are stressed on the first syllable in General American, and on the second in British RP.

6. *Been* rhymes with *bean* in a British accent 99 times out of a hundred, whereas in General American it always rhymes with *bin*.

7. In British RP *for* is often, though not always, pronounced with a schwa (fə) before a consonant or a semi-vowel, as in *for you* and *for me*: "fə yoo";

"fə mee." *For* is pronounced "ə" before a vowel, when the final "r" in *for* is linked to the vowel, as in *for us*: fə rus. *For* is not usually stressed. In General American *for* usually rhymes with the number "four"; the final "r" is lightly pronounced.

8. In British RP the following common words often take a schwa on the second pronounced syllable, whereas in General American the second syllable is pronounced "ee": *anything, everything* (the second "e" in the word's spelling is silent in both accents). The word *everybody* in British RP is often pronounced "E vrə bə dee" in General American "E vree BA: dee." The word *always* is often pronounced with a schwa on the second syllable in British RP, and with the full diphthong "ay" in General American.

9. In British RP *to* is almost always pronounced with a schwa (tə) before the semi-vowels "y" and "w" and before a consonant, as in *to you, to wait* or *to be*: tə yoo; tə wayt; tə bee. *To* is pronounced to rhyme with "too" and "two" before a vowel, as in *to act*: too akt. *To* in a verb infinitive is almost never stressed. The word *today* is usually pronounced "tə DAY" in both General American and British RP. In General American *to* usually rhymes with "too" and "two." The British actor's instinct is to say "Tə be aw not tə be"; the American's "Too be or not too be," with the "r" in *or* lightly pronounced.

Note: The first pronunciation in the list of examples below is British RP; the second is General American. The capitalized syllables indicate primary stress.

acrimony: ÆK ri mə nee; ÆK ri moh nee

advertisement: ad VÖ tis mənt (This is also General American, with "vör" instead of "vö."); ad vör TIZ mənt

apparatus: æ pə RAY təs; æ pə RÆ təs

aristocrat: Æ ris tə kræt; ə RIS tə kræt

clerk: kla:k; klörk

composite: KA:M pə zit; kəm PA: zit

controversy: kən TRA: və see; KA:N trə vör see (This is also British RP, with silent post-vocalic "r.")

demolition: DEE mə li shən; DE: mə li shən (This is also British RP.)

discriminatory: dis krim i NAY tə ree; dis KRIM in ə taw ree (This is also British RP, with "tə" instead of "taw.")

dynasty: This word is stressed on the first syllable in both British RP and General American, but the British RP pronunciation of the first syllable is "din"; the General American "deye."

glacier: GLÆS ee ə; GLAY shər, but note: "glacial" is GLAY shəl in both British RP and General American.

laboratory: lə BO: rə tree; LÆ brə TAW ree

lieutenant: ləf TE nənt; loo, or lyoo, TE nənt

maintain: mən TAYN; mayn TAYN (This is also British RP.)

medicine: MED sin; MED i sin

modernize: MO:D nize or MO:D ə nize; MA:D ər nize

nephew: NE vyoo; NE fyoo

privacy: This word is stressed on the first syllable in both Britsh RP and General American. In British RP the pronunciation is "pri" and in General American "prI.")

schedule: SHED yool; SKED yool, or, more vulgarly, dgool

thorough: THU rə; THU roh

vitamins: This word is stressed on the first syllable in both Britsh RP and General American. The British RP pronunciation of the first syllable is "vi" and the General American "veye."

Pronouncing Foreign Names, Words and Phrases

Many nineteenth-century authors assumed that their readers were educated people who knew Greek and Roman mythology, and could understand quotations, sometimes very long ones, too, in Latin, Greek, French and German, without translations. Consider the following opening of Edgar Allan Poe's story "The Purloined Letter":

> *Nil sapientiae odiosus acumine nimine.—Seneca*
> At Paris, just after dusk one gusty evening in the autumn of 18—, I was enjoying the twofold luxury of meditation and a meerschaum, in company with my friend, C. Auguste Dupin, in his little back library, or book-closet, *au troisième*, No. 33 *Rue Dunôt, Faubourg St. Germain.*

Nor does Poe stop there. There are French sentences and Latin phrases, none of them translated, scattered throughout the story, which ends as follows:

> "... and I just copied into the blank sheet the words—
> '—Un dessein si funeste,
> S'il n'est digne d'Atrée, est digne de Thyeste.'
> They are to be found in Crébillon's 'Atrée.' "

NOTES, COMMENTS, AND HINTS

Consider the amount of erudition required to understand these brief excerpts: Not only does Poe expect you to understand the untranslated quotations from Seneca and Crébillon, but he also expects you to know who they are, and, eventually, what these quotations mean to the story. The quotation from the tragedy *Atrée et Thyeste* in particular gives you a key to the whole affair of the purloined letter. In addition, you have to know the myths of Thyestes and Atreus in order to understand the ironic, wry allusion made to his opponent by Dupin (pronounced "dü PÆ*N*"), the character who wrote the note in which the quotation appears.

A "meerschaum" (pronounced "MEEə or MEER SHO:M" in English, with both syllables equally stressed; in German the word is pronounced "ME:ə SHOUM," with the digraph "ou" representing the sound in the word "out") is a kind of pipe with an ornately carved white bowl. The German name means "sea foam."

The address in the first paragraph of the story indicates that the narrator is visiting his friend Dupin in his fourth-floor apartment in the aristocratic quarter of Paris, the 16th arrondissement (pronounced "a: raw*N* di:s ma:*N*"; it means "district," literally "a rounding off"), which is the Faubourg St.-Germain (pronounced "fo: boor se:*N* zhe:r ME:*N*"). On the other hand, Poe may simply have meant the area of the 6th arrondissement now called St.-Germain. The church of St.-Germain, one of the oldest in Paris, is located there. The Paris of his day had not yet undergone the vast change brought about by Baron Haussmann's (pronounced "o:s MA:N") radical reconstruction of the city. The phrase *au troisième* means "on the third" and is pronounced "o: trwa:

zi: YE:M"; the ground floor of a Paris building is not numbered; floor number one is the name for the floor one flight up. The street name *Rue Dunôt* is pronounced "rü dü NO:"; but, in fact, there was and is no such street anywhere in Paris (there is a *rue Dunois* in the 13th arrondissement); Poe invented the name.

Seneca (ca. 3 BCE–65 CE) was a Roman philosopher, dramatist and statesman who espoused Stoicism, the philosophy which emphasizes, among other things, the point of view that all passion and self-indulgence are to be eschewed and (this is perhaps its most famous tenet, amounting to a cliché), that adversity is to be borne with patience and fortitude. Seneca was Nero's tutor. He was later out of favor with that sadistic, lunatic emperor and stoically committed suicide. The quotation Poe uses as an epigraph means: "Nothing is so odious to wisdom as too much cunning." According to a number of scholars Poe invented the saying, as it does not appear in Seneca's works. In the Classical system of Latin pronunciation the sentence is pronounced: "ni:l sa: pee EN tee eye oh dee OH soos a: KOO mee nay NI: mee nay."

The all but forgotten Prosper Jolyot de Crébillon (1674–1762) (pronounced "pro:s PAIR zho: LYO: də kré bi: YO:*N*"), was a classical dramatist. The quotation, from his revenge tragedy *Atrée et Thyeste* (1707), means: "So deadly a plan, if it is not worthy of Atreus (pronounced "AY tree us"), is worthy of Thyestes (pronounced "thigh ESS teez")." The French quotation is pronounced: " "u*N* de sæ:*N* si: fü NEST / si:l né di: nyə da: TRÉ / e: di: nyə də tee YEST."

In Greek mythology Atreus, the founder of the house of that name, was the father of Agamemnon and of Menelaus, who married Helen, on whose account the Trojan War was fought. Thyestes was Atreus' brother. He seduced Aerope, his brother's wife. In order to revenge himself, Atreus invited Thyestes, on the pretext of effecting reconciliation, to a feast at which Atreus served him a dish made of Thyestes' own children. Atreus was punished by the gods for his shocking behavior. There is a great deal more involved in the story of these two brothers, and of this tragic family. The stories connected with the House of Atreus have inspired great literature and great plays, from Aeschylus, Euripides, Sophocles, Seneca, Chaucer and Shakespeare to Racine, Goethe and Eugene O'Neill.

If you were asked to record Poe's story, you would have to pronounce the French as perfectly as you could, certainly with absolute correctness, even if you have an American or English accent. As for the Latin, there are several systems of pronunciation. Since nobody really knows how the ancient Romans pronounced Latin, you would have to choose one of them, depending on the era in which the Latin is used. You should learn the three systems of Latin pronunciation: Classical; Medieval, or Church; and the old English system, still used in legal Latin and, in a modified form, in scientific nomenclature. You may find knowing the different systems useful in all kinds of ways, from recording the classical quotations in Poe's story to reading the dialogue in a British law trial story or the role of a medieval clergyman speaking Latin in novels yet to be written, which—you never know—you may be called upon to record. For more on Latin pronunciation see the Introduction to the section on Romance Language accents in my book *Accents: A Manual for Actors* (Limelight Revised and Expanded Edition, 2002).

In contemporary fiction the use of foreign languages is all but nonexistent, but it is ubiquitous in nonfiction, especially in history and biography. It would have been far too difficult for me to record biographies of Toqueville, Philippe d'Orléans (Louis XIV's brother), Napoleon the First, Napoleon the Third, Marie Antoinette, Charles de Gaulle, Balzac, Baudelaire, and Rimbaud without knowing French; or an anthology like *The Norton Book of Travel* (travel literature from ancient Greek to contemporary accounts) without having a rudimentary knowledge of the phonetic systems of many languages. Nor could I have recorded Henri Troyat's biography of Turgenev without knowing French and some Russian, or the short stories of Anton Chekhov without knowing something about Russian phonetics so as to be able to pronounce the Russian names correctly, albeit in an anglicized manner. Histories of Brazil and numerous books about the Middle East required of me a working knowledge of Portuguese, Arabic and Hebrew pronunciation, if not of the languages themselves.

You are expected to, and of course you want to, pronounce foreign words and phrases correctly, fluidly, fluently, and authentically, although often the better-known ones are anglicized, as in the French *déja vu* (usually pronounced DAY zha: VOO, without the French "ü" sound, which would make it dé zha: VÜ). You must look them up if you don't know what they mean; there is no use in pretending you do when you don't. Even if you have learned at least the rudiments of other languages, or at least how to pronounce them, there can be unexpected obstacles in your path. Be aware, for instance, that the diacritical marks that indicate pronunciation in languages such as Czech, Polish and Serbo-Croatian are not always used in English or American books, so you will have to look up the names of people and places. Be aware as well that there is no uniform romanized transliteration from other alphabets, such as Cyrillic, Hebrew or Arabic. Authors use different systems of transliteration—sometimes of their own devising; the system is not always explained, and in such cases it will be up to you to figure out the phonetics, perhaps by looking up a word or name in a dictionary printed in the original alphabet, if necessary. You should learn the two different, but consistent systems for the romanization of Chinese (the earlier Wade-Giles system; the later Pinyin system); either may be used, but sometimes, inconsistently, an author uses both! And learning stress patterns for different languages is a big help where languages have uniform, invariable patterns: Polish words, for instance, are always stressed on the penultimate syllable; Hungarian on the first; French phrases on the last syllable, unless it contains a "mute e" (the equivalent of a schwa), and so forth. In languages where stress patterns are random, as in English or Russian, you have to check the stress on every word you don't know, and even some you think you do know. (For instance, the Russian name *Ivanov* can be stressed on any of its three syllables, depending on whose name it is!) In tonal languages, such as Chinese—Mandarin, Cantonese, etc.—or Vietnamese, you should try to learn and do the correct tones. (A *tonal* language uses tones, or pitches, that change the meaning of a word. The word *ma* in Mandarin, for instance, indicates a question, or means "mother," "scold," or "horse," depending on which tone is used. English is an example of an *intonational* language, where the a word can be uttered on any pitch without changing its meaning.) Familiarize yourself thoroughly with the phonetic system and pitch and stress patterns of any language you have to pronounce.

Practice Exercises for Good Diction

The object of these exercises is twofold: to relax the mouth, and to make the muscles into a flexible instrument. Exercise the muscles of the mouth by moving the lips from side to side with the mouth slightly open, then repeat with the mouth open wider. Open and close the jaw, and stick the tongue out and back in. Make chewing motions with your mouth closed. Do these exercises repetitively, at least ten times per set.

Distinct articulation of consonants and of clear, unclouded vowels is very important in all areas of vocal work. One good exercise is to take any consonant and follow it with all the vowels and diphthongs. Take "h," for example, and say: "ha, ha, ha, hay, hay, hay, heh, heh, heh, hee, hee, hee, hi, hi, hi, high, high, high, ho, ho, ho, hoh, hoh, hoh, hu, hu, hu, hoo, hoo, hoo," etc.

Be very careful when doing the exercises below to avoid consonant dropping, assimilation and coalescence. Assimilation and coalescence take several forms:

1. One consonant can disappear into another in such phrases as "quite determined," where the "t" in "quite" would simply be dropped and elided into the "d" of determined;

2. Similarly "s" or "z" coalesces with "sh" is such phrases as "this shoe" or "these should go here";

3. Assimilation also takes place when "t" or "d" is followed by "y" and changed into "tsh" or "dzh" in such phrases as "can't you tell" (kæn choo); or "get your book" (ge chər) or "did you see that?" (di dgoo);

4. Consonants in consonant clusters are frequently dropped in such phrases as "hold fast," where we should here the "d" and "t," or "the first thing I want to tell you," where we should hear all the final "t" sounds, even though in normal speech we would not hear the final "t" in "want" before "to," a phrase often heard as "wanna."

In normal speech, of course, some consonant assimilation is natural, and you would certainly use normal speech in recording dialogue, but for the purposes of these exercises be very aware of the phenomenon. Some of the most salient examples of consonant dropping, assimilation and coalescence are heard in certain regional accents: In New York City "Did you eat yet?" becomes "dgee che?" with the "t" in "yet" glottal stopped. And in a heavy London Cockney "That's all right, isn't it?" becomes "æss aw roy? ni?" with both the "t" in "right" and "it" glottal stopped. In Australia "Made your bed yet?" becomes "my dgə bi dgit" with the "t" in "yet" tapped or even glottal stopped.

Remember Hamlet's advice to the actors: "Speak the speech, I pray you, as I pronounced it to you, trippingly on the tongue; but if you mouth it, as many of your players do, I had as lief the town-crier spoke my lines." That is still good advice. The following exercises should be both educational and amusing.

A Tongue Twister

A flea and a fly in a flue
Were imprisoned, so what could they do?
Said the fly: "Let us flee!"
"Let us fly!" said the flea.
So they flew through a flaw in the flue.

From "Four Tricky Limericks" by Carolyn Wells

(Note: The word tutor should be pronounced "TYOO tər.")

I

A tutor who tooted the flute
Tried to tutor two tooters to toot.
Said the two to the tutor,
"Is it harder to toot or
To tutor two tooters to toot?"

II

A canner exceedingly canny,
One morning remarked to his granny,
"A canner can can
Anything that he can,
But a canner can't can a can, can he?"

From W. S. Gilbert's *Patience* (1881), music by Arthur S. Sullivan, Act One, *Chorus of Dragoons*

(Note: Consonants, consonants and more consonants, initial, middle and final! We ought to hear them all, including the "t" in not *in the first line, and the "d" in* and *wherever the word occurs. And don't forget all those "t" sounds in the line "Pretty sort of treatment for a military man!" Be sure to include the "t" in the middle of the word* treatment*!)*

Now is not this ridiculous, and is not this preposterous?
A thorough-paced absurdity—explain it if you can.
Instead of rushing eagerly to cherish us and foster us,
They all prefer this melancholy literary man.
Instead of slyly peering at us,
Casting looks endearing at us,
Blushing at us, flushing at us, flirting with a fan;
They're actually sneering at us, fleering at us, jeering at us!
Pretty sort of treatment for a military man!
Pretty sort of treatment for a military man!

From Gilbert and Sullivan's *Patience*, Act Two, *Duet*—Bunthorne and Grosvenor

(Notes: 1. The name Grosvenor *is pronounced* "GROHV nə"*; the "V" is sometimes followed by a schwa, giving the name three syllables. 2. The "d" sounds in the words* and *and* cultured *and the "t" in* it *in the line "If I pronounce it chaste" should all be clearly articulated. We want to hear all those consonants.)*

BUN. When I go out of door,
Of damosels a score
(All sighing and burning,
And clinging and yearning)
Will follow me as before.

I shall, with cultured taste,
Distinguish gems from paste,
  And "High diddle diddle"
  Will rank as an idyll,
If I pronounce it chaste!

BOTH. A most intense young man,
  A soulful-eyed young man,
An ultra-poetical, super-aesthetical,
  Out-of-the-way young man!

From Gilbert and Sullivan's *Ruddigore* (1887), Act One, *Song*—Robin Oakapple.

(Notes: 1. Crichton *is pronounced* CRY tən. *James Crichton (1560?–1583?) was a Scottish "Renaissance man," literally and figuratively, and apparently a charming, dashing adventurer. He was known as an erudite scholar when he traveled in Italy in 1579, and he supposedly spoke twelve languages. The Admirable Crichton, as he was called, was killed in a not so admirable street brawl. 2. Be sure to articulate clearly the "z" and "s" sounds in "man's saddled"; the "d" sounds in the line and "And hampered and addled" (we should hear all those "d" sounds); the "t" at the end of the word diffident; and all the "st" sounds in "You must stir it and stump it.")*

My boy, you may take it from me,
  That of all the afflictions accurst
    With which a man's saddled
    And hampered and addled,
  A diffident nature's the worst.
Though clever as clever can be—
  A Crichton of early romance—
    You must stir it and stump it,
    And blow your own trumpet,
  Or, trust me, you haven't a chance!

    If you wish in the world to advance,
    Your merits you're bound to enhance,
      You must stir it and stump it,
      And blow your own trumpet,
  Or, trust me, you haven't a chance!

From Gilbert and Sullivan's *Ruddigore*, Act Two, *Patter-Trio*, Robin, Despard and Margaret, second verse

(Notes: 1. All the "t" and "d" sounds in the first line, and throughout, should be strongly articulated. 2. In British RP the word suggestion *is pronounced* "sə DGEST chən"*; in General American the pronunciation is* "səg DGEST chən." *3. In the word* valuable *pronounce all the vowels:* VÆL yoo ə bəl. *4. In the words* excellent suggestions *make sure we hear all those clearly articulated consonants.)*

MAD MARGARET

If I were not a little mad and generally silly
I should give you my advice upon the subject, willy-nilly;
I should show you in a moment how to grapple with the question,
And you'd really be astonished at the force of my suggestion.
On the subject I should write you a most valuable letter,
Full of excellent suggestions when I feel a little better,
But at present I'm afraid I am as mad as any hatter,
So I'll keep 'em to myself, for my opinion doesn't matter.

Recommended Texts and Exercises for More Diction Practice

1. Anything from W. S. Gilbert's libretti for the Gilbert and Sullivan comic operas. The Patter Songs are perfect; for example, the Lord Chancellor's "Nightmare Song" from Act Two of *Iolanthe* (1882).

2. The lyrics of Noel Coward's songs are also excellent for diction practice. Try such songs as "Mad Dogs and Englishmen" and "Don't Put Your Daughter on the Stage, Mrs. Worthington," two of my favorites. Also, the crisp dialogue in his brilliant play *Private Lives* is admirable for diction practice.

3. The exercises in Edith Skinner's *Speak with Distinction* and the suggestions and exercises in J. Clifford Turner's *Voice and Diction for the Stage*, both mentioned earlier, are all ideal.

4. Use any of the entries in *Bartlett's Roget's Thesaurus* for diction practice. An example, chosen at random: "*attracting,* pulling, drawing, dragging,

tugging; adductive, associative, aducent." Repeat the entry at least three times in a row, as fast as you can, pronouncing all the consonants distinctly.

5. Use any of Shakespeare's *Sonnets*. For practicing the "s" sound, Sonnet XXX is a good one: "When to the sessions of sweet silent thought/I summon up remembrance of things past..." Say the "s" sounds quickly and lightly to avoid sibilance. You will find the sonnet on page 288.

6. Take any word; find all the words that rhyme with it and write them in alphabetical order. Repeat them slowly at first, then more rapidly, making sure to pronounce all the consonants distinctly. An example: at, bat, brat, cat, chat, DAT, drat, fat, flat, frat, gat, gnat, hat, mat, Nat, pat, prat, rat, sat, scat, shat, slat, spat, splat, sprat, tat, that, vat.

7. Certain well-known poems lend themselves very well to diction practice. Among them are Edgar Allan Poe's *The Raven* and *The Bells*; Alfred, Lord Tennyson's *The Charge of the Light Brigade*; Rudyard Kipling's *Boots*; the poems in Lewis Carroll's Alice books and his comic epic *The Hunting of the Snark*.

CHAPTER 3

Microphone and General Recording Techniques

A Brief History of Recording

In 1877 Thomas Alva Edison invented the "talking phonograph," which used a magnetic process to record the human voice on a tinfoil-wrapped cylinder. Within a few years the machine was refined, and recordings were made on longer lasting wax cylinders. By the late 1880s Edison finally felt enough confidence in his improved phonograph to begin recording the voices of the famous for posterity, and well-known actors such as Henry Irving, Edwin Booth, Joseph Jefferson, and Ellen Terry, wanting to have their performances immortalized, and poets and luminaries such as Walt Whitman, Robert Browning, Alfred, Lord Tennyson, Florence Nightingale, W.S. Gilbert and Arthur S. Sullivan, happily flocked to the recording studios, or recorded at home or in hotel rooms. Congratulating him on his "most wonderful discovery," Sullivan remarked jocularly, in the recording he made at Edison's request, that he was "terrified at the thought that so much... bad music may be put on record forever."

In 1887 Emile Berliner invented a flat disc, or record, which was to replace the wax cylinder as the preferred recording medium, especially as its surface became more durable. He coined the word "gramophone" for the machine he invented to play them. By 1915, flat shellac records, playing about four minutes of sound at 78 rpm (revolutions per minute), were the norm.

Before the sound engineers had learned how to regulate volume levels, in the first days of recording in the old acoustic studios, test recordings had to be made for distance, to hear what sounded best. Most of them were destroyed, of course. But there are acoustic test recordings made in London in 1910 of Dame Nellie Melba (1859–1931), the great Australian soprano, singing a few bars from Ophelia's Mad Scene from Ambroise Thomas's opera *Hamlet*, with the conductor Landon Ronald accompanying her on the piano. They are instructive for today's recording artists, since you can clearly hear the different distances each time she sings, as well as the talking in the background. With vastly more sensitive digital equipment, you have to be even more keenly aware of the correct distance from the microphone.

The floor in the acoustic studio was marked out as a grid, and, once the tests had been made, the singer was placed on a given square. A Stage Manager on the floor had the job of moving the singer around physically when necessary, usually on the engineer's signal. The Stage Manager would place his hands lightly on the singer's shoulders and move him or her back and forth, especially on loud high notes, when the singer had to be farther away from the acoustic horn, so as not to distort the recording.

Overtones and undertones did not record terribly well with this rather unsophisticated, primitive equipment, so that subtleties were often lost. Because of their lower timbres, men's voices, such as that of the Italian tenor Enrico Caruso (1873–1921), recorded better than women's voices. It is often said, in fact, that Caruso made RCA and the gramophone. Without his contribution, commercial recording might have been only a passing fad. His voice, which recorded superbly even in the acoustic era, was so uniquely beautiful that he became a household name. The gramophone loved him, as the camera loves an actor like Tom Cruise.

But the greatest tenor of the late 1800s, until Caruso came along, handsome, idolized Jean de Reszke (1850–1925), was so upset by what he heard on experimental recordings he had made for Fonotipia in their Paris studios in 1905 that he insisted they break the masters. He never made another record. Fortunately for us, however, there was Lionel Mapleson.

Mr. Mapleson (1865–1937) was the librarian at New York's Metropolitan Opera. In 1900 he borrowed recording equipment from Thomas Edison, and proceeded to record two-minute snatches on wax cylinders of live performances at the Met through 1903. He captured the voice of de Reszke in some excerpts from Wagner's *Siegfried* and Meyerbeer's *Les Huguenots* and *L'Africaine*. One has to listen several times, even to remastered recordings, to hear the voice. The recordings, made up in the flies (the prompt box, tried first, proved impossible because of the noise of the equipment), sound as if a locomotive is going across the stage. Still, one can hear de Reszke's spectacular, bewitching voice, and he must have been mesmerizing.

The distinguished American diva, Emma Eames (1865–1952) gave a radio interview in 1939 after she had already been retired from the opera stage for twenty-eight years. (You can hear it on *Emma Eames: the complete Victor recordings (1905–11)*, Romophone CD 81002–2, 1993.) She describes the difficulties of making acoustic recordings: "To a sensitive person the conditions were unnerving," she says, in her mellow, mellifluous speaking voice. The singer had to sing directly into the center of the horn, and everything was done in one take. The orchestra was almost "invariably out of tune." The gramophone may have loved some singers' voices, but it did not always love musical instruments: The piano is the star of the acoustic era, and recorded very well, but the violin often sounded squeaky, and tubas had to play the parts written for basses and cellos, whose wooden sounding-boxes recorded poorly.

Revolutionizing the recording industry, the electric microphone replaced the acoustic horn, and electric recording began late in 1925. After 1948 the 33-rpm vinyl LP (long-playing record), which played for about twenty minutes, replaced the more fragile 78s, and lots of people scrambled to replace their old 78 albums, just as, later on, people replaced their LPs and audiocassettes with the new compact discs.

It is instructive to listen to voices that spanned the eras from acoustic to electric recording. You can hear Dame Nellie Melba's 1926 Covent Garden farewell, and her electric studio recordings, and compare them to her earlier, acoustic recordings. Or compare one of the greatest of basses, Ezio Pinza (1892–1957), known to American musical comedy theatergoers as the original Emile de Becque in Rodgers and Hammerstein's *South Pacific,* and to generations of opera enthusiasts as one of the greatest Don Giovannis in Mozart's opera (he was a magnificent singing actor), in his acoustic days and in his later electric recordings. What you hear in comparing the two is: what you *don't hear,* although you are recognizably hearing the same voices. The timbre is there in the acoustic recordings, but the voices are not as rich, even though the performances are thrilling.

Meanwhile, by 1934 there had been another revolutionary development: the perfection of thin plastic magnetic reel-to-reel recording tape. The fragile tape was a long, thin strand wound onto a "feeder" reel, and the end of the tape was attached to a "take-up" reel, onto which the tape continued to wind as it recorded. For the first time, recordings could be edited and mistakes corrected. Tape was soon being used in studios to make master recordings, which were then transferred to records.

The early 1960s saw another technological advance: reduced in size, the tape was enclosed in a tiny protective rectangular plastic box, or cassette, that could be sold commercially and listened to on a cassette player. Some decades later, the CD, or compact disc, which was "read" by a lazar light, instead of coming into contact with a phonograph needle, replaced scratchy LPs.

Cassettes, which tended to deteriorate or develop annoying "tape hiss" after repeated playing, began to be far less manufactured. A newer invention, DAT (digital audiotape), has the same problems. A vast improvement over previous technologies, the digital CD is more or less permanent, sounds the same on every playing, and is not ordinarily susceptible to damage.

During Franklin D. Roosevelt's presidency, Helen Keller and Harry Hopkins came up with the idea of recording books on 78-rpm records for the blind. In 1936 the first Talking Books records were made, and they must have been very inconvenient and cumbersome, with many discs required for each book. The recording artist dared not make mistakes, because there was no way to edit the recording. Once reel-to-reel tape was used to make Talking Books, that situation changed. Although the results were good, the process of correcting mistakes using analog recording technology was clumsy: when the sound engineer had wound the tape to the correct place and pressed the record button, the reader had to be sure to come in exactly on cue, picking up her or his exact pace, in order to make a smooth transition, matching the new recording to the old, and not recording over into the next sentence, which would have necessitated further rerecording. And the sound engineer had to be adept with the buttons, stopping the tape in good time. In the 1960s cassettes replaced the less convenient LPs that had succeeded the 78s, and the contents of the edited reel-to-reel tapes were transferred onto them for distribution to the public after approval from the National Library Service. Digital recording has now replaced the analog reel-to-reel tapes.

Caedmon and, occasionally, other record companies had begun making and releasing recordings of poetry, fiction and plays, many of them original cast recordings, in the 1950s. Other complete plays had been done earlier, such as *Othello* in Paul Robeson's famous 1943 production. And the Shakespeare productions of Orson Welles and his Mercury Theatre (all now available on CD) had been recorded in the 1930s. It was only a question of time, then, before the idea of recording entire books for commercial release occurred to publishing companies as a way to increase their revenues.

Although the recording business was and is mostly involved with music of all kinds, the human speaking voice has always been recorded extensively. Thanks to compact discs, it is again possible to hear the voices of many historical figures and of great actors of the past. There are lessons to be learned about acting styles from recordings of nineteenth-century Shakespearean actors, as well as poets and authors talking about and reading from their works. Listen to recordings of Robert Browning positively shouting his poem "How They Brought the Good News from Ghent to Aix," perhaps because he didn't know how to read for the acoustic horn and thought his voice wouldn't record if he read more quietly; Walt Whitman, sounding very real and natural, not at all forced or artificial, and speaking with a slight

New York accent; and Alfred, Lord Tennyson pounding away at the rhythms of "The Charge of the Light Brigade." They are all absolutely fascinating. And political figures from presidents of the US to prime ministers of the UK also made records. Quite apart from their intrinsic interest, some of these recordings may be useful for character work; see the Bibliography for a list of relevant CDs.

The Microphone

The digital recording equipment and the microphones used nowadays are extremely sensitive. For this reason the microphone is usually covered with a cap, made of foam plastic. In front of it is often a finely meshed screen, called a "pop screen," mounted on a movable arm. Its purpose is to blot out or deaden slightly plosive noises, which might record as a popping sound. Microphones are either omni-directional, that is, they pick up sound from anywhere, or directional, and must be placed directly in front of, or just to the side of, the reader's mouth. Most studio microphones are directional.

Microphone and Recording Technique

1. Never touch the microphone. Do not tap it. Do not blow into it.

2. Let the sound engineer adjust the microphone for you.

3. You will be wearing headphones while you record. You can hear yourself talking, and if the volume is too loud or too soft, ask the sound engineer to adjust it. The volume you hear in the headphones does not affect the volume at which your voice records.

4. Before you begin recording, the sound engineer will do a "level check," asking you to read a bit so he or she can hear the volume of your voice and determine the levels at which he or she has to set the switches to capture your vocal range. If you go over or under the range, adjustments have to be made. When you read for the level check, speak with the actual volume you will be using during the recording. Depending on the results of the level check the sound engineer may readjust the microphone, and/or ask you to change your position by moving closer to or farther away from it.

5. Keep about five or six inches from the mike if it is directly in front of you; about three or four inches if it is slightly to the side.

6. The closer you are to the microphone, the less volume you have to use. You will automatically sound more intimate the closer you get. If you lean back, or move away from the microphone, you will sound less intimate, and the microphone will pick up "room tone" (ambient noise). However, the sound environment inside the studio, which is lined with soundproof materials, is designed to eliminate echoes and extraneous sounds.

7. Use your diaphragm to support the voice, just as if you were projecting on a stage, and place the voice correctly in the masque, but do not speak loudly.

8. Be careful of p, t, s, and plosive sounds generally.

9. Learn to breathe silently. Everything records, including breathing, which you may think is silent, but isn't. Do not take a loud breath before starting a sentence; those annoying "breath cuts," as they are called, make editing as tedious and sometimes as impossible as trying to edit a film in which an actor and the continuity person have not taken care to have the actor in the same physical position for different takes of the same scene. Breath cuts have to be corrected immediately by rerecording or else deleted by the editor later.

10. Sit as still and as quietly as possible. Try not to move while you are recording.

The Environment of the Soundproof Sound Studio

You will be recording in a two-room soundproof studio. The recording booth half of the studio is usually rather small, to avoid a lot of extra "air" in the sound being recorded. The furniture in the recording booth consists of a table with a reading stand and a lamp or lamps on it, and a chair in front of it. Next to the table is a microphone on a floor stand, and there may be a side table with a pitcher of water and some cups. You will be able to see the director and sound engineer on the other side of the booth's large window, as they sit at the digital soundboard.

Before or after the session the engineer usually records extra "room tone," which is ambient noise used as needed to make the recording sound full, and not hollow, and is especially necessary when editing corrections. The ambience, as heard on the recording, should be consistent, and since it varies slightly from day to day, it has to be recorded at the session for editing purposes, which shows you just how sensitive modern recording equipment is.

Preparing for the Recording Session

A commercial recording session can last anywhere from four to six hours, sometimes seven or eight. If the recording is noncommercial, sessions usually last two or three hours. Sometimes the actor will record for two two-hour sessions, with an hour break in between. Proper pauses and breaks are always taken, often at the reader's discretion.

It is a good idea not to eat or drink before a session. Stomach noise records very well, and the session will have to stop while you gurgle and growl. In any case, food and drink, especially dairy products, as I said earlier, can create phlegm that will interfere with the vocal cords by coating them, and you want to have them as clear as possible. On the other hand, drinking water or clear liquids can help moisten the vocal cords and the mucous membranes.

How to prepare the text, usually at home, on your own unpaid time, is explained in Chapters Five through Nine. This must be done before you are ready for the session, for which you must arrive on time, or, even better, early at the recording studio, so that you have time to relax after your trip to work, and to prepare for the session.

You will enter the recording booth, and place the script, whether loose pages, pages in a binder, or the printed book itself, on the adjustable reading stand, which you can set at the angle that is most comfortable for you. If you need to, use a "book prop," which is a wooden or metal bar placed at the bottom of the reading stand, to allow the book resting on the prop to sit higher on the stand. You may have to hold the book with your hands as you record to keep it steady, or it may be flat so that you can leave your hands free. If the book is in the form of loose pages, you will have room to place only two pages at a time on the reading stand, and you will have to stop after you have recorded them in order to place the next two. Put the pile of loose pages on the table to the left of the reading stand so you can glance at it sideways and finish a sentence started at the bottom of the second page and continued on top of the next, before you stop to put the new pages on the stand.

Sit down in what should be a comfortable chair, which may or may not have arms; the choice of seating is up to you, and several kinds of chairs will be available. (You will not usually be standing, as actors did in the old radio dramas, and still do for voice-overs and commercials.)

Keep your hair out of your face. Both men and women should wear comfortable, loose clothing, since even the noise of a man's stiff collar rubbing against the neck will be recorded. Some actors like to wear a cotton t-shirt, because there is no risk of its making a sound, but a long- or short-sleeved shirt or blouse made of any soft material will do. Do not rub your shoes against each other: the noise of leather or rubber records!

After you are comfortably seated, put on the headphones. The sound engineer will then adjust the microphone. When you feel that everything is ready, and you are comfortably in position and relaxed and ready to begin—and you should always inform the people you are working with if you are not yet ready, and tell them when you are ready—the sound engineer will do the level check, and when it is satisfactory, the engineer is ready for you to record.

What to Expect: How the Recording Session Works

Relax so that you can concentrate on the material you will be recording, just as you would if you were about to go on stage to perform in a play. The sound engineer will give you a signal to begin, which will be either a verbal signal ("We're rolling," or "Rolling," usually; illogical, perhaps, when reel-to-reel tape is no longer being used), or a hand signal, or both. You will then begin to read, perhaps taking a slight pause before commencing, if, for instance, you feel it necessary to readjust your concentration. You should take proper pauses of two seconds between sections of material: before a new chapter begins in a novel, for instance, or before a subheading in a chapter in a work of nonfiction. A director may tell you to take even longer pauses between chapters.

Try to keep a good even tempo, and pace yourself as you read, neither too slow nor too fast, although the pace will depend on the material. The calm, placid description of the Catskill Mountains at the opening of Washington Irving's *Rip van Winkle* (see page 176) will obviously require a different tempo from the frenetic chase over the moors in Conan Doyle's *The Hound of the Baskervilles* (see page 182). The text itself will more or less dictate the pace.

When you record, the booth will be darkened as an aid to concentration, while light from a reading lamp or lamps shines directly on the book. The director and engineer's side of the studio may be darkened also, or they may prefer to sit with overhead lights on.

Since you will be listening to your own voice through the headphones as you record, if you don't like what you hear, you can always stop reading and ask to record something again. As soon as you stop, the sound engineer will turn on his or her microphone and ask you what the problem is. Conversely, if extraneous sound is recorded the engineer will stop you and explain what has happened before picking up again from a place shortly before where the sound recorded.

Stopping often for noise may be deleterious to your concentration and to your sense of making the recording flow, especially if you are "on a roll," but is absolutely necessary, since no recording containing intrusive sounds will be approved for release to the public. When you have to turn a page, the recording stops, because the noise would be picked up. Do not break your concentration when turning pages. The engineer and director follow the text with you, and know when the page has to be turned, so that the engineer knows when to halt the process and wait for you. You will nod or say "OK" when you are ready to resume.

Even though you will have prepared the text thoroughly beforehand, mistakes are almost inevitable, since your eye is continually going ahead of what you are saying. Mistakes are not something to worry about. Some readers stumble a lot more than others. If you do stumble over a word, and the engineer stops the recording, try to keep your concentration on the text going, even while you wait for the recording to continue. Don't start joking around or laughing.

The director will usually tell the actor how correcting mistakes is to be handled, whether they be misreads or stumbles. Sometimes the director asks the actor before the session begins how he or she would like to handle mistakes, in which case the question is usually, "Do you want to be interrupted in the middle of things, and do the necessary correction immediately, or wait until the bottom of the page to do the pickups?" Editors don't like to get too far beyond the place that needs to be corrected, for a couple of reasons: First, the voice may sound quite different two hours later, let us say; and second, the farther away one is from a mistake, the more difficult it becomes to edit in a correction, since, among other things, allowance has to be made for how much time can fit on a cassette side or CD.

After you have stopped for a mistake, the engineer will bring you back to the place just before your gaffe, roll the recording, and you will then come in with the correct words and go on from there. This procedure is called a "punch-in." The punch-in method is used for recording Talking Books at the American Foundation for the Blind. Readers at Talking Books are paid for the recorded hour, which means that you may work for two hours and get only one and a half hours actually recorded, and that you are paid for the one and a half hours. In order to determine how much you are going to be paid, the time has to be ascertained based on what will actually be kept in the final recording, so the punch-in method of doing corrections immediately makes sense. This method is harder for the reader, because it requires a break, however brief, in his or her concentration on the text and on what is coming next; it gives the sound engineer/editor less work to do later.

Another way of correcting an error is just to take a brief pause, pick up where you want to, and continue reading; the editor will take care of the mistake later. You will have arranged this procedure with the director before the session begins. This method is sometimes preferred in commercial recordings (although punch-ins are used as well), when the reader is paid by the hour spent in the studio, regardless of how much is actually recorded. It saves time for the reader, and makes more work for the editor, of course.

A third method is to record all corrections on a separate track, to be edited in on the spot, or later.

There will also be times when you will have to stop for technical reasons having nothing to do with your reading. The stiffly bound book you are holding may make "book" or "page noise." A soundproof panel inside the recording booth may crack, or a distant door may slam. The computer may crash, or something may go wrong with the recording equipment, or the sound engineer accidentally press a button when none should be pressed, or accidentally press the wrong button, in which case the reader should try, as when he or she has stumbled, to maintain concentration.

After the finished recording has been proofed, that is, listened to by a sound engineer for mistakes, further corrections may have to be made, and corrections sessions are scheduled. The corrections sessions may take place a few days or even a few weeks after the original recording session. It is obvious that when doing corrections you will want to match your tone and vocal quality to the original, which necessitates listening to the part of the recording that needs to be corrected and recapturing your original pace and rhythm. Indeed, editing will be impossible if you don't, especially since corrections are usually done on a separate track.

The recordings are saved to a computer's hard drive, and usually backed up on another, attached hard drive, and/or burned onto a CD. Every session should be saved in this way, since recordings can be lost because of technical problems, such as the computer's crashing. Should a recording, or part of one, be lost, you will be paid both for material already recorded, and for rerecording whatever is necessary.

You will have been asked either before you begin to record the text or at the end of a commercial recording to record a list of opening and closing side announcements, which will then be inserted into the recording at the appropriate places by an editor. You will be recording in terms of sides of a cassette, and/or of individual CDs.

In the case of noncommercial, public service recordings on cassette—many noncommercial recordings are not yet available on CD—which are tone indexed (that is, the listener can hear a beep, which enables her or him to stop and listen to, for example, the beginning of a chapter or short story; the beep is only heard when a cassette player is in fast forward or rewind mode), you will record the list of tones (such as "Side One, Tone One"), during the recording of the table of contents. This list will inevitably have to be changed when you have finished the recording, and new numbers recorded on a separate track, which the editor will insert later.

In a commercial situation, aside from recording the side announcements on a separate track, you will not have to think about where the sides begin and end. The editor and engineer will divide the recording into sides later. But in the noncommercial sector, such as the Talking Books recorded at the American Foundation for the Blind, you will usually have to make opening and closing announcements as you go, taking proper pauses after the opening announcement, before beginning the text, and before the closing announcement. The engineer will tell you when the side is finished.

Talking Books cassettes are not commercially available. They are released by the National Library Service, are specially formatted and can only be played on a special machine; both the cassettes and the cassette player are available free to qualified subscribers through the NLS. Each cassette has two tracks on each side, or four "sides." When Side One is finished the tape is turned over, so that Side Two can be played. At the end of Side Two the tape is turned over again, and the side selector switch is pressed so that Side Three can be played. Side Four, on the other side of the cassette, can be heard by using the same process of turning the tape over. This format allows books to be released on fewer cassettes than commercial recordings. The Talking Books are always unabridged, and include footnotes and notes (only explanatory notes are usually included, and bibliographical ones left out), and bibliographies in nonfiction works. Many commercial recordings of nonfiction books eliminate that material altogether.

The director runs the commercial recording session, and everything is done for the convenience of the actor, since it is important that the actor feel comfortable and relaxed. However, some directors are much more hands-on than others, and you will have to learn to deal with directors who interrupt the recording to make points clear, while others would let things slide.

As noted previously, breaks are at the actor's convenience, although if the director feels that the actor is getting tired, she or he may ask the actor to take one. Breaks are very important, obviously, in a six- to eight-hour session. Also, many actors prefer to take a short lunch break of about twenty minutes to a half hour, if everyone's schedule permits, so that they don't lose their concentration on the material. It is not a good idea to eat a heavy lunch. A light salad or a sandwich is usually the best sort of choice, and soup is excellent, especially clear soup. Green or black tea without milk or sugar is also a good liquid to consume, and if you wish to avoid the caffeine you can always drink decaffeinated or herbal tea. Try to avoid liquids that are too hot or too cold.

If you need to, use a throat lozenge during a break. Some readers like a fairly strong lozenge, like Fisherman's Friend or Ricola. I prefer a mild, soothing pastille, such as Grether's Blackcurrant Pastilles and then only rarely. A glass of cold water to help restore dried mucous membranes is actually better for your throat than a lozenge, if you are in normal health. If you do use a lozenge, don't keep it in your mouth, as some readers do, during a recording session; it actually interferes with the recording, even if it helps keep the mouth moist, and the extra "mouth noise" it sometimes makes can be picked up.

One of the director's jobs is to make sure that the right words are emphasized, which is usually what the actor who has prepared the text well will do anyway. However, the director may want certain things said in certain ways, and the actor must be able to "take direction," that is, to accept and implement the instructions given by the director.

It is also the director's job to ensure that words (particularly difficult or abstruse words) are correctly pronounced, and, again, you must take direction. Do not say to a director, "I never pronounced it that way in my life!" First, remember that dictionaries often have multiple pronunciations for words (see Chapter Two), and there may be a pronunciation that the company or the director prefers. And secondly, remember that you are working for the company that hired you, and you should pronounce the words as they wish, even if you think they are wrong.

The director also makes sure that the actor knows how to pronounce foreign names and phrases correctly. In commercial recordings a researcher usually prepares a list of such pronunciations for the actor. In a noncommercial situation it is often, but not always, the actor who does his own dictionary research. This is the case, for instance, at the American Foundation for the Blind, where shelves of dictionaries of all kinds are available for both actors and proofers to use.

Readers/actors should note the following difference between work in the theater and in the book recording studio: In the theater the director is in charge of telling the story of the play, and the actor's job is to fulfill her or his part of the director's vision of how the story is to be told. But in the recording studio it is the actor who tells the story, with the help of and suggestions from the director, if necessary. Casting the right reader/actor is half the battle, so it is often unnecessary for the director to intervene, except on technical matters, such as sounds being too plosive, mouth noise being picked up by the microphone, or sound levels set by the engineer being too high or too low. Ordinarily the director will go over difficult areas of the text before the session begins and give his or her direction on words to be stressed and on particular pronunciations.

To conclude, one hopes the recording session will go smoothly. Most of them do. But in the event that things do not go well—either for you personally, or because of technical difficulties (a computer can crash, for instance, right in the middle of a sentence you are recording)—maintain your composure. There is nothing you can do about technical problems anyway, and it is in everyone's interest to fix the problems as soon as possible. If the problem is a personal one, take a break. Drink a glass of water, compose yourself, and begin again. To get the best results—the best product, as the producers say—the important thing is that the recording session should be enjoyable, for everyone. So . . . enjoy!

CHAPTER 4

Acting Methods and Techniques

The preceding chapters have dealt with some of the concrete, technical aspects of book recording. Now we enter a realm that is more nebulous, where nothing is predetermined or predictable, as we approach the art of interpreting literary texts and reading them aloud, which every actor will do in his or her intimately personal manner. But before we get there, we must explore how your particular method of working as an actor determines how you work to prepare and perform a text. In this chapter you will find a discussion of a number of approaches and tools useful in book recording.

One of the first questions an actor asks after reading a script in preparation for a role is, "Who am I?" meaning "Who is this person, the character I am about to play?" My name is Hamlet or Romeo or Vanya, Ophelia or Juliet or Yelena, but who am I as a person? What is my background, my personality? What are my wants, my needs, my desires? When preparing a work of fiction for recording, you must ask yourself the same questions about each of the characters. In a novel or short story the author usually gives you most of the answers, whereas in a play you have to deduce them, based on your analysis of the dialogue and stage directions. But to the questions—as relevant for recording as for the stage—"In what ways do I identify with the character?" and "How do I bring the character to life?" only the actor can supply the answers.

As Stanislavsky told us, elaborating on the well-known definition of acting as "doing something with a purpose," acting is the correct action correctly performed, "as if" the actor were in the situation and circumstances in which the character lives. In other words, what audiences want to see on the stage when they see actors doing something with a purpose is behavior, and what listeners to recorded books want to hear is behavior, reflected vocally.

In real life, as in a play or a novel, behavior is conditioned by internal psychological characteristics and needs, and by external circumstances such as temperature (hot, cold, warm, comfortable, uncomfortable); place (the character's own room or space, someone else's place, a hotel room, on the deck of a boat, a clearing in a forest, a park, etc.); time (morning, afternoon, evening, night); and by such circumstances as being drunk, tired, wide awake or ill. Unlike real life, where situations can be ambiguous and behavior difficult to analyze, fiction distils and crystallizes behavior so that we can understand it more easily.

The actor's goal is always to incorporate all the given circumstances into his or her performance, to personalize and internalize them. But the actor never forgets, indeed, cannot ever forget that he or she is performing on a stage or in front of a camera or a microphone, and not actually living the character's life. Even while going through the play or recording the book and living from moment to moment "as if" the actor were the character, the actor must have an inner censor that controls awareness of real, external circumstances during a performance. If the actor were to forget them, we would have an unfortunate situation, like that in the film *A Double Life* (1947), in which Ronald Colman plays an actor performing Othello, and finds the role taking over his life.

This necessary dichotomy is part of the craft of acting. The art of acting, on the other hand, consists of the distinctive way in which the talented individual uses her or his training, the way in which that person analyzes and interprets characters. The actor's entire background and life experience come into play, as well as the actor's intellect as it has developed through self-awareness, knowledge of life, and general education.

There are two seemingly opposed ideas about basic acting technique, and two approaches to creating a character:

1. The internal, so-called organic system of building a character, which is often called the Method, where the actor works on the character's inner emotional life before dealing with such things as the character's appearance and distinctive manner of speaking. The actor seems to become the character, so close is his or her identification with that person, and, when performing, lives in the moment, without anticipating the next event—which the character (although not the actor) is not in a position to know—"as if" what happens next is a spontaneous occurrence;

2. The external, so-called technical way of working, from the outside in. Not appearing to anticipate the next moment is equally necessary in the

> external approach, in which the actor seems to imitate or "present" the character to the audience. The actor begins by asking such questions as "What does the character look like?" and "What does the character sound like?"

The external approach appears to some to result in "acting" in the sense of playacting; the internal in "behaving." Actually, both approaches are technical (they use techniques), but the vexed question of which is real acting is hotly debated. Either one is frowned upon and derided, and often misunderstood, by those who believe in the other. In Britain and in the United States both systems have their exponents.

The seeming opposition between the two approaches is not as cut and dried as it appears, since every actor needs to take into account and assimilate aspects of both, no matter how the actor proceeds when initiating preparation of a role. Vocal technique, movement and other technical disciplines, such as fencing and stage combat, are as much a part of every acting school and drama department program as acting and scene study classes. Ultimately every actor puts all he or she has learned together to form a specific, individual method of working.

Surprisingly, both approaches have their origin in the theories and practices of Constantin Stanislavsky (1863–1938), the actor, director and teacher who, together with Nemirovich-Danchenko, founded the Moscow Art Theatre in 1898.

Stanislavsky's methods changed over time. His earlier approach seems to be more prized in the United States, and his later theory to be generally more valued in Britain. He always taught, in both his earlier and later phases, that the actor must behave "as if" he were in the circumstances dictated by the play. The question is, however, what that means: Should the actor behave "as if" it were he, himself, in those circumstances (how would he, as opposed to the character, behave?), looking within himself and using his affective memory (substitutions) to project himself into the circumstances of the play, which is what Stanislavsky believed at first? In other words, finding the correct emotion gives rise to the correct action. Or should the actor analyze the character's behavior and behave as he thinks the character would (not "imitate" the behavior, but simply "behave"), finding the correct internal and external actions in the given circumstances of the script, based on the character's (not the actor's) "internal monologue," and feeling whatever emotions arise from within, which is what his later teaching was all about? In other words, finding the correct action gives rise to the correct emotion. What does it mean, then, to personalize a script? And how does one personalize a script?

These theories were the source of the bitter debates and disagreements between the highly influential teachers Lee Strasberg (1901–1982), an actor as well as a teacher and theorist, and Stella Adler (1901–1992), an actress from a great and notable theater family with decades of experience in the Yiddish theater, where Stanislavsky's methods were revered even before they were well known in the English-speaking theater. Stella Adler and Lee Strasberg, who also spoke Yiddish and knew the Yiddish theater, each believed the other had misunderstood and misinterpreted Stanislavsky. Briefly, for Mr. Strasberg it was the first approach (using the actor's own affective memory and internal life to find and do correct actions correctly, in the service of the script) that was important; for Ms. Adler the second approach (finding and doing correctly the internal and external actions in the script itself, and letting the emotions happen) was paramount. If you read their books, which are well worth reading, you discover that in some ways their ideas converge. They both believe, for instance, that the actor must relax in order to concentrate and allow emotions to happen. But their methods deal with internal techniques in diametrically opposite ways, and in their approaches to personalization Strasberg and Adler remain far apart.

But before Stanislavsky, Adler and Strasberg there was Delsarte.

François Delsarte (1811–1871) began his life in the theatre as an actor and singer. When he secured a position as a tenor at the Opéra Comique, his career looked promising, but he damaged his vocal cords, had to retire from the stage altogether, and decided to become a teacher. (It is an interesting, if trivial sidelight of history, that Delsarte was the uncle of the composer Georges Bizet, who wrote *Carmen* [1875].)

The teaching of acting in the mid-nineteenth century was a disorganized, haphazard affair, until Delsarte decided to devise what became a very popular system for actors to follow, a system which he taught to actors and opera singers both. In an age when scientific thought was becoming important Delsarte wanted acting to be a scientific study, its methods and techniques codified and classified as if acting were like the natural sciences.

His basic principal was that all emotion, all feeling, all ideas could be expressed on stage by a series of gestures and poses, which, however calculated and studied they might be, must appear to be real and natural. Emotion gave rise to gesture, and his elaborate system described in minute detail how to use all of the body to project to the audience the feelings and attitudes of the character. In untalented hands the results must have seemed terribly mechanical. However, it was the first time in the history of modern acting that an attempt had been made to systematize a method for teaching actors. Three centuries earlier, in the Elizabethan era, there had been an elaborate system of gestures and poses used to express emotion, sometimes on every word, but it had long been forgotten. (See B. L. Joseph's *Elizabethan Acting* [Oxford University Press, 1964].)

The aim of Delsarte's system was to train actors in the art of being graceful and poised, all in the service of expressing the emotional life of the character. To that end he divided the human body into zones: the head, seat of the mind and the intellect; the trunk of the body, seat of the emotions; and, finally, the limbs, which would express the body's emotions and the mind's thoughts. In order for the body to have the flexibility that the system required, training in gymnastics was prescribed for all actors.

His system became so popular that even nineteenth- and early twentieth-century society ladies studied it. In their salons in Europe and the United States they provided a great deal of entertainment, from vocal and instrumental concerts to "tableaux," in which the hostess and her male and female friends would don costumes and create a famous scene from history or art, such as "Queen Elizabeth the First Knighting Sir Francis Drake." Delsarte gestures and poses in these tableaux were as *de rigueur* as the French phrases thrown into conversation in English and American drawing rooms. The salon devotees were also very fond of poetry recitations and interpretive dances, and the hostess or someone invited to perform would dance or give recitations using the appropriate Delsarte gestures. The contents of Genevieve Stebbins's very rare book, *Delsarte System of Expression* (Edgar S. Werner Publishing & Supply Co., 1902) includes "Part III: Theory and Practice of Delsarte System, Pantomime, Physical Culture, and Statue-Posing." There are also "32 illustrations from Greek art." The statue-posing must have been very popular at society parties!

Early sound movies of some well-known opera singers show them using gestures that are pure Delsarte. And you can hear the results of his teaching on some of the recordings of nineteenth-century actors listed in the Bibliography, even if not all those actors studied with him. Listening to such recordings can give you a sense of period that might be useful in recording nineteenth- and early twentieth-century works of fiction, especially when an old-fashioned, declamatory style is required.

The Delsarte system was the epitome of a "technical" approach to acting: you don't have to "feel" anything, just look as if you do. Similarly, Berthold Brecht in the 1920s and 1930s, with his idea of the "Verfremdungseffekt" (pronounced "fe:r FRE:M doongs e: FE:KT"; the alienation effect), wanted actors to take the external approach completely, and not to be involved emotionally in any way with their characters, but to "present" them to the audience.

What is usually meant by "technical" is "calculated" as opposed to "experiential." No moment is spontaneously lived behavior; no emotion arises from what is actually happening to the actor, and every moment will be played the same way in every performance, even if the scenery is collapsing. The audience is asked nevertheless to believe that the actor feels the character's emotions, even though both the tears and the laughter are faked, often quite expertly. For practitioners of this system, the so-called spontaneous, organic behavior of the Method actor, who wants to "live" the part, is merely undisciplined and self-indulgent, unpredictable from performance to performance, serving not the play but the actor and failing to tell the author's story.

Some American actors wrongly consider the calculated, external approach to be the classic British way of creating a character from the outside in, using vocal and physical techniques. I must emphasize here that such a view is a cliché, and that British actors, like all actors everywhere, want audiences to believe entirely in the truthfulness of their behavior and emotions, and that they use internal emotional techniques, as well as external techniques, to achieve that end—just as American actors do.

The experiential, internal approach to the creation of a character from the inside out is exemplified in one American form by the sense memory and private moment substitution methods taught by Lee Strasberg at the Actor's Studio, in which the actor theoretically "becomes" the character (although, arguably, the actor substitutes himself for the author's character). But that is a clichéd perception of the results of Strasberg's teaching. To correct misconceptions about the Studio, you have only to read Lee Strasberg's own writings, as well as books by others who wrote about what went on there. Despite the cliché that Method actors "mumble," vocal technique is important, and the Method is meant very much for the actor to serve the play.

You will find either approach, or an approach combining aspects of the two, serviceable when creating and recording characters in works of fiction. You might use internal techniques of sense memory for visualizing where you are, what the time of day is, what the weather is like, and so forth, that will allow you to project yourself into the story you are telling. The use of personalized substitutions will give an emotional reality to any character you portray. And you must simultaneously remember the importance of vocal technique and good diction, both of which come under the heading of external techniques. Either Stella Adler's or Lee Strasberg's approach to personalization will be serviceable, but whatever method you use when recording a work of fiction, you have to prepare the arc of the story and of all the characters' stories in it using a similar method to the one described in the next paragraph, before you begin to personalize the material.

The actor begins by reading the script of a play—a book or story, if we are talking of recording—in order to discover the plot of the story, and then how his or her character fits into it, what the character's "journey" through the play is, and what the character's main goal is (the through-line and superobjective). She or he studies how and if the character changes and where the character's internal journey takes him or her. After the general arc for the character is traced, and the actor has developed an idea of the overall shape of the character's story, he or she looks for the "spine" or core of the character (every scene in the play has its own "spine" as well). But no attempt is yet made to analyze the specific beats or moments, or to "orchestrate" or "score" the beats. That will happen in the rehearsal process, as the actor "finds" the character, and breaks the story down into its specific moments. And there the external and internal approaches begin to diverge.

In the external school, an actor playing Shakespeare's Richard the Third begins by asking what the character looks like, by working on his physical posture and deformities, on his makeup, and on the character's special voice and his hunchbacked gait. He may work technically on speaking the verse. He may even leave much of the process described in the previous paragraph until after he has done some of the external work described here. Eventually the actor arrives at the character's thought processes and objectives, at the character's behavior and way of being in the world, and at an analysis of the character's circumstances, which include the character's physical attributes (already worked on). His speaking of the verse will not necessarily project felt emotion (it may appear to the audience to do so), but may be technically beautiful, with cadences and vocal modulations, which "indicate" (a dirty word to those of the opposite school) the character's emotions. But the actor's aim is still to "present" the character truthfully, which is why this school of acting is also called "presentational."

If your approach to book recording is purely external, you may begin by asking what the character sounds like, choose a character's voice based on your character analysis, and work on the dialogue technically, consciously choosing intonation patterns and inflections. And the results may be excellent and convincing, similar to those of the Shakespearean actor just described.

In the internal—also called the "representational"—approach to creating a character, an actor playing Richard the Third begins, reads through the play as described above, then begins to analyze the thought processes and emotional life of the character and to find substitutions from the actor's own emotional life and past that are in some way analogous to those of the character and the character's given circumstances in some way (the physical attributes of Richard the Third being part of the circumstances, to find them truthfully the actor may, for instance, use as sense memory a time when he sprained his ankle and had to limp around). Such substitutions are meant to lead the actor to the truthful emotional life of the character. The character's behavior should appear to be natural and spontaneous; to arise organically from the situation and the circumstances the character is in, even though the behavior may be calculated, as a result of the rehearsal process, to the nth degree. Eventually, in rehearsal, more substitutions for individual beats or moments may be discovered and the actor finds the physical life of the character with his hunched back and crippled arm, his deportment, movement, demeanor, and makeup. He deals with the problems of speaking the verse (or should deal with them;

this aspect of the craft is often given too short shrift by actors taking this approach), which may be differently spoken from performance to performance, but may also end up being as wonderfully modulated as it is in the so-called technical or presentational school.

If you choose the purely internal approach when preparing a work of fiction, you may begin by finding substitutions for the characters' situations and emotional life, without thinking of what the character sounds like or what inflections to use, except in a specifically necessary situation, and the result may be a convincing, engrossing and spontaneous reading in which the listener hears organic behavior.

Some actors refer to the character they are playing as "I" ("I come into the room"), and some as "he" or "she" ("He, or she, comes into the room"). The use of third-person pronouns can tend to distance the actor from the role, although it does not have to do so, and many actors prefer it. Often, although not always, the internal approach is the one used by the actor who says "I," and the external approach by the actor who says "she" or "he."

You will find more techniques useful for recording in the works of Michael Chekhov, Anton Chekhov's nephew, who was a charismatic actor; you can see him as the psychiatrist in Alfred Hitchcock's *Spellbound* (1945). He taught acting and wrote *To the Actor on the Technique of Acting* (Harper and Row, Publishers, 1953), and other books. Two of his principal methods involve the use of the imagination: there are exercises where the actor invents all kinds of external circumstances, which the audience will never know about, such as imagining that you have a ball and chain attached to your leg when you are supposed to be walking through desert heat; and the "Psychological Gesture," which the actor finds for the character as a way into the character and as a means of awakening the life of the character. It might consist of a jump up and down, or of hugging oneself, or, indeed, of any meaningful gesture. You might find it useful in creating a character for a book recording to develop such a gesture to help launch you into reading a character's dialogue in an organic, spontaneous way.

A truly great actor, Morris Carnovsky (1897–1992) explained his approach to the art in *The Actor's Eye*, which he wrote with Peter Sander (Performing Arts Journal Publications, 1984). This simple and insightful book sums up the necessary bases of acting method: You have to concentrate on the action (what you are doing; the action may be mental as well as physical), the object (whether physical or something desired), and the self (who you are as a character). Those simple bases are, of course quite full and quite complicated and demanding. The approach is also quite fulfilling, and demands of the actor that she or he think deeply about the character. Again, you will find it useful in creating characters vocally, because it will help you to find a character's center.

Carnovsky's career was a long one, and he was a founding member of the Group Theatre (so influential in the 1930s and afterwards; Stella Adler, Sanford Meisner and Lee Strasberg were also founding members), as was his wife, Phoebe Brand. I saw him in that usually overlooked role of Firs in Anton Chekhov's *The Cherry Orchard* in 1987 at the Long Wharf Theatre, and he was extraordinary and impressive even while playing a man who is self-effacing. But then his riveting, memorable performances as King Lear, Prospero, and Shylock at the American Shakespeare Festival in Stratford, Connecticut were breathtaking, and astounding in their profound insights into the roles; and he had one of the great, gorgeous voices—flexible, expressive, deep and sonorous. He had been blacklisted in the 1950s during the horrible McCarthy witch-hunts, when the paranoid maniac senator went after anyone even remotely suspected of Communist sympathies. Someone gave Carnovsky's name to the committee, so his career in Hollywood was cut short; eventually he returned to the stage to do his magnificent Shakespearean performances, and he also taught acting at Brandeis University.

When I knew him I was a young actor at the American Shakespeare Festival. He was playing Prospero and I watched every performance, and learned endlessly from him. When I was cast to play Malvolio in the journeyman production of *Twelfth Night* I asked his advice, which was pithy and to the point. He said, "To Malvolio, everybody smells slightly." In Michael Chekhov's terms, a giant sniff might be the psychological gesture that awakens the actor to the character. Once again, you might use this sort of technique to help you create the voice of a character, because such a sniff will lead you to use your voice in what the listener might hear as a snobby or aloof character, whose visceral withdrawal from other people we can actually hear.

Sanford Meisner taught for more than fifty years at the Neighborhood Playhouse, and eventually published an informative, important book, which he wrote with Dennis Longwell: *On Acting* (Vintage Books, A Division of Random House, 1987). One of his basic and vital exercises is the repetition exercise. Two actors observe each other and one makes a remark about something she or he has noticed about the other actor, who then repeats exactly what the first one has said. The first actor must then repeat what the second one has said, and they continue to go back and forth. The subtext may change: perhaps one of the actors feels foolish and begins to giggle, for instance. The acting partner must pick up on this, and repeat it, perhaps feeling silly in turn, or perhaps angry, which will add another element to the repetition. This exercise demands concentration, and the actor is taught to listen not only to the words, but also, most importantly, to the subtext, which is of supreme importance in book recording. Sanford Meisner's approach emphasizes specificity and reality. Your emphases in creating characters for book recording should be the same.

Another noted acting teacher of the internal, organic method is Uta Hagen, whose main idea about acting is that everything the actor does and thinks, and all of the actor's circumstances, should be absolutely specific, and that every internal and external object should have specific meaning, just as in real life. She deals with the use of substitutions as a primary tool, and with the necessity to be specific in every moment of a performance. For instance, when preparing an entrance the actor has to know where the actor (the character) has just been, what the actor has been doing just before entering, what the actor is doing now, and what the first thing is that the actor wants, as well as the specifics of time, place and weather. This can all be quite important in creating the feeling a character has in a work of fiction. David Copperfield walking down a London street or along a country lane behaves and sounds differently in each place. Jane Eyre coming in from a walk in the cold countryside or sitting alone in her warm bedroom feels and behaves differently, depending on the circumstances. For more about Uta Hagen's methods, see below, under Circumstances; and see the Bibliography for her books.

A Glossary of Some Common Terms

1. Action:
   a. External action: What the character does to get what he or she wants; actors "play" actions, not emotions.
   b. Internal action: Thought processes, including the "interior monologue," which is a running series of thoughts in a "stream of consciousness," worked out in rehearsal (perhaps) and scored (see below). The internal action is exteriorized as behavior.

   Stanislavsky came to believe that the correct action, correctly performed, based on the given circumstances in the play, and arrived at in the rehearsal process, would awaken the emotion of the character. He had previously believed almost the exact opposite, namely that the correct emotion, when found, would lead to the correct action to be played in fulfillment of the objective. The opposite approaches are at the heart of the disagreement between the Stella Adler and the Lee Strasberg interpretations of Stanislavsky's Method.

2. Affective memory: This term means the memory of emotions and feelings in any situation, whether emotionally charged or not (emotional memory); and the memory of physical sensations—hot, cold, drunk, sick, tired, attracted to something or someone, etc.—(sense memory). Emotional and sense memories can overlap. Affective memory is one of the actor's most

important tools; it is used by analogy to understand a character's situation and/or the particular circumstances in a scene.

3. Beat, or Unit:
   a. The beginning of a specific moment during which an action is played;
   b. A longer amount of time in which a conflict in a scene is played out.

   If and when an objective has been attained, or if and when it has not, there is a change of beat. When one beat comes to an end, another begins. Characters can have individual beats that differ from the longer beats in a scene. A beat, in other words, can represent a change in a character's sub-objective.

4. Circumstances: The factors that condition a character's life. (See also Relationship.) Emotional circumstances are internal, and include how the character feels in his or her relationships with the other characters, as well as the character's state of emotional health, and what the character needs emotionally. Physical circumstances include time, place, the weather, the temperature, and the character's state of physical health. Place, that is, where one is located in space, is very important: We behave differently in a public place than at home. Time is also a very specific conditioning circumstance, not only the general time of day, but also the specific moment. In her acting class, which I had the pleasure of attending, Uta Hagen did a very instructive and entertaining exercise to demonstrate the specificity of time's conditioning of behavior: She was in her apartment on Washington Square and was about to go teach a class at the HB Studio on Bank Street. Looking at her watch she discovered she had only ten minutes to be there on time. Could she make it? She hurriedly packed her purse, put on her coat and ran out the door, shouting "Taxi! Taxi!" The second time she did the exercise she looked at her watch and saw that she now had only five minutes to make it to her class on time. Now she was really in a hurry! She rushed around like a mad person, and frantically shouted, "Taxi!" as she almost fell. She did the exercise a third time. Now it was already the exact time the class was supposed to begin. So, what's the use? In disgust, muttering obscenities, she packed her purse and got the necessary things together, then walked fairly swiftly out the door, and suddenly broke into a run and yelled "TAXI!"

5. Intention: The underlying, or subtextual, meaning of a line, delivered with the idea of expressing something a character wants to express in a particular way, or something a character feels. An intention may be to express anger, sadness, or happiness. Intentions may be for the purpose of accomplishing an objective.

6. Object:
   a. An internal or external area of concentration, whether it is a teapot from which one is pouring tea, or the person one loves; objects, such as the teapot, can awaken memories;
   b. Objective, as in the definition below.

7. Objective: What the character wants; the character's goal. A sub-objective is a smaller objective on the path to achieving or accomplishing an objective.

8. Obstacle: What is in the character's way; the obstacle may be physical, another character, emotional, internal, etc. Work on obstacles is extremely important in preparing a character.

9. Organic: Spontaneous, unanticipated behavior resulting from living in the moment and proceeding as the character would from one moment to the next. Such organic behavior must be carefully prepared for during the rehearsal process, in part by scoring the beats, which must then be "forgotten."

10. Relationship: The nature of the character's connection to other characters, as well to internal and external objects; how and why the character relates. Relationships are part of the important internal and external circumstances in a character's life; they condition behavior. Here are some of the sorts of questions the actor has to ask when considering relationships (the questions use the word "I," which you may understand to mean the character the actor has to play; if you wish you may substitute the words "he" or "she"): How do I behave when I am in love with someone? How do I behave if I hate someone? How do I behave in the presence of my parents, spouse, lover, partner, children, friends, acquaintances, neighbors, teammates, colleagues, bosses, teachers, doctors, or lawyers? How do I feel about them? How do I relate to them? How do I relate to or react to a change in the temperature, i.e., am I more comfortable in hot weather or in cold, for example? How do I relate to a body of water, if I can or can't swim? Do I have allergies, so that I relate in a specifically fearful way to even the sight of a certain flower or of someone smoking a cigarette? Do I have vertigo, claustrophobia, agoraphobia, or acrophobia? Am I afraid of something or someone? How do I relate to my possessions, to my environment?

11. Score:
    a. (Noun) the way the story (in other words, the life) of the character proceeds, with its high and low points and its changes of beat, much like a piece of music;

   b. (Verb) to put together the basic line of development of the part, with its climaxes and changes of beats.

12. Spine:
   a. The psychological core of the character; what makes the character tick, and determines the overall objective of the character.
   b. The core of a scene; its overall aim or thrust.

13. Substitution: The use by the actor of emotions and/or events or people or relationships, etc., from his or her own life, analogous in some way to the emotions or events experienced by the character, in order to bring reality to the portrayal of the character. This is one of the most important acting techniques, and involves the use of affective memory (see above.)

14. Subtext: The underlying meaning of the text; the intention and/or desire of the character as expressed by manner, intonation patterns and behavior.

15. Super-Objective: a character's ultimate goal.

16. Through-line: the ultimate thrust of the story in the play, into which all the individual characters of the play fit. Each scene has its own through-line. So does each character, with her or his story's arc, or shape, and super-objective.

Subtext and Intentions: An Exercise

This is one of the most useful exercises for creating characters in recorded books. Say the words "Here I am" with the subtextual meanings/intentions listed below. You can also come up with any number of different ways to say the phrase for yourself.

1. Aren't you glad to see me?

2. Sorry I'm late!

3. Oh, damn, not again! [as if talking to yourself]

4. I've wound up in the same old place I started out from.

5. Take comfort! I'll make sure you are all right.

6. You villain! Just you wait one second, and you'll see!

7. And now I will be on my way.

8. Isn't that strange?

9. Answer the question "Where are you?"

10. Where are you? (Stress the word "I.")

11. Look this way! (Stress the word "Here.")

12. And here I stay. (Stress the word "am.")

13. And that is a definite fact, which I want to emphasize. (Stress every word.)

CHAPTER 5

Reading Techniques

Manuel Garcia, the famous teacher of the bel canto method to generations of opera singers, wrote in *Hints on Singing* (1894), "The pupil must read the words of the piece again and again till each finest shadow of meaning has been mastered. He must next recite them with perfect simplicity and abandonment. The accent of truth apparent in the voice when speaking is the basis of expression in singing." And Shakespeare's Hamlet gives the following famous advice to the players: "... but use all gently: for in the very torrent, tempest, and—as I may say—whirlwind of your passion, you must acquire and beget a temperance, that may give it smoothness. O! it offends me to the soul to hear a robustious, periwig-pated fellow tear a passion to tatters, to very rags..." This is all excellent counsel for today's recording artists. Rehearse your text assiduously. Be smooth and temperate in your reading. That, coupled with simplicity and "abandonment," which means giving yourself over to the material and allowing it to filter through you as you give a voice to what has been silent, endowing texts with a kind of life in sound, will make for an enjoyable, sometimes even enthralling experience for the listener.

Even in a dynamic action-filled scene in a work of fiction where you might have to shout and become emotional, smoothness and temperance are demanded. In practical terms you cannot be so loud and uncontrolled that a) you sound like you are overdoing it, and b) you go past acceptable sound levels set by the sound engineer. You must still maintain a sense of where you are—in the recording studio—and what you are doing: reading aloud, even while giving yourself up to the scene and making it come alive.

Some Important General Hints

The principal technique you need to develop for recording texts is to read ahead as you are speaking. Your eye must take in the next line or lines, and you must unconsciously prepare to say them. You must not anticipate what is coming. Instead, concentrate on what you are reading at the moment, while always staying aware of what is coming next. This technique will make the reading smooth, and not choppy. To practice it, sit quite still, as you would in the recording studio. Rest a text, a book, a newspaper or a magazine, comfortably on a table and hold it steady in front of you. Record it, then listen to the recording for smoothness. As you listen to the playback, follow the text, so that you can judge whether your reading sounds as you intended it to when you planned your interpretation. Being able to critique what you hear in a spirit of objectivity and without being self-deprecating is very important. Listen to see if you have made any mistakes: When you are reading ahead, certain kinds of mistakes are common: the substitution of "this" for "that," "these" for "those," and "but" for "and." These mistakes are nothing to worry about; almost everybody makes them. They will either be corrected immediately or later in a corrections session or during the editing process. (See Chapter Three: Recording Techniques, pages 69-70.)

Here are some more techniques and methods for you to use in the recording studio. You can practice them at home by selecting any text, recording it and listening to yourself:

1. Mean what you say. The best way to do this is to make the words your own. Make them mean something to you personally, which will make them come alive.

2. In both fiction and nonfiction select a person you are talking to (it could be the director, or the sound engineer who would be listening to you do the recording). This will help you sound as natural as possible and not stilted or academic or theatrical, unless the material calls for the latter. You need not be aware of your chosen fictitious listener during the entire course of your reading—in fact you will inevitably forget that person as you go on reading—but choosing someone to read to will help launch you into the text.

3. As a good general rule, don't drop your voice in volume or pitch at the ends of sentences. There will, of course, be times when you will want or need to drop your voice. But avoid it as a habit.

4. Unless specifically needed for a character, avoid a singsong or droning quality, either of which is monotonous and difficult to listen to.

5. Sometimes words that appear inessential, words you would not ordinarily think of stressing or emphasizing, such as a conjunction or a preposition, can be used to make a point or to portray character. For example, Sir Michael Redgrave as Andrew Crocker-Harris in the film of Terence Rattigan's *The Browning Version* (1951) almost invariably pronounced the word "to" in a verb infinitive as "too," whereas British RP speakers usually pronounce it "tə" before a consonant. Redgrave used this overly precise pronunciation as a vocal trait or "signature" to emphasize the pedantry, reserve, hesitation and shyness of the character.

6. Keep character voices and accents fairly light, or the story you are telling may be difficult to listen to. In easily sustainable or necessary cases, however, you should do heavier voices and accents. (See Chapter Six, Recording Fiction.)

7. You must play attitudes when recording characters. The author has entered the character's mind, and so must you. (For more detail, see Chapter Six.) Attitudes are subtextual, even if they are directly stated in the text. If we are told that a character is petulant, we have to hear that petulance, so you as a reader interpreting the text have to know a) why the character is petulant, and b) how petulance is conveyed vocally. You must read the character's dialogue "as if" you were petulant. You must understand and adopt the character's point of view. We have to hear what the character is feeling and going through, just as we would in a theater.

8. If you are called on to convey humor, read it as if you were deadly serious or it will not be funny. This requires you to be an actor-comedian, and if you are telling a story with punch lines, means quite literally that you have to "punch" or emphasize vocally, by pitch and by volume, the line with the joke in it. You have to know that what you are saying is funny and why it is funny, and at the same time you have to keep that knowledge to yourself, in the back of your mind, as it were. And you have to be able to time the delivery of the punch line for maximum effect, so as to surprise the audience. Humor that is telegraphed to the audience is no humor at all. You may laugh, but chances are they won't.

9. Adopt the point of view of the author when recording nonfiction, and make it your own (at least temporarily). This may be difficult if you dis-

agree with the author's politics or ideas on religion, for example, but it is an obligation you must assume.

10. A corollary: Do not comment on the material you are interpreting, whether it is fiction or nonfiction. In other words, do not show by your voice or intonation pattern that you think it ridiculous, stupid or unseemly. It is your obligation to make the material come alive. I once recorded what I considered two execrably written, manifestly lunatic, off-the-walls books by Texe Marrs, *Mystery Mark of the New Age: Satan's Design for World Domination* and *Dark Secrets of the New Age: Satan's Plan for a One World Religion*. When the National Library Service (NLS) at the Library of Congress reviewed the recordings for approval before releasing them to the subscribing public, many of whom would no doubt disagree with my assessment of those books, they approved of the tone and style I had adopted, which were sincere, committed, and real. I had given myself over to the material and adopted the author's point of view. I must admit that during the recording sessions the sound engineer and I not infrequently burst out laughing, but we did get through the books.

11. For any work you are assigned to record, learn as much as you can about the author and the era in which he or she wrote, and about the actual living conditions of the day, so that they become almost viscerally familiar to you. Situating a work in its historical, literary and social context will help you give the book its proper significance and bring it to life. You need to know the kind of information you will find in many of the "Notes, Comments and Hints" sections following the practice texts.

12. Relax and concentrate, just as you would in preparing an entrance for the stage or an appearance on camera. Only by relaxing can you concentrate and focus on the material to be recorded.

Preparing the Text for Recording

Take as central to the process of preparing and recording your interpretation of a text the idea that you are telling a story, whether you are reading fiction or nonfiction. You tell different kinds of stories in different ways.

Some listeners enjoy hearing an expressive, dramatized reading of a work of fiction, complete with the characters' voices, as if they were at a play; others prefer listening to a flat, neutral reading, so that they can themselves supply the characters' voices and visualize the incidents of the story, as they would if they were reading the book silently to themselves. You may be called on to adopt either manner of reading, depending on both the particular text and the requirements of the producer and director of the recording. The director will usually tell you what style and manner are wanted for a particular book, or are required by the company or organization you are working for. For instance, I recall being told by a director running an audition for a rather abstruse, somewhat dry book on the history of science not to sound academic or pedantic, but to try to sound as if I were just talking to someone. If you are not informed or instructed, you can always ask the director what she or he wants or requires.

The first thing you have to do when preparing a text for recording is to read it. That statement may seem extremely obvious, but it is a fact that texts are not always as well prepared as they ought to be. (Reading a text cold after glancing through it in a cursory manner is a not uncommon practice, and it may be all right when a very experienced recording artist does it, but it is not a practice that I can recommend.) I repeat with Stanislavsky his famous double entendre (and the title of his most famous book) "an actor prepares," a motto that ought to be taken very seriously by an actor getting ready to do a recording. You owe it to the producer, the director, the sound engineer, the eventual listener, and to yourself to be thoroughly conversant with the shape of the story you are telling and with where the author is leading you. You certainly don't want to find out on page twenty that a character whose dialogue you have been reading with a General American accent since he appeared on page one comes from Dublin and has retained his Irish brogue. Not only would it be a rather bad surprise, but it would also necessitate rerecording the twenty pages. One thinks of Kaufman and Hart's hilarious satirical comedy about Hollywood, *Once in a Lifetime,* where the Producer says to the Director, after the wrong movie has been shot by mistake, that from now on, whenever a movie is made, someone has to read the script first!

Equally obvious, but necessary: As you read through the text, if you see a word you don't know, or an obscure word you think you know, look up its pronunciation in a dictionary. In *The Adventure of the Creeping Man* Sherlock Holmes sends the following telegram to Dr. Watson: "Come at once if convenient—if inconvenient come all the same." To paraphrase: If you need to look up a word, look it up. If you don't need to look up a word, look it up all the same. You may think you know the pronunciation of a word when you don't, so look it up! Refer to Chapter Two for information on some of the difficulties of English, and to the Bibliography for a list of some useful dictionaries.

Your second step is to begin making decisions about interpreting the text, about how to tell the story, whether it be fiction or nonfiction. Decide what the story is about, what its themes are, and what you wish to emphasize thematically. Decide how you are going to read it, whether dramatically or more quietly, for instance. You need to decide on a general tone for the narration, which will be determined by the way in which the author has told the story. Think about the style in which the text is written. If you have fiction to interpret, you will have to decide how to make the characters come alive vocally. If this all seems rather vague and amorphous at the moment, remember how much of a mystery a play seems to the actor on his or her first contact with it. The subjects of how to create specific characters vocally and how specifically to tell the story, including how to open it, are covered in later chapters of this book.

When readying a text, you are usually permitted to mark it up as you wish (or you may prefer not to mark it up, and simply remember what you have planned). Underline words you wish to emphasize. Draw up or down arrows over or under a phrase to remind you of intonations you wish to use. When you have looked up a word you are not sure of, write the pronunciation in the margin.

You may find it useful to rehearse by reading some of the book aloud and/or recording it, or parts of it, at home, so that you can critique and correct yourself before you go into the studio. I think too much reading aloud is perhaps harmful for a final performance: You want to leave some room for spontaneity. On the other hand, it is certainly a good idea to discover how easily the text can be read aloud, so by all means do some experimentation. A good text, like a good reading, should flow. If the text is awkwardly written it won't really flow, and your task may be more difficult. You have to figure out how to make it flow anyway.

How much time you devote to rehearsal is up to you. Once you get into the studio you are expected to be prepared to do the actual recording, so you will usually not be rehearsing there, unless a director requires you to do so, or unless you request it.

Charles Dickens: His Public Readings

In 1853 Charles Dickens (1812–1870), the much-loved and prolific novelist known for his humor, his compassion, his sentiment, and for a gallery of memorable characters created on a scale not seen since Shakespeare, gave his first public reading, *A Christmas Carol*, for charitable purposes. He later embarked on a highly popular series of quite dramatic paid public readings of his works, using scripts that he prepared himself. He rehearsed them thoroughly, and performed them with incredible energy and commitment. The readings, which continued until shortly before he died, took him to

Ireland and the United States of America, as well as all over England. One would love to have heard them on record, but, alas, it was not until 1877 that Thomas Alva Edison invented the phonograph.

Simon Callow, the gifted English actor, has recently performed an absolutely extraordinary "living biography" of Charles Dickens by Peter Ackroyd (see the Bibliography for his magisterial biography, *Dickens*), called *The Mystery of Charles Dickens*. Previously done to great acclaim in London, on tour in Britain, and on Broadway in New York, the play was taped for television at the Albery Theatre in London in 2001. The show includes many readings from the novels, and Simon Callow succeeds beautifully in his goal of having the audience "encounter" Dickens. A DVD of the show is available from Kultur Video, and I recommend it very highly.

Back in 1983 Emlyn Williams made a television program of his one-man show of Charles Dickens's public readings, as well as an LP of them. I heard the long-playing record, saw the television broadcast, and finally saw him do the show on stage. His makeup as Dickens was flawless, as was his rendition of the selections from the novels. I can still see and hear him in my mind's eye, and I imagine his readings must have been very much like those of Dickens, himself, complete with the sorts of gestures and physical playing of characters, which we know Dickens, a great actor, did, both from various accounts by friends, and from newspaper reviews of his performances. A recording artist will find it very instructive to listen to Williams's readings.

We are fortunate to have copies of the scripts Dickens used; he published them in twenty-one individual booklets (they were later published in a one-volume edition in 1868). These scripts were the actual published volumes of his works, which Dickens abridged, and then marked up to indicate stress and emphasis, with occasional marginal notes as to volume and pitch. The scripts are not only very instructive for the student of Dickens, but also provide a very useful tool for study by anyone preparing a text for recording today. There were several facsimile editions published, among them *Nicholas Nickleby* and *A Christmas Carol*, and twelve of the scripts, not in facsimile, have been published in a paperback: *Sikes and Nancy, and Other Public Readings* by Charles Dickens (edited with an Introduction and Notes by Philip Collins; Oxford University Press, 1983).

Dickens underlined once words that he wished to stress in an ordinary way. Words or phrases that he wished to emphasize particularly he underlined twice. In the margins he wrote indications such as "Driving" or "low" or "Cheerful narrative"; these stage directions to himself were also underlined, usually twice.

One interesting stage direction in the margin of Dickens's script for *Nicholas Nickleby* (1838) is "Slapping the desk," underlined twice. (Dickens had a reading lectern specially constructed to his specifications. An exact copy of it was used by Emlyn Williams in his performances.) The stage direction is meant to be carried out at the precise point when Squeers, the dreadful, tyrannical, sadistic, avaricious schoolmaster and owner of Dotheboys Hall in the lonely wilds of Yorkshire, enters the classroom and addresses the students with the line: "Let a boy speak a word without leave... and I'll take the skin off that boy's back." In his book *Charles Dickens as a Reader* (Chapman and Hall, 1872) Charles Kent says that Dickens would make a "ferocious slash on the desk with his cane." The recording artist could make a similar slash with his voice by spitting out the word "Let" in the harshest, sharpest tone, for a highly melodramatic effect.

Sometimes words which appear inessential, words would not think of stressing or emphasizing ordinarily, can be used to make a point or to portray character, as in the case of Dickens's stressing the word "Let" in characterizing the appropriately described "ferocious" Mr. Squeers. Dickens himself sometimes stressed repeated adjectives, such as "very" or "rather" in a series such as the one in *Dombey and Son;* see the excerpt below, on page 109.

Here, as practice exercises for you, are three excerpts from Dickens's tour manager George Dolby's book about the man he called "The Chief." It is called *Charles Dickens as I Knew Him: The Story of the Reading Tours in Great Britain and America (1866–1870)* (T. Fisher Unwin, 1887).

From Chapter VII: "Christmas and the New Year"

During our stay in New York for the Brooklyn Readings, Mr. Horace Greeley had accepted an invitation to dine with Mr. Dickens at the Westminster Hotel on Saturday, January 18th [1868]; and in expressing his delight at the success of the Readings took occasion to question the advisability of Mr. Dickens reading in Washington, giving as his reasons that the political horizon was a little hazy, and that "trouble" with the President (Andrew Johnson) might accrue at any moment, in addition to which the "rowdy" element was more largely represented in the city at that moment, in view of the supposed difficulties with the President. It was his opinion that the "rowdies" would make themselves obnoxious to Mr. Dickens. I had just returned from Washington, and had secured the only available hall there (the Carol Hall), which held but seven hundred and fifty or eight hundred people, and intended charging five dollars a ticket for the Washington Readings; a proceeding Mr. Dickens disapproved of at first, but to which he eventually yielded on my pointing out to him that there were more people in New York, Boston, Philadelphia and Brooklyn than there were in Washington, and that these people on an average paid (thanks to the "noble army of speculators") that price to hear him in those cities. As to the "rowdy" element, I thought nothing of that...

NOTES, COMMENTS AND HINTS

Dickens was persuaded, and went to Washington, where he was very well received. Dolby says: "The Washington readings were among the most brilliant given in America. At the first reading every class of society was represented, the President himself being present, with his family..."

The president at the time was Andrew Johnson (1808–1875), seventeenth president of the United States, succeeding Abraham Lincoln. For purely politically partisan reasons he was impeached—this is the impending "trouble" Dolby refers to—in February 1868, but not convicted.

A humanitarian and a pacifist, Horace Greeley (1811–1872) founded the *Tribune* in 1841 to provide an inexpensive paper for all New Yorkers. He was famous for his editorials, and for the advice often attributed to him: "Go west, young man! Go west, and grow up with the country!" That statement was actually made by another journalist, John Babson Lane Soule (1815–1891) in an article reprinted by Greeley in the *Tribune*. But Greeley was fond of repeating it.

Five dollars a ticket was an awful lot of money in those days; think in terms of hundred-dollar tickets on Broadway today for some musicals. You will not be surprised to learn that even back then a "noble army of speculators" sold tickets at exorbitant prices to those people who were just dying to attend the readings.

Dolby mentions New York and Brooklyn in the same sentence. At the time he wrote his book Brooklyn was a separate city, only being incorporated as a borough into New York City in 1898.

This autobiographical/biographical memoir is pretty straightforward nonfiction writing. Dolby was not a writer by profession and the writing itself is not very interesting; one might even characterize his style as a bit dull and plodding, but serviceable. If you were to record this book you would have to play against the plodding style, and to make it sound interesting and real by reading the text with variety and liveliness.

The book's only attraction lies in the well-known personages it puts on stage. This is life at its most mundane, but lived by famous people. Dickens's readings may have been compelling, but the details of his business arrangements are less than thrilling.

The good-hearted and loyal Mr. Dolby is obviously a bit overawed by his "Chief," and you may want to reflect that in your reading. Although nonfiction, this book, is a first-person narrative, with George Dolby telling us his story, so there is room for some interpretation of the text.

As one way of reading the excerpts from Dolby's book, adopt a self-effacing attitude, even when saying "I." It is Charles Dickens who is important, from Dolby's point of view. You must always think of the narrator's or character's point of view. Here, Dolby feels subservient to Dickens, and that attitude should be reflected in your deferential tone. For instance, whenever you say "Mr. Dickens" the tone should be one of admiration, and the thoughts underlying and informing your reading of the name—your subtext—should be something like: "He is the important one. He is the one you want to hear about. Isn't this interesting?"

Here is the same text again, marked as I might do if I were preparing it for recording. (Usually I simply remember how I wish to read a text.) These purely technical notes indicate my own possible interpretation of the text and of the character of George Dolby, and I have gone much farther than one would usually do for nonfiction. Other interpretations of this character and other readings of this text are possible, and I encourage you to explore them. Even a straight, neutral reading of the text, without the kind of characterization I have indicated below, would be entirely appropriate, since this is a memoir and not a novel. If spontaneity seems to be absent in my "scoring" of the text, my reading of it was originally spontaneous, and these are simply indications of what happened organically.

Normally, any notes I made would be much abbreviated from what you see here. For instance, I might simply put an exclamation mark in the margin where I wished to remind myself that I want to say "Mr. Horace Greeley" in the way I have indicated in the long note preceding his name. The notes shown in brackets below would be in the margins in the book; here they precede the text they are meant to interpret. Underlined words are meant to be stressed. Pauses are indicated by a bar (|).

> During our stay in New York for the Brooklyn Readings, | [*Tone of voice: very impressed; expect the listener to be impressed that you have met Mr. Greeley. Speak the name on an upper pitch, so it stands out.*] Mr. Horace Greeley had accepted an invitation to dine with Mr. [*Speak his name reverentially, lowering the pitch slightly.*] Dickens at the Westminster Hotel on Saturday, January 18th; and in [*Of course he was delighted! Who wouldn't be?*] expressing his delight at the success of the Readings took occasion to question the [*Let the voice rise in pitch.*] advisability | of Mr. [*deferential tone*] Dickens reading in [*Speak this on a falling tone.*] Washington, | giving as his reasons that the political horizon was a little hazy, and that [*higher pitch*] "trouble" with the President (Andrew Johnson) might accrue at any moment, in addition to which | the [*Speak this word on an upper pitch.*] "rowdy" element was more largely represented in the city at that moment, in view of the supposed difficulties with the [*upper pitch*] President. [*Just who does Greeley think he is?*] It was his opinion that the "rowdies" would make themselves

obnoxious to [*deferential tone*] Mr. Dickens. [*In a slightly nervous way speed up the rhythm here. Uh oh! Will all my plans fall apart, after the trouble I have taken? Trouble on the horizon if we have to cancel these readings!*] [*Ego, ego!*] I had just returned from Washington, and had secured the only available hall there (the Carol Hall), which held but seven hundred and fifty or eight hundred people, and intended charging [*Impressive!*] five dollars a ticket [*No pause here, even for the semi-colon*] for the Washington Readings; a proceeding Mr. [*deferential tone; lower pitch*] Dickens disapproved of at first, but to which he eventually yielded on [*Ego, ego!*] my pointing out to him [*This phrase should gradually rise in pitch.*] that there were more people in New York, Boston, Philadelphia and Brooklyn | than there were in [*upper pitch*] Washington, | and that these people on an average paid [*the whole phrase lower in pitch, to indicate parentheses*] (thanks to the "noble army of speculators") that [*upper pitch*] price to hear him [*rising inflection on the following words, ending on an upper pitch*] in those cities. [*Speak the following words on a falling tone, ending low.*] As to the "rowdy" element, [*airily dismissive; ego, ego!*] I thought nothing of that...

When you record a first-person narrative autobiographical memoir, you are, in effect, playing a character, but you may not use a character voice. Nonfiction generally demands a straight read. There should be no acting in the sense we mean when we talk about bringing a work of fiction to life. Your objective is simple: to relate the story in a varied and interesting way, and to keep the attention of your listeners. But you cannot afford to be so lively that you indulge in overly dramatic readings of scenes such as the tale of a momentous battle in the English Civil War that brought Oliver Cromwell to power and caused Charles I to lose his head. You are not recording Captain Ahab's titanic fight with Moby-Dick! Also, when you record nonfiction, an imitation of the well-known people who are depicted in it, should their voices be available to be heard on record, is absolutely forbidden. The same advice holds true for the recording of a third-person narrative biography, memoir or history. Just read what Churchill or Franklin D. Roosevelt said in your own voice; you should play their attitudes, without overdoing it.

Two excerpts from Chapter XIV: "Hyde Park Place—The Chief's Last Days in Town"

Slipping his arm in mine, we passed through the arcade and proceeded at once to our dining-place, where I had caused his favorite corner to be kept for him. Having settled down to our dinner, I was naturally anxious to hear from his own lips what Her Majesty and the Chief could have found to talk about for an hour and a half.

"Tell me everything," I said, modestly.

"Everything! my dear fellow, everything! I tell you what, it would be difficult to say what we did *not* talk about," was his reply.

"Well, then," I said, "let me have *some* of it, unless they were all state secrets."

He then went on to tell me that Her Majesty had received him most graciously, and that, as Court etiquette requires that no one, in an ordinary interview with the Sovereign, should be seated, Her Majesty had remained the whole time leaning over the head of a sofa. There was a little shyness on both sides at the commencement, but this wore away as the conversation proceeded.

Her Majesty expressed her deep regret at not having heard one of the Readings, and although highly flattered at this, Dickens could only express his sorrow that, as these were now finally done with, and as, moreover, a mixed audience was absolutely necessary for their success, it would be impossible to gratify Her Majesty's wishes in this particular. This, he said, the Queen fully appreciated...

• • •

...The price of provisions, the cost of butcher's meat, and bread, were next lightly touched upon, and so the conversation rippled on agreeably to an agreeable end. But the interview did not close until the Queen, with gracious modesty, had begged Mr. Dickens's acceptance at her own hands of a copy of the "Journal to the Highlands," in which Her Majesty had placed an autograph inscription, and her own sign manual. This was the book which the coachman had been so particularly enjoined to give into Miss Dickens's own hands.

The Queen, on handing the book to Mr. Dickens, modestly remarked that she felt considerable hesitation in presenting so humble a literary effort to one of the foremost writers of the age. She had, Her Majesty said, requested Mr. Helps to present it for her; but as he had suggested that the gift would be more highly prized by Mr. Dickens if he received it from Her Majesty's own hands, she had resolved herself on this bold act. After asking Mr. Dickens to look kindly on any literary faults of her book, Her Majesty expressed the desire to be the possessor of a complete set of Mr. Dickens's works, and added that, if possible, she would like to receive them that afternoon.

Mr. Dickens, of course, was only too pleased to gratify the wishes of the Queen, but begged to be allowed to defer sending his books until he had had a set specially bound for Her Majesty's acceptance...

NOTES, COMMENTS AND HINTS

The phrase "and her own sign manual" means that Queen Victoria (1819–1901) signed it by hand. "Miss Dickens" refers to one of Dickens's daughters. Mr. Arthur Helps, later Sir Arthur, was one of Queen Victoria's private secretaries.

Again we have Dolby's awkward writing style to contend with: "Slipping his arm in mine, we passed through the arcade and proceeded at once to our dining-place, where I had caused his favorite corner to be kept for him." In the first place, we have a dangling participle: "Slipping his arm in mine, we..." doesn't really make grammatical sense; "he" is the correct reference (he passed through the arcade with me). In the second place, "caused his favorite corner to be kept for him" is decidedly plodding. "Reserved his favorite corner table" would have been better. Dolby thinks he is being elegant, but he is merely being deferential and even fawning, and this should be reflected in the tone of even a neutral reading, but not too heavily. Dolby is by no means Uriah Heep in *David Copperfield*.

Apparently it doesn't take much for someone in the Queen Victoria's presence to feel flattered; isn't it a rather negative compliment, after all, that the queen regretted not having attended a reading? And Queen Victoria talking about the price of groceries must have been a bit odd. It is possible that she had no very clear idea what they cost.

One can read between the lines and determine what Dickens's real attitude about this meeting with Queen Victoria was; it may not have been quite what Dolby says it was. Dolby, himself, however, is a bit like Dobby, the subservient house elf in the Harry Potter series; he doesn't dare to be less than deferential, or he might have to punish himself: "Bad Dolby!" No doubt the stolid Dolby was a very efficient and well-organized tour manager, partly because of his need for approval.

We have in Dickens's attitude to Queen Victoria, as Dolby tells it, the somewhat naïve adoration of the flunky for the master, an admiration similar to Dolby's of Dickens. It might be going too far to call what Dolby describes "sycophantic obsequiousness," and such an attitude would be a bit surprising, coming from an author who made no bones about excoriating the capitalist class system of Victorian England, although Dickens did have a properly respectful and dignified attitude to the queen, as the occasion demanded. In a way a servile attitude on Dickens's part would be quite understandable, both because of the awe anyone might feel in the presence of so revered a figure, and also because Dickens came from a poor background and was a self-made man; no doubt something of servility remained part of his character when he was in the presence of those born to wealth. Dolby, himself, is clearly very conventional in his views, and his acceptance of the class system of the day is quite apparent in his writing. In fact it comes leaping out at the reader with every word. Dickens, nevertheless, even if he felt slightly awestruck and flattered by the royal attention—and this is what gives away some of his real attitude—is quite firm in his refusal to do a command performance for the queen. One rather wonders as well what he must have thought of the queen's book.

If all of the above were to represent your interpretation of the text (and, once again, it is open to other interpretations), the question is how to convey Dickens's attitude through the morass of Dolby's narration of what Dickens said. One answer is to convey it by taking a slightly belligerent tone of voice, a bit truculent, with an upward pitch at the ends of the clauses in the lines "as these were now finally done with, and as, moreover, a mixed audience was absolutely necessary for their success, it would be impossible to gratify Her Majesty's wishes in this particular." Let the voice rise challengingly—don't overdo it; you are not about to be involved in a pugilistic match—on the words "done with," and "necessary" and "success." Lower the pitch slightly, and read "it would be impossible to gratify Her Majesty's wishes" in a neutral tone. Then take a very slight pause before saying in a lower voice that lets us hear you draw back and that sounds deferential, "in this particular," as if you were bowing; you might stress either "this" or "particular," or both words. You could then read the line "This, he said, the Queen fully appreciated" on a slightly higher pitch and in a very flat, dry, somewhat cold tone, with very little affect. Perhaps she said she did, but perhaps she didn't.

From Queen Victoria's *Leaves from the Journal of Our Life in the Highlands from 1848 to 1861* (1868).

BLAIR CASTLE, BLAIR ATHOLE, THURSDAY, SEPTEMBER 12

We took a delightful walk of two hours. Immediately near the house the scenery is very wild, which is most enjoyable. The moment you step out of the house you see those splendid hills all round. We went to the left through some neglected pleasure-grounds, and then through the wood, along a steep winding path overhanging the rapid stream. These Scotch streams, full of stones, and clear as glass, are most beautiful: the peeps between the trees, the depth of the shadows, the mossy stones, mixed with slate, etc., which cover the banks, are very lovely; at every turn you have a picture.

NOTES, COMMENTS AND HINTS

And what a picture it is! The *Leaves* go on like this for 287 pages, to be followed years later by its equally vapid sequel, *More Leaves from the Journal of a Life in the Highlands* (1884). Incidentally, the hero of the first book is Victoria's adored Prince Albert "who made the life of the writer bright and happy." In fact, the book is dedicated to the memory of Albert, who carries a rifle when they go out riding in a carriage, and shoots every animal in sight whenever he can. The second book is dedicated to "My Loyal Highlanders," and to the memory of John Brown, the hero of the book and the man whom she loved.

Queen Victoria's books are quite conventional, and actually tell us nothing. The hills are beautiful, the streams flow and the sky is bright or cloudy. Anything more insipid or vacuous could hardly be imagined. "So humble a literary effort" rather understates the case; it is not a literary effort at all, really. What you have just read is a typical passage, chosen absolutely at random.

The movie *Her Majesty Mrs. Brown* (1997) is worth seeing, not only for itself, but because the conditions of life in the Victorian era are so well observed and so authentically reproduced, from the costumes to the behavior to the sense of what it meant to travel long distances to the way in which food was eaten, and so forth, that it gives us a real feeling for what life must have been like back then. *Mrs. Brown*, as the movie is known in the US, is useful in situating Victorian texts in the sociopolitical atmosphere that is their background, and that should inform your reading of them.

Lytton Strachey's irreverent biography *Queen Victoria* (1921) is useful as well. Strachey informs us that "the Princess's main achievement during her school-days was linguistic. German was naturally the first language with which she was familiar; but English and French quickly followed; and she became virtually trilingual, though her mastery of English grammar remained incomplete." Queen Victoria is said to have made two recordings for Edison, one of which she had sent to the Negus of Ethiopia. Neither recording has survived, if indeed they ever existed. Presumably she had a slight German accent, which would not be surprising, since both her mother and her governess were German, and she grew up speaking the language. And she and Albert spoke German when alone together. You might try using a slight German accent when practicing this passage, just as an exercise. See page 243 for some information on German accents.

As a second exercise, read this little excerpt "straight." Imagine the scenery in your mind's eye, and convey the beauty of it to the listener through the tone of voice which results from your visualization.

From Lytton Strachey's *Queen Victoria* (1921), Chapter I: "Antecedents," III.

The fourth son of George III was Edward, Duke of Kent...

What his political opinions may actually have been is open to doubt; it has often been asserted that he was a Liberal, or even a Radical; and, if we are to believe Robert Owen, he was a necessitarian Socialist. His relations with Owen—the shrewd, gullible, high-minded, wrong-headed, illustrious and preposterous father of Socialism and Co-operation—were curious and characteristic. He talked of visiting the Mills at New Lanark; he did, in fact, preside at one of Owen's public meetings; he corresponded with him on confidential terms, and he even (so Owen assures us) returned, after his death, from "the sphere of spirits" to give encouragement to the Owenites on earth. "In an especial manner," says Owen, "I have to name the very anxious feelings of the spirit of his Royal Highness the Late Duke of Kent (who early informed me that there were no titles in the spiritual spheres into which he had entered), to benefit, not a class, a sect, a party, or any particular country, but the whole of the human race, through futurity." "His whole spirit-proceeding with me has been most beautiful," Owen adds, "making his own appointments; and never in one instance has this spirit not been punctual to the minute he had named." But Owen was of a sanguine temperament. He also numbered among his proselytes President Jefferson, Prince Metternich, and Napoleon; so that some uncertainty must still linger over the Duke of Kent's views. But there is no uncertainty about another circumstance: his Royal Highness borrowed from Robert Owen, on various occasions, various sums of money which were never repaid and amounted in all to several hundred pounds.

NOTES, COMMENTS AND HINTS

Edward, Duke of Kent (1767–1820) was the ne'er-do-well, prideful father of Queen Victoria. Robert Owen (1771–1858) was a pioneer socialist, who turned the town of New Lanark in Scotland into a model industrial community, and, going to the United States, founded the community of New Harmony in Indiana along cooperative lines; it was an unfortunate failure. "Several hundred pounds" was a great deal of money in those days. A "necessitarian" Socialist was one who believed in the inevitability of Socialism.

Lytton Strachey (1880–1932), biographer, literary critic, and a member of the Bloomsbury Group, which included Leonard and Virginia Woolf, is often extremely ironic, as he is here. As far as Strachey was concerned, religion was anachronism and superstition, and spiritualism he viewed as particularly ludicrous. Politics was the history of petty intrigues, and the only important aspect of life was personal relationships.

Everything Strachey tells us is the absolute truth; it is his way of putting it that makes it funny. The sarcasm is evident, but nobody could accuse him of being sarcastic, so deadpan is his comedy, and that gives you a clue as to the "straight," dry tone to take when reading this text. Let Strachey's humor speak for itself. Don't telegraph it or give it away. But do savor the language, and stress the adjectives describing Robert Owen, for instance, but without being labored. Keep it light and keep it moving along. Even while maintaining a dry reading, enjoy yourself and relish Strachey's elegant turns of phrase. You might bring out the irony slightly—without losing the deadpan delivery—of the words "so Owen assures us," "the sphere of spirits," and "also numbered among his proselytes." Be very serious when reading about the spirit of the Duke of Kent being punctual for his appointments with Robert Owen. Strachey has chosen his facts very carefully indeed.

Even if you just read this text completely straight, you can hardly help sounding sarcastic, without trying to. The last sentence of this excerpt simply drips with sarcasm: Strachey is having his fun, puncturing holes in the balloon of foolish pretensions. The text is so well written that it simply flows when read aloud, so allow it just to take you with it.

Here is the opening of the only account of Dickens's readings authorized by the writer himself, compiled by his willing friend, Charles Kent.

From Charles Kent's *Charles Dickens as a Reader* (1872)

> A celebrated writer is hardly ever capable as a Reader of doing justice to his own imaginings. Dr. Johnson's whimsical anecdote of the author of The Seasons admits, in point of fact, of a very general application. According to the grimly humourous old Doctor, "He [Thomson] was once reading to Doddington, who, being himself a reader eminently elegant, was so much provoked by his odd utterance, that he snatched the paper from his hand, and told him that he did not understand his own verses!" Dryden, again, when reading his Amphytrion in the green-room, "though," says Cibber, who was present on the occasion, "he delivered the plain meaning of every period, yet the whole was in so cold, so flat, and unaffecting a manner, that I am afraid of not being believed when I affirm it." . . .

NOTES, COMMENTS AND HINTS

Dr. Johnson is Samuel Johnson; see the excerpts from Boswell's famous biography on page 302.

The Seasons (each "season" first published separately, then as an entire poem in 1740), by the Scottish poet James Thomson (1700–1748), was a long poem about nature, and had no plot or story, thus challenging the Aristotelian notions of poetics considered sacrosanct by the Neoclassicists. Thomson was a precursor of Romanticism.

There is a great deal of debate about the meaning of the terms Neoclassicism, often simply called Classicism, and Romanticism, which are usually applied to literary periods. Neoclassicism, which is said to last roughly from the Restoration of King Charles II in 1660 to about the start of the French Revolution in 1789, supposedly includes a respect for the classical values of Horace's *Ars Poetica* (*The Art of Poetry*) and Aristotle's *Poetics*, such as unity of time and place, simplicity, elegance and attention to detail, and Romanticism, lasting roughly from the 1790s to about 1830, when Realism set in, is supposedly opposed to the rigidity of the Neoclassicists and calls for new forms and experimentation and freedom of stylistic approach. How true is all this? It seems problematic, given that we have writers like Thomson almost fifty years earlier than Romanticism, and an incredibly versatile, far-ranging group of innovative authors in both periods. See the section on style in Chapter Six, page 144. Nothing is that simple when it comes to pinning down literary style.

John Dryden (1631–1700) was a major English poet, literary critic and dramatist, and, supposedly, a Classicist. The era in which he lived is often called the Age of Dryden, so important was he. His translation of Virgil's *Aeneid* became the standard, much admired and often quoted. Amphytrion (pronounced "æm FI: tree on") was a mythological hero who accidentally killed his uncle, Electryon (pronounced "e LEK tree on"), King of Mycenae (pronounced "my SEE nee"), and fled with the king's daughter Alcmene (pronounced "alk MEE nee"), with whom he was in love, to Thebes for safety and was there absolved of his guilt. Dryden's *Amphytrion* (1690), with music by Henry Purcell, was a great success.

In the eighteenth and nineteenth centuries authors in England and France customarily read a play aloud to the assembled company before they began rehearsing it, or to a board of directors who were to pass judgment on it. In 1848 Balzac, for instance, read his play *Le Faiseur* (*The Jobber*) to the board of the Comédie Française, and was quite ineffective, so nervous and terrified was he.

Colley Cibber (1671–1757) was a well-known actor and playwright who wrote his own plays and revised some of Shakespeare's. His version of *Richard the Third* was popular, and Sir Laurence Olivier even used several of Cibber's lines in his film version in 1955.

Before the age of recording we can only discover how well known people sounded by reading descriptions of them, just as, before the age of film, we can read in a Shakespeare variorum edition an exact description of how Edwin Booth played Hamlet, every gesture, every intonation, every move. And no doubt there is some truth in what Kent has to say about authors reading their own works, but there are marvelous exceptions, aside from Dickens himself, such as Dylan Thomas or John le Carré. In any case, it is always interesting to hear an author read, if only to hear the voice that created the writing.

To read this little selection aloud requires dexterity with language, and a delight in its use. Adjectives and phrases such as "whimsical" and "grimly humourous," applied to Dr. Johnson, or Johnson's own "eminently elegant," can be nicely emphasized by drawing out the vowels in them ever so slightly. Read this high-toned writing with excellent diction, but without any kind of pedantic or labored delivery. Rather, play a bit against the pedantry, which is inherent in the language, and will be there for the listener simply on hearing the words.

As an amusing exercise, read this selection in any kind of accent you can think of, whether foreign or native to the language. This will also have the effect of freeing you up, and helping you to avoid a pedantic, or too precise, tone.

Another way of practicing this text is to ignore what I said above and exaggerate the pedantry. Give it a slight mincing touch, with just a bit of a superior attitude. This would no doubt not be a final interpretation if you were actually to record this text.

And now for the master who did the readings: Charles Dickens prepared his texts thoroughly and rehearsed assiduously, as he told Charles Kent:

> "Whatever thought was lavished thus upon the composition of the Readings, was lavished quite as unstintingly upon the manner of their delivery. Thoroughly natural, impulsive, and seemingly artless... So thorough and consistent throughout his reading career was the sincerity of Dickens, in his impersonations, that his words and looks, his thoughts and emotions were never mere make-believes, but always, so far as the most vigilant eye or the most sensitive ear could detect, had their full and original significance."

Kent, surprised at the ease with which Dickens read the rapid dialogue of the voluble Doctor Marigold, the title character of a short story, was enlightened when the elated Dickens explained "half-weariedly, yet half-laughingly," "There! If I have gone through that already to myself once, I have gone through it two—hundred—times!"

Dickens's sincere approach and the results he achieved as a consequence of it are still desirable today; we still want reality, and "never mere make-believes." And as Kent tells us:

> "The secret of his original success, and of the long sustainment of it in each of these two careers—as Writer and as Reader—is in a great measure discoverable in this, that whatever powers he possessed he applied to their very uttermost. Whether as Author or as Imperson-

ator, he gave himself up to his appointed task, not partially or intermittingly, but thoroughly and indefatigably."

Here are three unabridged excerpts, one from *A Christmas Carol,* one from *Dombey and Son,* and one from *The Pickwick Papers.* If you were to record these books, you would be recording either a specially abridged or an unabridged version, whether commercial or for an organization that uses volunteers. Dickens himself abridged all three for his own readings, but I have not used his versions here. More selections from Dickens will be found on page 119 in this chapter, and on pages 169, 192, 198 and 199 in Chapter Six.

The opening of *A Christmas Carol, In Four Staves* (1843); from "Stave One: Marley's Ghost."

Marley was dead, to begin with. There is no doubt whatever about that. The register of his burial was signed by the clergyman, the undertaker, and the chief mourner. Scrooge signed it. And Scrooge's name was good upon 'Change for anything he chose to put his hand to.

Old Marley was as dead as a door-nail.

Mind! I don't mean to say that I know, of my own knowledge, what there is particularly dead about a door-nail. I might have been inclined, myself, to regard a coffin-nail as the deadest piece of ironmongery in the trade. But the wisdom of our ancestors is in the simile; and my unhallowed hands shall not disturb it, or the Country's done for. You will therefore permit me to repeat, emphatically, that Marley was as dead as a door-nail.

Scrooge knew he was dead? Of course he did. How could it be otherwise? Scrooge and he were partners for I don't know how many years. Scrooge was his sole executor, his sole administrator, his sole assign, his sole residuary legatee, his sole friend, and sole mourner. And even Scrooge was not so dreadfully cut up by the sad event, but that he was an excellent man of business on the very day of the funeral, and solemnized it with an undoubted bargain.

NOTES, COMMENTS AND HINTS

Our narrator is "I" (presumably Charles Dickens), a first-person narrator telling "you," a word he uses often, a story. But in this case "I" is not telling "you" his own story, so in effect we have a third-person narrative. And "I" is an excellent storyteller, who makes his points with emphasis and variety, including an occasional touch of irony ("... or the Country's done for"), all of which you must do when you practice this selection.

Dickens underlined "Scrooge" twice, on the first and third (but not the second) mentions of the name. And the manner in which he read that name, according to what Charles Kent, who certainly heard it more than once, tells us, evoked the miserly and feared personality of the character very vividly and made the audience see "Scrooge in the flesh." I would imagine that he lengthened the "oo" sound and perhaps articulated the consonants more strongly than would usually be done, while dropping his voice, or perhaps raising it, just slightly in pitch. Perhaps he trilled the "r" as well. It may have been a bit melodramatic for our taste, but doing something similar, if toned down, would, I think, be highly effective in a recording for contemporary listeners.

The words "Old Marley" in the second, one-sentence paragraph were apparently uttered in a very soft, low tone, almost a whisper, perhaps, and this tone was meant no doubt to evoke a sort of secretive, creepy, and not exactly reverential (for even at the outset we sense that Marley is not a character to be revered) view of the dead man whose ghost we will soon meet.

The adjective "sole" was possibly emphasized every time Dickens said it, and given more importance than the nouns it modifies, if one may judge by the excerpt from *Dombey and Son*, just below, and his way of reading "very" and "rather," as you will see. The idea of being alone, and of what being alone means, is a very important theme of the story, so that it makes some thematic as well as stylistic sense to stress "sole." You could, of course, do the exact opposite, and not emphasize the word "sole" at all. This is the sort of choice you will have to make, and sometimes it will be spontaneous and unplanned, arising from the moment; such choices can be quite as effective as any calculated choice.

A later paragraph begins: "Oh! But he was a tight-fisted hand at the grindstone, Scrooge! a squeezing, wrenching, grasping, scraping, clutching, covetous, old sinner!" When Dickens read the "Oh!" which begins this line, he drew that word out to some length, for some three seconds or more. That would perhaps be a bit too much for today's listeners, but lengthening a word is clearly an effective technique, and an excellent way of making a point, if it is not overdone. However, it is permissible to overdo it just a bit for a character's way of speaking. It would make a very specific sound signature for a particular personage, so that the listener could instantly identify the character.

Dickens's rhythms are very pronounced, his rhythmic structure being his way of telling the story and driving it forward, which makes it easy to read this excerpt aloud. The passage should be delivered somewhat slowly, with all deliberate speed. Do not make it labored, or it will be deadly, and difficult to listen to. Lines like "Of course he did. How could it be otherwise?" would be more ironic and pointed for being "thrown away," that is, not emphasized, but delivered rather casually, in a slightly offhand manner, almost as an aside.

This opening should intrigue us, and it should flow, and lift us up and into the story. We should wonder, as Dickens means us to in this masterful beginning, why he is telling us that Marley is dead, and who Marley was when he was alive.

From *Dombey and Son* (1848), Chapter One: Dombey and Son.

Dombey sat in the corner of the darkened room in the great arm-chair by the bedside, and Son lay tucked up warm in a little basket bedstead, carefully disposed on a low settee immediately in front of the fire and close to it, as if his constitution were analogous to that of a muffin, and it was essential to toast him brown while he was very new.

Dombey was almost eight-and-forty years of age. Son about eight-and-forty minutes. Dombey was rather bald, rather red, and though a handsome well-made man, too stern and pompous in appearance, to be prepossessing. Son was very bald, and very red, and though (of course) an undeniably fine infant, somewhat crushed and spotty in his general effect as yet. On the brow of Dombey, Time and his brother Care had set some marks, as on a tree that was to come down in good time—remorseless twins they are for striding through their human forests, notching as they go—while the countenance of Son was crossed and re-crossed with a thousand little creases, which the same deceitful Time would take delight in smoothing out and wearing away with the flat part of his scythe, as a preparation of the surface for his deeper operations.

Dombey, exulting in the long-looked-for event, jingled and jingled the heavy gold watch-chain that depended from below his trim blue coat, whereof the buttons sparkled phosphorescently in the feeble rays of the distant fire. Son, with his little fists curled up and clenched, seemed, in his feeble way, to be squaring at existence for having come upon him so unexpectedly.

"The house will once again, Mrs. Dombey," said Mr. Dombey, "be not only in name but in fact Dombey and Son; Dom-bey and Son!"

The words had such a softening influence, that he appended a term of endearment to Mrs. Dombey's name (though not without some hesitation, as being a man but little used to that form of address): and said, "Mrs. Dombey, my—my dear."

A transient flush of faint surprise overspread the sick lady's face as she raised her eyes towards him.

"He will be christened Paul, my—Mrs. Dombey—of course."

She feebly echoed, "Of course," or rather expressed it by the motion of her lips, and closed her eyes again.

"His father's name, Mrs. Dombey, and his grandfather's! I wish his grandfather were alive this day!" And again he said "Dom-bey and Son," in exactly the same tone as before.

Those three words conveyed the one idea of Mr. Dombey's life. The earth was made for Dombey and Son to trade in, and the sun and moon were made to give them light.

NOTES, COMMENTS AND HINTS

Dombey and Son is a searing indictment of heartless, selfish capitalism and of the corrosive effects of money. Its theme is apparent on the very first page, in the last bald statement of this excerpt. The omniscient third-person narrator of the story is filled with compassion and sadness even for the stolid, morally obtuse, ethically blind Dombey, for his sick, suffering wife and for the baby boy born into the lap of luxury, into a world and destined to a fate of which he as yet knows nothing, and of which, in his sensitive, perceptive soul, he will be horrified to learn; into a cruel world of perfidy and meanness in which human beings treat each other like objects, because they know no better; and yet into a world where love and compassion can flourish and must be made to flourish. The story, which begins to unfold through the eyes of the little boy, the innocent Paul Dombey, makes one think of the early days of Dickens himself, born into poverty, forced to be a child laborer in a factory, and faced with a world created in part by the Dombeys (often unwittingly and unconsciously) who inhabit the mansions and choose to know nothing of the plight of the impoverished masses. Dickens understands people, and condemns not so much them as the system under which they live, even though they have helped to create something so cruel and so heartless.

A sadness should underlie the telling of the story, without the reader's acting that sadness, so that the listener, caught up in and fascinated by it, should have a gradually instilled sense of longing for a better world as the story unfolds. The recording artist should adopt a fairly neutral tone in the narrative passages, but with a fine sense of the language and of the theme.

An article in the June 18, 1870, *Spectator* said that Dickens in his reading of this excerpt "made the most painful impression of pathos feeding upon itself." He made quite a point of the phrase in the first paragraph, "and it was essential to toast him brown while he was very new," which he underlined in his script, and he must have gotten quite a laugh from his audience. As Kate Field, his American admirer, tells us in her book *Pen Photographs of Charles Dickens's Readings, Taken from Life* (James R. Osgood and Company, 1871), Dickens emphasized the adjectives "rather" and "very" in the second paragraph, instead of the other adjectives they modify; he also stressed the adjectives "crushed" and "spotty": "Dombey was rather bald, rather red, and though a handsome well-made man, too stern and pompous in appearance, to be prepossessing. Son was very bald, and very red, and though (of course) an undeniably fine infant, somewhat crushed and spotty in his general effect as yet." Also in the second paragraph he emphasized "Dombey" and "Son," both of which he underlined once.

Finding a voice for Dombey, when he speaks, is a very nice task. Apparently Dickens had a deep, rich voice, which he could make deeper and richer when he wished, that must have helped him enormously in his characterization. Don't overdo the vocal characterization and make him so insufferably pompous that he becomes merely ridiculous; that would betray the material. Dombey is incapable of really enjoying anything in life, despite his immense wealth; he wouldn't even know how to begin enjoying what life has to offer. The smug self-satisfaction and triumphant attitude of Dombey should help you find his voice. Dombey's obtuseness, his narrow view of the world, his unctuousness and his reserve should all come through from his first utterance. He is self-contained, he needs nobody; yet he is happy to have his line and his way of life continue, a way of life he doesn't even think about, because he considers it simply the natural order of things and takes it for granted, as he does everything. He is incapable of doing anything else.

Some long time ago, in his childhood, Dombey learned to be afraid of his own feelings, and of emotion generally. Expressing his feelings became almost impossible. He learned to fear punishment, to fear that he would be hurt if he expressed the truth about what he felt. In short Dombey is remote, reserved, and restrained in his expression. These qualities, these aspects of his character are the obstacles against which Dombey struggles in order to achieve his sub-objective of expressing his feelings, and they must be apparent in his voice. These are inner obstacles, however, and should result not in a flat, neutral delivery of what he has to say, but rather in a tight, somewhat repressed, restrained tone. Dombey does have feelings, as is apparent from what he does manage to say, but those feelings are interred as deeply as possible. Even his happiness at having a son is rather remote, and Dickens makes a point of telling us how little, save with an effort, he is able to express affection, and even then, quite unsuccessfully. That he is able even to say the words "my dear" comes as a great surprise to his wife and one can quite imagine the complete lack of any sense of sexual fulfillment on Dombey's part, as though he wishes to conceive a son merely out of duty, and then to escape internally as well as externally from what must be to him the guiltiest of pleasures. His wife, too, one imagines, submits to her husband out of duty and without feeling anything much, in the kind of behavior we have come to look upon as typically mid-Victorian (not always particularly accurately, as a matter of fact).

When you prepare a text, this is the sort of character analysis you have to do. As a personal substitution for all of the above find that place in yourself where you have felt repressed and unhappy. Perhaps you have had unhappy experiences in love that you can use to inform your reading of the excerpt, "as if" Dombey's happiness and unhappiness and his inability to express himself were your own. In addition, as you read this third-person narrative, you might imagine that you are actually talking about yourself, which will personalize the reading.

From *The Posthumous Papers of the Pickwick Club* (1837), Chapter XXXIV: "Is wholly devoted to a full and faithful Report of the memorable Trial of Bardell against Pickwick"

"You have heard from my learned friend, gentlemen," continued Serjeant Buzfuz, well knowing that, from the learned friend alluded to, the gentlemen of the jury had heard just nothing at all—"you have heard from my learned friend, gentlemen, that this is an action for a breach of promise of marriage, in which the damages are laid at 1,500l. But you have not heard from my learned friend, inasmuch as it did not come within my learned friend's province to tell you, what are the facts and circumstances of the case. Those facts and circumstances, gentlemen, you shall hear detailed by me, and proved by the unimpeachable female whom I will place in that box before you."

Here, Mr. Serjeant Buzfuz, with a tremendous emphasis on the word "box," smote his table with a mighty sound, and glanced at Dodson and Fogg, who nodded admiration of the Serjeant, and indignant defiance of the defendant.

"The plaintiff, gentlemen," continued Serjeant Buzfuz, in a soft and melancholy voice, "the plaintiff is a widow; yes, gentlemen, a widow. The late Mr. Bardell, after enjoying, for many years, the esteem and confidence of his sovereign, as one of the guardians of his royal revenues, glided almost imperceptibly from the world, to seek elsewhere for that repose and peace which a custom-house can never afford."

At this pathetic description of the decease of Mr. Bardell, who had been knocked on the head with a quart-pot in a public-house cellar, the learned serjeant's voice faltered, and he proceeded, with emotion:

"Some time before his death, he had stamped his likeness upon a little boy. With this little boy, the only pledge of her departed exciseman, Mrs. Bardell shrank from the world, and courted the retirement and tranquillity of Goswell Street; and here she placed in her front parlour window a written placard, bearing this inscription—'Apartments furnished for a single gentleman. Inquire within.' " Here Serjeant Buzfuz paused, while several gentlemen of the jury took a note of the document.

"There is no date to that, is there, sir?" inquired a juror.

"There is no date, gentlemen," replied Serjeant Buzfuz; "but I am instructed to say that it was put in the plaintiff's parlour window just this time three years. I entreat the attention of the jury to the wording of this document—'Apartments furnished for a single gentleman!' Mrs. Bardell's opinions of the opposite sex, gentlemen, were derived from a long contemplation of the inestimable qualities of her lost husband. She had no fear—she had no distrust—she had no suspicion—all was confidence and reliance. 'Mr. Bardell,' said the widow; 'Mr. Bardell was a man of honour—Mr. Bardell was a man of his word—Mr. Bardell was no deceiver—Mr. Bardell was once a single gentleman himself; to single gentlemen I look for protection, for assistance, for comfort, and for consolation—*in* single gentlemen I shall perpetually see something to remind me of what Mr. Bardell was when he first won my young and untried affections; to a single gentleman, then, shall my lodgings be let.' Actuated by this beautiful and touching impulse (among the best impulses of our imperfect nature, gentlemen), the lonely and desolate widow dried her tears, furnished her first floor, caught her innocent boy to her maternal bosom, and put the bill up in her parlour window. Did it remain there long? No. The serpent was on the watch, the train was laid, the mine was preparing, the sapper and miner was at work. Before the bill had been in the parlour window three days—three days, gentlemen—a being, erect upon two legs, and bearing all the outward semblance of a man, and not of a monster, knocked at the door of Mrs. Bardell's house. He inquired within; he took the lodgings; and on the very next day he entered into possession of them. This man was Pickwick—Pickwick, the defendant."

NOTES, COMMENTS AND HINTS

I suggest you get a copy of Dickens's book and use the whole chapter for practice. You can use it to help develop the skill of sustaining character by reading it straight through without stopping.

This central episode is a hilarious trial for breach of promise of marriage, a civil suit brought against the innocent, likable, naïve Mr. Samuel Pickwick by his landlady, Mrs. Martha Bardell, who is infatuated with her lodger and fancies herself in love with him. She believed, based on certain things he had said, and which she misinterpreted, that her affections were returned, and that Mr. Pickwick had actually proposed marriage. When the horrified

Pickwick realized her mistake and refused to marry her, she was so deeply offended and outraged that she took him to court. Her rascally solicitors (lawyers) are Messrs. Dodson and Fogg, and her barrister (the lawyer who actually pleads the case in court) is Serjeant Buzfuz.

The pompous, self-centered, self-important Buzfuz's objective is not simply to persuade the jury of the justice of his client's case, but "to be admired." He is a narcissistic personality with an incredible sense of his own importance not merely in the trial, but in the entire scheme of things in the universe. In short, he has a monumental ego. His oration is full of sententious, tendentious moralizing, and of course, ultimately, there is nothing in it. It is a tissue of fabrications and false allegations and sanctimonious misinterpretations of so-called evidence.

Dickens's reading of this trial scene was one of his most effective and appreciated performances. Charles Kent tells us that it was greeted with "peals of laughter." "Every point, however minute, told and told effectively," he tells us. And he continues: "... there was something eminently absurd in the Serjeant's extraordinarily precise, almost mincing pronunciation." Later on he refers to "the bland and melancholy accents of Serjeant Buzfuz," to "his cruelly, matter-of-fact precision," and to his "gravity." All of this is wonderful grist for the recording artist's mill.

Dickens's internal "stage directions" are perfect: "with a tremendous emphasis on the word 'box' " and "in a soft and melancholy voice" are phrases that tell us not only how to read that particular section of the text, but also how to indicate the complete phoniness of the speaker, as do "the learned serjeant's voice faltered, and he proceeded, with emotion..." and "Serjeant Buzfuz paused" for effect.

Kate Field actually gives us Dickens's intonation patterns for certain lines in the Pickwick trial reading. Dickens imitated very closely a lawyer's manner of delivery in a classical oratorical style. (See Anthony Sher as Disraeli in the movie *Mrs. Brown* for a superb rendition of parliamentary oratory, very much in the old-fashioned style.) And see the wonderful English movie *The Pickwick Papers* (1952), available on videocassette from United Home Video, with Donald Wolfit as an orotund, almost vicious Serjeant Buzfuz and Nigel Patrick as that delightful scamp, Mr. Jingle.

Here are the lines from Kate Field's book relevant to the above excerpt from *Pickwick Papers*; I have added notes in brackets. Dickens stressed the words in italics.

1. [There is a rising tone on the word "afford."]

   never *ford*!
   ... which a custom-house can
   af-

2. [There is a rising tone on the word "boy."]

   stamped his likeness upon a *hoy*
   bo-
   lit-tle

3. [There is a falling tone on the syllables "*sin-*" and "*In-*" and a rising tone on "*within.*"]

   Apartments furnished for *In-* *in*!
   sin- gentleman.
   a gle quire *with-*

For purposes of practice, I propose some purely technical suggestions. The suggested line readings below are based on my organic reading of this text. Readings of lines must always be based on the internal circumstances and life of the character, because external manifestations are the result of internal processes. In the case of Serjeant Buzfuz the internal process and its external manifestations include the circumstance that he is a professional trial lawyer who has rehearsed his speech:

On the line " 'The plaintiff, gentlemen,' continued Serjeant Buzfuz, in a soft and melancholy voice, 'the plaintiff is a widow; yes, gentlemen, a widow.' " try a falling intonation pattern both times you say the word "widow." Suggesting finality and almost with a tear in the voice, the word "widow" should be lower in pitch the second time than the first.

The line to the jury "There is no date, gentlemen" could be delivered so as to give it significance, as if it meant something to the case Buzfuz is making, and as if he were saying, "This, gentlemen, is an important point!"

Draw out the vowels in "long" and "lost" in the line "a long contemplation of the inestimable qualities of her lost husband." Say the word "inestimable" on a higher pitch, and stress both the words "lost" and "husband."

The name "Mr. Bardell" should be said every time as if he were a saint.

In the line "Actuated by this beautiful and touching impulse (among the best impulses of our imperfect nature, gentlemen), the lonely and desolate widow dried her tears" the word "touching" should be spoken on an upper pitch, and the word "impulse" should begin on a lower pitch and should be spoken on a rising tone. Stress both words in the phrases "best impulses" and "imperfect nature," and say "imperfect nature" on either a higher or a lower pitch, to differentiate it from the surrounding pitches. Say "dried her tears" on a falling tone, with great finality, even though a comma follows it, then begin the following section of the text immediately at a slightly quicker pace.

On "Did it remain there long? No." lower the pitch and say the line in a voice of growling thunder. Take a slight pause after the words "The serpent," drawing out the vowels and speaking the rest of the phrase somewhat harshly and on a higher pitch.

In his Preface to *A Tale of Two Cities* (1859) Dickens wrote the following:

> When I was acting, with my children and friends, in Mr. Wilkie Collins's drama *The Frozen Deep*, I first conceived the main idea of this story. A strong desire was upon me then to embody it in my own person, and I traced out in my fancy the state of mind of which it would necessitate the presentation to an observant spectator, with particular care and interest.

The recording artist could with profit take what Dickens did for himself as a good approach to the preparation of a text. You can also use the two sentences quoted from the Preface as a little practice exercise, making his nineteenth-century grammar clear and intelligible to a twenty-first century listener.

Helen Potter's Impersonations

In 1891 Helen Potter, the American actress, published a book called *Impersonations* (New York: Edgar S. Werner). She was famous for her dramatic recitations and readings from the concert platform, and especially for her impersonations of famous people, men and women, in full costume and makeup: She performed as Oscar Wilde, lecturing on aesthetics, and as Henry Ward Beecher, giving a sermon about Lincoln's death. Photographs of her show that she was a superb makeup artist, who really looked the parts. She toured with her own company, which she called the Pleiades "A Groupe [*sic*] of Seven Stars," which included the Eichberg String Quartet. The Pleiades performed scenes from well-known plays, and Helen Potter did her impersonations of well-known actors in the roles identified with them: Edwin Booth as Hamlet; Charlotte Cushman as Meg Merrilies in Sir Walter Scott's *Guy Mannering*, and so forth. In her book she indicates all the tones and gestures she used in all her performances, and she includes introductory material on how to prepare such impersonations, how to care for the voice, and so on.

She devised a system of annotation for indicating intonation patterns and gestures, and proceeded to reconstruct the speeches and dramatic performances of a number of her famous contemporaries, on whom she had taken detailed notes, using her system. She explains in the book how to take such notes, what to listen for and what to observe. The people she knew and had heard, aside from those mentioned above, included Fanny Kemble (the English actress who married a Southern plantation owner and became an ardent abolitionist), Ellen Terry, the French actress Sarah Bernhardt (Potter impersonated her in French—of course), Elizabeth Cady Stanton and Susan B. Anthony.

Her technical indications for a scene she performed in Italian from a play about Queen Elizabeth, which had been done by the Italian actress Adelaide Ristori, are very revealing of theatrical practice in her day: "RENDITION: Breathe fast and heavy; voice sometimes aspirate, sometimes half guttural; hand to the heart, eyes wide open, and now and then turned upward in the sockets." Can you imagine? Very Delsarte! (See Chapter Four.) She even learned a speech from a Chinese play, in Mandarin, and performed it dressed in full regalia!

Here, as an exercise, is part of a speech given in her own defense by Susan B. Anthony (1820–1906), the great champion of women's rights, and especially of the right to vote. Taken from the court transcripts, Anthony's impassioned defense was given at the trial at which she was convicted of the offence of voting in the 1872 election for Ulysses S. Grant. She was fined $100, which she refused to pay, but she was not imprisoned. It is unclear to me whether Helen Potter, who deeply admired Susan B. Anthony and writes as if she knew her personally, actually attended the trial in Canandaigua, New York, but she had certainly seen Miss Anthony speak and knew her voice and manner, which she was able to recreate as part of her show.

The single vertical line [|] represents a brief pause after a word. A backward slash [(\ )] represents a falling tone, from high to low; it precedes the word uttered on the falling tone. The sign [<] represents an increase in vocal force lasting to the next change; it precedes a word which is pronounced with greater force. The sign [o] represents a high note on the syllable that follows it. A forward slash [(/)] means that the following syllable is spoken on a rising tone; this is the only sign not actually used by Ms. Potter, who draws a rising sign over the syllable.

From Helen Potter's *Impersonations* (1891)

[The judge says, "Has the prisoner anything to say why judgment should not be pronounced?"]

Miss A. [*rising.*] Yes, your honor, | I have (\ ) many things to say; | for in your ordered verdict of guilty, you have trampled underfoot | every | vital | principle | of our (\ ) government. < My (\ ) o natural rights | my (\ ) o civil rights, my o political rights, | my (\ ) o judicial rights | are all alike | ignored. Robbed of the fundamental privilege of citizenship, | I am degraded | from the status of a citizen to that of a subject; | and not only myself indivi (/) dually, but all of my (\ ) sex, | are, by your honor's verdict, doomed to political sub o (\ ) jection | under this so-called Re o publican form of (\ ) government. < Your denial of my citizen's right to (/) vote, | is the denial of my right to consent | as one of the (\ ) governed | the denial of my right of representation | as one of the (\ ) taxed; | the denial of my right | to a trial by a jury of my o (\ ) peers | [the word "as" is spoken on a low note] as an offender against (\ ) law | therefore, | the denial of my sacred rights | to life, | liberty,—property. |

[Judge's Voice: The court orders the prisoner to sit down.]

Miss A. [*still standing.*] But your honor will not deny me this one and only poor privilege against this high-handed outrage | upon my citizen's rights. May it please the court to remember | that since the day of my arrest last Novem (\ ) ber | this is the first time | that either myself or o any [the word "person" is spoken on a low note] (\ ) person | of my disenfranchised (/) class | has been allowed a word of defense before judge or jury—

NOTES, COMMENTS AND HINTS

Just follow Helen Potter's indications until they feel comfortable and real to you. Try to see what is underneath the words, and make the emotions your own by using substitutions if necessary. After the judge's interruption there are no indications of intonation patterns or pauses until after the word "outrage," which shows us that the sentence is meant to be spoken fairly rapidly and on one breath, as a hurried protest. In Susan B. Anthony's speech all the phrasing is indicated by Helen Potter's markings. It clearly arises from deep emotion and anger and is a passionate expression of her political and personal feelings. We are shown its surface, like the tip of an iceberg. But if we are to make it mean anything we must personalize it and make it real from below the surface, from the inside.

Helen Potter's final advice to anyone performing this speech on stage: "If recalled, enter quickly, bow abruptly and retire."

Phrasing and Rhythm

Phrasing depends on the style in which the material is written, and breath control is important in controlling phrasing. The long, sinuous sentences of Marcel Proust and the short, curt periods of Ernest Hemingway require different phrasing, and different breath control.

Phrasing and rhythm go hand in hand. The nature of the scene will often dictate the rhythm and pace at which you read, with the result that they will be natural. It should not be necessary to calculate the phrasing or the rhythm or pace, but if you are having difficulty getting a text to flow, you may want to do just that.

Throughout this book you should consciously consider phrasing only if you have to, when working on all the illustrative texts and exercises. Phrasing is of paramount importance not only for the sake of clarity, for making points clearly, whether in fiction or nonfiction, but also for creating atmosphere. Pauses, hesitations, delays all contribute to the communication of meaning and to the feeling of what is going on in a scene. The sinister atmosphere of dread in the excerpts from *Dracula* (see page 121) and *Jane Eyre* (see page 131) is created partly as a result of phrasing, as is the intimate, confiding atmosphere of the opening of *Swann's Way*, (see page 164) and the placid, lordly ambience of the opening of *Rip van Winkle* (see page 176).

The rhythm of a scene, like that of a musical piece, can be legato or staccato, and the pace or tempo of a scene can be fast or slow. Everything depends on the nature of the scene, whether it is languid or dynamic, filled with reverie or filled with physical action, full of rambunctious humor or replete with imminent danger.

Here are some examples of texts, each of which demands different phrasing and a different kind of rhythm.

From Charles Dickens's *The Posthumous Papers of the Pickwick Club* (1837), Chapter II: "The first Day's Journey, and the first Evening's Adventures; with their Consequences.

"Heads, heads; take care of your heads!" cried the loquacious stranger, as they came out under the low archway, which in those days formed the entrance to the coach yard. "Terrible place—dangerous work—other day—five children—mother—tall lady, eating sandwiches—forgot the arch—crash—knock—children look round— mother's head off—sandwich in her hand—no mouth to put it in—head of a family off—shocking, shocking! Looking at Whitehall, sir?—fine place—little window—somebody else's head off there, eh, sir?—he didn't keep a sharp lookout enough either—eh, Sir, eh?"

"I was ruminating," said Mr. Pickwick, "on the strange mutability of human affairs."

"Ah! I see—in at the palace door one day, out at the window the next. Philosopher, sir?"

"An observer of human nature, sir," said Mr. Pickwick.

"Ah, so am I. Most people are when they've little to do and less to get. Poet, sir?"

"My friend Mr. Snodgrass has a strong poetic turn," said Mr. Pickwick.

"So have I," said the stranger. "Epic poem,—ten thousand lines—revolution of July—composed it on the spot—Mars by day, Apollo by night—bang the field-piece, twang the lyre."

"You were present at that glorious scene, sir?" said Mr. Snodgrass.

"Present! think I was; fired a musket—fired with an idea,—rushed into wine shop—wrote it down—back again—whiz, bang—another idea—wine shop again—pen and ink—back again—cut and slash—noble time, sir..."

NOTES, COMMENTS AND HINTS

This scene practically reads itself, as Mr. Jingle talks incessantly, and enthusiastically, but rarely in complete sentences. As a general rule he doesn't seem to think verbs are necessary. He speaks in a staccato rhythm, and rather rapidly. The phrasing and the rhythm are given to you in no uncertain manner, and you will rarely find such an obvious, and easy, rhythm to play. Mr. Jingle is delightful and macabre at the same time. There are no gaps in his thinking and his ideas come tumbling out of him; the dashes in the text do not represent pauses, but, rather, the compression of his ideas and thoughts, because he thinks so quickly, shallow though he may be. Mr. Jingle is rather in love with himself and with his language. You should run the plethora of phrases onto each other, without too many gaps (you do need some pauses, in order to make points). It is here, if ever, that breath control is important. It is also especially important to breathe through the nose, and not through the mouth, or you will never get through this text.

Mr. Alfred Jingle is an impudent strolling actor, a ne'er-do-well who convinces the gullible Mr. Samuel Pickwick and the members of the Pickwick Club that he is a gentleman of consequence. He cadges dinners and generally sponges off them. In the scene above he has just rescued Mr. Pickwick (they are meeting for the first time) from an altercation with a cabman, who had taken him for an "informer," because Mr. Pickwick, who is always taking notes and making observations about everything he sees, took down the number of the cab and information about the cabman's unusual horse.

Mr. Pickwick's rhythm is slower, more dignified and more stately than Jingle's, without being in the least pompous. Pickwick is a very friendly, likable and somewhat naïve sort of chap. Mr. Jingle overawes Mr. Snodgrass, the poet of the club, and, indeed, takes in the whole group of Pickwickians, including Mr. Tupman, the lover of the group, and Mr. Winkle, the club's sportsman, even though Jingle is a consummate and obvious liar.

As an exercise try reading Jingle's dialogue as rapidly as you can, then slow it down. Everything he says makes sense, and his train of thought is logical, at least to him.

Mr. Jingle simply loves what he has to say. He is so energetic, enthusiastic, bubbling over with life and merriment and delight that he gets carried away with his thoughts and images, which are frequently nonsensical to us, although not to him. That should give you plenty of vocal energy, which is what you need when you record! A caveat: Don't be so enthusiastic that you overdo it! You still have to be real. You have to be down on the earth and not floating in the clouds. Find an apt substitution for this character, perhaps a situation in which you had to do some fast talking. Jingle actually turns out to be quite a con man, but you just can't dislike him. He's a scamp, but he's not a villain. Use the entire chapter in Dickens's book for practice.

From Bram Stoker's *Dracula* (1897), Chapter Two: "Jonathan Harker's Journal—continued"

. . . The old man motioned me in with his right hand with a courtly gesture, saying in excellent English, but with a strange intonation:—

"Welcome to my house! Enter freely and of your own free will!" He made no motion of stepping to meet me, but stood like a statue, as though his gesture of welcome had fixed him into stone. The instant, however, that I had stepped over the threshold, he moved impulsively forward, and holding out his hand grasped mine with a strength which made me wince, an effect which was not lessened by the fact that it seemed cold as ice, more like the hand of a dead than a living man. Again he said:—

"Welcome to my house! Enter freely. Go safely, and leave something of the happiness you bring!" The strength of the handshake was so much akin to that which I had noticed in the driver, whose face I had not seen, that for a moment I doubted if it were not the same person to whom I was speaking. So to make sure, I said interrogatively, "Count Dracula?"

He bowed in a courtly way as he replied, "I am Dracula, and I bid you welcome, Mr. Harker, to my house. Come in, the night air is chill, and you must need to eat and rest." As he was speaking, he put the lamp on a bracket on the wall, and stepping out, took my luggage. He had carried it in before I could forestall him. I protested, but he insisted.

"Nay, sir, you are my guest. It is late, and my people are not available. Let me see to your comfort myself." He insisted on carrying my traps along the passage, and then up a great winding stair, and along another great passage, on whose stone floor our steps rang heavily. At the end of this he threw open a heavy door, and I rejoiced to see within a well-lit room in which a table was spread for supper, and on whose mighty hearth a great fire of logs, freshly replenished, flamed and flared.

The Count halted, putting down my bags, closed the door, and crossing the room, opened another door, which led into a small octagonal room lit by a single lamp, and seemingly without a window of any sort. Passing through this, he opened another door, and motioned me to enter. It was a welcome sight. For here was a great bedroom well lighted and warmed with another log fire, also added to but lately, for the top logs were fresh, which sent a hollow roar up the wide chimney. The Count himself left my luggage inside and withdrew, saying, before he closed the door.

"You will need, after your journey, to refresh yourself by making your toilet. I trust you will find all you wish. When you are ready, come into the other room, where you will find your supper prepared."

The light and warmth and the Count's courteous welcome seemed to have dissipated all my doubts and fears. Having then reached my normal state, I discovered that I was half famished with hunger. So making a hasty toilet, I went into the other room.

I found supper already laid out. My host, who stood on one side of the great fireplace, leaning against the stonework, made a graceful wave of his hand to the table, and said:—

"I pray you, be seated and sup how you please. You will I trust, excuse me that I do not join you, but I have dined already, and I do not sup."

NOTES, COMMENTS AND HINTS

Of course the temptation to imitate Bela Lugosi is almost irresistible. And why resist it? Especially if you are doing this selection as an exercise. Dracula's rhythm and his phrasing are conditioned by his Transylvanian (it could be Romanian or Hungarian) accent—if you ever record this, you would do well to keep it light, for the sake of audience comprehension. One of the important characteristics of the Hungarian accent in English is stressing the first syllables of words, a habit that is hard to break, because in Hungarian itself first syllables are always stressed. You would also avoid doing an imitation of anyone, and find your own way of doing the character and the accent; a light Romanian accent, with a slight trilled "r," would be a good choice.

Count Dracula's English is "excellent, but with a strange intonation." He knows the difference between "dine" and "sup," for instance, but his grammar is somewhat faulty: in the last sentence of this excerpt he means "sup *as* you please" and "*if* I do not join you." But his inaccuracy does not prevent us from knowing exactly what he means. Read his lines with the very polite, courtly intention of making his guest feel welcome. The tone of Dracula's dialogue could be described as silky, with perhaps a slight suggestion of seduction, implied rather than acted outright.

The phrase "with a courtly bow" gives you a clue as to how to read this scene: in a stately rhythm, not hurried. There is all the time in the world. A slightly slow pace may add to the sense of brooding menace that hangs over this whole scene, even before Dracula offers Harker his icy hand. Experiment with pace, and record this text at different tempi, all of which should be organically based on your (Harker's) internal and external circumstances. Remember a time during which you felt uneasy and vaguely threatened, perhaps when you were alone in a dark room, and use it to inform Harker.

Telling us his own story, our first-person narrator, Jonathan Harker, is not yet terrified to the point of being driven mad; he merely finds everything in this alien, unfamiliar world a bit strange and slightly forbidding, and he attributes his feelings to the fact that he is in a part of the world that is so different from the familiar world and staid culture of Victorian England. Of course the Count strikes him as odd; after all, he is a vampire, even though Harker does not yet know that. And their walk down the cold corridor and up the stairs is so disquieting and sinister that Harker "rejoices" to see the brightly lit bedroom. Place is a very important circumstance in this text: the menacing, dark rooms of the crumbling old castle create an eerie sense of foreboding. Think of a place in which you felt threatened, and use it to inform Harker's uneasiness.

What we should hear in your voice, then, during the narrative sections is a sense of tense exploration and of mild surprise, when, for instance, Harker sees that supper has been prepared. He might think 'Oh, isn't that nice?' were it not for the slightly forbidding strangeness of the whole proceeding, as if one were being offered an unfamiliar and repellent dish to taste—the chilled monkey brains in the film *Indiana Jones and the Temple of Doom* (1984) come to mind—which one was obliged to accept out of politeness. Substitutions don't always have to come from something you have lived through directly; they can also come from remembered reactions to others' experiences.

Abraham ("Bram") Stoker (1847–1912) became manager and general factotum for his idol, Henry Irving, in 1878, and served him faithfully for twenty-seven years. During that time he wrote many novels, but *Dracula* is the one by which he is best remembered. The theater had fascinated him since his boyhood in Dublin, so it is not surprising that the book is so theatrical and has lent itself well to many stage and cinematic adaptations. You can afford to be quite theatrical in your reading of this material.

Listen to the Caedmon recording, *Spine Chilling Tales of Horror*, which includes an abridged version of *Dracula*, performed by Carole Shelley and David McCallum (see the Bibliography). McCallum reads the part of the story excerpted above. He fulfills the convention admirably of playing different characters, even though he is actually playing Harker, and would not be imitating Dracula. We hear McCallum as Harker living (or reliving: he is writing the journal, which is one of his "actions") through the story from moment to moment. When McCallum suddenly becomes Dracula it is quite a startling event. He has just the right accent for the Count, not overdone at all but very real. He also does some excellent things technically, such as stressing the adjective "massive" the several times it occurs, describing the castle doors; and on the line "... I do not sup," he stresses the pronoun "I."

From Sir Walter Scott's *Ivanhoe* (1819), Chapter XXIX

"What dost thou see, Rebecca?" again demanded the wounded knight.

"Nothing but the cloud of arrows flying so thick as to dazzle mine eyes, and to hide the bowmen who shoot them."

"That cannot endure," said Ivanhoe; "if they press not right on to carry the castle by pure force of arms, the archery may avail but little against stone walls and bulwarks. Look for the Knight of the Fetterlock, fair Rebecca, and see how he bears himself; for as the leader is, so will his followers be."

"I see him not," said Rebecca.

"Foul craven!" exclaimed Ivanhoe; "does he blench from the helm when the wind blows highest?"

"He blenches not! he blenches not!" said Rebecca, "I see him now; he leads a body of men close under the outer barrier of the barbican."

Every Gothic castle and city had, beyond the outer-walls, a fortification composed of palisades, called the barriers, which were often the scene of severe skirmishes, as these must necessarily be carried before the walls themselves could be approached. Many of those valiant feats of arms which adorn the chivalrous pages of Froissart took place at the barriers of besieged places.

"They pull down the piles and palisades; they hew down the barriers with axes. His high black plume floats abroad over the throng, like a raven over the field of the slain. They have made a breach in the barriers—they rush in—they are thrust back! Front-de-Boeuf heads the defenders; I see his gigantic form above the press. They throng again to the breach, and the pass is disputed hand to hand, and man to man. God of Jacob! it is the meeting of two fierce tides—the conflict of two oceans moved by adverse winds!"

NOTES, COMMENTS AND HINTS

This novel, extremely popular in its day—it sold ten thousand copies on its first printing, within a matter of weeks—takes place in medieval England against the background of the conflict between the Normans and the Saxons—even though the Normans had now been masters of the realm for two hundred years. Historically, in fact, one may question whether such deep hostility actually still existed between the two groups. As in the familiar Robin Hood stories, the wicked King John sits on the throne of England while the heroic Richard the Lion-Hearted is away in the Holy Land on a crusade. (Incidentally, for a fascinating and truer account of the Crusades than westerners are usually presented with read Amin Maalouf's *The Crusades through Arab Eyes,* translated from the French by Jon Rothschild; Schocken Books, 1989.) Jean Froissart's (1333?–1400/01) *Chronicles* is a major source of information on warfare and chivalric customs during the feudal era.

Sir Walter Scott (1771–1832) told a rousing tale and told it well, and he had an enormous influence on art and literature. Artists painted scenes from his books, and many of his books were adapted for the opera stage (Donizetti's *Lucia di Lammermoor* [1835] and Sir Arthur Sullivan's *Ivanhoe* [1891], to name but two; *Ivanhoe* had already been adapted for the opera stage several times). Scott was a progressive thinker for his era, a product of the European Enlightenment, and he believed in tolerance and in the basic goodness of all human beings. He was rare for his day and age in usually portraying Jews sympathetically. Isaac of York, though somewhat stereotyped, and his beautiful, generous daughter Rebecca are both sympathetic characters, who suffer under anti-Semitic prejudice and restrictive laws.

The plot is complicated; briefly, it is as follows: Cedric of Rotherwood, the Saxon chieftain, chafes under the oppressive rule of the conquering Normans, and dreams of a restored Saxon kingdom. To that end he wishes to unite his ward Rowena to the last scion of the Saxon ruling house, Athelstane. But Rowena loves Cedric's son Wilfred of Ivanhoe, whom Cedric has disinherited, because Ivanhoe returns Rowena's love. He went off to the Holy Land to fight in the Crusades with King Richard I, and has returned to England in disguise as a simple pilgrim. He learns of the villainous treachery of John, King Richard's brother, who rules in his absence with an iron hand, and determines to help Richard. Isaac of York, a wealthy Jewish merchant, whom Ivanhoe rescues from an attempted robbery, befriends him. Isaac's beautiful daughter Rebecca falls hopelessly in love with the handsome knight.

There are two central events in the novel: the tournament at Ashby, in which King Richard, returned from the Holy Land, in disguise as the Black Knight, defeats John's Norman knights with the Saxon Wilfred of Ivanhoe's help (he is disguised as the Disinherited Knight, and has been given arms and armor by Isaac and Rebecca); and the siege of the castle of Torquilstone, where Isaac, Rebecca and the wounded Ivanhoe are held prisoner by the Normans, one of whom, the villainous Templar knight, Sir Brian de Bois-Guilbert, is in love with her. A siege is mounted to rescue them, during which Locksley (Robin Hood) and his merry men come to the assistance of King Richard. Bois-Guilbert carries Rebecca off, but she is accused of witchcraft, condemned, and is about to be burned at the stake, when Ivanhoe courageously appears and fights Bois-Guilbert in order to save Rebecca's life. (See part of that scene in Chapter Six, on page 157.) At the end of the book King Richard unites Ivanhoe and his beloved Rowena and sets all to rights.

The melodramatic scene during the siege of Torquilstone is informed by the tremendous excitement of the battle being described. The stakes for both characters are very high. Ivanhoe and Rebecca are both extremely anxious about the outcome of the siege. Fortunately, you do not have to utter Rebecca's "loud shriek," but your voice should rise in pitch on those words, so that the listener seems to hear the shriek.

The rhythm is fierce, and the pace accelerated. The many exclamation points give you clues as to the pacing of the scene and the headlong rhythm which informs it. The wounded knight's urgent question "What dost thou see?" which he has asked more than once, gives you an immediate sense of urgency, especially since he is demanding "again." The descriptive phrases such as "cloud of arrows flying so thick as to dazzle mine eyes" and the strong verbs such as "hew down" and "pull down" also give you a sense of the hectic pace and rhythm of the battle. "They rush in—they are thrust back!" show you that the actions follow pell-mell, and your voice should go with them. "Two fierce tides" is Scott's powerful metaphor for the entire battle scene; use the image to help you as you read it. You might imagine that you are in the ocean being buffeted by the powerful waves that come rushing headlong onto the beach even near the shore.

Read Ivanhoe's very first line with a sense of anxiety. He is not merely asking what the distant trees and hills look like. Remember the subtext exercise at the end of Chapter Four. A line like "What dost thou see, Rebecca?" could have any number of subtexts. Choose a strong one, especially since Sir Walter Scott tells us that Ivanhoe "demanded" to know. Where in French the word simply means to ask (a *demande* is simply a question), its connotation in English is "to insist on an answer or an action," even though in the English of Scott's day and in the context of the sentence it means simply "to ask."

For more on the Elizabethan language, which passes in *Ivanhoe* for medieval speech, see the Notes, Comments and Hints following the excerpt on page 157.

Personalize the Text

Make the text real and meaningful for yourself, whether it is history, autobiography, biography or fiction. To personalize a text means to identify with it, so when recording fiction substitute relevant and analogous events and people from your own life for scenes and characters and situations in the book. The substitutions are a tool to help you get into the material. It may be that you will not need that tool, and can simply rely on the power of your imagination and on vocal technique, but it is there to be used as needed; and I recommend its constant use. If ever a text demanded to be personalized with deeply felt emotional substitutions from your own life, it is Marcel Proust's book, *Swann's Way* (see selections on pages 164 and 265). And see again the excerpts from Dickens.

The following exercises are simpler that the excerpts from Proust, but they still demand substitutions, as even the first line of Captain Meadows Taylor's book shows.

From Captain Meadows Taylor's *Confessions of a Thug* (1839), Chapter One

You ask me, Sahib, for an account of my life; my relation of it will be understood by you, as you are acquainted with the peculiar habits of my countrymen; and if, as you say, you intend it for the information of your own, I have no hesitation in relating the whole; for though I have accepted the service of Europeans, in my case one of bondage, I cannot help looking back with pride and exultation on the many daring feats I have performed. Often indeed does my spirit rise at the recollection of them, and often do I again wish myself the leader of a band of gallant spirits, such as once obeyed me, to roam with them wherever my inclination or the hope of booty prompted.

But the time is past. Life, Sahib, is dear to everyone; to preserve mine, which was forfeited to your laws, I have bound myself to your service, by the fearful tenure of denouncing all my old confederates, and you well know how that service is performed by me. Of all the members of my band, and of those with whom chance has even casually connected me, but few now remain at large; many have been sacrificed at the shrine of justice, and of those who now wander broken, and pursued from haunt to haunt, you have such intelligence as will lead to their speedy apprehension.

Yet Thuggee, capable of exciting the mind so strongly, will not, cannot be annihilated!

NOTES, COMMENTS AND HINTS

One of the more bizarre books to come out of the Victorian era, this sensational novel is about a hitherto obscure sect in colonial India, and it shocked the British public. On the other hand, they were not usually shocked by the harsh actions committed by their own British administrators and soldiers, actions which they considered simply a matter of course when subduing the "uncivilized" Indian population, to whom they were supposedly bringing the benefits of European civilization. In reality, of course, they conquered and brutally exploited India for their own gain. Twenty years after India had finally achieved independence, in 1947, thanks to Gandhi and his non-violent resistance movement, my brother Richard was in Calcutta, and from descriptions in the letters he wrote to me I could see that the rotten legacy of imperialism was still apparent: whole families living homeless in the streets against a background of crumbling colonialist architecture, and the air rife with the odors of cooking and marijuana. If you have had similar experiences or have seen movies or documentaries about India you can use them to inform your reading, keeping them in the back of your mind. In any case, you must place the book in its historical and social context, and find visceral substitutions.

Captain Philip Meadows Taylor (1808–1876) was an officer, amateur archaeologist and novelist (he dropped the name Philip when publishing his books) who served in British-occupied India, where, as superintendent of police at Bolarum, it fell to him to investigate Thuggee. He drew on the accounts and confessions of an actual informant in writing his novel. When writing *The Moonstone* (1868), Wilkie Collins drew on Captain Taylor's book for general information about India, and specifically for the bloodthirsty practices of Thuggee, which serve as a background to Collins's novel. Charles Dickens also used information from Captain Taylor's novel for *The Mystery of Edwin Drood* (1870), in which the rituals and signs and portents associated with Thuggee may provide clues to the solution of the mystery. Since Dickens died before completing it we will never really know what he had in mind, although valiant attempts, based on his notes, to write endings for the book have been made. See the selection below from Charles Mackay's book, from which Collins and Dickens also culled information.

In these opening paragraphs of Captain Taylor's novel there is a great deal of information about the character who is our first-person narrator, the Thug Ameer Ali. And there is a good deal of room for anyone reading this book to substitute all kinds of personal things for the actual facts being narrated, because those facts are very general. However, it is also a good idea to inform yourself about Thuggee, and then to substitute something from your own life that might be analogous to belonging to an in-group with its own secrets and rituals; not, of course, a group of murdering thugs, but perhaps a club or an organization of some sort.

Actually, the novel goes back and forth between two first-person narrators: Ameer Ali, who is confessing his crimes; and the British officer to whom he is confessing. You might want to use a very slight Indian accent for Ameer Ali. And, as an experiment, try something you would not ordinarily dream of doing: Dwell slightly on the "s" sounds from time to time, starting with the word "Sahib," to give the character a hissing, snake-like feeling. This trait can be done technically (just do it!); or you could arrive at the result through rehearsal, when any number of reasons (such as the difficulty the character has pronouncing "s"), could be adduced to account for it and make it real and organic.

Take a very quiet, mesmerizing approach to the listener when reading this narrative. It should be compelling and somewhat sinister, but the man is already old and less menacing than he was. Bring out the sense of weariness in the narrative. Substitute some time in your life when you were very tired and felt like giving up on something, because Ameer Ali has given up the fight and decided simply to talk about his life. Talk softly, and directly into the microphone "as if" an interlocutor were sitting right in front of you and very, very close.

From Charles Mackay's *Memoirs of Extraordinary Popular Delusions and the Madness of Crowds* (1841), "The Thugs, or Phansigars" (last section of Volume I, omitted in later editions)

The followers of this sect are called Thugs, or T'hugs, and their profession Thuggee. In the south of India they are called Phansigars: the former word signifying "a deceiver"; and the latter, "a strangler." They are both singularly appropriate. The profession of Thuggee is hereditary, and embraces, it is supposed, in every part of India, a body of at least ten thousand individuals, trained to murder from their childhood; carrying it on in secret and in silence, yet glorying in it, and holding the practice of it higher than any earthly honour. During the winter months, they usually follow some reputable calling, to elude suspicion; and in the summer, they set out in gangs over all the roads of India, to plunder and destroy. These gangs generally contain from ten to forty Thugs, and sometimes as many as two hundred. Each strangler is provided with a noose, to despatch the unfortunate victim, as the Thugs make it a point never to cause death by any other means. When the gangs are very large, they divide into smaller bodies; and each taking a different route, they arrive at the same general place of rendezvous to divide the spoil. They sometimes travel in the

> disguise of respectable traders; sometimes as sepoys or native soldiers; and at others, as government officers. If they chance to fall in with an unprotected wayfarer, his fate is certain. One Thug approaches him from behind, and throws the end of a sash round his neck; the other end is seized by a second at the same instant, crossed behind the neck, and drawn tightly, while with their other hand the two Thugs thrust his head forward to expedite the strangulation: a third Thug seizes the traveller by the legs at the same moment, and he is thrown to the ground, a corpse before he reaches it.
>
> But solitary travellers are not the prey they are anxious to seek. A wealthy caravan of forty or fifty individuals has not unfrequently been destroyed by them; not one soul being permitted to escape. Indeed, there is hardly an instance upon record of any one's escape from their hands, so surely are their measures taken, and so well do they calculate beforehand all the risks and difficulties of the undertaking.

NOTES, COMMENTS AND HINTS

The word *Phansigar* is pronounced "FAN si ga:r." To differentiate between the pronunciations of "Thug" and "T'hug" say "thug" for the first, and "t [slight breath pause] hug" for the second.

Your main task in reading this imperialistic text is simply to make the clear points the author makes and to give us information.

Charles Mackay (1814–1889), a British poet and journalist whose great hobby was collecting all kinds of facts, describes the sect of the worshipers of Kali, the Hindu goddess of destruction. His book, which details everything from financial schemes and panics to "tulipomania" and alchemy, has become a great classic.

Look at a number of films that have been based on or around the story of the sect of the Thugs, among them *Gunga Din* (1939), *Indiana Jones and the Temple of Doom* (1984), and *The Deceivers* (1988).

Even in certain works of nonfiction you can personalize the text to some extent. This terrifying description of some of the practices of the Thugs lends itself to personalization, but, since this is nonfiction, you may not infuse or inform the text with a real sense of terror, as you would in a work of fiction. Instead, remember a time in your life when you were terrified, and allow it to filter through very slightly into your reading. If you have never been terrified, you must certainly have had moments of nervousness, perhaps before taking an exam you weren't sure you would pass. Even such a comparatively mild state of fear, which may have loomed larger at the time than it does in retrospect, might be useful as a substitution.

In using a substitution you reveal yourself without actually doing so: The substitution is your "actor's secret." The audience has no idea what your substitution is—and it is best not to dissipate its power by telling anyone what it is, since talking about troubling things can often be a relief, which is exactly what you don't want; you want the substitution to retain its power and hold over you. The listener will hear simply what is in the text, while the tone of your voice, informed by an underlying attitude of awed fear, will communicate a kind of fascination that will make the listener want to hear more.

Two excerpts from Charlotte Brontë's *Jane Eyre* (1847).

FROM CHAPTER 13

I and my pupil dined as usual in Mrs. Fairfax's parlour; the afternoon was wild and snowy, and we passed it in the schoolroom. At dark I allowed Adele to put away books and work, and to run downstairs; for, from the comparative silence below, and from the cessation of appeals to the door-bell, I conjectured that Mr. Rochester was now at liberty. Left alone, I walked to the window; but nothing was to be seen thence: twilight and snowflakes together thickened the air, and hid the very shrubs on the lawn. I let down the curtain and went back to the fireside.

In the clear embers I was tracing a view, not unlike a picture I remembered to have seen of the castle of Heidelberg, on the Rhine, when Mrs. Fairfax came in, breaking up by her entrance the fiery mosaic I had been piercing together, and scattering too some heavy unwelcome thoughts that were beginning to throng on my solitude.

"Mr. Rochester would be glad if you and your pupil would take tea with him in the drawing-room this evening," said she: "he has been so much engaged all day that he could not ask to see you before."

"When is his tea-time?" I inquired.

"Oh, at six o'clock: he keeps early hours in the country. You had better change your frock now; I will go with you and fasten it. Here is a candle."

"Is it necessary to change my frock?"

"Yes, you had better: I always dress for the evening when Mr. Rochester is here."

• • •

FROM CHAPTER 20

I had forgotten to draw my curtain, which I usually did, and also to let down my window-blind. The consequence was, that when the moon, which was full and bright (for the night was fine), came in her course to that space in the sky opposite my casement, and looked in at me through the unveiled panes, her glorious gaze roused me. Awaking in the dead of night, I opened my eyes on her disk—silver-white and crystal clear. It was beautiful, but too solemn; I half rose, and stretched my arm to draw the curtain.

Good God! What a cry!

The night—its silence—its rest, was rent in twain by a savage, a sharp, a shrilly sound that ran from end to end of Thornfield Hall.

My pulse stopped: my heart stood still; my stretched arm was paralysed. The cry died, and was not renewed. Indeed, whatever being uttered that fearful shriek could not soon repeat it: not the widest-winged condor on the Andes could, twice in succession, send out such a yell from the cloud shrouding his eyrie. The thing delivering such utterance must rest ere it could repeat the effort.

NOTES, COMMENTS AND HINTS

Charlotte Brontë (1816–1855) was the daughter of a Yorkshire pastor originally from Ireland, and the sister of Emily Brontë (1818–1848), who wrote *Wuthering Heights* (1847) and of Anne Brontë (1820–1849), who wrote *The Tenant of Wildfell Hall* (1849).

At the beginning of the story Jane Eyre is an orphan who is being raised by her aunt, Mrs. Reed, who is quite hostile to her. See page 173 for the opening of the novel. Mrs. Reed sends Jane away to Lowood School, where the pupils are treated sadistically. Leaving the school, she is engaged by the strange and forbidding Mr. Rochester, who appears to have some secret sorrow, as a governess for his ward, Adele, at Thornfield Hall. When he makes advances to Jane, she leaves his employment, although she loves him: that is not, of course, the end of the story.

Mrs. Fairfax, the housekeeper at the Hall, is kind and welcoming to Jane, so read her lines with a gentle smile, and even with a sense of love, which should all be heard in your voice. Think of a moment in your life when you treated someone with love and kindness, perhaps helping someone preparing to go out with someone you knew they were in love with.

The cry Jane hears is that of Mr. Rochester's insane wife, kept out of the way in a distant room in Thornfield Hall, and looked after by a keeper.

Two important symbols are used throughout the book, and help condition the way you read and personalize this text:

1. Food is a metaphor both for need and for something lacking. At Lowood School the food is served in skimpy portions, and older girls often steal it from Jane. She is hungry not merely for food, but for personal fulfillment as well. At Thornfield Hall she eventually finds the latter, and, while there, she never lacks for food either. So the section about dining with her

pupil should be read as the memory of something very pleasant, despite the miserable afternoon weather. Think of a pleasant meal you anticipated having, perhaps in a restaurant with a friend. Being invited to tea by the man she loves is an exciting prospect, and Jane is more than a little nervous about it. Read her dialogue with that in mind. Choose as a substitution a moment in your life when you were about to meet someone you were attracted to. Remember your nervous anticipation. You will then not have to worry about how to read the lines technically. Let the mental substitution simply allow you to give yourself over to the text; the nervousness should filter through into your voice, and the listener will then hear your behavior in your intonation patterns.

2. The moon is a metaphor for change, and is looked at many times in *Jane Eyre*. Every time, a change is about to take place. In the second excerpt there is something ominous about the moon, something eerie that sends a chill up and down the spine, and that should be reflected in the voice. Jane is not merely frightened; she is so terrified that she is paralyzed with fear. Use a substitution from a time in your life when you were truly afraid and didn't quite know why. Allow the terror to simply be there, and it will be reflected in your intonation patterns. Once again, the listener will hear your behavior.

Some Recommendations for Further Reading and Listening

1. In Appendix B of Richard Ellmann's splendid biography *Oscar Wilde* (Alfred A. Knopf, 1988) you will find a lecture of Oscar Wilde's, reprinted from *Helen Potter's Impersonations*.

   Helen Potter gives the reader an exact indication of how Wilde—a superb lecturer and conversationalist, and one of the wittiest men of his or any other age—sounded, and of his delivery, with the pauses he took, and with information on both his pronunciation and his intonation patterns. It is most instructive reading (and it is easier to find Richard Ellmann's book than the scarce volume by Helen Potter).

   Wilde speaks in a very measured, deliberate, musical way. One important thing for you to notice is that he never drops his voice at the end of a sentence. Here is a brief excerpt:

   > We | in our Renaissance | are seeking to create a sovereignty | that shall o still (/) be (\ ) England's [spoken on a low pitch] | when her

> yellow leopards | are weary of (/) wars [Wilde pronounced it "wa:z"]..."

In British RP—Oscar Wilde, born and bred in Dublin, learned to speak with an upper-class English accent while at Oxford—the word *Renaissance* is pronounced "rə NAY səns," or "sa:Ns"; the latter pronunciation was prevalent in the Victorian era, when French phrases were used in conversation as a matter of course. In General American it is pronounced "REN ə sa:ns."

The pronunciation of the word *wars* is much the same as it was in General American in the Victorian era, except the final "r" was pronounced by American speakers ("wa:r"), as one can hear on the recordings made by Woodrow Wilson, Theodore Roosevelt, William Howard Taft and William Jennings Bryan on *In Their Own Voices* (see the Bibliography). The pronunciation is still heard in areas of the Middle West.

2. Listen to Ruth Draper's monologues (she called them "monodramas," and wrote them all herself), originally recorded in 1954 and 1955. She was a truly great actress, and it is very instructive and inspiring to hear her magnificent performances, full of tender love and delightful humor, which she recorded reluctantly, because she was sure only a live theater audience could appreciate them. Ruth Draper (1884–1956) was a humanist who understood and loved people from all walks of life, even though she herself came from the world of "high society"; she was a friend of both Edith Wharton and Henry James, who set their novels in that milieu. More recently Patricia Norcia, a worthy successor to Ms. Draper, has performed Ruth Draper's monodramas, and recorded some of them, with great success. (See the Bibliography for further information on the recordings.)

3. Dylan Thomas was not only a wonderful writer, but also an impassioned performer of his own work. (See the Bibliography for information on his available recordings.)

4. Edgar Allan Poe's short stories and poems, as well as stories and poems by many other authors, have been recorded, often quite memorably. (See the Bibliography for a list of some available recordings.) Use any of his stories for practice.

5. For practicing nonfiction, use any of the biographies by Graham Robb or Antonia Fraser. William Doyle's *The Oxford History of the French Revolution* (Oxford University Press, 1989) is also excellent for practice. They all have

the virtue of being very well written, and they all read very well and very fluently aloud. It is not that they are easy to record: A great deal of dictionary research has to be done, looking up names of places and people, but the reading flows because the writing is fluid. For the same reasons I would also recommend for practice any books by Mark Kurlansky or Simon Winchester.

A Final Exercise, from Charles Kent's *Charles Dickens as a Reader* (1872)

> Herodotus, then in his fiftieth year, reflected for a long while seriously how he might, with the least trouble and in the shortest time, win for himself and his writings a large amount of glory and reputation. Shrinking from the fatigue involved in the labour of visiting successively one after another the chief cities of the Athenians, the Corinthians, and the Lacedæmonians, he ingeniously hit upon the notion of appearing in person at the Olympian Games, and of there addressing himself simultaneously to the very pick and flower of the whole Greek population. Providing himself beforehand with the choicest portions or select passages from his great narrative, he there read or declaimed those fragments of his History to the assembled multitude from the stage or platform of the theatre. And he did this, moreover, with such an evident captivation about him, not only in the style of his composition, but in the very manner of its delivery, that the applause of his hearers interrupted him repeatedly—the close of these recitations by the great author-reader being greeted with prolonged and resounding acclamations.

NOTES, COMMENTS AND HINTS

Called the "Father of History," Herodotus (pronounced "he: ROD ə təs") lived from ca. 485-ca. 425 BCE and was famous for his history of the Persian Wars, which lasted from 499 to 479 BCE and ended in Greek victory over Persia. Herodotus's *Histories* are known for their wealth of detail about life in ancient Greece. The Lacedæmonians (pronounced "LÆ sə dee MOH nee ənz") are the Spartans.

The florid and elegant (perhaps top-heavy) style we associate with the Victorian period is much in evidence here, and in Kent's writings in general. Play against the floridity when reading this aloud, otherwise you risk sounding pompous. It may be difficult to make this sound natural, but the sentences do flow, because the grammar is so correct. Most contemporary actors would have to rehearse this material a lot, however.

Your attitude, reflected in your tone of voice, without overdoing it, might be "Isn't that wonderful?" that "...he ingeniously hit upon the notion of appearing in person..." To tell the story you have to make clear points, just as the author does. The story goes from verb to verb, as it were: Herodotus *reflected* on how to win a reputation (his objective), he *shrank* from the laborious task of traveling from city to city (an obstacle), he *hit on the notion* of appearing at the Olympian Games, he *provided* himself with his texts, he *appeared* there and *read* his texts aloud (three actions in support of his objective), and the audience loved the show. Objective accomplished!

To proceed with any material, fiction or nonfiction, break down the text in this way so that the skeleton or outline of the story emerges. You have to know what story you are telling. Kent's sentences are complex, but the ideas in them are easy to grasp, so although his syntax complicates the way the story is told, once you have made that syntax your own, and it feels natural to you—once you own the syntax—the job of telling the story when reading it aloud is ultimately quite simple and straightforward.

CHAPTER 6

Recording Prose Fiction

General Advice: Telling the Story

"A man may see how the world goes with no eyes. Look with thine ears," says Lear to the blinded Gloucester as they stand on the "extreme verge" of the cliffs at Dover in Shakespeare's *King Lear* (Act IV, Scene 6).

If you have ever seen the chalky white, sheer cliffs of Dover or a picture of them, you will have an immediate clear image in your mind's eye as soon as someone mentions them; an image that may be reinforced and clarified by a writer's description of them, or by the famous song in which the bluebirds fly over them. When someone mentions a historical event like the D-Day invasion of June 6, 1944, you will remember dramatizations you may have seen or a documentary film, with ships looming on the gray horizon, and you can immediately picture events taking place before your eyes. When you talk with someone on the telephone you have an immediate, visceral sense of that person's emotional state and of what she or he is living through from moment to moment during your conversation. It is exactly these visual and aural senses that you must bring to the telling of a story. In other words, when you bring the beauty and music of a story to life with your voice alone, you must read it in such a way as to allow the listeners to visualize the places and events and people in it as they follow the narrative. You have to make the listeners hear the people in the story thinking, and living through each event in their lives from moment to moment. In order to do this you must project yourself into the story. You must see the places and events and hear the people in it, and really act it. Since listeners obviously cannot see Sherlock Holmes running across the moors in *The Hound of the Baskervilles*, they have to be able to visualize and thus experience the chase, and to feel its urgency in every word you say; see page 182. Nor can they see the despairing Félix taking the feverish Henriette in his arms in Balzac's *The Lily in the Valley*, but they must hear his desperation and her pain; see page 189. And you are your listeners' guide through the labyrinth of the story's plot.

A good story is at the heart of any deathless literary work. Some might say it is the most important element in any work of fiction, its sine qua non. A story is written with a particular order of development—usually chronological; although some stories go back and forth in time—as well as its own pace and rhythm, and these will shape your reading, whether you are recording a novel or a short story. Many stories contain secondary plots, or subplots, each of which has its own shape. An often-used plot sequence is:

1. An introduction to the setting of the story, and to the characters, principal (there is usually more than one principal character) and secondary, each of whom has her or his individual story, within the context of the larger story in which they play their parts;

2. A rising development of the action, taking us forward;

3. A crisis, or conflict (perhaps more than one), which may have been apparent early in the plotting, or been hinted at and occur later on;

4. A resolution of the climactic crisis or crises after which there is a downward falling development of the action;

5. Finally, the dénouement (the French word means, literally, "unknotting") or final unfolding of the plot and sub-plots (if any), leading to the resolution of the story.

When the story is over, we should have a satisfying sense of completion. At the end of Dickens's *Great Expectations*, for instance, we read the last line "And I saw no shadow of another parting from her," and we don't need to know more. (But see the Notes, Comments and Hints to the excerpt from *Great Expectations*, which is a specific case when it comes to endings, on page 193.)

Many of the short stories of Edgar Allan Poe and Conan Doyle's short stories and novels about Sherlock Holmes, however intricate their plot details and however unexpected their developments; as well as such relatively simply plotted novels as Sir Walter Scott's *Ivanhoe* (simple, despite its many characters and plot strands); Herman Melville's *Moby-Dick*; and Robert Louis

Stevenson's *Kidnapped* with its sequel *David Balfour* (called *Catriona* in the UK), follow this basic sequence.

In a more complicated novelistic plot structure there may be *several major* stories, which are not subplots, as in the model presented above; each major story may nevertheless be subordinate to an overarching story, and each may be developed (perhaps) along the simple plot lines described in the previous paragraph, yet may be interwoven in unexpected ways and tied together by some theme(s) or character(s) that is/are common to them all. Alexandre Dumas' *The Count of Monte Cristo* is a case in point, as are some of Charles Dickens's and Balzac's greatest works, and also Marcel Proust's *Remembrance of Things Past*.

Because the author has chosen to tell a particular story for reasons that go beyond the mere sequence of events we call a plot, a story also includes a theme or themes. They might perhaps be moral, philosophical, political, or psychological in nature, but when the story is over, the events in it will be seen to have fit into its underlying theme or themes.

In preparing a text for recording, you have to understand clearly the themes, and how they are developed, as well as each thread, each strand of the story's plot, and the warp and woof and weave of its tapestry. You have to find the overall arc, the through-line of the plot, and pace the story, as well as each sequence, action and event within it, as it seems to demand internally.

What is interesting in prose fiction is not just the plot of the story or its themes, but the people in it, the characters upon whom the plot and themes depend, without whom the story would have no meaning. Very often the plot opposes two principal characters, called the "protagonist" and the "antagonist," because they play these roles for each other, as in Robert Louis Stevenson's *The Master of Ballantrae;* see page 246. An antagonist may or may not be a villain out to destroy the protagonist.

And what is interesting about the characters is their emotional affective life, their relationships, and their behavior. The words they speak, which by themselves give us a clue to that affective life, are only a part of the picture: It is the meaning behind or beneath the words, the subtext (intentions, desires and attitudes) that we have to convey to the listeners. People want to be able to identify with the characters and the story in some way, and to get caught up in the narrative. You as a recording artist will have to be as specific in interpreting the material and creating the characters' lives, and in adopting the characters' point of view, as you would be if you were playing a character on stage.

Reading dialogue is like a doing a scene in a play, and you must make it sound as if the people are really talking, and really talking to each other. If the text is a first-person narrative you are playing the narrator, who is usually also a character in the story she or he is telling, and who sometimes has dialogue, as in the cases of Jane Eyre or Dr. Watson. And in a first-person narrative you will usually want to use the convention of playing the other characters fully, even though, logically speaking, the person telling us the story would probably not be playing other characters in it.

You have to ask yourself questions as an actor about all the circumstances in which the character finds himself or herself. For instance: Where am I when I begin telling the story? Where am I at various points in the story? Am I at home, and in my living room? Or am I in bed? Or am I having dinner in my own or someone else's dining room, or in a restaurant? Am I in a public place? Where a person is conditions how she or he behaves.

The author doesn't always tell you where you are. For instance, perhaps the first-person narrator in Marcel Proust's *Swann's Way* is telling us his story while he is in bed and we are seated opposite him, or even on the edge of his bed, or perhaps not. We, the listener, don't really know where he is, which creates a kind of deliberate and interesting limbo. But you as a reader/recorder should decide where he is. Perhaps he is sitting in front of a microphone, recording his memories. Perhaps he is nervous. Perhaps he is relaxed. Remember: It is you who will embody the character and therefore it is actually you who will be nervous or relaxed. A character doesn't actually exist in terms of being able to speak aloud, until you make that character exist. In other words, you bring yourself and who you are to the creation of the character.

More questions: Am I suffering from the weather out on the cold, damp marshes, like Pip in *Great Expectations*; see page 199? Am I in the heat of the desert, or on the seashore? Am I on a whaling ship in the middle of the freezing ocean, as in Herman Melville's *Moby-Dick*; see page 233? Even if the story is told in retrospect (most stories are), we often relive it, especially for the purposes of recording, as we tell it, as in Edgar Allan Poe's *The Cask of Amontillado*; see page 203, where the nitre-encrusted walls of the damp catacombs are almost a character in the story.

You must also ask yourself what time of day it is. When, for instance, is Proust's Narrator beginning to tell us the story? Is it late at night? Certainly it feels as if it is, because the narrative is concerned, quite intimately, with that time of day. But we could be sitting together in a living room in the middle of the afternoon. Once again, we are in a kind of temporal limbo, just as we are in a spatial limbo. If you record Poe's *The Tell-Tale Heart* you will relive the midnight hour at which you entered the old man's room; see page 225. Dr. Watson is on the moor in *The Hound of the Baskervilles* at different times of day or night, and the behavior described is different each time; consequently, the tone of the narrative will vary, from cheerful to fearful.

Further questions for the actor to ask are "What do I want (what is my objective)?" followed by, "How much or how little do I want what I want?" In other words, how much does the *character* want what he or she wants? How high are the stakes, and how important is the objective? Two more questions:

"What stands in my way, that is, what is/are the obstacle(s)?" "What do I do to get what I want, that is, what is/are my action(s)?"

The use of substitutions, which enables you to bridge the gap between your life and the character's, is not only essential, but also one of the most interesting and enjoyable techniques from the actor's point of view. For more on the creation of characters vocally see page 202; and see Chapter Four on acting methods.

Listening to dialogue in films with your eyes closed, and to recorded plays in prose and in verse, are very instructive exercises for demonstrating how we hear behavior and interactions and relationships reflected vocally. If you go browsing in your local bookstore or library or on the internet you will find many such plays, and there are some listed in the Bibliography.

You will also find recordings of literature of various genres (prose fiction in the form of novels and short stories; poetry), as well as a great deal of pulp fiction of various genres. Listen to as much of it as you can.

Whether you are recording a novel or a short story, an epic like Homer's *Iliad* or *Odyssey*, or the medieval saga *Beowulf*; a mystery, a romance, a classic panoramic historical novel like Leo Tolstoy's *War and Peace*; a science fiction tale like H. G. Wells's *War of the Worlds*; a medieval romance like Sir Walter Scott's *Ivanhoe*; one of J. K. Rowling's delightfully imaginative Harry Potter books, a charming, beautifully told Andersen fairy tale, a children's book like *Babar the Elephant*, a tale of the sea like the C. S. Forrester's Hornblower series or Patrick O'Brian's Maturin novels, a saga about pirates like Robert Louis Stevenson's *Treasure Island*, an American cowboy western, a spy, a thriller, or an action-adventure tale, or a piece of badly-written, ludicrous pulp fiction meant for a public brought up on soap operas, your responsibility as a recording artist is the same: To be true to your listening public, and to record the book in a lively and truthful manner, fulfilling what the author has written and making it come alive for the audience who wish to listen to it. You may dislike the book you are recording, but, as I said in Chapter Five, you must not comment on the material by allowing your contempt for it to be apparent in the tone of your voice. You may often be called upon to record pulp fiction instead of real literature, and you will probably have fun doing it. But when you are chosen to record a work of real literature, you will be confronted with a very exciting prospect indeed, as you do the research necessary to situate a work of literature in its historical and social context, and read with your actor's eye so that you can bring your interpretations to life.

Don't confuse pulp fiction with popular literature. Many great authors, such as Dickens, Dumas and Balzac, have been very popular in their own lifetimes. This chapter will deal only with literature.

What is the difference, then, between literature and pulp fiction? In a piece of pulp fiction of the melodramatic "bodice ripper" genre known as gothic romance, for instance (and one could discuss certain science fiction, mystery, fantasy or horror novels as well), the handsome, sophisticated and unscrupulously caddish seventeenth-, eighteenth-, or nineteenth-century English Duke of Whatchemecallit, or the French Duc de Jenesaisquoi, rips the bodice off the innocent village maiden Mary, or Marie, who is madly in love with him, but knows they can never marry because of the difference in their stations. It is written with the most ordinary, banal, trite dialogue and has the most hackneyed descriptions of scenery, or of sunsets over the sea or over the mountains or reflected off the roofs of the castle turrets; and the scenes and situations in it are also ordinary, banal and trite. The unreal characters have no psychology, and no attempt is made to do anything except tell the rip-roaring, swashbuckling story in the most lurid manner possible. Pulp fiction's stock in trade is ultimately an unexciting, tedious, formulaic tale of mayhem and romance, whatever the genre (although much science fiction contains very little romance, being devoted as it is to fictitious science). Even the faintly ludicrous sex scenes, verging on bad pornography, fail in their attempts to titillate and arouse the reader. The books are written in language that is an abysmal travesty of literary English, to the point sometimes of being floridly purple prosy. The pulp fiction story has no theme, merely the parody of a theme. It has no statement to make and nothing of consequence to impart. I don't even think it is good entertainment. One sometimes has the impression that these mawkish, maudlin, saccharine books were written by computer, or by the same method as paint-by-the-numbers oil paintings, that is, by the method of fill-in-the-blanks. Although pulp fiction is ephemeral, it has existed for a couple of centuries, because there is a market for it.

Even with a similar story to tell, a piece of literature has fully developed characters with real personalities, real conflicts and themes—personal or political or psychological, for instance—is written beautifully, and is often memorable. The author knows grammar and observes its rules, while manipulating the language and using it in a personal, individual manner, which is called the author's style. In short, such a piece of literature is the opposite of a piece of pulp fiction in almost every way.

Nevertheless, it remains true that literature, even great literature, has something in common with pulp fiction: Melodrama is often common to both, and they both have characters and dialogue and scenes and situations. But there the comparison ends. When it comes to the mystery novel, for example, there is a world of difference on the one hand between a beautifully crafted, superbly written mystery novel by P. D. James, Christiana Brand, Dorothy Sayers, Julian Symons or Edmund Crispin, with its rounded, fully observed characters, and on the other a murder mystery novel in which the trite story, arousing perhaps a modicum of interest in the clichéd characters, is told in a formulaic, and ultimately banal way, like the arithmetic problems in a child's schoolbook. This is not to say that such a novel cannot be entertaining. And there is certainly room for both kinds of mystery stories.

And there is also a vast difference between a swashbuckling romance or rousing historical intrigue by Alexandre Dumas, and the work of some hack scribbler of syrupy pulp Gothic love stories, although the prolific Dumas himself was accused in his day by the envious, and often racist writers of such pulp romances (Dumas' father was a black general in Napoleon's army), of being just such a hack, but his novels include *The Three Musketeers* and its multi-volume sequels, and *The Count of Monte Cristo*, which are, like all his books, immortal classics, while his jealous attackers' works are long forgotten.

Whatever the genre, there are two basic forms of narrative:

1. First-person narrative, in which the story is told by a character who says "I" and therefore participates in the story. "I" may be telling her or his own story, or someone else's story from the point of view of "I." "I" is a character you have to play when recording the story. The first-person narrator often has a great emotional investment in the story, especially if it is her or his own story, as in *Jane Eyre, Moby-Dick, Great Expectations* or *Remembrance of Things Past.*

2. Third-person narrative, in which the narrator tells the story of someone other than the narrator (usually). The narrator functions as a character, whether in the persona of a character in the story the narrator is telling, or of the author of the story. The narrator, who says "she" or "he," may or may not be an actual participant in the story, but the narrator is certainly looking at the story from the outside. A third-person narrator may have less emotional investment in the story than a first-person narrator, depending on whose story the third-person narrator is telling. But you as the actor still have to play the third-person narrator as a character, just as you would a first-person narrator. You might tell us the story less emotionally than if it were the story of your own life, as you would Irving's *Rip van Winkle* or Lewis Carroll's *Alice in Wonderland*; or you might have a great emotional investment in the story, even if it is not your own, as in Dickens's *Dombey and Son* or *A Tale of Two Cities.*

Seldom does one find that rather daring form of narrative, second-person narrative, in which the author, or some character narrating the story says "you," making the reader a direct participant in the story, telling the reader what he or she is doing: "You are walking down a path. You turn to your right," etc. Some novelists, notably Michel Butor, of the mid-twentieth-century French "New Wave," and the Italian writer Italo Calvino, have attempted second-person narrative, and their books are interesting experiments, which work strikingly well.

When you are recording a text, the question of the narrator's, particularly a first-person narrator's, intended audience is also important, more so than if you were simply reading the text silently for yourself. You should choose someone to "talk" to, at least in order to launch yourself into the story. You will find suggestions for choosing your fictitious audience, depending on the nature of the story, in some of the Notes, Comments and Hints sections following some of the texts.

"...o'erstep not the modesty of nature," Hamlet counsels the Players in Act III, Scene 2. But there will be times when extreme melodrama is demanded, and then you must perhaps, o'erstep nature's modesty just a bit. On most occasions, however, Hamlet's advice will serve you well when recording fiction. Be economical and simple in your means, and you will allow the listener to enter the world of the story with you.

After you have prepared your interpretation, just talk to us when you perform a text. Tell us the story. Don't pontificate, even if you are the omniscient narrator, like Honoré de Balzac, so often accused, with some justice (but he is still fascinating) of pretending to "know it all," as in his plethoric discourse on the technology of printing books and manufacturing paper at the opening of *Illusions perdues* (*Lost Illusions*) (1837). (This somewhat tedious, yet somehow intriguing opening has a purpose, of course, which only becomes apparent later on, and Balzac, who loved knowing it all, did have an intimate knowledge of these things, since he had once owned a printing shop.)

Another important consideration to bear in mind when preparing a text is the question of period (when the work was written), and the style of writing associated with the period, which conditions how you will read the material aloud.

Understanding Style and Period

The word "style," when used in literary criticism, has at least three applications:

1. Style means the distinctive and personal manner of expression, including the vocabulary, the grammar and the length or brevity of sentences, of a particular author. Style can be so individual and recognizable that it lends itself to parody. Robert Benchley, for example, did hilarious parodies of Marcel Proust and Charles Dickens; Max Beerbohm parodied Henry James and many other authors, in his droll *A Christmas Garland* (1922); and Marcel Proust did a whole series of clever parodies of various French authors, including Balzac and Saint-Simon.

2. Style is also seen as having several levels, meant to guide the writer. The levels depend on a) the character or person speaking, whether an aristocrat or an artisan; b) the occasion, whether formal and solemn, as in a funeral oration, or informal, as in a conversation; c) the literary genre, whether tragedy or comedy. Orators and upper-class characters and heroes in tragedies used "high" style. More ordinary speakers used "middle" or "plain" style for general occasions, and in comedy. And "low" style was used by working-class characters in comedy, and by servants and underlings in tragedy. The idea of this stylistic hierarchy comes from Cicero, and was much in force until about the end of the eighteenth century, but after that it ceased to have much influence or value. An example: In Shakespeare's *Hamlet* Claudius, Gertrude and Hamlet often, though not always, speak in "high" style (Claudius's speech to the court; Hamlet's soliloquies; Gertrude talking with Hamlet in the court scenes), while Polonius usually speaks in "middle" style (except when giving his famous advice—a sort of parody of the "high style—to his departing son, Laertes), and the Gravedigger and other servile characters speak in the "low" style.

3. The concept of "style" is also applied to literary periods, that is, a certain style of grammar, and of writing, is said to be used by many authors in a particular period, and therefore to predominate in and to be characteristic of that period. But when literary critics write about "style" they often include in their concept of the word the notion that a particular set of values and/or ideas "in the air at the time" is common to those authors who wrote during the period, that is, content and form seem to be, if not inseparably, at least intimately linked. Whether the existence of such a link is or is not real has been much debated. One speaks, for example, of a "Romantic" period and of the Romantics' attitudes and style (love and idealization of nature, distrust of civilization, the influence and importance of the subjective, of the imaginative and of the irrational, as opposed to the importance of rationality and level-headedness; convoluted, flowery prose, heightened effects, and lurid melodrama on occasion), or of a "Realistic" period following the "Romantic" period, and of the Realistic writers' attitudes and style (truthful portrayal of character and of nature, no idealization, rationality, objectivity and the minimizing of the importance of subjectivity; straightforward prose, containing real descriptions without flowery coruscation).

Literary styles, like literary periods, overlap: Baroque slides almost imperceptibly into Rococo; Classicism into Romanticism into Realism into Naturalism, and the historical periods in which those styles and schools of literature predominated slide almost imperceptibly into each other as well, marked off for the sake of convenience by certain political events, so that, for instance, the French Revolutionary era slides into the Napoleonic era. The idea of "style" applied to a "period" is therefore difficult to pin down in an absolutely definite way.

What do we mean, for instance, when we say that many Victorian writers have a "stilted" style and use "stilted" language? What, first of all, do we mean by "stilted," surely a loaded, condemnatory, judgmental word? We mean that their language is "old-fashioned" in its diction—syntax, vocabulary and expression—and that the effect of their clunky, top-heavy, "stilted" language is to make it difficult to read. A Victorian book, we think, sounds awkward and stiffly formal when read aloud. Victorian writers use what to us is archaic vocabulary and their sentences have too many clauses in them. We mean that such writers are prolix, verbose and repressed, stodgy, stiff, pedantic stick-in-the-muds. They are starchy, formal and rigid. They are also artificial, affected, mannered, pretentious and precious, self-conscious and pompous. There is something unnatural, repressed, puritanical and deceptive about their thoughts and about the way they are expressed. These authors are like someone perpetually seen in formal dress, instead of in a relaxed sport jacket and no cravat, or a casual dress or pantsuit. We associate all of this with that one word "stilted." And to whom does it really apply? And why would anyone read books by these "stilted" authors? (The word might apply more to certain Edwardian writers than to the Victorians.)

If you examine the works of such writers as Charles Dickens, Wilkie Collins, William Makepeace Thackeray, George Eliot, Anthony Trollope, Lewis Carroll, or Robert Louis Stevenson, you will see that the word "stilted" certainly doesn't generally apply to any of them, even though there are parts of works by any one of them to which the word might apply in terms of writing style, but not necessarily in terms of their ideas or attitudes. Yet they all lived and wrote during the Victorian era; sometimes their syntax seems to give them commonality, and sometimes they seem to have certain social and political ideas in common. All of them are critical of the times in which they lived, and they express their criticisms more or less overtly, and sometimes with humor. The word "stilted" is actually much more applicable to a great many Victorian writers we no longer read, partly because of that quality in their writing. We also no longer read them because they don't seem to have much to say to us. The three-volume "sensation" novel, filled with lurid melodrama and cardboard, stereotypical characters is more or less the equivalent of today's pulp fiction; only it's a lot longer, and written in a remote, inaccessible, "stilted" style.

But what does this disquisition on the meaning of style have to do with the art of reading a book aloud? The question for the recording artist is how to read books written in styles that are not contemporary without sounding foolish, stilted or pompous. And the problem for recording artists is that they might sound like they have their noses in the air simply because the writing style of the author is archaic. In other words, how does a reader take on the attributes and elements of such a style so that they sound natural and real?

To begin with, knowledge of literature and of history is necessary if you wish to record fiction written in different periods. How did people go about their daily lives? What was the technology with which they had to deal? Social and sexual attitudes and mores are all important factors, and the more you have informed yourself about them, the better and more convincing will your reading be, because you will have made all those attitudes and attributes your own. You will inhabit them. You will live inside them. (Temporarily, of course.)

Second, since grammar is part of style, the period's grammar must become second nature; you must master it and make it your own. Even if you say that the narrative style, no matter what the period, is artificial, in that it is not usually the way people speak, even in a first-person narrative, still there is the dialogue to deal with, and it is meant to reflect real human speech. "Egad, sir" from an eighteenth-century character, and "Gee whiz, mister" from a twentieth-century character, may mean similar things, but they cannot be delivered in quite the same tone. To us today the first might be slightly more formal in feeling, colloquial as it is, without necessarily being pompous (unless the character is), while the second is more relaxed and informal, colloquial and familiar in tone, even if delivered to a stranger. If you are recording *Jane Eyre* or *Treasure Island* you don't want to sound like you just walked in from buying chewing gum at the corner store. But you might want to sound just like that if you are recording J. D. Salinger's *Catcher in the Rye.*

Since style means an author's singular and individual manner of expression, one would never confuse, say, Charles Dickens's expansive, rich, sometimes ornate style with Ernest Hemingway's terse, lean, often spare style. One might describe the style of many a Charles Dickens sentence as "hypotactic," that is, full of connected clauses with their connections made apparent by the use of such words as "when" and "because." Dickens does write short, pithy, pointed sentences as well, sometimes to humorous effect. An Ernest Hemingway sentence, on the other hand, could often be described as "paratactic" in style, that is, full of clauses with no necessary or indicated connection, except perhaps the word "and." Hemingway is known for his short, simple, seemingly unconnected sentences, the cumulative effect of which is quite evocative. You have to approach each author differently, and to make each author's style your own.

Ernest Hemingway's mentor and friend, Gertrude Stein, who influenced him greatly as far as his general cultural education was concerned, has a completely different style from his. For learning dexterity and flexibility, read anything of hers aloud. Despite her reputation for obscurity and bizarre stylistic tricks, Stein was an accomplished stylist, and her writing always makes sense, and makes even clearer sense when read aloud. Although her style seems convoluted, it is really elegant and translucent.

To help you see clear differences in style, look at the world of the musical theater, and of music in general, where different styles are easy to hear and experience, just as styles in painting are easy to recognize. Listen to the music of a period for which you have a book to record, look at the paintings of that period, and you will learn a great deal about the period, because music and painting have an immediate impact and can thus help to give you a visceral sensation and feeling for the era.

For instance, the comic operas of Offenbach and of Gilbert and Sullivan, written in the nineteenth century, are quite different in style, tone and content from that of the mid-twentieth-century American musical comedies of Rodgers and Hammerstein or Lerner and Loew, which are different again in style, tone and content from the early-twentieth-century Viennese operettas of Lehar and Kàlman. The musical idioms in which these composers wrote are different from each other, as are the styles in which they are performed, and the sensibilities and choice of subject matter were also quite as different as the cultures that gave rise to them. In the France of Napoleon III, a repressive regime in which the ruling classes were much given to luxury and extravagance, Offenbach's rollicking 1858 comic opera *Orphée aux Enfers* (*Orpheus in the Underworld*), with its mythological and outspoken political satire, was received with great acclaim by all social classes, although Offenbach outraged the more pedantic, stick-in-the-mud critics of his day. His comic opera assumes the same classical education and knowledge on the part of even the most ordinary members of his Parisian audience that nineteenth-century authors assume when they quote Roman and Greek authors in their original languages. *Orphée aux Enfers* is still much loved today, its sparkling, jaunty dances and its hauntingly beautiful melodies every bit as appreciated as they were when it was first produced, but nobody would write a musical comedy on such a subject or in such a style nowadays.

For the sake of convenience the different periods of English literature are divided roughly as follows:

1. Old English (Anglo-Saxon) 450–1066 [*Beowulf*];

2. Middle English, 1066–1500 [Chaucer];

3. Renaissance, 1500–1660, including the Elizabethan (1558–1603) [William Shakespeare, Christopher Marlowe, Ben Jonson], Jacobean (1603–1625) [John Donne; King James Version of the *Bible*], Caroline (1625–1649) [the

Cavalier poets]; and the Puritan Interregnum or Commonwealth (1649–1660) [Thomas Hobbes's *Leviathan*] periods;

4. Neoclassical Age, from 1660 to roughly 1785, divided into the Restoration (1660–1700) [John Milton's *Paradise Lost*; John Dryden], the Augustan Age, or the Age of Alexander Pope (1700–1745) [Jonathan Swift, Daniel Defoe], and the Age of Sensibility or of Samuel Johnson (1745–1785) [Henry Fielding's *Tom Jones*], which includes Neoclassicism (also called Classicism) and the Enlightenment in Europe;

5. The Romantic period, from approximately 1785 to 1830 [Jane Austen, Lord Byron, William Wordsworth, Samuel Taylor Coleridge], includes the school of Gothic literature [Mary Shelley's *Frankenstein*];

6. The Victorian era (1832 to 1901) [Charles Dickens, George Eliot, Thomas Hardy, Alfred Lord Tennyson], includes the school of the Pre-Raphaelites (1848 to 1860) [Dante Gabriel Rossetti], and the Aesthetic and Decadent schools (1860 to 1901) [Walter Pater, Oscar Wilde]; this is also the era of Realism [Honoré de Balzac 1799–1850], and, especially in France, of Naturalism [Emile Zola (d. 1902)];

7. Modern periods (1901 to the present), including the Edwardian (1901 to 1910) [H. G. Wells, George Bernard Shaw, Max Beerbohm; Joseph Conrad]; the Georgian (1910 to 1936); the Modern period (1914 to 1945); and the Post-Modern period (1945 to the present). The Modern period includes such writers as Virginia Woolf, William Butler Yeats, James Joyce, D. H. Lawrence, Marcel Proust in France, Anton Chekhov (1860–1904) in Russia, and Thomas Mann (1875–1955) in Germany.

In American literary history the periods are slightly different:

1. Colonial (1607–1776) [Cotton Mather];

2. Revolutionary (1776–1790) [Thomas Paine, Thomas Jefferson, James Madison, Benjamin Franklin];

3. Early National (1790–1828) [Washington Irving, James Fenimore Cooper];

4. Romantic, also called the Age of Transcendentalism or the American Renaissance (1828–1865) [Ralph Waldo Emerson, Henry David Thoreau, Edgar Allan Poe, Herman Melville, Nathaniel Hawthorne, Harriet Beecher Stowe, Henry Wadsworth Longfellow, Emily Dickinson, Walt Whitman];

5. Realistic (1865–1900) [Mark Twain, Henry James, Edith Wharton, Louisa May Alcott];

6. Age of Naturalism (1900–1914) [Jack London, Theodore Dreiser, Stephen Crane, James Weldon Johnson];

7. Modernist period (1914–1939), including the Jazz Age [F. Scott Fitzgerald], the Harlem Renaissance of the 1920s [Langston Hughes, Zora Neale Hurston], and the "Lost Generation" of the 1920s and 1930s [Gertrude Stein, Ezra Pound, T. S. Eliot];

8. Contemporary (1939 to the present), including the Beat writers of the 1950s [Jack Kerouac, Allen Ginsberg] and the Counterculture of the 1960s and 1970s. Modern and contemporary writers include Eugene O'Neill, Ernest Hemingway, Eudora Welty, Lilian Hellman, John Updike, Kurt Vonnegut, Jr., Sylvia Plath, Arthur Miller, Tennessee Williams, Ralph Ellison, W.E.B. DuBois, Lorraine Hansberry, Alice Walker, Toni Morrison and Maya Angelou.

Many of the authors listed lived through more than one period: Benjamin Franklin, for instance, lived and wrote in both the Colonial and the Revolutionary periods; and Edgar Allan Poe lived in both the early National and the Romantic periods, but is usually considered a Romantic writer. James Weldon Johnson lived in the Age of Naturalism and in the Harlem Renaissance, and is associated with both, although he is more a realistic than a naturalistic writer. The more you know about the period in which a writer lived, the better equipped you will be to empathize with that writer and to enter into the spirit and ethos of her or his works.

To demonstrate what I mean by reading with a specific and particular style in mind I have chosen some illustrative texts for practice exercises from the seventeenth, eighteenth and nineteenth centuries. One of the most important elements for you to consider—I repeat—is grammar, which must become second nature to you. The text's grammar must become a habitual way of expressing yourself, just as your own contemporary grammar is. Personalize the grammar and make it your own way of talking. "Own" the grammar. Make the manner in which the story is told your manner.

It is very interesting to see how grammar changes with the centuries, usually in the direction of simplicity, and to realize that, despite the changes, the language is in many ways the same, and that it is generally easily comprehensible. Occasionally, of course, one needs a footnote. Although you can ignore variations in the spelling of words that we still use, paradoxically, you may have to learn new vocabulary in the form of words that are now fallen into desuetude.

Seventeenth Century—Restoration Period

From Richard Head's *THE LIFE and DEATH OF THE English Rogue OR, HIS LAST LEGACY TO THE WORLD. CONTAINING Most of his Notorious Roberies, Cheats and Debaucht Practices. With a full Discovery of a High-way Rogue; also Directions to all Travellers, how to Know Rogues, and how to avoid them. And an Infallable Rule how to take them, when Robb'd by them. Directing all Inn-keepers, Chamberlains and Ostlers, how to Distinguish Rogues from honest Guests. The manner of his being Apprehended and his Behaviour in Prison, which was very Remarkable To which is added an Alphabetical Canting Dictionary; English before the Canting for the better understanding of Mumpers and Manders, Priggers and Prancers, Rum Pads and Rumpadders. Part Four, (1667),* Chapter II: *They are ship'd from Palermo to Naples, by the way Mistress Dorothy continues the Story of her Hostess who was hanged with her Husband for a Murder, the like was never heard of, her notorious confession at the Gallows of all her former Villanies: Latroons reflections on it. Mistress Dorothy and her Companion the Soldier, return for London.*

A single Gentleman came as a Traveller to lodge in her Inn, having set up his Horse, and his Portmantua carried to his Chamber, he knocks for his Landlady, who coming up to him he acquaints her that he thought he should make a stay for two or three days, and therefore delivers into her hands a bag of one hundred pounds, desiring her to lay it up safe for him; she took the Bag and promised to keep it safe, and so she did from him: The Devil was one of her Privy Council, who advised her to perswade her Husband to murder the Gentleman for his money, which thus they cunningly effected as they thought, but he that did set them at work will pay them their wages.

At midnight she and her Husband entred the Gentlemans Chamber through a private door which was hid behind the Hangings, a Sally-port for a thousand Roguerie they committed; mine Host with a pillow he had brought with him, and the assistance of his wife, smothered the Gentleman as he lay in his bed, having so done and putting on his

Cloaths, they laid him down into the Stable, and there with a Rope ty'd to a beam they hung him up, and so went to bed; In the morning the Hostler going into the Stable found a Gentleman there hanging, upon sight whereof he ran into the house with an Out-cry, which quickly reacht the ears of the Neighborhood, so that in an instant the house was fill'd with people, every one giving his Verdict as his imagination prompted him; the general Vogue was that for some discontent he had thus desperately made away with himself. This old Beldame had the impudence to come into the Throng of the people, and there declare her Hypocritical sorrow for the death of her Guest, protesting that she would have given an hundred pounds with all her heart, that no such thing had hapned in her house. I took notice, said the Host, of his extraordinary melancholly last night, and reproving him for his unsociableness, he clapt his hand upon his brest and with erected eyes to heaven, he groaned so loud and long that I thought it would have bin his last. This prodigious lye would have wrought wonderfully upon the belief of the people, being a strong Circumstance of his despair or great discontent, had not this unlucky boy which I told you of before, cryed out, true good people, I heard him groan too, but it was when my Master and Mistress were hanging him up in the Stable, what they had been doing with him before I know not, but I saw them as I lay under the Manger bring in his body which seem'd to me as dead, and had they seen me I believe I had not been now living, my Mistress had the chiefest hand in this work as I judge, for she got up into the Rack and stradling the beam tyed the Rope, then did my Master raise the body in his Arms for her to put the noose about his neck; this is a truth said he, for which I will rather dye than deny.

His Master hearing this, and being conscious to himself that this was no ly which the boy said, betook himself to his heels, whilst his wife with a brazen countenance was justifying her innocence. The people seeing the flight of one, and the matchless impudence of the other, concluded them guilty; and laying hands on her first, and hold of him after, they secured them with the boy till the Constable was fetched, who came immediately and carried them before a Justice, where being examined they stood out stiffly in their own vindication, maugre the boys peremptory and undaunted accusation; In fine their guilty consciences would not let them longer persist in their justification, but confest the Fact that it was an hundred pounds which was committed to their charge by the Gentleman, that first tempted them to smother him, the Devil helping them to a way they thought indiscoverable. They were committed to Goal [*sic*], where they lay till Assizes, at which time they were both sentenced to dye.

NOTES, COMMENTS AND HINTS

The first thing you will notice, once you have got past the incredible title (quite a title, eh? And typical of the seventeenth century), is that the punctuation is not at all what we would use today. Commas or semicolons separate sentences that should be separated by periods. For instance, notice the comma in the very first sentence after the word "Inn," where nowadays we would certainly put in a period and make a new sentence. The not yet standardized spelling and grammar, natural back then, are also extraordinary to us in the twenty-first century. If you have to record such a text, first repunctuate it so that the sentences make sense, and do not, as they do in the excerpt above, simply run into each other. Second, you have to understand the words we no longer use: The word "maugre" (pronounced "MAW gər") is from the French word *malgré*, meaning "in spite of," or "despite." The word "Portmantua" (pronounced "pawrt MAN chew ə") is, of course, *portmanteau*, meaning "a suitcase." A "Sally-port" (today two separate words: sally port) is a gateway in a castle from which soldiers sally forth to battle. The word "Beldame" (pronounced "BEL dam"), means "an old hag." The word "Goal" is simply a misspelling of "gaol," for American "jail," which is how "gaol" is pronounced.

The slang words in the title for crooks and petty confidence tricksters of all sorts can be found in Eric Partridge's fascinating *A Dictionary of the Underworld: British and American* (The Macmillan Company, 1950). The word "canting" means "slang," but in the seventeenth century it was also a general word for "begging." The word "cant" (pronounced "kænt" in both British RP and General American) means "underworld slang" even today, as well as what we more usually mean by that word, which is "insincere piety." Partridge tells us that a "Mumper" is a beggar of the more genteel variety, who appears well off; a "Mander" is a beggar, usually a paroled prisoner without means; "Prigger" and "Prancer" are both words for horse thieves; "Rum Pads" and "Rumpadders" are highwaymen.

The grammar mixes past and present tenses, which would not be permitted today. (It reminds me of the line in Lewis Carroll's *The Hunting of the Snark*: "Then the bowsprit got mixed with the rudder sometimes.") But you must not allow the grammar to throw you off. Simply accept it as it is; it gives the excerpt a somewhat colloquial feeling for its day and age. Once you have mastered the grammar technically and are comfortable with it, you can then simply tell the story.

You have in this text a gruesome, grisly tale to tell. It is all narrative, and you should make us see the events in our mind's eyes by starting slowly at first, then reading the later part of the text at a brisker pace, so that the events build to a climax. Experiment by recording it at different paces, and find the one that is most comfortable for you. You and your listeners should have a growing sense of horror, as you would when looking at any good horror film, especially those that deal with real-life horror, as opposed to those great old films with fictitious monsters. But think of any horror film to help you get into this narrative. You might look, for instance, at the real-life murder story *10 Rillington Place* (1971), with Richard Attenborough as a chilling John Christie, and an altogether excellent cast. And we should have a real sense of that poor, terrified stable-boy who saw the murder from his hiding place, and whom you, the narrator, "heard... groan too." Your, the narrator's, attitude of compassion should be reflected vocally, and you can do that by substituting a time in your own life when you felt sorry for someone, which should make the circumstances in the story real to you as you narrate them. Choose another time as well, when you either went through something awful yourself, or heard of some terrible event.

You might want to pick someone to talk to in whom you could confide, because you want to get this harrowing story off your chest. You'll feel better after you've told that friend or confidant.

This is a picaresque novel, from the word "picaresque" (pronounced "PI:K ə RESK"; derived from the Spanish *picaro* (pronounced "PI: ka: ro:"), meaning a rogue. Picaresque novels recount the escapades of a roguish, rakish hero, usually in a series of episodes that take the hero all over the map. *The English Rogue* takes its rascally hero on his adventures all over Europe, and the book proved so popular when it was published in 1665 that three more "parts" were published, through 1667, and the original book was renamed as "Part One." The purported autobiography is the story of the cynical rogue Meriton Latroon, an Irishman (despite the book's title), a confidence trickster, and an amoral seducer of women, one of whom he gets pregnant and ships off to Virginia. Despite the implications of the title, he is not punished, but lives happily off his ill-gotten gains, at the end of Part One. Retribution comes later on, but the next parts are full of interpolated stories before we arrive at the rogue's end. This book influenced Henry Fielding, who wrote his own picaresque novel, but with a likable hero, *Tom Jones*, instead of the usual rogue.

Eighteenth Century—Age of Sensibility.

From Henry Fielding's *The History of Tom Jones, a Foundling* (1749), Part XVII, Containing Three Days, Chapter Two: The Generous and Grateful Behaviour of Mrs. Miller

Mr. Allworthy and Mrs. Miller were just sat down to breakfast, when Blifil, who had gone out very early that morning, returned to make one of the company.

He had not been long seated before he began as follows: "Good Lord! my dear uncle, what do you think hath happened? I vow I am afraid of telling it you, for fear of shocking you with the remembrance of ever having shewn any kindness to such a villain." "What is the matter, child?" said the uncle. "I fear I have shown kindness in my life to the unworthy more than once. But charity doth not adopt the vices of its objects." "O, sir!" returned Blifil, "it is not without the secret direction of Providence that you mention the word adoption. Your adopted son, sir, that Jones, that wretch whom you nourished in your bosom, hath proved one of the greatest villains upon earth." "By all that's sacred, 'tis false," cries Mrs. Miller. "Mr. Jones is no villain. He is one of the worthiest creatures breathing; and if any other person had called him villain, I would have thrown all this boiling water in his face." Mr. Allworthy looked very much amazed at this behaviour. But she did not give him leave to speak, before, turning to him, she cried, "I hope you will not be angry with me; I would not offend you, sir, for the world; but, indeed, I could not bear to hear him called so." "I must own, madam," said Allworthy, very gravely, "I am a little surprized [*sic*] to hear you so warmly defend a fellow you do not know." "O! I do know him, Mr. Allworthy," said she, "indeed I do; I should be the most ungrateful of all wretches if I denied it. O! he hath preserved me and my little family; we have all reason to bless him while we live. And I pray Heaven to bless him, and turn the hearts of his malicious enemies. I know, I find, I see, he hath such." "You surprize [*sic*] me, madam, still more," said Allworthy; "sure you must mean some other. It is impossible you should have any such obligations to the man my nephew mentions." "Too surely," answered she, "I have obligations to him of the greatest and tenderest kind. He hath been the preserver of me and mine. Believe me, sir, he hath been abused, grossly abused to you; I know he hath..."

NOTES, COMMENTS AND HINTS

You will notice immediately that the title is simpler and shorter than the seventeenth-century title (not always true of eighteenth-century titles), and that the sentences are punctuated largely as we would punctuate them today. Paragraphs would be divided differently now, and each separate bit of dialogue would be a separate paragraph. Nor would we mix verb tenses as Fielding does (Blifil "said" and Mrs. Miller "cries" in the same paragraph for an event taking place in the present), but as it stands this selection presents no great difficulty.

The grammar in the spoken dialogue seems quite close to our own. In the narration Americans would say, of course, "We had sat down to breakfast," but in Britain you would still be apt to hear "We were sat down to breakfast." English intransitive verbs were often conjugated with the auxiliary "to be", and not, as they mostly are today, with "to have." Fielding had great feeling for and excellent observation of real eighteenth-century speech. Even with the few unfamiliar terms—such words as "hath" instead of "has," and "nay" instead of "no"—you can easily make this language your own. After all, you don't stress "hath" any more than you do "has" in a sentence such as "... what do you think hath happened?" " It is easy to read the dialogue in a conversational tone, and to adopt the attitudes of the characters. Squire Allworthy is indignant; Mrs. Miller is earnest; and Mr. Blifil, conniving and sniveling as usual, hides his manipulative nature under a mask of sincerity, which he apes very well.

The plot of *Tom Jones* is simple:

The kindly, benevolent, compassionate and wealthy Squire Allworthy—his name indicates his character, as names often do in eighteenth-century literature—finds a baby boy on his bed and, out of pity, adopts the child, whom he names Tom Jones, because Allworthy has been led to believe that Jenny Jones, a servant girl, is the mother. Jenny leaves the village in disgrace. In reality the mother is Squire Allworthy's sister Bridget, who has managed to keep her pregnancy secret from her brother. Bridget marries Captain Blifil. They have a son, and Tom and young Blifil are raised together. Squire Allworthy treats them with equal kindness, until the jealous, spiteful, malicious young Blifil—the antithesis of the good-hearted, naïve Tom Jones—leads Allworthy to believe that Tom has been carrying on with the neighboring squire's daughter, Sophie Western, whom Blifil wants to marry. Tom and Sophie are indeed in love, but the naïve Tom is innocent of any wrongdoing. Nevertheless Squire Allworthy banishes him from his estate. Tom's adventures now begin, and eventually take him to London, where he finds lodgings with the amiable Mrs. Miller, who is an acquaintance of Allworthy. At the end of the book Blifil gets his comeuppance, and Tom and Sophie are married.

The scene of conflict in the excerpt above is an easy one to play. The narration is minimal. The scene is mostly dialogue, and therefore requires you to act as if you were in a play. Each of the three characters' objectives is also quite clear: Blifil wants, in his malicious way, to continue to smear Tom Jones; Mrs. Miller wants to undeceive Squire Allworthy; and Allworthy, convinced of Tom's villainy by the conniving Blifil, wants to believe what he believes, and he simply cannot accept that his beloved nephew Blifil is lying to him. Find substitutions for all three characters. You might remember a time when you refused to believe something about someone you knew, despite the energetic attempts of a third person to convince you. You might have been deceived about someone, and later discovered the truth.

The pace of this scene should be fairly quick, and the tone and mood energetic and playful, despite the seriousness of the conflict. Enjoy Fielding's dialogue and savor his language. Enjoying the language in any text is always a key to making the listener enjoy it.

See the 1963 movie *Tom Jones* directed by Tony Richardson, if you haven't done so, with Albert Finney as the perfect Tom Jones, Susannah York as a delightful Sophie, and David Warner as a sly Blifil. The narration by the Abbey Theatre's Michael MacLiammoir is a lesson in itself.

Henry Fielding (1707–1754), along with Samuel Richardson, whom Fielding parodied, was one of the first English novelists to write a real story with a through-line, and not an episodic collection of tales, like *The English Rogue*, on which it nevertheless built. The novel is full of bawdy and open sexuality, and quite different in its frankness from books soon to be written by more reticent Romantic and Victorian writers. Contributing to the book's delightful humor is the endless pursuit of Tom by various characters, and his own pursuit of the wealthy London society aristocrat, Lady Bellaston. And Tom and Sophie are perpetually chasing each other as well. The pace and rhythm of many of the scenes depends on the chase, which adds a quickness and enjoyment to the story. The book reminds one of the satiric paintings and drawings of William Hogarth (1697–1764) or the engravings of the caricaturist Thomas Rowlandson (1756–1827) later in the century. Take a look at them to help give yourself a feeling for the atmosphere and the life portrayed in *Tom Jones*.

Early Nineteenth Century—Romantic Period.

From Sir Walter Scott's *Ivanhoe: A Romance* (1819), Chapter XLIII

To the summons of the herald, who demanded his rank, his name, and purpose, the stranger knight answered readily and boldly, "I am a good knight and noble, come hither to sustain with lance and sword the just and lawful quarrel of this damsel, Rebecca, daughter of Isaac of York; to uphold the doom pronounced against her to be false and truthless, and to defy Sir Brian de Bois-Guilbert, as a traitor, murderer, and liar; as I will prove in this field with my body against his, by the aid of God, of Our Lady, and of Monseigneur Saint George, the good knight."

"The stranger must first show," said Malvoisin, "that he is a good knight, and of honourable lineage. The Temple sendeth not forth her champions against nameless men."

"My name," said the Knight, raising his helmet, "is better known, my lineage more pure, Malvoisin, than thine own. I am Wilfred of Ivanhoe."

"I will not fight with thee at present," said the Templar, in a changed and hollow voice. "Get thy wounds healed, purvey thee a better horse, and it may be I will hold it worth my while to scourge out of thee this boyish spirit of bravade."

"Ha! proud Templar," said Ivanhoe, "hast thou forgotten that twice didst thou fall before this lance? Remember the lists at Acre—remember the Passage of Arms at Ashby—remember thy proud vaunt in the halls of Rotherwood, and the gage of your gold chain against my reliquary, that thou wouldst do battle with Wilfred of Ivanhoe, and recover the honour thou hadst lost! By that reliquary and the holy relic it contains, I will proclaim thee, Templar, a coward in every court in Europe—in every Preceptory of thine Order—unless thou do battle without farther delay."

Bois-Guilbert turned his countenance irresolutely towards Rebecca, and then exclaimed, looking fiercely at Ivanhoe, "Dog of a Saxon! take thy lance, and prepare for the death thou hast drawn upon thee!"

NOTES, COMMENTS AND HINTS

Of course, Ivanhoe saves the day and rescues Rebecca.

Bois-Guilbert is pronounced "bwa: gi:l BARE." Malvoisin is pronounced "mæl vwa: ZÆ:N; the name means "bad neighbor."

Ivanhoe is a Romantic historical novel. And with a one-word title and a two-word subtitle! In the seventeenth century the title might have been *The Most Tragicall and Elevating Historie of the Valliant Knight Sir Wilfred of Ivanhoe, CONTAINING an account of his Journey to the Holye Lande and Backe, together with his most Doughty Deeds in Rescuing the True and Glorious English King Richard the First Plantagenet and in rescuing Fair Damsels in Distress, with the Story of Robin of Lockesley, known as Robin Hood and Other Divers Matters, All of a Moral Character, Such as to Give the Reader an Idea of True Moralitie*. In the eighteenth century it might have been *The Adventurous History of Wilfred of Ivanhoe, a Knight*. Later in the nineteenth century it might have had a longer title than the one Scott gave it, and in the twentieth and twenty-first centuries it would be simply *Ivanhoe*.

Even though this novel is a medieval romance, the style is nineteenth-century Romantic. Sir Walter Scott wrote retrograde dialogue in an attempt to sound antiquated by being vaguely Shakespearean and using the second person singular subject pronoun "thou" with verbs ("thou hast"; "thou hadst"), and the adjective "thy" ("thy lance"), forms long gone. To get his antique effect Scott also uses unusual syntax that even the Elizabethans might have found a bit odd: ". . . hast thou forgotten that twice didst thou fall before this lance?"

The Romantics didn't really believe that people spoke that way, because they knew—at least I think they must have known—that Early Modern English (the language of Shakespeare) didn't exist in the era in which the story is set, but they did think people ought to speak in an archaic idiom, to give the dialogue the flavor of long ago and far away. Even though the effect is Elizabethan, rather than medieval, it was all one to Sir Walter Scott and his impassioned readers.

The effect is also melodramatic, with lines like: "Ha! Proud Templar..." and "Dog of a Saxon! take thy lance..." So get out your old melodrama caps, and have fun! You can overdo it just a bit with material like this. It is stylistically fitting.

The conflict between the characters, and their opposite objectives, are very clear and easily played. Sincerity and high stakes are the keys here. This is a matter of life and death, quite literally, so play that in your reading of Ivanhoe and Bois-Guilbert's confrontational dialogue. Malvoisin is very much in charge of the proceedings, and the tone of his one line should be authoritative. His objective is to cool tempers and to make sure that everything goes according to the rules.

For another excerpt from *Ivanhoe* and more information about the book, see page 124.

Later Nineteenth Century—Victorian Realistic Period.

Two excerpts from George Eliot's *Daniel Deronda* (1876); Book I: The Spoiled Child, Chapter One

Men can do nothing without the make-believe of a beginning. Even Science, the strict measurer, is obliged to start with a make-believe unit, and must fix on a point in the stars' unceasing journey when his sidereal clock shall pretend that time is at Nought. His less accurate grandmother Poetry has always been understood to start in the middle; but on reflection it appears that her proceeding is not very different from his; since Science, too, reckons backwards as well as forwards, divides his unit into billions, and with his clock-finger at Nought really sets off in medias res. *No retrospect will take us to the true beginning; and whether our prologue be in heaven or on earth, it is but a fraction of that all-presupposing fact with which our story sets out.*

Was she beautiful or not beautiful? and what was the secret of form or expression which gave the dynamic quality to her glance? Was the good or the evil genius dominant in those beams? Probably the evil; else why was the effect that of unrest rather than of undisturbed charm? Why was the wish to look again felt as coercion and not as a longing in which the whole being consents?

She who raised these questions in Daniel Deronda's mind was occupied in gambling not in the open air under a southern sky, tossing coppers on a ruined wall, with rags about her limbs, but in one of those splendid resorts which the enlightenment of ages has prepared for the same species of pleasure at a heavy cost of gilt mouldings, dark-toned colour and chubby nudities, all correspondingly heavy—forming a suitable condenser for human breath belonging, in great part, to the highest fashion, and not easily procurable to be breathed in elsewhere in the like proportion, at least by persons of little fashion.

• • •

The Nereid in sea-green robes and silver ornaments falling back over her green hat and light-brown hair, was Gwendolyn Harleth. She was under the wing or rather soared by the shoulder of the lady who had sat by her at the roulette-table; and with them was a gentleman with a white mustache and clipped hair: solid-browed, stiff and German. They were walking about or standing to chat with acquaintances; and Gwendolyn was much observed by the seated groups.

'A striking girl—that Miss Harleth—unlike others.'

'Yes, she has got herself up as a sort of serpent now, all green and silver, and winds her neck about a little more than usual.'

'Oh, she must always be doing something extraordinary. She is that kind of girl, I fancy. Do you think her pretty, Mr. Vandernoodt?'

'Very. A man might risk hanging for her—I mean a fool might.'

'You like a *nez retroussé* then, and long narrow eyes?'

'When they go with such an *ensemble*.'

'The *ensemble du serpent*?'

'Woman was tempted by a serpent. Why not man?'

NOTES, COMMENTS AND HINTS

Instead of a long title we have a long epigraph, but this is not typical of nineteenth-century novels, although there are often shorter epigraphs, which are usually apt quotations from philosophers, historians, and the like, at the heads of chapters. George Eliot wrote this one herself. It states one of the themes of the book in the neutral, scholarly tone with which you should read it, just as the paragraphs which follow set the narrative tone. George Eliot's writing is complicated, and will strike some as being stilted, as in the manner discussed earlier. You might have to read the epigraph several times to grasp its meaning, and it may be difficult to make that meaning clear when reading it aloud, but a fairly slow rhythm, with an emphasis on the words that make the points, will make it as clear as possible.

Here is my technical suggestion for one way to read the epigraph: Take a brief pause after the first sentence, to let the point sink in. That point is intriguing enough to make us want to hear more. Take another pause after the word "measurer," another after the word "unit," then read on without pausing until you get to the word "pretend," and stress it and almost all of the following words; finally, pause again at the end of the sentence. Your next pause should not be until after the word "his." Stress the words that make salient points, but do not pause again until after the Latin phrase *in medias res*. Stress the words "true beginning," and the other words in boldface, and read the rest of the epigraph without pausing:

> Men can do nothing without the make-believe of a beginning. [Pause] Even Science, the strict measurer, [Pause] is obliged to start with a make-believe unit, [Pause] and must fix on a point in the stars' unceasing journey when his **sidereal clock** shall **pretend** that **time is at Nought**. [Pause] His less accurate grandmother Poetry has always been understood to start in the middle; but on reflection it appears that her proceeding is not very different from his; [Pause] since **Science, too,** reckons **backwards** as well as **forwards**, divides his **unit** into **billions**, and with his clock-finger at **Nought** really sets off *in medias res*. [Pause] No retrospect will take us to the **true beginning**; and whether our prologue be in heaven or on earth, it is but a fraction of that **all-presupposing fact** with which our story **sets out**.

The whole tone and feeling of the book then changes immediately as we go into the narrative mode, and enter into the mind of our hero, Daniel Deronda, in this third-person narrative.

Gwendolyn Harleth immediately intrigues us, as she intrigues those watching her. She is as yet a mystery. We have yet to hear her speak and we know nothing about what she is really like. We have seen her only from the outside. Daniel Deronda, about whom we also know very little as yet, is deeply attracted to her, or at least deeply intrigued by her, and he does not know what to think of her. George Eliot is a genius at maintaining a suspenseful attitude towards this young lady, who must indeed have something more going on than we see. What is it? Who is she? (Eliot characterizes her as a Nereid, a sea nymph who, in Greek mythology, was one of the sea god Poseidon's attendants, wont to flit in and out and roundabout.) And who is he: Daniel Deronda? Why should we be interested in him and in what he thinks of her?

So the novel opens, piling unknown, mysterious circumstance on mysterious circumstance. The sense of mystery should come through in your reading, but without assuming a tone of voice that says "mystery." Rather, you should narrate in a simple manner and lead us onward into the story. We, the listeners, should want to find out who these people are, exactly as we would if we were reading this passage silently to ourselves. The thoughts revealed to us at the very beginning, however, are those of Daniel, so you must narrate them in a slightly different tone, even though Daniel's thoughts are also being narrated, and we are outside his mind, and in the mind of our omniscient narrator (who is actually ourselves as we tell the story). But the narrator's simple "narrative" voice actually comes into play only at the beginning of the second paragraph. As a general substitution for this scene as a whole use a time when you fell in love with someone, perhaps when you saw that person for the first time.

Daniel Deronda, Eliot's last novel, is one of her most fascinating stories. One of its themes is the discovery of the self, of who and what we are. The complicated, intricate plot takes us from this opening scene at a casino in the resort of Leubronn to the highest aristocratic circles in England, and follows the story of Gwendolyn, who is trapped in a miserable marriage, which she contracted for money, to Grandcourt, a man she cannot abide—this man had abandoned a mistress and children in order to marry Gwendolyn (Gwendolyn knew about the mistress, who had begged her not to marry Grandcourt)—and of Daniel, the adopted son of Sir Hugo Mallinger. Daniel rescues Mirah, a young Jewish girl, from drowning, and falls in love with her, while Gwendolyn falls in love with Daniel. All the worlds of the story—the aristocratic circles, the country-house scene, the Jewish quarter in London, Italy—overlap each other and are interdependent in this moving story, a major theme of which is anti-Semitism, which George Eliot found deeply horrifying. If you were to record this novel, you should know, in order to give it the background which would inform your reading, that other Victorian writers were not always as sensitive or as intelligent as Eliot was on the subject of the recently emancipated Jews, whom they saw as alien, intrusive outsiders. Eliot writes with these other authors, whom she opposes, in the front of her mind. Even some of the most famous Victorian writers have a streak of anti-Semitism in their books, which abound in negative stereotypical portraits and snide references. Charles Dickens, for instance, in spite of all his compassion, progressive politics, and humanitarianism, created the stereotypical Jewish villain Fagin in *Oliver Twist* (1837), a miserly fence who trains boys to be pickpockets; Fagin is by no means the most villainous character in the book, and he is not unkind to the boys. But every time Fagin appears, Dickens refers to him in almost every sentence as "the Jew" or "the old Jew," so that the tone of those passages is nauseatingly anti-Semitic. Dickens, to his great credit, tried to make amends when his insensitivity was pointed out to him, notably with the kindly (not always successfully written) Jewish characters in *Our Mutual Friend* (1865), and always protested that he had nothing but goodwill and good feelings towards Jews.

Is *Daniel Deronda*, written in the Realistic Period, a Romantic or a Realistic novel? I would say it is both: A mid-Victorian Realistic novel, with a Romantic sensibility. It is Romantic in that it is idealistic, and explores the nature of subjectivity; it is Realistic in that it portrays its characters and milieus in an objective, faithfully real way. George Eliot, the pen name of Mary Anne Evans (1819–1880), was known as a realistic novelist. Her books emphasize the inner psychology of characters and analyze their actions from a psychological perspective, almost for the first time in the history of the English novel.

By now you will have noticed how style changed in the course of the century. And it was to change even more, going in the direction of simplicity in syntax and vocabulary and punctuation, as the nineteenth century drew to a close. *Daniel Deronda* is a contemporary story for its time, written in a style quite different from that of Sir Walter Scott. The use of French is typical of the period and of the high society circles in which part of this novel takes place, so there is a great deal of French in the dialogue, just as there is in Poe's *The Purloined Letter* (see Chapter Two, page 52). In *Ivanhoe*, too, there is a great deal of French, but, since it concerns the conflict between the Norman French aristocrats who rule England and the Saxons whom they have dispossessed, it is natural that there should be, particularly in the names of the characters.

A *nez retroussé* (pronounced "né rə troo SÉ") is a "turned-up," or "snub nose." The word *ensemble* (the French pronunciation is "a:*N* SA:*M* blə") means in this excerpt exactly what it means today in one of its senses (the whole outfit); the word is obviously new to the English language in Eliot's day, and is still considered French, just as such an English word such as *partner* was new to French when Balzac used it. He spelled and presumably pronounced it in the English way, but it is now a French word: *partenaire*. The phrase *ensemble du serpent* (pronounced "a:*N* SA:*M* blə dü sayr PA:*N*") means "the serpent's ensemble," because the person talking has said that Gwendolyn looks like a serpent.

The dialogue in the second excerpt is idle, malicious gossip. Rather than reading it maliciously, however, take a slightly bored, but amused tone. The issues in the dialogue are not life and death, and the speakers don't care all that much. In other words, the stakes are not terribly high. They are simply whiling away the hours, idling about the casino. We have no idea who is speaking, since we are meeting Mr. Vandernoodt for the first time, but we know that they are people of the upper crust, so the tone should be snobby, without being overdone. Pronounce the French correctly, although you may give it a slight English accent if you wish, to reflect the character of the people speaking. When you prepare such a text as this opening, you must know who these people are, which is why you must read the whole story before making decisions about what voice, tone and attitude to adopt.

With the dialogue we are already closer to the style of our own time than we were even in the excerpt from *Tom Jones*. Of course the faux medievalism of the dialogue in *Ivanhoe* has nothing to do with the reality of people's speech, and is clearly not a reflection of how people spoke in Scott's day. For that we have to go to someone like Jane Austen; see pages 171 and 226 for excerpts from *Pride and Prejudice*.

Setting the Scene: The Opening

You have to set the scene, just as the author does. The images must be clear in your mind so that you can convey them to the listener. You have to draw the listeners into the story and make them see the action, or the place or person, in their mind's eye, as if they were reading the printed text for themselves, and as if you were yourself involved in the story—as if you were at the place and with the people you are describing.

Some Openings: How to Read Them

Here are some examples of openings of different kinds and styles, together with some ideas on how to read them aloud. You will find other openings elsewhere in this book: Stephanie Cowell's *The Physician of London: A Novel* on page 200; Charles Dickens's *A Christmas Carol* on page 107; George Eliot's *Daniel Deronda*, above; Charles Kent's *Charles Dickens as a Reader* on page 104; Edgar Allan Poe's *The Purloined Letter* on page 52 and *The Tell-Tale Heart* on page 225; and Captain Meadows Taylor's *Confessions of a Thug* on page 127.

All openings have the same basic purpose: to take the reader into the story in a way that will be intriguing and make the reader want to continue reading.

From Marcel Proust's *Remembrance of Things Past* (also known as *In Search of Lost Time*), Volume One: *Swann's Way* (1913); my translation

For a long time I got into bed early. Sometimes, my candle hardly extinguished, my eyes closed so quickly that I had no time to tell myself "I'm falling asleep." And half an hour afterwards the thought that it was time to try to go to sleep woke me up; I wanted to put down the volume I believed I still had in my hands and to blow out my light; I had not stopped while sleeping to reflect on what I had just read, but those reflections had taken a slightly particular turn; it seemed to me that I, myself, was what the work spoke about: a church, a quartet, the rivalry of François I and Charles V. This belief survived my awakening by several seconds; it did not shock my reason, but weighed like scales upon my eyes and prevented them from realizing that the candle was no longer lighted. Then it began to become unintelligible to me, like the thoughts of a prior existence after metempsychosis; the subject of the book detached itself from me, I was free to attach myself to it, or not; immediately I recovered my sight and I was most astonished to discover an obscurity around me, sweet and restful for my eyes, but perhaps even more so for my mind, to which it appeared as something without a cause, incomprehensible, something truly obscure. I asked myself what hour it could be; I heard the whistling of trains, which, more or less far away, like a bird singing in a forest, leaped over the distances, depicting for me the extent of the deserted countryside where the traveler is hastening towards the next station; and the little path which he takes will be engraved in his memory by the excitement he owes to new places, to unaccustomed acts, to the recent conversation and the farewells under the unfamiliar lamp that follow him still in the silence of the night, and to the approaching sweetness of his return home.

NOTES, COMMENTS AND HINTS

This opening immediately involves the reader in intimate complicity with its first-person narrator. Prospective publishers misunderstood the opening, every image of which foreshadows what is to come, and because of it (in part) Proust had great difficulty in finding a publisher for his innovative book. It was rejected time after time, for various reasons. M. Humblot, who read it for the publishing house of Ollendorff, wrote a letter to Louis de Robert, a friend who was trying to help Proust find a publisher: "Dear friend, I may be thick as a plank, but I cannot understand how a gentleman could take thirty pages to describe how he tosses and turns in his bed before being able to fall asleep."

The opening is introspective. Who is telling this story? You are! It is you who says "I" to us, the listeners. I am not being facetious when I say that it is you who are the "I" of the story; part of Proust's purpose is to have the reader identify with the Narrator, or at least to take the Narrator's side and to understand him; one of the Narrator's objectives is to be known and understood. You actually have to read the whole book to find out who this "I" is. Not only is the Narrator a character in his own story; he is also the character telling that story. A listener to a recording would be invited to identify or to empathize with "I," but a listener is one step further removed from the story than you, and it is up to you to draw the listener into the circumstances and events as they evolve, since the listener cannot do this for her or himself, as someone reading the text silently would. As a reader, you must realize that the author Marcel Proust, and his character the Narrator are plunging themselves, and you, immediately into a world both familiar and strange: Their world becomes your world.

The quiet, calm atmosphere of this opening passage, which, apart from it being about something we have all experienced—falling asleep, waking up unexpectedly and being confused for a moment—sets the scene for the entire novel. Consequently, this opening paragraph should be read quietly, intimately, perhaps almost mesmerically. Your action as an actor/ reader/interpreter of this passage is "to draw the reader/listener into your world."

To make sense of the last sentence in the paragraph requires good breath control and some technical skill in taking proper pauses, so that the meaning and the images, for each of which as well as for the whole scene, you should find substitutions, become clear. Pauses are indicated by semi-colons, but the commas separating the last clauses also indicate pauses. The clauses must be spoken in a legato way, not staccato at all. The effect will be haunting, dreamlike. I have marked the passage below with bars to indicate the pauses I suggest you might take, but you should feel free to find your own:

> I asked myself what hour it could be; | I heard the train whistles, which, more or less far away, like a bird singing in a forest, leaped over the distances, | depicting for me the extent of the deserted countryside | where the traveler is hastening towards the next station; | and the little path which he takes will be engraved in his memory by the excitement he owes to new places, | to unaccustomed acts, | to the recent conversation and the farewells under the unfamiliar lamp that follow him still in the silence of the night, | and to the approaching sweetness of his return home.

Keep the voice up at the ends of clauses, on the words before the pauses I have indicated. I have not suggested a pause between "follow him still" and "in the silence of the night," but you may want to take one there, as long as the listeners still have a sense of continuity, because the final clause—"to the approaching sweetness of his return home"—is linked to "the little path which he takes will be engraved in his memory by the excitement he owes..." To make this link clear the intonation (the pitch pattern) must be much the same as in the previous clauses.

If you speak French, listen to the beautiful recording by André Dussollier (see the Bibliography). His reading of this opening is very soothing, very restful. In general, M. Dussollier separates clauses by very brief breath pauses, so that we can really listen for the meaning of the words. He varies the rhythm for the same reason. You will notice that, having read the phrase "I had not stopped while sleeping to reflect on what I had just read" at a medium slow tempo, with a suggestion of reflective thinking in his intonation (his voice stays up and does not drop at the end of the clause), he pauses very briefly (just time enough for a breath to be taken), then speeds up, and takes no pauses at all in the phrases "but those reflections had taken a slightly particular turn; it seemed to me that I, myself, was what the work spoke about." He then takes another breath pause, slows down and takes a pause after each clause separated by commas in the phrase "a church, a quartet, the rivalry of François I and Charles V," dwelling slightly with an upward intonation on each image, and allowing the listener to absorb each one.

Even though this analysis describes what Dusollier does technically, you will have the impression that his reading itself is not technical, but organic; that it comes from inside, that he has invested his emotions in it, and that the pauses and intonations arise naturally from the way in which the narrator thinks and the way in which he wants to tell us what he thinks. As a reader you must make the listeners believe that you are telling us the opening events of the story "as if for the first time"—using that Stanislavskian principle which is the sine qua non of good acting.

The Narrator's intimate revelations continue beyond the passage quoted above, and begin to deal with the Narrator's sexuality. In the last clause of the sentence that follows, one of the Narrator's thoughts will carry us through the book, remaining in the back of our mind, haunting us: it concerns the thoughts of the Narrator as he awakens from his dream of a beautiful woman:

> If, as sometimes happened, she had the features of a woman whom I had known in my waking life, I vowed to give myself over entirely to this goal: to find her again, like those who leave on a trip to see with their own eyes a longed-for city, imagining that one can taste in reality the charm of a dream.

Can one or can one not taste the charm of a dream in real life? What is reality? The text is beautifully poetic, and the words, announcing one of Proust's major themes, deserve to be savored, by you and by your listeners. A caveat: Beware of sounding labored. By taking an organic approach to this material you should be able to avoid that.

You must personalize the text. The traveler returning from a journey—who is he? Who is he to you? Is this description of the traveler a mere generality? The themes of sleeping and waking, and of travelers on journeys, of love and desire recur throughout the book.

You should pick someone to read to in your imagination with whom you might wish to share your most intimate thoughts and feelings. Your tone should be ruminative, but with something in it that says to us "I am leading you somewhere. Please follow me, and you will see that what I have to say will mean a great deal to you." Talk quietly and intimately into the microphone. Tell us. Don't read to us. Don't narrate. Don't talk at us, talk to us. Quietly. Soothingly. Evocatively. Be yourself!

Marcel Proust (1871–1922), having translated two of John Ruskin's books into French and written essays and newspaper columns and published a book of short stories and poems, made at least two attempts, which he discarded, at writing what was to become his masterpiece, *A la recherche du temps perdu*, which some consider the twentieth century's greatest work of fiction.

Proust's book is, among other things, an autobiographical story told by its first-person narrator (a character whose name we don't actually know, although it may be Marcel; we call him the Narrator), who, in the course of the book, discovers his vocation to be a writer, and, as we learn at the end of the book, has actually written the book we have just been reading.

Proust thought that a work of art should be enjoyed and understood for itself, without reference to the author's life. In Proust's case it has been easy for some people to confuse author and Narrator, because the book contains many autobiographical elements. However, the aspiring writer who is the Narrator and Author of *In Search of Lost Time* is emphatically not its actual author, Marcel Proust, a very different person in so many ways from his character. Among other things, the Narrator, who wants to be a writer, has the greatest difficulty in sitting down and writing.

Proust used so many incidents, people and elements of his life in creating the Narrator that it is relevant to ask who Proust was, even though the author is not the Narrator, because the background of Proust's life informs the character. Marcel Proust was a somewhat enigmatic, mysterious person, despite the endless books and articles that have been written about him (one can speak of a Proust industry), including the memoirs of his friends and family and the famous *Monsieur Proust* by Céleste Albaret, the confidante and "gouvernante" who knew him and did not know him. He knew so many people, and he wrote thousands of letters. Everything and everybody fascinated Proust. He was deeply loved, and perhaps he never really knew it. At least he lived to see his life's work beginning to be crowned with glory, even if he died before the last volumes of his masterpiece were published. They were edited for publication by his brother, Dr. Robert Proust and by Jacques Rivière, a writer and editor who was a friend of Marcel's. For more information, read *Marcel Proust: A Life* by William Carter; see the Bibliography.

It is a shame that Proust never recorded himself reading from his book. One would love to have heard him. We don't know what his voice sounded like, but there have been many descriptions of it, and some people apparently mistook his housekeeper Céleste's for his on the telephone, so much had their almost symbiotic relationship made her voice resemble his. We do know what she sounded like, because she can be heard in filmed and taped interviews. When she tells us what he said to her, her voice changes, she almost imitates him unconsciously, and we certainly hear Proust's style of talking and his intonation pattern. When she tells us how he called her "ma chère Céleste" (my dear Céleste; pronounced "ma: she:r sé LEST"), her voice drops on the second word, which is drawn out slightly, and is very tender, almost seductive. Léon-Pierre Quint, who knew Proust, says, "Céleste spoke with the plaintive tones of her master." Some of his other friends described Proust's voice as being slightly veiled and nasal (due perhaps to his chronic asthma), a bit quavering, soft and, as the poet Anna de Noailles says, "extremely sweet."

And in Paul Morand's book *Le visiteur du soir* (*The Evening Visitor* or *Visitor of the Evening*, La Palatine, 1949) Morand recreates Proust's actual conversation, not dissimilar to his writing. Morand also appears in a documentary reading that conversation, and imitating Proust. Many of his friends claimed that when they read Proust's book they could hear his voice in their heads, just as I could hear in my mind the voices of the actors in the first two Harry Potter films when I read *Harry Potter and the Order of the Phoenix* (Arthur A. Levine Books/Scholastic, 2003). You can see both Morand and Céleste on a CD-ROM called *Marcel Proust: une découverte multimedia de l'oeuvre de Marcel Proust* (*Marcel Proust: A Multimedia Discovery of the work of Marcel Proust*) by noted Proust scholar Jean-Yves Tadié (Éditions Gallimard, 1999). All of this information about Proust's voice and about the way he talked may give us a clue as to how to read Proust's book aloud.

I had the deeply felt pleasure and privilege of reading a brief excerpt from one of the most famous episodes in the book—where the Narrator dips a piece of the little cake known as a Petite Madeleine in some tea, thus involuntarily awakening childhood memories—at a PEN evening called "Proust Regained" at Alice Tully Hall in the fall of 2001, with such notables on the stage as William Carter, Roger Shattuck, Nadine Gordimer, Edmund White, Lydia Davis, and André Aciman. I read it in French to open the program, and the great actress Zoë Caldwell read the English translation, so beautifully, and in such a heartfelt, yet simple narrative manner, that the audience wept. That is the manner I recommend to you. There is something so profoundly moving when you read it in that way, and all the powerful emotional depth that is in the book comes through to the audience.

From Charles Dickens' *A Tale of Two Cities* (1859); Book the First: Recalled to Life; Chapter One: The Period.

It was the best of times, it was the worst of times, it was the age of wisdom, it was the age of foolishness, it was the season of Light, it was the season of Darkness, it was the spring of hope, it was the winter of despair, we had everything before us, we had nothing before us, we were all going direct to Heaven, we were all going direct the other

> way—in short, the period was so far like the present period, that some of its noisiest authorities insisted on its being received, for good or for evil, in the superlative degree of comparison only.
>
> There were a king with a large jaw and a queen with a plain face, on the throne of England; there were a king with a large jaw and a queen with a fair face, on the throne of France. In both countries it was clearer than crystal to the lords of the State preserves of loaves and fishes, that things in general were settled forever.

NOTES, COMMENTS AND HINTS

This is a very different beginning in every way from Proust's. To begin with, it does not appear at first glance to be a first-person narrative, although it might be one; we won't know until we get past the opening. Secondly, its somewhat grand tone is meant to set a grand historical scene and to sum up, in admirable language, an entire period, and to evoke a long-gone era, far away in time even when Dickens wrote this opening. But he brings it into the present by his comparison with "the present era," and we can still relate to it, even though he wrote in 1859, because the same phenomena he mentions as existing then exist now, and people have the same attitudes about how well or how badly things are going politically and economically. There are extremists and moderates of every description. This opening is immediately active and awake, and involves us in the meshes of the net of time, but not as Proust sees time in his opening, from an individual perspective, but rather as seen from a grander historical perspective. The coming revolution is in the air. Even if we have never seen portraits of the French and English monarchs, the visual, imagistic opening of the book bring pictures into the mind,. You must see those pictures, so that the listener can see them.

Everything in this opening is done in terms of opposites, and opposites are wonderful to read, since they do half the job for you. This passage should be done with tremendous variety and never in a labored way, or it will be monotonous and difficult to listen to. Compare it to another piece of writing that is full of opposites, Hamlet's famous soliloquy "To be or not to be."

Read this text just a wee bit grandly, but not grandiloquently. Infuse it with some passion and your own interest in it. Keep it as simple as you can, even though the periods are elaborate—though not so florid as to be "a coruscation of impromptu epigram," as Tarara, the Public Exploder, says in Gilbert and Sullivan's *Utopia, Limited* (1891). Bear in mind Dickens's phrase "the superlative degree of comparison" (the -est endings for adjectives) as a hint on how to read this excerpt.

The allusion to Shakespeare's Richard the Third's "the winter of our discontent" in Dickens's line "...it was the spring of hope, it was the winter of despair" is surely meant. There is thus an implicit comparison between the dark world of pre-revolutionary France, about to explode, and bring an era to an end, and the similarly terminal era of the reign of Richard the Third and the Wars of the Roses, about to change England forever.

From Jane Austen's *Pride and Prejudice* (1813), Chapter 1.

It is a truth universally acknowledged, that a single man in possession of a good fortune must be in want of a wife.

However little known the views of such a man may be on his first entering a neighborhood, this truth is so well fixed in the minds of the surrounding families, that he is considered as the rightful property of someone or other of their daughters.

"My dear Mr. Bennet," said his lady to him one day, "have you heard that Netherfield Park is let at last?"

Mr. Bennet replied that he had not.

"But it is," returned she; "for Mrs. Long has just been here, and she told me all about it."

Mr. Bennet made no answer.

"Do not you want to know who has taken it?" cried his wife impatiently.

"*You* want to tell me, and I have no objection to hearing it."

That was invitation enough.

""Why, my dear, you must know, Mrs. Long says that Netherfield is taken by a young man of large fortune from the north of England; that he came down on Monday in a chaise and four to see the place, and was so much delighted with it, that he agreed with Mr. Morris immediately, that he is to take possession before Michaelmas, and some of his servants are to be in the house by the end of next week."

"What is his name?"

"Bingley."

"Is he married or single?"

"Oh! Single, my dear, to be sure! A single man of large fortune; four or five thousand a year. What a fine thing for our girls!"

"How so? How can it affect them?"

"My dear Mister Bennet," replied his wife, "how can you be so tiresome!..."

NOTES, COMMENTS AND HINTS

Jane Austen was, as E. B. White called her, "a deeply humorous woman." Here she talks directly to you, the reader, and expects you to agree that her opening statement is ironic, as is made clear in her second sentence. She is very tongue-in-cheek and delightfully wry. To convey the irony, you should not read the opening sentence in a didactic tone, nor even in a particularly humorous tone; you don't want to telegraph the idea that the listener should laugh. One choice would be to deliver the opening line somewhat drily and "straight," to use the comedian's term, and to let the humor come out that way, although the lightest of slightly ironic tones would also be a most agreeable possibility. In fact, the tone throughout is best kept light, partly so that the more serious scenes will stand out in contrast, like the chiaroscuro effects in a Rembrandt painting.

As the opening introduces two characters and the names of two others, plus revealing of the existence of the Bennets' daughters, our interest in all these people is aroused. The theme, the direction, and a hint as to the possible subsequent events of the story are also stated quite directly at the outset.

It is immediately apparent that Mrs. Bennet is rather excitable and that stolid, down-to-earth, wry Mr. Bennet, with his dry sense of humor, knows just how to get at her, albeit with kindness and love, despite his teasing. Mrs. Bennet is revealed as a good, loving mother, ambitious in the interests of her daughters, but at the same time somewhat naïve, and even gullible. In some dramatized versions she is overplayed as flighty and hysterical. If you are recording this book you should avoid overdoing her character. You have a very nice contrast to play between the two characters of husband and wife. Choose as a substitution a time when someone was pulling your leg, or having you on, and you then realized it.

Consult the section of this chapter on how to do vocal characterizations (page 202). The listener must have as immediate a sense of who the characters are as if he or she were reading the text silently from the printed book.

Jane Austen (1775–1817) began writing what proved to be her most enduringly popular novel in 1796, under the title *First Impressions*. Her father, a rector, offered it to a publisher, who refused even to read it. She put it aside, and in 1811, encouraged by the success of *Sense and Sensibility*, she picked it up and started working on it again. In 1813, seventeen years after she had first begun it, she finally published this polished, witty, psychologically astute, charming book, originally in three volumes. She lived long enough to enjoy the great success of her books, although all of them were published anonymously, and it was only after her death that her brother Henry revealed their authorship. In a letter dated January 29, 1813, to her sister, Cassandra Elizabeth, Jane Austen calls *Pride and Prejudice* "my own darling child," and with regard to the character of Elizabeth Bennet, the novel's heroine, she continues: "I must confess that I think her as delightful a creature as ever appeared in print, and how I shall be able to tolerate those who do not like *her* at least, I do not know." For another excerpt see page 226.

From Charlotte Brontë's *Jane Eyre* (1847), One.

There was no possibility of taking a walk that day. We had been wandering, indeed, in the leafless shrubbery, an hour in the morning; but since dinner (Mrs. Reed, when there was no company, dined early) the cold winter wind had brought with it clouds so somber, and a rain so penetrating, that further out-door exercise was now out of the question.

I was glad of it: I never liked long walks, especially on chilly afternoons: dreadful to me was the coming home in the raw twilight, with nipped fingers and toes, and a heart saddened by the chidings of Bessie, the nurse, and humbled by the consciousness of my physical inferiority to Eliza, John, and Georgiana Reed.

NOTES, COMMENTS AND HINTS

Jane Eyre herself is the first-person narrator, telling us her own story. Her character must be immediately established. She begins in the middle of a conversation with the reader, as it were, and the first line might almost be her answer to the question, "Did you not take a walk that day?" If you were reading it as if answering that question your pitch might rise on the word "possibility" and the words "of taking a walk that day," being a repetition, would be delivered without emphasis. But if you are beginning it as if to tell a story, and not in answer to a question, then the words "possibility" and "taking a walk that day" would all be stressed, with perhaps an emphasis on the word "that."

The second sentence tells us what time of year it is, and that it is cold, and leads us into the cheerless, bleak atmosphere of the story. In reading this aloud it would be good not to adopt a cheerless, bleak, mournful, depressed tone, however. Since the words give us the depressive atmosphere, and since Jane Eyre, the character whom you are playing, is, to say the least, not describing terribly happy events or a terribly happy day, you should allow the listener into the story by adopting a somewhat neutral tone. Let the listeners supply the unhappiness; do not reflect it in your voice, or the listener may not be drawn into the story.

And avoid any tone of self-pity, since self-pity is an unattractive quality, particularly if you try to sustain it over the course of a long narrative, although self-pity may be called for at a specific moment in a story. In this case, assume the character's attitude of "things just were the way they were, and there was nothing to be done about them, and at least I didn't have to go for a walk, which I hated to do when it was cold outside, and there is some cheer in that."

Jane's sense of inferiority is immediately stated—she says it is physical, but we instantly feel it must be a general character trait—and we feel as well that it must be unwarranted. In other words, we are on her side; but we won't be if you have taken a self-pitying tone.

We also realize, when shortly into the story, that she is a young girl in a helpless situation, so that we have a certain sense of sympathy and empathy for her, since she is obviously suffering, and, as we soon find out, is treated unjustly and dismissed as if she were nobody, as if she were a nonentity and unworthy of love or even of consideration, as if she has no feelings or desires that need be attended to.

Jane Eyre is rather a brave girl, and capable of great endurance and great forbearance, even of tolerance for those who make her suffer, because she feels inferior, which means that she feels they have a right to make her suffer, since she is so unworthy and undeserving. She is terribly abused psychologically, yet we discern that she is in some way a gifted child. To understand more about the psychology of individuals such as Jane Eyre, who has absorbed the image of herself as unworthy from the people who treat her as if she were, read Alice Miller's *The Drama of the Gifted Child* (Basic Books, 1996).

It is a good idea to do some additional research into the general situation of women, the general circumstances of their lives in that era. See the excerpt from Mary Wollstonecraft's *A Vindication of the Rights of Woman: with Strictures on Political and Moral Subjects* (1792) on page 339. In Chapter 12 Jane herself tells us:

> Women are supposed to be very calm generally: but women feel just as men feel; they need exercise for their faculties, and a field for their efforts as much as their brothers do; they suffer from too rigid a restraint, too absolute a stagnation, precisely as men would suffer; and it is narrow-minded in their more privileged fellow-creatures to say that they ought to confine themselves to making puddings and knitting stockings, to playing on the piano and embroidering bags.

Jane is very aware of what being a woman means in the society of her day, and is very strongly, even fiercely independent and proud. She refuses to give in to societal pressure, and will only have a relationship with a man who will treat her on equal terms. So the tone of the reading of this brief excerpt from the novel's opening should be centered, and we should sense—vaguely at this point—that there is some way in which Jane will overcome the sense of inferiority with which she begins her life, and arrive at the attitude she has in Chapter 12. Indeed, since she is telling her story to us a long time after it happened, she has actually already attained the maturity she lacks in the beginning.

For more excerpts from *Jane Eyre* and for more information about the book see page 131.

From Mark Twain's *The Adventures of Tom Sawyer* (1876), Chapter I: Tom Plays, Fights, and Hides

"Tom!"

No answer.

"TOM!"

No answer.

"What's gone with that boy, I wonder? You TOM!"

No answer.

The old lady pulled her spectacles down and looked over them about the room; then she put them up and looked out under them. She seldom or never looked *through* them for so small a thing as a boy; they were her state pair, the pride of her heart, and were built for "style," not service—she could have seen through a pair of stove-lids just as well. She looked perplexed for a moment, and then said, not fiercely, but still loud enough for the furniture to hear:

"Well, I lay if I get hold of you I'll—"

She did not finish, for by this time she was bending down and punching under the bed with the broom, and so she needed breath to punctuate the punches with. She resurrected nothing but the cat.

NOTES, COMMENTS AND HINTS

The rhythm of this opening is deliberately staccato, propelling the action forward. Mark Twain launches us into the story *in medias res*, or, as my grandparents might have said, *in mitske derinnen*, which is colloquial Yiddish for *in medias res*.

The first word is shouted, getting the listener's attention immediately. The second "Tom" is even louder. Aunt Polly is very annoyed, as if she were saying "Drat! Where *is* that boy? He's always doing this to me!"

Even though this is a third-person narrative, you can put yourself as a narrator into the role of Aunt Polly, as you describe her actions. One way of making the listeners see the action is to stress certain words: "The old lady <u>pulled</u> her spectacles <u>down</u> and <u>looked over</u> them about the room; then she <u>put</u> them <u>up</u> and <u>looked out under</u> them." But that is merely technical. If you can project yourself into that room with feeling and imagine yourself doing what she is doing, you should not have to worry about which words to stress; the emphasis should be natural and organic. The ironic statement about what the glasses mean to Aunt Polly should be delivered with Twain's typical dry wit, without telegraphing to the listener that you think it is funny.

Twain gives you clues as to how to read the lines: "she said, not fiercely," muttering under her breath. You can punch the word "punching" in "punching under the bed with a broom." Just playing Aunt Polly's action of looking for Tom Sawyer, who she is sure is hiding somewhere in the room, will help you get the correct rhythm and momentum for the scene.

Samuel L. Clemens (1835–1910), whose pen name was Mark Twain, was America's preeminent humorist and a humanitarian commentator on the events of his day. And he wasn't only funny back then. He is still funny, because the targets of his satire are unfortunately still in operation. They include hypocrites and charlatans of all kinds, including the purveyors of fake spirituality and false religion, racists and bigots. For his satirical look at literary criticism see the excerpt from his essay *Fenimore Cooper's Literary Offenses* on page 347. For a continuation of the opening of *Tom Sawyer*, see page 235, to follow how Twain develops the story.

From Washington Irving's *Rip van Winkle* from *The Sketch Book* (1819–1820)

> Whoever has made a voyage up the Hudson must remember the Kaatskill mountains. They are a dismembered branch of the great Appalachian family, and are seen away to the west of the river, swelling up to a noble height and lording it over the surrounding country. Every change of season, every change of weather, indeed, every hour of the day, produces some change in the magical hues and shapes of these mountains, and they are regarded by all the good wives, far and near, as perfect barometers. When the weather is fair and settled, they are clothed in blue and purple, and print their bold outlines on the clear evening sky; but sometimes, when the rest of the landscape is cloudless, they will gather a hood of grey vapours about their summits, which, in the last rays of the setting sun, will glow and light up like a crown of glory.
>
> At the foot of these fairy mountains, the voyager may have descried the light smoke curling up from a village, whose shingle-roofs gleam among the trees, just where the blue tints of the upland melt away into the fresh green of the nearer landscape.

NOTES, COMMENTS AND HINTS

There is something very peaceful and benign in this description of the lordly and majestic scenery of the Catskill Mountains. This opening sets the scene for a rather pleasant, and, indeed, engrossing and entertaining moral tale. The scenery goes from the general to the more localized setting of the little village where Rip van Winkle lives. Compare this literary opening to the cinematic opening sequence of *Vanilla Sky* (2002), where we see an aerial shot of New York, zoom in on the Dakota apartment house, then on the bedroom and the sleeping

Tom Cruise. Irving's beginning has something in common also with Victor Hugo's elaborate opening description of medieval Paris in *The Hunchback of Notre Dame,* which is called in French simply by the name of the cathedral, *Notre Dame de Paris.* You might take a look at it, and compare it to *Rip van Winkle.*

Enjoy the language and the scenery. Project yourself in your mind's eye into some of the beautiful mountain landscapes you have enjoyed. If you have ever had occasion to take a train ride from New York City heading north up the right bank of the Hudson, with the river to your left and the mountains in front of you looming up far away as the train curves round the bends in the river, you know how apt Washington Irving's description is. The Catskills still look as he described them, despite the addition of bridges across the Hudson and many built-up towns along the riverbanks. And if you take the train around sunset, you still see the glow over the mountains "like a crown of glory." Savor this lovingly evocative excerpt, and let yourself be swayed and carried along by the language, and the listeners will go with you. Very soon there will be more humorous matter with which to entertain them, and the tone of the story will change. By that time you will have gotten their attention and made them want to hear more.

Washington Irving (1783–1859), diplomat, traveler, historian, satirist and writer of short stories, was America's first man of letters, the father of American literature. We still read his two classic short stories, *Rip van Winkle* and *The Legend of Sleepy Hollow*, but much of his voluminous output now gathers dust on library shelves, unfortunately.

From Thomas Hardy's *The Woodlanders* (1887), Chapter One

> The rambler who, for old association's sake, should trace the forsaken coach-road running almost in a meridional line from Bristol to the south shore of England, would find himself during the latter half of his journey in the vicinity of some extensive woodlands, interspersed with apple-orchards. Here the trees, timber or fruit-bearing as the case may be, make the wayside hedges ragged by their drip and shade, their lower limbs stretching in level repose over the road, as though reclining on the insubstantial air. At one place, on the skirt of Blackmoor Vale, where the bold brow of High-Stoy Hill is seen two or three miles ahead, the leaves lie so thick in autumn as to completely bury the track. The spot is lonely, and when the days are darkening the many gay charioteers now perished who have rolled along the way, the blistered souls that have trodden it, and the tears that have wetted it, return upon the mind of the loiterer.

> The physiognomy of a deserted highway expresses solitude to a degree that is not reached by mere dales or downs, and bespeaks a tomb-like stillness more emphatic than that of glades and pools.

NOTES, COMMENTS AND HINTS

Fair sends a shiver up and down your spine, don't it? This is a description of the kind of scenery that is symbolic of loneliness and conducive to bleak imaginings, and very much in contrast with Irving's opening to *Rip van Winkle*. Irving's is majestic and mysterious, where Hardy's is brooding and portentous and grim, and not at all majestic. Hardy's opening sets the scene for the terrible gloomy story to come.

Grace Melbury, daughter of the wealthy timber merchant George Melbury, is betrothed to Giles Winterbourne, her father's employee, and she is returning from school along this road to the village of Hintock to marry him. Giles adores Grace, but she does not return his affections deeply. She is forced by her father to marry Giles to make up for a wrong her father had done to his father. But Grace meets and falls in love with the new village doctor, Edred Fitzpiers, a ladies' man who flirts with all the village maidens. Grace and Edred marry. Fitzpiers has a passionate love affair with the seductive Felice Charmond, and when Grace learns about it she is furious and deeply upset. She and her father hear that there is a "new law" regarding divorce, which has hitherto been an ecclesiastical matter, the courts of the Church of England being able to grant a divorce upon securing a special private act of Parliament making the divorce legal. Grace wants to divorce Fitzpiers and marry Giles. However, the Divorce and Matrimonial Causes Act of 1857 turns out entirely to favor men, and does not provide women with the possibility of instituting divorce proceedings, unless they can prove, in addition to adultery, desertion, unusual cruelty, bestiality, incest or bigamy. There are further plot complications as this fascinating, passionate story dealing with love, betrayal and women's rights unfolds.

To read this opening aloud, make us see the deserted road and all the scenery of the open and exposed Dorset downs. The gloom will be there, so you need not do more than read the description clearly, imagining yourself there, and substituting an analogous experience from your own life. Even if you have never been on a deserted country road during the late afternoon when the day is darkening, you must surely have walked home through deserted streets late at night, so use that or any similar experience to launch you into reading this narrative, and to give you a feeling of loneliness and trepidation. You might also look at a book of photographs of Dorset.

Thomas Hardy (1840–1928) was known as a poet and as a realistic novelist, but it might be more accurate to describe him as a pessimistic novelist who believed in a stoic attitude to life in the face of its tragedies. His great series of novels is set in the fictitious, but generic, English county of "Wessex," in some of what is now Dorset, the country of John Fowles, and the setting for Jane Austen's *Persuasion*. *The Woodlanders* is one of the Wessex novels.

From Herman Melville's *Moby-Dick; or, The Whale* (1851), Chapter One: "Loomings"

> Call me Ishmael. Some years ago—never mind how long precisely—having little or no money in my purse, and nothing particular to interest me on shore, I thought I would sail about a little and see the watery part of the world. It is a way I have of driving off the spleen, and regulating the circulation. Whenever I find myself growing grim about the mouth; whenever it is a damp, drizzly November in my soul; whenever I find myself involuntarily pausing before coffin warehouses, and bringing up the rear of every funeral I meet; and especially whenever my hypos get such an upper hand of me, that it requires a strong moral principle to prevent me from deliberately stepping into the street, and methodically knocking people's hats off—then, I account it high time to get to sea as soon as I can. This is my substitute for pistol and ball. With a philosophical flourish Cato throws himself upon his sword; I quietly take to the ship. There is nothing surprising in this. If they but knew it, almost all men in their degree, some time or other, cherish very nearly the same feelings towards the ocean with me.

NOTES, COMMENTS AND HINTS

"Call me Ishmael" is one of the most famous opening lines in American literature. It immediately invokes the Biblical story of Ishmael and Hagar, and consequently the idea of an outcast, of a search for home and what home means, and it tells us as well that the first-person narrator of this story is not telling us his real name. Thus, the theme of alienation is also metaphorically stated in this opening line. We realize immediately that we will be dealing with symbols and signs, but as a reader, you cannot play symbols and signs: You simply have to let them be there for the listener to discern.

When you read these first three words, read them very simply. Give no hint of portent, of what is to come, and which is past by the time "Ishmael" is telling us his story. The only thing we should sense, and then only dimly, is a feeling of restlessness and, especially, loneliness. And do savor the language at the same time.

Herman Melville (1819–1891) knew when he wrote what turned out to be his masterpiece, that he was creating an epic story, akin to those in the Bible, to the ancient Homeric epics, the *Iliad* and the *Odyssey*, and to the Oedipus cycle of Sophocles. Melville's themes—the fusion of the desire to murder with the desire to create, the mystery of the universe and its origins, the nature of the gods that control humanity's destiny, and the battle against one's fate—are also found in the ancient literature.

"Cato" is the Roman Stoic philosopher Cato the Younger (95–46 BCE) who committed suicide by running himself on his sword upon learning of one of Caesar's victories. The allusion announces ancient classic themes, foreshadows the suicidal mission of Captain Ahab, and tells us that "Ishmael" is an educated man.

The actual opening of the book is not "Call me Ishmael," but a long disquisition on the etymology of whales and literary allusions to whales, all of which is meant to set the scene for the great conflict to come: the hunt for the great white whale, Moby-Dick. Melville based his novel on an article he had read in the *Knickerbocker Magazine*, which recounted the chase after a whale named "Mocha Dick." Apparently this whale was found near the isle of Mocha, and Dick, like Tom or Harry, was a name often given to whales, prefaced by a geographical name. Why Melville changed the name, and how he came up with the name "Moby" remain mysteries.

Melville felt that he had to use heightened language, and to invent new words, in order to tell his colossal, innovative saga in the monumental style it deserved, for his themes are vast, dealing with man's aloneness in the unresponsive, indifferent universe. And his metaphors are also monumental—the whaling ship *Pequod*, commanded by Captain Ahab, named for a wicked king in the Bible, is the world in microcosm. Melville's style is elemental in its power; it rolls along in huge sentences like the sea itself, and, like the sea, it can be very dramatic, very bizarre, very strange and unsettling, and extremely unpredictable. He invents words: "leewardings," "domineerings," and uses strange phrases, such as "my keeled soul." The word "hypos," on the other hand, is simply ordinary nineteenth-century slang for "very low spirits"; it derives, apparently, from "hypochondriac." See Eric Partridge's useful *A Dictionary of Slang and Unconventional English* (Macmillan, 1961).

In the Book of Genesis Ishmael is the son of the patriarch Abraham by his wife Sarah's handmaiden Hagar. Sarah, being too old to conceive, has allowed her husband to father a son with her servant; then, by a miracle, Sarah also conceives, and gives birth to Isaac. Jealous of Hagar and Ishmael, Sarah prevails upon Abraham against his will to drive them out into the desert (Genesis: XXI), where God, the omniscient, omnipresent, omnipotent literary character in the Bible, protects them. So here we have a story in which a son is driven away by his own father, and in which jealousy and injustice prevail, although in the end Ishmael and Hagar are saved through divine intervention.

In *Moby-Dick* we are asked to call the person telling us the story of his survival after the whale hunt in the desert/ocean Ishmael. Think of all the ramifications of that name and of the Bible story that we associate with those opening three words. Those ramifications must inform your characterization of the narrator, otherwise unnamed, telling us his story. Has our first-person narrator had an analogous experience to that of the Torah's Ishmael? Or is he referring to later events in the story he is telling us, and does Captain Ahab have something in common with Abraham, who, in another story, was prepared to sacrifice his son Isaac at God's command? Did "Ishmael" view him as a father figure? If so, he was a strange, forbidding and distant father. At any rate, "Ishmael," like the Biblical character is saved from death, perhaps also by divine intervention. Is his sensibility numbed and deadened by what he has been through? Is he past caring? He cares enough to tell us his story. Why? Perhaps he wishes to bear witness, like a survivor of the Holocaust or the Rwandan genocide, to a horrendous, traumatic event.

We don't know very much about "Ishmael" and his prior life. We know he is probably fairly young, like Ishmael in the Torah, and that he was a teacher before he got a yen to go to sea. He remains mysterious even after we get to know him better, as if he wished to tell us his story and remain hidden at the same time. That sense of secrecy and a lack of openness should be reflected vocally; it should inform your reading. While you are preparing and reading this excerpt, think of parts of yourself that you do not wish to reveal, and see how that makes you feel. The resulting reading may be a bit startling to you. Remember, this is subtext, so don't play the action "I want to hide and not reveal myself," which would reveal the subtext to the listener. Keep it hidden. Ask yourself, as Gandalf asks Frodo in Tolkien's *The Lord of the Rings*, "Is it secret? Is it safe?"

For another excerpt and more information about this book see page 232.

Reading Different Kinds of Scenes

Scenes in works of fiction fall into certain categories, and require different techniques to bring them to life. Those techniques have to do with rhythm and pace, tone and level of voice, and the actions and attitudes of the characters.

Action Scenes

Action scenes should be done excitedly, that is, with an internal sense of excitement. And they should be done fairly quickly, the rhythm, the pace, and the velocity of the scene, being determined by the material. Be very careful, however, not to rush action scenes. Reading too quickly does not allow the listeners to follow the scene clearly, let alone get involved in it, which is what you would like them to do. If you want your listener to get caught up in the scene, you will read from the inside, feeling emotionally what is going on. An action scene is not a mere mechanical or technical exercise. You must bring a sense of reality and life to the scene. Read clearly, with great energy, carrying the scene forward, making it vivid in the mind's eye, and you will automatically read such scenes at a correct, quick, energized pace, without rushing the tempo. Your objective as an actor is to recreate the characters' actions in order to make the events of the scene clear and visual for the listener. Remember the scene in Chapter Five, on page 124, from Sir Walter Scott's *Ivanhoe,* in which Rebecca describes a battle scene to the wounded Ivanhoe, whom she has been tending. She makes what is happening vividly clear to him, and this is what you must do for your listeners.

What you are doing in an action scene is creating suspense with the voice. You do that not only by reading at a correct tempo, but also by stressing certain kinds of words that tell you graphically what is happening, especially verbs, sometimes nouns, prepositions or adjectives. If you have a repeated series of words of a certain kind, you will find it helpful to stress them, because the rhythm thus created gives the impression of headlong, pell-mell action, whether it is a swashbuckling sword fight, a battle scene, or a run across the moors, as in the following example.

From Sir Arthur Conan Doyle's *The Hound of the Baskervilles* (1902), Chapter 12: "Death on the Moor"

"The hound!" cried Holmes. "Come, Watson, come! Great heavens, if we are too late!"

He had started running swiftly over the moor, and I had followed at his heels. But now from somewhere among the broken ground immediately in front of us there came a last despairing yell, and then a dull, heavy thud. We halted and listened. Not another sound broke the heavy silence of the windless night.

I saw Holmes put his hand to his forehead like a man distracted. He stamped his feet upon the ground.

"He has beaten us, Watson. We are too late."

"No, no, surely not!"

"Fool that I was to hold my hand. And you, Watson, see what comes of abandoning your charge! But, by heaven, if the worst has happened we'll avenge him!"

Blindly we ran through the gloom, blundering against boulders, forcing our way through gorse bushes, panting up hills and rushing down slopes, heading always in the direction whence those dreadful sounds had come. At every rise Holmes looked eagerly round him, but the shadows were thick upon the moor, and nothing moved upon its dreary face.

NOTES, COMMENTS AND HINTS

There are a number of ways of indicating the action in this scene and thus bringing the listener along in the excitement. The frequent exclamation marks in the dialogue give you an obvious and, dare I say it, elementary clue as to how excited these characters are, and, consequently, as to how to read their spoken lines. I have underlined the words that I would suggest you stress in that last verb-filled paragraph, as an indication of one way of conveying action:

> Blindly we ran through the gloom, blundering against boulders, forcing our way through gorse bushes, panting up hills and rushing down slopes, heading always in the direction whence those dreadful sounds had come. At every rise Holmes looked eagerly round him, but the shadows were thick upon the moor, and nothing moved upon its dreary face.

On the other hand, you could emphasize the nouns, and still give yourself and the listener the sensation of a headlong rush over the moor. Emphasizing the verbs shows more of the struggle of Holmes and Watson, and less of the scenery, while emphasizing the nouns allows us to see the scenery. Both readings would work quite well:

> Blindly we ran through the gloom, blundering against boulders, forcing our way through gorse bushes, panting up hills and rushing down slopes, heading always in the direction whence those dreadful sounds had come. At every rise Holmes looked eagerly round him, but the shadows were thick upon the moor, and nothing moved upon its dreary face.

You will no doubt be able to find other ways of conveying the action. What you don't want to do in such a scene is to take any kind of indifferent tone or slow, deliberate pace, which would simply kill it.

However you choose to read such a scene, the reading must come from feeling what the characters are living through from moment to moment. The characters' objectives and the obstacles in their way must be in your mind. The reasons for wanting to attain, or to accomplish, those objectives inform the scene. In this case we may state the objective as: "We want to save Sir Henry Baskerville from certain death! And we are the only ones who can do it! And it has to be done in a fearful hurry, because the danger is at hand!" The obstacles are the distance and the difficult terrain they have to traverse. And the action is "to run across the moor."

"We halted and listened." Suddenly the action comes to a standstill, and this change of beat should be reflected vocally by a slight pause after the line, as if you are indeed standing there and listening. There is a chill in the line that follows this one, and then the rhythm, which has slowed slightly (I am talking of both the writing and the reading of the story) picks up again, becomes quicker, as Holmes puts his hand to his forehead and stamps his feet. From there the intensity of the action simply takes you along. You have only to let yourself go with it. The sense memory of times when you have run, gone jogging, or even chased someone down a street, with the remembered sensations of breathlessness and purpose, should inform your reading.

Here is another example of Sherlock Holmes in a different action, concentrated on his work examining the rooms where Mortimer Tregennis died, from "The Adventure of the Devil's Foot":

> One realized the red-hot energy which underlay Holmes's phlegmatic exterior when one saw the sudden change which came over him from the moment that he entered the fatal apartment. In an instant he was tense and alert, his eyes shining, his face set, his limbs quivering with eager activity. He was out on the lawn, in through the window, round the room, and up into the bedroom, for all the world like a dashing foxhound drawing a cover. In the bedroom he made a rapid cast around and ended by throwing open the window, which appeared to give him some fresh cause for excitement, for he leaned out of it with loud ejaculations of interest and delight. Then he rushed down the stair, out through the open window, threw himself upon his face on the lawn, sprang up and into the room once more, all with the energy of the hunter who is at the very heels of his quarry.

Try stressing the prepositions in "... down the stair, out through the open window," etc. to give a feeling vocally for the "red-hot energy" with which Holmes carries out his actions. Ordinarily you might be inclined to stress the nouns, but in this case they will not serve your turn as well as the prepositions will.

Sir Arthur Conan Doyle (1859–1930) was a prolific writer of historical romances and science fiction, aside from the famous canon of fifty-six Sherlock Holmes short stories and four novels. He was also a believer in spiritualism—see page 103, for some information on Lytton Strachey, who was not. On pages there are more excerpts from *The Hound of the Baskervilles.*

From Robert Louis Stevenson's *Treasure Island* (1883), Chapter 21: "The Attack"

> The boarders swarmed over the fence like monkeys. Squire and Gray fired again and yet again; three men fell, one forwards into the enclosure, two back on the outside. But of these, one was evidently more

frightened than hurt, for he was on his feet again in a crack and instantly disappeared among the trees.

Two had bit the dust, one had fled, four had made good their footing inside our defences, while from the shelter of the woods seven or eight men, each evidently supplied with several muskets, kept up a hot though useless fire on the log-house.

The four who had boarded made straight before them for the building, shouting as they ran, and the men among the trees shouted back to encourage them. Several shots were fired, but such was the hurry of the marksmen that not one appears to have taken effect. In a moment, the four pirates had swarmed up the mound and were upon us.

The head of Job Anderson, the boatswain, appeared at the middle loophole.

"At 'em, all hands—all hands!" he roared in a voice of thunder.

At the same moment, another pirate grasped Hunter's musket by the muzzle, wrenched it from his hands, plucked it through the loophole, and with one stunning blow, laid the poor fellow senseless on the floor. Meanwhile a third, running unharmed all around the house, appeared suddenly in the doorway and fell with his cutlass on the doctor.

Our position was utterly reversed. A moment since we were firing, under cover, at an exposed enemy; now it was we who lay uncovered and could not return a blow.

The log-house was full of smoke, to which we owed our comparative safety. Cries and confusion, the flashes and reports of pistol-shots, and one loud groan rang in my ears

"Out, lads, out, and fight 'em in the open! Cutlasses!" cried the captain.

NOTES, COMMENTS AND HINTS

This rousing, rip-roaring, swashbuckling tale of pirates and treasure hunting is a perennial favorite, even with adults. All the characters are memorable, from our narrator, young Jim Hawkins, to the one-legged Long John Silver, so admirably portrayed by Robert Newton in what is still, to my mind, the best version of the story ever filmed, Walt Disney's 1950 *Treasure Island*. To help you visualize the fight at the stockade, look at that scene in the film, and use the sensations you experience in bringing the written scene to life. Newton, by the way, has such great fun hamming it up and rolling his eyes and his Rs that we have great fun along with him. When you record a book, enjoying yourself is a big part of the process, and the listener will enjoy the book so much more if you have taken pleasure in recording it. Your enjoyment will communicate itself without your being aware of it.

Some technical advice: Stress the strong verbs in the opening paragraph that show us what actions are taking place ("swarmed," "fired," and "fell"). Where the wounded men fell is less important than the effect of the plethora of verbs allowing us to hear the action taking place, so as you tell us where they fell make your voice sound incidental: You will thus add visually to our picture of the scene, without slowing the action down. If you emphasize every little thing that happens and make everything important, paradoxically we will lose the sense of anything's being important, as well as the narrative thread of the scene, and the sense of action taking place.

Continue stressing those verbs or verbal phrases: "was on his feet again"; "made straight before them for the building, shouting as they ran," etc.

The cumulative effect of the headlong rhythm is to let us feel the heat and smoke and confusion of the fight. For another excerpt from *Treasure Island* see page 218.

Love Scenes

Reading love scenes, whether they are scenes of passion, conversations, or lovemaking, requires the use of affective memory: the remembrance of moments of tenderness and pleasure. Such scenes—intensely personal, intimate, private, quiet or passionate, perhaps all at the same time—absolutely require personalization and substitution. To sound natural, when you are in essence talking to yourself, and to read so that the scenes do not sound contrived or artificial, is a demanding task. Depending on how intimate the text is, you almost have to make love to the microphone, or at least into the microphone. For certain scenes you should sound "as if" you were leaning forward and talking very softly into your beloved's ear, confiding a secret perhaps over a late glass of wine, "as if" you were sitting in front of a fireplace, talking to the one person you can really talk to on the deepest level.

Love scenes, and very effective ones, too, often leave the explicit details of sexual encounters to the readers' imaginations; they imply and suggest, rather than describe, which allows the reader to supply the details—a good thing, since everyone is turned on in her or his own way.

Sexuality and its pleasures have a major place and play a pervasive role underlying all of literature, of course. The psychology of love and how people deal with their sexuality, as well as the repression of sexuality, which reflects the repression prevalent in society, are major themes in literature.

Read Balzac's *Lost Illusions* (1837–1843), and its sequel *The Splendors and Miseries of the Courtesans* (1843–1847) if you want a complicated story that displays all kinds of sexuality and sexual passion and deals with their psychological complications; the books have plenty of love scenes to use as practice texts. Love and passion are two of Balzac's major themes, and his treatment of them makes him rather different from many other nineteenth-century writers, like Charles Dickens, whose love stories, while full of passion, are so often about repressed feeling, where Balzac's are usually so open in their expression. There is a prudishness about Dickens that is absent in Balzac.

In Balzac sexuality can be sordid and mercenary, and occasionally comic, as in the pursuit of the beautiful Esther Gobseck by the baron de Nucingen in *The Splendors and Miseries of the Courtesans*, but it can also be wonderful and passionate and fulfilling. There are numerous sexual encounters of all kinds in Balzac, and the range of sexuality and sexual passion and even obsession he is willing to portray is astonishing. Homosexuality is part of his portrayal of human love, for instance, although he was not quite as open on the subject as he might have been if he had been writing a century later. There is virtually no treatment of that subject in Dickens, but there are occasional vague intimations and implications of it, particularly in *Great Expectations*. However, Dickens is not interested in portraying the gamut of human sexual experience.

Much of the treatment of love in Dickens makes it appear as if love exists on some ethereal, otherworldly plane. Love is innocent and pure (whatever that means; not inspired by sexual desire, I presume), and sexual encounters are nonexistent in Dickens—he deliberately avoids them—although tender, romantic love scenes abound. Love is sweet and unselfish, and rather akin to the courtly love of the Middle Ages, when sexual fulfillment was not to be expected, and the lovers pined away, or if they did not, they met with dire consequences. Deep sexual passion is something to be suppressed, perhaps by an effort of the will. It is an unfit subject for literature, apparently, although *Great Expectations* is the great exception to that last statement. But in Dickens's books sexual passion results in misery, as it does in *Great Expectations*, or in ruin, as it does in *Bleak House* (1853), one of his greatest works. Emotional devastation, affliction, heartache, and wretchedness are the price of desire—these are dire warnings against indulging in sex—despite the sentimental, romantic happy endings for which Dickens is also noted, and sometimes loved or decried; seen as moving, or mawkish and maudlin, depending on the reader's taste.

The closest Dickens and Balzac approach each other in their treatment of love is in Balzac's early love story, full of repression and melodramatic overtones, *Le Lys dans la vallée* (*The Lily in the Valley*) (1835), which has some vague similarities to the sort of passion described in *Great Expectations*, but even in that story, the closest Dickens came to dealing with obsessive, masochistic love, sexual passion is unfulfilled, and Pip's obsessive love for Estella is contrasted with the so-called purity of Biddy's unselfish love for Joe Gargery. Do Biddy and Joe even have a sexual relationship?

Charles Dickens lived from 1812–1870; Balzac from 1799–1850. Their different attitudes about sexuality, at least as expressed in their books, may, some critics would maintain, show a cultural difference between mid-nineteenth-century France and England, with its puritanical social roots. It would be inaccurate, however, to generalize in that way, because repression crosses cultural lines. And sexual feelings and sexuality are more often described in Victorian literature than they are usually thought to be by those for whom Victorianism and prudery are often perceived as going hand in hand.

Nevertheless, it remains true that what was acceptable in Balzac's France as an explicit literary subject was unacceptable in Dickens's England, except in restricted terms. Wilkie Collins, for instance, put the following passage in his 1875 novel *The Law and the Lady*:

> He caught my hand in his, and devoured it with kisses. His lips burned me like fire. He twisted himself suddenly in the chair, and wound his arm around my waist. In the terror and indignation of the moment, vainly struggling with him, I cried out for help.

The editors of *The Graphic*, in which the novel was serialized, rewrote it considerably, reducing it to: "He caught my hand in his and covered it with kisses. In the indignation of the moment I cried out for help." They then inserted a footnote explaining why they had rewritten the offensive paragraph.

Collins, within his contractual rights to have the book serialized without any alterations, maintained that the scene was "perfectly innocent." He was furious, and felt obliged to remonstrate with the editor, who thought that the passage in question was "an attempted violation of the heroine of the story." Nowadays we would say, "Yes, and . . . ?" (It was restored when the novel was published in book form.) *The Graphic* ran an article the day after the last episode of *The Law and the Lady* appeared, and particularly objected once again to the passage quoted above. Wilkie Collins published a rebuttal in *The World*, a newspaper edited by a friend of Collins. But many people must have felt that the novel was not suitable for "family reading." (See the excerpt on page 252.)

Despite Balzac's freedom to write what he chose, he, too, felt obliged to treat certain forms of sexual behavior in a veiled manner (Cousin Bette's lesbianism; Vautrin's homosexuality, to some extent), and there was a sort of puritanical streak in French culture as well as in that of Victorian England. When Gustave Flaubert's *Madame Bovary*, the story of a middle-class woman's adultery, was published in 1857, it so scandalized the French authorities that Flaubert was put on trial for obscenity. Marcel Proust, writing more than half a century later, thought the same thing might happen to him, and maintained that people would never speak to him again once they had read certain sexually explicit episodes in his book. For his treatment of some aspects of later nineteenth- and early twentieth-century repressed, prurient sexuality, see the selection from *Swann's Way* on page 255. Swann himself is very shy and does not dare to embrace the woman he loves, because he is so afraid that he might lose her if he is too bold. The psychology of this character, as of all the characters in *Remembrance of Things Past,* is explored in detail and in depth.

Knowing the kind of background information discussed here should help you find a tone and a style of reading that will reflect the kind of behavior, passion, general ethos and atmosphere that we find in the books of nineteenth- and early twentieth-century authors in England and France. The foregoing brief discourse is the result of the sort of research you should do into the culture that informs a book you are asked to record. You want to plunge yourself, insofar as possible, into the world in which the authors and their characters lived. You would do the same thing with any culture and any era.

When we come to pulp fiction and pornography (which some people certainly enjoy), we are very far from love scenes, and into purely sexual scenes. You will have to cope with bad writing in which a quality of cheap tawdriness and mercenary sexuality invades the stories. Imply lubricity, in recording such pornographic scenes, by a leering tone of voice and by using all the other techniques we have already discussed (affective memory, and the conveying of action through the voice by stressing certain words, and so forth), but that is not the sort of scene I propose to deal with here.

Two scenes from Honoré de Balzac's *La Comédie humaine (The Human Comedy): Le Lys dans la vallée (The Lily in the Valley)* (1835), my translation.

Notes: The novel is written in the form of a letter to Countess Natalie de Manerville, whom Count Félix Vandenesse loves, and who has asked him to tell her of his past life. Balzac writes in The Lily in the Valley: *"The unknown battle which is unleashed in a valley of the Indre between Mme. de Mortsauf and passion is perhaps as great as the greatest known battles." Madame Henriette de Mortsauf, although unhappily married to a nice man, refuses to give herself physically (she would not wish to violate her marriage vows in that way, and she has to think of the effect of doing so on her children), to Félix Vandenesse, who is madly in love with her, although she loves him and gives herself to him emotionally on condition that he accept the terms she offers, and remain faithful to her. Their constant encounters are thus inflamed by passion, and yet innocent of any conduct that would violate her marriage vows.*

FROM "II: FIRST LOVES."

To set the scene: The two children are occupied; Monsieur de Mortsauf has just left: "He went away as if he were conscious of the trouble his presence

> *would have brought to my conversation with Henriette, or else because, out of chivalrous regard for her, he knew that it would give her pleasure if we were left alone. His character presented inexplicable aspects, because he was jealous, as all weak people are; but at the same time his confidence in the saintliness of his wife was limitless . . ." Félix Vandenesse speaks:*
>
> "Beautiful human flower that caresses my mind and kisses my soul! Oh, my lily!" I said to her, "always intact, and upright on your stem, always white, proud, perfumed, solitary!"
>
> "Enough, monsieur," she said, smiling. "Talk to me about yourself. Tell me everything."
>
> We had then, under that mobile vault of trembling leafy branches, a long conversation full of interminable parentheses, taking up one subject, leaving off, taking it up again, in the course of which I brought her up to date on my life and my occupations; I described my Paris apartment to her, since she wanted to know everything; and since (happiness as yet unappreciated), I had nothing to hide from her. Knowing thus my soul and all the details of an existence filled with crushing work, learning thus the extent of those functions that I exercised with such exactitude that the King, I told her, called me "Mademoiselle de Vandenesse," she seized my hand, and kissed it, letting fall a tear of joy. This subtle transposition of roles, this magnificent praise, this thought expressed rapidly, and understood still more rapidly: "You are the master I would have wished for, you are my dream," in short, everything that there was of confession in such an action, in which abasement was greatness, in which love betrayed itself into entering a region forbidden to the senses, all that storm of celestial things, fell upon my heart and crushed me. I felt myself to be as nothing. I wanted to die at her feet.

In the following scene (which I have abridged slightly) from "III: The Two Women," Félix, having returned after a long absence, visits Mme. de Mortsauf as she is dying. She has taken ill because of the news she has received that Félix had been unfaithful to her, and had had an affair, now over, with the English Lady Dudley, whom he had not really loved, but with whom he had experienced physical passion.

> "As in the old days you will give me health, Félix, and my valley will be of benefit to me. How could I not eat what you will offer to me? You are such a good nurse! And then you are so rich in strength and in health, that, near you, life is contagious. My friend, prove to me that I will not die, not die deceived! They think my greatest pain is my

thirst! Oh! Yes, I am very thirsty, my friend. The waters of the Indre are so painful to gaze upon, but my heart feels a more ardent thirst. I was thirsty for you," she said to me in a choking voice, taking my hands in her burning hands, and drawing me to her so she could throw these words into my ears: "My agony has been not to see you. Did you not tell me to live? I want to live! I want to go horseback riding, too! I want to know everything, Paris, parties, pleasures!" . . .

She threw her arms around my neck, kissed me violently, and hugged me close, saying, "You shall not escape me any more! I want to be loved, I will commit follies, like Lady Dudley, I will learn English so I can say "my dee." She nodded her head to me as she used to do when she was leaving me, to let me know she would be back in an instant. "We will dine together," she said to me, "I'll go tell Manette . . ." She was stopped by a sudden attack of weakness, and I laid her down, completely dressed, on the bed.

"There was one other time when you carried me like that," said she, opening her eyes. She was very light, but above all very ardent; picking her up I felt her body burning with fever . . .

NOTES, COMMENTS AND HINTS

"In a choking voice" not only gives you an exact and perfect indication of how to read Henriette's lines in the last excerpt, but also absolutely conditions the way the rest of her lines should be read.

In both scenes, act the dialogue. But do not act the narration in a very emotional way, because the story told by Félix is in the past, so that there is some distance between him and the events he describes. In other words, don't relive them as if they are presently occurring events. They have to be told to us, not dispassionately or unemotionally (there is clearly a great deal of complicated, layered affect there), but with the distancing effect that hindsight imparts, even though you read through them from moment to moment.

In general, avoid a melodramatic approach to this text, which is so full of melodrama. This is a text where playing down will bring out what is actually there more strongly than if you played it up.

Also, remember that Henriette is dead, and it is to Natalie that Félix is telling the story of his relationships with Henriette and Lady Dudley. He is as honest as he can be, and wishes to conceal nothing from Natalie, for her decision as to whether or not to accept his hand in marriage depends on his telling his story completely and straightforwardly. (If you want to know her decision, read the book.) So his intended audience has to be dealt with carefully and with kid gloves. The objective of self-justification is clearly very important. Choose as an imaginary audience someone you want to justify yourself to, and then be as honest as you can in reading this text. Psychologically, despite the melodrama, this is a very real story, based on some of Balzac's psychological reactions in particular relationships, although not on his actual experiences. Just as he used what was inside him as a writer, you as an actor/recording artist must use what is inside yourself.

From Charles Dickens's *Great Expectations* (1861), Chapter XLIV

"Estella," said I, turning to her now and trying to command my trembling voice, "you know I love you. You know that I have loved you long and dearly."

She raised her eyes to my face, on being thus addressed, and her fingers plied their work, and she looked at me with an unmoved countenance. I saw that Miss Havisham glanced from me to her, and from her to me.

"I should have said this sooner, but for my long mistake. It induced me to hope that Miss Havisham meant us for one another. While I thought you could not help yourself, as it were, I refrained from saying it, but I must say it now."

Preserving her unmoved countenance, and with her fingers still going, Estella shook her head.

"I know," said I, in answer to that action: "I know. I have no hope that I shall ever call you mine, Estella. I am ignorant what may become of me very soon, how poor I may be, or where I may go. Still, I love you. I have loved you ever since I first saw you in this house."

Looking at me perfectly unmoved and with her fingers busy, she shook her head again.

"It would have been cruel in Miss Havisham, horribly cruel, to practice on the susceptibility of a poor boy, and to torture me through all these years with a vain hope and an idle pursuit, if she had reflected on the gravity of what she did. But I think she did not. I think that in the endurance of her own trial, she forgot mine, Estella."

I saw Miss Havisham put her hand to her heart and hold it there, as she sat looking by turns at Estella and at me.

"It seems," said Estella very calmly, "that there are sentiments, fancies—I don't know how to call them—which I am not able to comprehend. When you say you love me, I know what you mean, as a form of words; but nothing more. You address nothing in my breast, you touch nothing there. I don't care for what you say at all. I have tried to warn you of this; now, have I not?"

I said in a miserable manner, "Yes."

"Yes. But you would not be warned, for you thought I did not mean it. Now, did you not think so?"

"I thought and hoped you could not mean it. You, so young, untried, and beautiful, Estella! Surely it is not in Nature!"

"It is in *my* nature," she returned. And then she added, with a stress upon the words, "It is in the nature formed within me. I make a great difference between you and all other people, when I say so much. I can do no more."

NOTES, COMMENTS AND HINTS

"I love, I adore Estella," Pip tells his friend Herbert Pocket, who tells him it is obvious.

The orphaned Philip Pirrip, nicknamed "Pip," since he could only pronounce his name as "Pip" when he was a child, has grown up on the North Kent marshes, raised by his sister and her husband, the kind, loving blacksmith Joe Gargery. Pip helps an escaped convict from one of the "Hulks," the prison ships moored near the marshes, to make good his flight. Pip is sent to keep demented, but wealthy old Miss Havisham, company. She had been jilted on her wedding day, and, in despair, keeps her house as it was on that day so many years ago. While there, Pip meets Estella, whom Miss Havisham is raising. He falls in love with the haughty young girl, who treats him with contempt. When he grows older, Pip receives the news that an anonymous benefactor has given him money and desires him to go to London to become a "gentleman," which he proceeds to do, eventually rejecting Joe Gargery in the process. Sure that his benefactor is Miss Havisham, Pip pursues Estella, whom he thinks Miss Havisham has destined for him, but Estella spurns him. His benefactor turns out to be Abel Magwitch, the convict he helped, who had escaped to Australia and made a fortune. Pip tries to help him escape from the country again, but they are caught and Magwitch is killed. The forgiving Joe Gargery nurses the desperately ill Pip, and he recovers. Pip knows he will never be with Estella, although he sees her one last time. That is the original ending, but in deference to some of his more sentimental, outraged readers, who wanted a happy ending, Dickens changed it so that they remain together: "...I saw no shadow of another parting from her."

In the scene above, which takes place before the return of Magwitch to England to see his "gentleman," Pip has returned to his Kentish town, and is visiting Miss Havisham and Estella, who is about to marry the odious Bentley Drummle.

Great Expectations is concerned with guilt and with snobbery, the guilt and snobbery of its hero and first-person narrator Pip, and the guilt and snobbery of the society that Dickens describes and evaluates. The novel is also concerned with the nature and psychology of love and with suffering through unrequited love. Pip's experience of love leads him from pessimism to disillusionment, and consequently to an understanding of himself. Yet, while he is in the grip of his fatal love for Estella, who has made it honestly clear to him that she does not and cannot love him, he feels powerless. As he says earlier in the book, in Chapter XXIX:

> ...Once for all; I knew to my sorrow, often and often, if not always, that I loved her against reason, against promise, against peace, against hope, against happiness, against all discouragement that could be. Once for all; I loved her none the less because I knew it; and it had no more influence in restraining me, than if I had devoutly believed her to be human perfection.

In practicing this brief passage try a technical experiment: Stress the nouns after "against" (that would be my final choice for an actual reading). Then try stressing the preposition "against," and not the nouns, every time it occurs. See what the results mean to you.

I cannot repeat enough that, as usual, you must personalize the material. Substitution of some real love or analogous emotional situation will empower you to make this material real, passionate, and moving. You must rip your heart asunder. The listener won't know what is passing through your mind, or whom you are thinking of, so you remain safe, but you must still tear yourself apart. Of course this does not mean you should "tear a passion to tatters"; you must remain not only within the emotional bounds set by the text, but also within the bounds of the level set by the sound engineer. That is why recording can be such hard work. As when performing a play on stage, you must be involved both internally and externally at the same time, aware of the exigencies of the external, while still being inside your performance.

There are a number of clues in the main text as to how to approach this material: Pip's "trembling voice," which he tries to control; Estella's "very calm" and cold manner of speaking; Pip's reply to Estella in "a miserable manner"; and the way in which Estella lays "stress upon the words." These hints are so important, and you must follow all of them. They inform the rhythm and dynamic and the changes of beats in the scene. Convey the contrast between the attitudes of Pip and Estella, his passion and her coldness, which are the heart of the scene, vocally by internally adopting the attitudes of the characters as you read—no mean feat, since you have constantly to go back and forth between the two.

"Trying to control my trembling voice" is an excellent stage direction: Pip wants to communicate his love (his immediate objective; his overall or superobjective is to have his love accepted and to be happy); the obstacle is his nervousness, as shown in his "trembling voice," which he has to try to control (his action).

Chances are that if you record *Great Expectations* you will not be doing it with someone else playing Estella, so you will have to address Pip's intimate remarks to the microphone. This is an instance where you must make love to the microphone, and act "as if" you were talking to Estella, and she to you, when she speaks. In other words, you must bring to the scene a real sense of intimacy and privacy, as you would if you were doing this scene in the theater or in front of a camera.

David Lean's 1946 film of this book is a masterpiece. It can be helpful to see what other interpreters have done with the same material, and seeing the marshes and Miss Havisham's rooms can give you a feeling for Dickens's descriptions of them. You will find another excerpt from *Great Expectations* on page 199.

Two excerpts from Stephanie Cowell's *The Players: A Novel of the Young Shakespeare* (1997), "The Lovers"

Watching her across the room, William felt his body begin to ache from the length of wanting her and his repressed fury. Madness to have come! Should he not this evening depart quietly and leave her alone with this dear cruel Earl who stood apart, slowly unbuttoning the embroidered doublet, his stomach slightly thrust forward in weariness, and drinking the last of someone's wine? As the player sat on the window seat he saw the two of them draw together, the young man bending to kiss the Italian girl, his fingers searching her bodice for the nipple of her breast. He sat in a daze of sorrow and disillusionment until he looked away, stood suddenly, and made to go.

Within seconds she was standing beside him, having taken his hands.

"Will," she said eagerly, "come up! Come up with us"

Compressing his lips, he shook his head, but still she tugged at his hand. "Come!" she said. "I love you. I want you to…" She came into focus with her sweet, childish smile, and he reached up to touch her hair, which was half unpinned, and then the exposed right nipple. It seemed to call to him intimately, and he claimed it as his.

"Madness," he muttered, but let himself be pulled. "What are you doing, sweet?…Wait, I can but stand…well, then, have your way." He gazed at Southampton, who had stripped off his doublet and stood with shirt unlaced…

• • •

The farthingale creaked slightly as he let it drop upon the Turkish rug and helped her step from its center. Next their fingers moved to unfasten the satin corset which had bitten into her flesh over her plain linen shift. Barefoot, she shook out her hair so that it tumbled down past her thighs and then held out her arms, first to one man and then the other, with a sweet, childish smile on her face. She had never looked so contented and so sweet.

With one sweep, William lifted her and carried her to the bed. Even as he kissed and bit her he kept one hand to loosen his doublet buttons and untruss his breeches. They too dropped to the floor. He knew nothing but his desire, though he had somehow partially drawn the bed hangings. "Stay off!" he shouted, his voice unclear in the direction he felt the Earl stood. Again and again his body thrust into hers, and the bed ropes creaked and pulled. Feathers floated up, the room smelled of warm candles and the moisture between her legs.

Someone was shouting and he knew it to be himself. The cries came from a place so deep in him that he had never known it before, and he thrust and thrust inside her until he had spent himself entirely. He rolled from her to the side with his arm over his eyes and heard the bed creak, and her sigh and the murmurs of his friend, whose boyish grunts and rough bawdy language seemed an echo of his own. Jealousy rose up, and a violence which frightened him, for he had always thought himself a gentle man...

NOTES, COMMENTS AND HINTS

There has always been a mystery connected with the identity of Mr. W. H., to whom William Shakespeare (1564–1616), the Bard of Stratford-Upon-Avon, dedicated his Sonnets (published in 1609), as there has been over the identity of the Dark Lady mentioned in them. Of the many possible solutions, Stephanie Cowell has chosen one with which to fashion an exquisite love story, in which the young Shakespeare learns about the pain and the ecstasy of love. If "W. H." becomes "H. W.," we have Henry Wriothesley, the Earl of Southampton (1573–1674), Shakespeare's patron. Emilia Bassano (1570–1674), Ms. Cowell's choice for the Dark Lady of the Sonnets, was a musician, and the daughter of an English mother and an Italian Jewish father. She and Shakespeare knew each other well, and it is said that he may have based the character of the seductive Cleopatra on her. The homoerotic element in the Sonnets has often been remarked, but nothing is known of Shakespeare's actual sexual life or proclivities. Speculation as to the identity of the young man and the Dark Lady of the Sonnets includes the possibility that they may have been simply fictitious inventions of the author. For more information and for background see A.L. Rowse's *Shakespeare the Man* (St. Martin's Press, revised edition, 1989).

A contemporary writer of great sensitivity and delicacy, Ms. Cowell has written moving, involving descriptions of love, and of lovemaking. Evocative, fragile and explicit all at the same time, her descriptions preserve the dignity and beauty of sexuality, and show an admirably respectful tenderness for it and for the characters. Tender, passionate, sensual and fun, this scene is exquisite in its sensibilities.

To read it aloud, substitute not only your own experiences of love, but think also of how it feels to be in a darkened, candle-lit room with people whispering in it, slightly drowsy, slightly drunken, perhaps. As an exercise useful for sense memory, if you have never been in a room lit entirely by candles, give yourself the experience. It will be useful for imparting a tenderness to the voice, and it should also beget a quietness of tone which will allow the listener into the scene, not in a prurient way, but with the respect and dignity the author has shown for the situation and for the characters. This scene is as much about the emotions of love as it is about their sexual fulfillment. Personalize the underlying emotions as you read these scenes aloud. You must, as with all love scenes, speak as privately as you can into the microphone, "as if" you were in bed talking intimately with your beloved. Imagine that you are alone with the other person or persons in the scene, and that there is nobody else around to hear you. And it is quite clear that you could never read such a scene convincingly if you have had no experience of love, so, I repeat, as always, use substitutions of analogous situations drawn from your own life to help you understand the feelings and the situation and circumstances in the scene. The audience won't know what your substitutions are, but they will have a sense of reality, which they would not have otherwise.

Descriptions

Descriptions of people, of domestic, artificial or natural scenes, and of natural phenomena, such as rainstorms and sunsets, abound in nearly every work of fiction. In the following examples we have, first, a satirical, humorous description, which must be read straight, but with a sense in the back of your mind that what you are reading is terribly funny. This is followed by selections illustrating descriptions of nature, which are similar to setting the opening scene of a book. Whatever the nature of the description, you have to make the reader feel and see the scene you are describing. Added to that necessity is the concomitant need to make clear the underlying, subtextual attitudes of the person describing the scene, which can range from bleak and forbidding to happy and inspiring. You want the listener to experience the scene in the way the character, whether participant or third-person narrator, experiences it.

Elsewhere in this book you have already encountered more descriptive passages, among them George Eliot's *Daniel Deronda* on page 159; Thomas Hardy's *The Woodlanders* on page 177; and Washington Irving's *Rip van Winkle* on page 176.

From Charles Dickens's *Our Mutual Friend* (1865), two excerpts from Chapter II: "The Man from Somewhere."

Mr. and Mrs. Veneering were bran-new people in a bran-new house in a bran-new quarter of London. Everything about the Veneerings was spick and span new. All their furniture was new, all their friends were new, all their servants were new, their plate was new, their carriage was new, their harness was new, their horses were new, their pictures were new, they themselves were new, they were as newly married as was lawfully compatible with their having a bran-new baby, and if they had set up a great-grandfather, he would have come home in matting from the Pantechnicon, without a scratch upon him, French polished to the crown of his head.

• • •

The great looking-glass above the sideboard reflects the table and the company. Reflects the new Veneering crest, in gold and eke in silver, frosted and also thawed, a camel of all work. The Heralds' College found out a crusading ancestor for Veneering who bore a camel on his shield (or might have done if he had thought of it), and a caravan of camels take charge of the fruits and flowers and candles, and knelt down to be loaded with the salt. Reflects Veneering: forty, wavy-haired, dark, tending to corpulence, sly, mysterious, filmy—a kind of sufficiently well-looking veiled prophet, not prophesying. Reflects Mrs. Veneering: fair, aquiline-nosed and fingered, not so much light hair as she might have, gorgeous in raiment and jewels, enthusiastic, propitiatory, conscious that the corner of her husband's veil is over herself. Reflects Podsnap: prosperously feeding, two little wiry wings, one on either side of his else bald head, looking as like his hairbrushes as his hair, dissolving view of red beads on his forehead, large allowance of crumpled shirt collar up behind. Reflects Mrs. Podsnap: a fine woman for Professor Owen, quantity of bone, neck and nostrils like a rocking-horse, hard features, majestic head-dress in which Podsnap has hung golden offerings.

NOTES, COMMENTS AND HINTS

This excerpt evokes first an entire household, and then some of the individuals in it and their guests at a grand, formal dinner party. Your listeners should *see* the looking-glass, the phony heraldic crest, the groaning sideboard, and the heavy, constrictive, massive, ornate, overdone environment in which the people exist, encrusted with jewels and weighted down with velvets. Think of something monolithic and ponderous as you prepare this text. To use a technique developed by Michael Chekhov, imagine that you have heavy weights on your shoulders, and that you are slowly sinking into the floor.

The Veneerings, whose name indicates their superficial character and behavior—everything in their home and lives is meant for show, and there is little beneath the glossy surface—are the epitome of nouveau riche, parvenu, *arriviste* capitalists, immensely wealthy, immensely self-contained and self-sufficient. The Podsnaps are also enormously rich members of high society, and Mr. Podsnap, pompous and self-satisfied, is rigorous in his habits, leading his life by the clock.

Professor Owen was a well-known phrenologist. Developed by Francis Joseph Gall around 1800, phrenology, greatly believed in during much of the nineteenth century, was the pseudo-science of determining a person's character or psychology or mental characteristics by studying the bumps on his or her forehead and skull, the shape of the skull, etc. Although for us today it is hard to believe that anyone of sense could take such quackery seriously, we must remember that phrenology was devised before modern scientific psychology, and seemed to provide logical answers to psychological questions.

The repetition of the word "bran-new" gives us an obvious clue as to how to read the opening material. You might stress it for ironic effect every time it occurs. Repeated words or kinds or words can determine how you read a description just as much as how you read an action scene.

From Charles Dickens's *Great Expectations* (1860–61), Chapter I

Ours was the marsh country, down by the river, within, as the river wound, twenty miles from the sea. My first most vivid and broad impression of the identity of things, seems to me to have been gained on a memorable raw afternoon towards evening. At such a time I found out for certain, that this bleak place overgrown with nettles was the churchyard; and that Philip Pirrip, late of this parish, and also Georgiana wife of the above, were dead and buried; and that Alexander, Bartholomew, Abraham, Tobias and Roger, infant children of the aforesaid, were also dead and buried; and that the dark flat wilderness beyond the churchyard, intersected with dykes and mounds and gates, with scattered cattle feeding on it, was the marshes; and that the low leaden line beyond, was the river; and that the distant savage lair from which the wind was rushing, was the sea; and that the small bundle of shivers growing afraid of it all and beginning to cry, was Pip.

NOTES, COMMENTS AND HINTS

Pip, the first-person narrator, who speaks of himself in this paragraph in the third person, tells us his experience from a child's point of view. This description, by the way, is beautifully realized visually in David Lean's 1946 film.

When reading descriptions of places, think in terms of colors; in this case shades of dull gray; Dickens gives you the word "leaden." The gray sea reflects the gray clouds. You might also remember paintings that such descriptions remind you of, if you need to go further in visualizing the scene. In this case I think of some of Rembrandt's landscapes, with lonely windmills on isolated rises of land.

The miserable, penetrating wind blows off the North Sea and chills Pip to the bone. To help you feel the shivers and the cold remember a raw winter day with the wind blowing, and how uncomfortable the frigid blasts made you.

For another excerpt from and more information about this book see page 192.

Two excerpts from Stephanie Cowell's *The Physician of London: A Novel* (1995), "One: The Young Priest"

Slightly above St. Paul's near the stone entrance of the city called Cripplegate, in the year of Our Lord 1617, was a half-timbered house. It lay below the fields and farmlands which encircled the city in the parish of St. Mary Aldermanbury, whose streets wound down to the river Thames.

London at that time was already an ancient, crowded town of one hundred and fifty thousand people. Daily from the country came men in search of work: they found dwellings in the twisting lanes hung with washing, scattered with flowers, and threaded with leaking sewage until the very city walls, which had first been raised by the Romans, seemed to want to thrust into the fields and pastures beyond for want of space. In this particular fragment of the city and in this particular house lived a physician called Nicholas Cooke. He was also priest, but that so recent that if anyone called him parson he could not help but look about to see if it were addressed to anyone other than himself.

• • •

FROM "TWO: BY THE THAMES IN WINTER"

Nicholas Cooke was at that time in his thirty-seventh year a well-built, fine-looking and tender man somewhere above six feet who moved lightly, shoulders slightly rounded, and with a sense of fierce shyness, as if he would cover his face with his arm if looked at too deeply. He wore a short beard, which he trimmed occasionally, and his thick brown hair, which curled slightly some inches below his ears, was tinged with grey. His eyes were large and brown. He was regarded by the older physicians of the city as rash and presumptuous, for though he was but three years a doctor, he would not keep his peculiar ideas to himself. Still, they could not help but admit he was strangely wise.

NOTES, COMMENTS AND HINTS

These excerpts are from the second of a trilogy of historical novels about the life of Nicholas Cooke, actor, soldier, physician and priest. He is such a real character that it is difficult to believe he did not actually exist. Ms. Cowell brings the London of the Elizabethan era in all its riotousness, its charged atmosphere, its colorful theater, and its bustling, venturesome people, vividly to life. Stephanie Cowell's gift for writing poetic prose is extraordinary. By her selection of images she takes the reader into the world she portrays so deftly, so meticulously, so accurately, that we seem to smell the smells in the London streets and to experience the extremes of temperature before the era of central heating and air conditioning. Your reading should make the listener feel all that, by emphasizing such words as "twisting lanes" and "leaking sewage," and by clearly contrasting the town and the countryside with your voice, as Ms. Cowell does with her writing.

In the very first sentence, with its slightly antiquated phrase "in the year of Our Lord," a phrase which few people would use nowadays, we are taken back several centuries, to an era when such a phrase was in common use. And as we continue, simply with the use of the word "parish," we are taken into a world where religion pervaded most people's lives. In Britain the word is still widely used, and there are still "parish councils" in some places, and religious Americans also belong to parishes, but the word still has an old-fashioned feeling to it.

At the opening of Chapter Two we have a description of Nicholas Cooke that sets him vividly before us. We seem to see those shy brown eyes, that handsome face, and to feel an attitude of compassion and tenderness. Read this passage simply, so as to allow the listener to experience what you would experience if you were reading it silently for yourself. Substitute someone you find attractive for Cooke, to give the reading of the description reality. Or you might look for inspiration at an Elizabethan miniature, one by Nicholas

Hilliard (1537–1619), for instance. Look also at paintings by Pieter Brueghel the Elder (1520?–1569) of Flemish peasants and the Flemish countryside, not so different from the landscape of Elizabethan England. Look at reproductions of stained-glass windows and photographs of English cathedrals, and at period engravings of scenes. The art of any historical period can help to give you an immediate feeling for the way life was lived back then.

The Character's Voice: Creating a Character Vocally

William Hazlitt, in his book *Characters of Shakespear's Plays* (1817), wrote, "Hamlet is a name: his speeches and sayings but the idle coinage of the poet's brain. What then, are they not real? They are as real as our own thoughts. Their reality is in the reader's mind. It is we who are Hamlet." And it is you as a recording artist who must bring the reality of a character's existence to vocal life.

When we were discussing my recording of Sherlock Holmes analyzing a case, Gordon Gould said to me, "You have to hear him think." Gordon played Sherlock Holmes in radio drama and recorded more than five hundred Talking Books for the American Foundation for the Blind. And he is exactly right: The listener has to hear the characters' actions, attitudes and intentions—the subtext—which you convey by using the intonation patterns we have learned unconsciously as children to associate with particular meanings. And do make strong choices! The listener should hear you shaking with rage, quaking with fear, trembling with anticipation, restraining your tears or your laughter, bubbling over with joy and merriment or collapsing into the depths of despair.

To explain subtext further: The words "How are you?" have an apparent simple meaning. Those words could be loving, angry, joyous, tender, indifferent, casual, serious, sarcastic, or any number of other things. They could be whispered or shouted, or simply spoken. They could be spoken to one's self. Any of the three words could be stressed, and that would change part of their subtextual meaning. But that meaning depends on who is saying them, and to whom. It depends on the relationship of the people talking, and all the circumstances in which those words are said. See Subtext: an Exercise in Chapter Four on page 86.

As I said earlier, how much you vary your voice depends partly on how many characters you have to portray, and how good your memory of them is. You may wish to change your voice only slightly. Bear in mind that as you play the characters' attitudes, attributes (male or female, old or young, weak or strong, authoritarian or submissive, etc.), and actions, your voice will automatically change anyway.

You may wish to develop a sort of "sound signature" for a character, that is, an instantly recognizable way of expressing him or herself that the character uses. For instance, when I was recording Sir Arthur Conan Doyle's *The Complete Sherlock Holmes,* I developed a distinctive way for Holmes to say "No" and "Yes": I prolonged the "n" and the "y" very slightly before finishing the word. "No" was usually said with a slight downward intonation. Actually, I was inspired by Michael Kitchen's performance as Detective Foyle in the BBC television series *Foyle's War* (2002) by Anthony Horowitz. He did just what I have described (he didn't do it all the time, of course; nor did I), and I am sure it was a completely spontaneous, organic response on his part, a result of his work on the character. For Holmes I frequently made that "No" more contemptuous than Michael Kitchen's "No," which was usually more a reflective response. I thought, too, of Dr. Watson telling us about Holmes's coldness and irony, reflected in his somewhat high-pitched voice (not to be made too high, or outlandish in any way). I certainly did not wish to imitate anyone else's performance of either Holmes (Basil Rathbone's peerless, distinctive characterization and unique, recognizable voice comes instantly to mind), or Watson, even if I had been capable of doing so; such imitations would have been impossible to sustain over many hundreds of pages. A fairly neutral, listenable voice is required for the narration of a text, even when the narrator is a character.

The important question to address is: How does the voice play the action and attitude?

Here is a simple example of a direct, physical action: A character shouts, so the action is "to shout," but the character's attitude may be anything: happy, sad, pleading, warning. This attitude of the character, and the reasons for shouting, as well as the person to or at whom the character is shouting, will determine what you do vocally, as will the actual physical circumstances in which the shouting takes place. If the character is shouting from a distance, for instance, you may lean back from the microphone and imagine that you are shouting from across a mountain gorge, cup your hands over your mouth, and shout, but in a voice that will not take you over the acceptable level set by the sound engineer. If you go over that level you will only have to record the line again anyway. To summarize, ask yourself the following questions: Why is the character shouting, under what physical and emotional circumstances, and to whom? And see the section on "Paralinguistics" on page 24.

From Edgar Allan Poe's *The Cask of Amontillado* (1846)

A succession of loud and shrill screams, bursting suddenly from the throat of the chained form, seemed to thrust me violently back. For a brief moment I hesitated—I trembled. Unsheathing my rapier, I began to grope with it about the recess; but the thought of an instant reassured me. I placed my hand upon the solid fabric of the catacombs, and felt satisfied. I reapproached the wall. I replied to the yells of him who clamored. I re-echoed—I aided—I surpassed them in volume and in strength. I did this, and the clamorer grew still.

It was now midnight, and my task was drawing to a close. I had completed the eighth, the ninth, and the tenth tier. I had finished a portion of the last and the eleventh; there remained but a single stone to be fitted and plastered in. I struggled with its weight; I placed it partially in its destined position. But now there came from out the niche a low laugh that erected the hairs upon my head. It was succeeded by a sad voice, which I had difficulty in recognizing as that of the noble Fortunato. The voice said—

"Ha! ha! ha!—he! he!—a very good joke indeed—an excellent jest. We will have many a rich laugh about it at the palazzo—he! he! he!—over our wine—he! he! he!"

"The Amontillado!" I said.

"He! he! he!—he! he! he!—yes, the Amontillado. But is it not getting late? Will not they be awaiting us at the palazzo, the Lady Fortunato and the rest? Let us be gone."

"Yes," I said, "let us be gone."

"For the love of God, Montresor!"

"Yes," I said, "for the love of God!"

But to these words I hearkened in vain for a reply. I grew impatient. I called aloud:

"Fortunato!"

No answer. I called again:

"Fortunato!"

No answer still. I thrust a torch through the remaining aperture and let it fall within. There came forth in return only a jingling of the bells. My heart grew sick—on account of the dampness of the catacombs. I hastened to make an end of my labor. I forced the last stone into position; I plastered it up. Against the new masonry I re-erected the old rampart of bones. For the half of a century no mortal has disturbed them. *In pace requiescat!*

NOTES, COMMENTS AND HINTS

This story is very effective when read aloud, and can be horrifying for an audience, even when they are familiar with it. Poe gives you everything clearly and concisely: The rhythms (of the story, and of the two different characters), the pace; everything is there, like ripe fruit waiting to be plucked from the branch. Of course, I have begun this exercise near the end of the story. Poe builds his sinister tale all the way from the beginning to the terrifying climax at the end and I suggest you get a copy of the whole story to use for practice.

Our first-person narrator is the wealthy aristocrat Montresor, who begins his story by telling us: "The thousand injuries of Fortunato I had borne as I best could; but when he ventured upon insult, I vowed revenge." He is already old when he says that line, but his deep bitterness, and his remembered satisfaction at having accomplished his objective, can hardly be exaggerated. When you read it, talk to us simply nevertheless. The bitterness is subtext; it is internal, and its reality will be apparent without vocal pyrotechnics, such as a snarl or a delivery of the line through gritted teeth.

The story takes place in Venice, "during the supreme madness of the carnival season." On the pretext that he has come into possession of a rare cask of Amontillado sherry, Montresor, his almost manic glee suppressed until, near the end of the story, it is no longer necessary to suppress it, but full of ironic quips at the expense of his victim nonetheless, lures the pompous, contemptuous and drunken Fortunato, who fancies himself a connoisseur of rare vintages, to his death.

Your first task, if you don't know how to pronounce it, is to look up the word "amontillado" (pronounced "a: MO:N tee YAH doh, or thoh"), unless this has been done for you. After all, you have to say it enough. The well-known Latin phrase at the end ("Rest in peace!") should be pronounced using the medieval, or Church, system, which would have been the natural one to use in Italy at the time when the story was written: "in PA: cheh reh kwee ES ka:t."

The scene of Montresor echoing Fortunato's screams reminds me of the scene in which the psychopath echoes the yells of his prisoner in the movie *The Silence of the Lambs* (1991). Although the character is very different from Montresor, the aged aristocrat telling us this tale of his youth, it might be helpful for you to take a look at it. But find your own substitutions, whether from your own life or from another work of art.

Questions to ask yourself are: Who are these two characters? What are they like? What are their objectives and attitudes? What are the obstacles in the way of Montresor taking his revenge? How are the characters' attitudes reflected vocally? What are their actions, and how are they reflected vocally? How do you do the laughs at the end? How do you do the screams? One answer to that last question is that you do them organically, from the inside, by using as a substitution an incident from your own life where you were absolutely terrified, even if it were only by being startled by someone's unexpectedly entering a room. You said something like, "You scared me!" You may not have screamed, but you probably wanted to. Another answer is: Just scream! The sound engineer will tell you if it's too much.

For some more answers to those questions, listen to the spine-chilling recording of this story by Basil Rathbone; see the Bibliography. As Montresor he is positively thrilled and gleeful (but restrained; he doesn't overdo it), not merely satisfied, to be taking his revenge. His screams as Fortunato are real, and as terrifying as they are terrified. As Montresor, Rathbone shouts on "I replied to the yells of him who clamored. I re-echoed—I aided—I surpassed them in volume and in strength," then grows suddenly quiet on "I did this," and continues reading with a sense of satisfaction, which we can hear in his voice. And this is not a mere technical exercise in melodramatic delivery that you can simply imitate: It comes from a place deep inside Rathbone, as it must from you when you practice this text.

As Fortunato, for whom he does a different voice from Montresor's (a slightly deeper, slightly slurred drunken voice), he coughs and laughs at the same time on the last lines; Fortunato has been ill with a bad cold and a cough throughout the story, and his cold is aggravated by the damp of the catacombs. And Basil Rathbone doesn't seem to have worried at all about sound levels. He just read the story the way he wanted to. The reading seems completely organic and spontaneous, and Rathbone rings all the changes in the story. He makes you experience the flickering of the torches, and the damp and darkness of the catacombs into which Montresor has led the unsuspecting Fortunato to his doom. I started to write "into which *he* has led the unsuspecting Fortunato," because Rathbone is so real in his reading that he seems to have incarnated Montresor perfectly. The effect throughout is chilling, and I found myself laughing with satisfaction when it was over, because the story had been so well read. "Wonderful!" is what I said to myself.

Edgar Allan Poe (1809–1849) led a complicated, sometimes tortured life, and his vivid imagination spawned memorable grotesque and arabesque tales (some of them, perhaps induced by alcohol or drugs) that are still thrilling to read and that speak to our subconscious minds. He was erudite, read Latin and Greek, and studied ancient and modern languages. People were fascinated by his public readings of his most famous and popular poem, "The Raven." As a background to his stories you might visit the cottage in Fordham, New York, where he lived with his young, very ill wife, who died there. The cottage is now the Poe Museum in Poe Park in the Bronx. Its forbidding, gloomy atmosphere and lack of comfort are a terrible inspiration. If you are in New York City, take the "D" train to the Kingsbridge Road stop. The museum is just across the street from the subway entrance.

Here is an example of a different kind of action:

From Sir Arthur Conan Doyle's *The Hound of the Baskervilles* (1902), Chapter One.

...He now took the stick from my hands and examined it for a few minutes with his naked eyes. Then with an expression of interest he laid down his cigarette, and, carrying the cane to the window, he looked over it again with a convex lens.

"Interesting, though elementary," said he as he returned to his favorite corner of the settee. "There are certainly one or two indications upon the stick. It gives us the basis for several deductions."

"Has anything escaped me?" I asked with some self-importance. "I trust that there is nothing of consequence which I have overlooked?"

"I am afraid, my dear Watson, that most of your conclusions were erroneous. When I said that you stimulated me I meant, to be frank, that in noting your fallacies I was occasionally guided towards the truth. Not that you are entirely wrong in this instance. The man is certainly a country practitioner. And he walks a good deal."

"Then I was right."

"To that extent."

"But that was all."

"No, no, my dear Watson, not all—by no means all. I would suggest, for example, that a presentation to a doctor is more likely to come from a hospital than from a hunt, and that when the initials 'C.C.' are placed before that hospital, the words 'Charing Cross' very naturally suggest themselves."

"You may be right."

"The probability lies in that direction. And if we take this as a working hypothesis we have a fresh basis from which to start our construction of this unknown visitor."

"Well, then, supposing that 'C.C.H.' does stand for 'Charing Cross Hospital,' what further inferences may we draw?"

"Do none suggest themselves? You know my methods. Apply them!"

NOTES, COMMENTS AND HINTS

The first part of Holmes's dialogue shows that he is thinking as he moves to sit down. It should be read in a tone of slight thoughtfulness, the action being "to begin analyzing what he has seen; to make sense of what he has observed." In general the action in this scene is: "To analyze"; or "to try to make sense of."

When Holmes says "I am afraid, my dear Watson..." the rhythm and pace become slightly faster, as he begins to tell us his conclusions, in a slightly excited, or at least concentrated, manner. He may tease Watson, but he is not malicious—Watson himself describes Holmes's manner as "mischievous"—although Holmes is, despite his brilliance, somewhat insecure and rather tense and highly-strung on occasion, and certainly erratic and eccentric in his habits and attitudes. In other words, when reading Holmes's conclusions about the cane do not take a tone of voice which would imply that Watson is an idiot. And don't be at all nasty on the speech beginning "I am afraid, my dear Watson..." Just deliver the following lines in a matter-of-fact manner. "This is what I have deduced, and why." Remember, he has not yet met Dr. Mortimer, whose cane he is examining, and who will start him on his pursuit of the devious, malevolent villain in this well-known tale of intrigue and murder.

Holmes's voice should be slightly higher in general pitch than Watson's, which should be more neutral. I base this on descriptions by Watson of Holmes's voice, which should also have a bit of an edge to it, a slight touch of sharpness. Watson's description of Holmes's voice in *The Hound of the Baskervilles* is that his voice is "cold, incisive, ironical" (opening of Chapter 12). In the short story "The Adventure of the Cardboard Box" he tells us that the voice is high-pitched.

Watson's descriptions of Holmes and of his behavior when they first meet, and as they are getting to know each other when they begin sharing rooms in Baker Street, in *A Study in Scarlet* (1887), will tell you all you need to know to begin interpreting these characters.

Dr. Watson, our good-hearted, well meaning first-person narrator, is rather different in the stories from the many portrayals of him in film and on television. Nigel Bruce, wonderful in his own right in the old Basil Rathbone films, is not really the Dr. Watson of Conan Doyle. As we can see in the excerpt above, Watson may not have Holmes's quick grasp of the meaning of events or his deductive powers, but he is not bumbling. He is, rather, an erudite medical man and a former soldier with the courage and determination to act promptly in dangerous situations, and with quite a literary bent; after all, he has supposedly written the very engrossing stories we are reading. Dr. Watson is a quiet and rather calm man, not easily ruffled, a man of equanimity and balance. He has unbounded admiration for Holmes, on whom he is often a steadying influence, and he is sometimes slightly hurt by Holmes's occasional humorously sarcastic remarks. You should give Watson the emotional life he has, and become emotional when he does.

Holmes admires Watson, too, for all the qualities I just mentioned, and even envies him a bit, perhaps, for his ability to take life with a rational, balanced view. James Mason played Dr. Watson insightfully in *Murder by Decree* (1979), with Christopher Plummer as a forthright Sherlock Holmes. If you look at that film, you will see in James Mason's Dr. Watson a dignified, somewhat withdrawn, shy, conservative and retiring man, slightly hurt on occasion by Holmes's occasional sarcasm, but reliable and a loyal friend always.

I highly recommend the following Sherlock Holmes short stories for general practice. They all contain finely drawn, unique, sometimes eccentric characters, and are excellent practice for finding characters' unique voices, for action scenes and for dialogue, so much of which is simply written from paragraph to paragraph, from reply to reply, without even a "he said" or a "she said" to interrupt its flow, since we have learned who they are at the beginning of the conversation: "The Adventure of the Norwood Builder"; "The Adventure of the Priory School"; "The Adventure of Charles Augustus Milverton"; "The Adventure of the Dying Detective"; "The Adventure of the Devil's Foot." Sometimes reading these stories is very much like reading a play aloud, a play in which you get to act all the parts.

More excerpts from *The Hound of the Baskervilles* are on pages 182 and 211.

Attitudes Are Adjectives

In adopting the character's attitude, look for the adjectives that describe it. They will help you to enter into the character's psyche, and assume the character's mental attitudes and point of view, just as the author has. Bear in mind that whereas in acting on stage you play not attitudes (you have, or embody, attitudes), but only actions, which are always expressed as verbs, in acting with the voice alone, when nobody can see you, you have to keep the character's attitude in mind.

An adjective applied to a character is a description not only of the character's attitudes and feelings, but also sometimes of actions to be played vocally, as when, for instance, a character can be described as excited. See "Actions Are Verbs" on page 221.

Attitudes may also give you clues as to rhythm and pace, besides providing clues as to how a character might speak. Also, the attitude in a character's dialogue is intimately linked to the intentions of that character, which depend on what the character wants (the objective), and how the character expresses the want (the vocal action).

More than one adjective may apply to any character, even at a given moment, and be generally descriptive of the character, or apply only to specific moments in the story. Sometimes the author gives the adjectives to you, thus facilitating your task. Sometimes you will have to come up with them yourself, based on your character analysis. Try to find strong adjectives that are suggestive and emotionally loaded, as in the illustrative texts in this section. A character may be "ecstatic" or "blissful," rather than simply "happy";

"despondent" or "upset," rather than merely "sad." You might want to find the full stories from which the texts below are excerpted, and use them for practice. For a marvelous, abundant store of adjectives and verbs refer to *Bartlett's Roget's Thesaurus* (Little, Brown and Company, 1996), an invaluable book, and the best thesaurus available, in my opinion.

1. Petulant, impatient (Culverton Smith)

From Sir Arthur Conan Doyle's
The Adventure of the Dying Detective

"Yes, Mr. Culverton Smith is in. Dr. Watson! Very good, sir, I will take up your card."

My humble name and title did not appear to impress Mr. Culverton Smith. Through the half-open door I heard a high, petulant, penetrating voice.

"Who is this person? What does he want? Dear me, Staples, how often have I said that I am not to be disturbed in my hours of study?"

NOTES, COMMENTS AND HINTS

When it comes to Mr. Culverton Smith, there are obviously lots of clues here, even in this very brief selection (and as always, of course, you must read the whole story in order to know the character and make choices), as to how to develop a voice for the character, and how to read this character's dialogue. And even in this short selection you are playing three characters, each one in a different paragraph! So there should be no problem with variety, even if you do a fairly neutral reading, as opposed to really acting each character vocally.

Culverton Smith's voice should have a sharp edge to it, and be perhaps slightly high in pitch. His diction is too precise, with strong, clipped consonants, overly articulated. The adjective "petulant," which describes his generally annoyed, impatient manner, as well as his voice, tells you exactly how to read Culverton Smith's lines. The action he plays can be described as "getting rid of his unwanted visitor."

Watson has, as usual, a neutral voice, but you should still play his intentions and his actions, which will give you all the vocal and subtextual variety you need. The butler could perhaps a slight working-class touch to his accent, since he is not the butler in one of the great stately mansions; he is working for a crook.

Staples the butler's action is "to serve," and his attitude can be described as "accommodating," while Dr. Watson's action is "waiting to be received," and his attitude as "hopeful," "determined" to succeed in his quest, and a bit "apprehensive," even "anxious," because Culverton Smith is the only man who can save Sherlock Holmes from dying of the dreadful disease on which Smith is the greatest expert. But don't play Watson's anxiety vocally so much as his determination (which is informed by his anxiety), because the next part of the story shows him barging into Culverton Smith's consulting room despite Smith's refusal to see him.

2. Truculent, litigious, irascible, belligerent (Frankland)

From Sir Arthur Conan Doyle's *The Hound of the Baskervilles*

To set the scene: Dr. Watson has gone to the village of Coombe Tracy, and is returning to Baskerville Hall when he encounters a local character, Mr. Frankland, who invites him into his home for a drink. Watson reluctantly accepts, as he doesn't particularly care for Frankland, who is the first person to speak in this excerpt.

"It is a great day for me, sir—one of the red-letter days of my life," he cried with many chuckles. "I have brought off a double event. I mean to teach them in these parts that law is law, and that there is a man here who does not fear to invoke it. I have established a right of way through the centre of old Middleton's park, slap across it, sir, within a hundred yards of his own front door. What do you think of that? We'll teach these magnates that they cannot ride roughshod over the rights of the commoners, confound them! And I've closed the wood where the Fernworthy folk used to picnic. These infernal people seem to think that there are no rights of property, and that they can swarm where they like with their papers and their bottles. Both cases decided, Dr. Watson, and both in my favour. I haven't had such a day since I had Sir John Morland for trespass because he shot in his own warren."

"How on earth did you do that?"

"Look it up in the books, sir. It will repay reading—Frankland v. Morland, Court of Queen's Bench. It cost me £200, but I got my verdict."

"Did it do you any good?"

"None, sir, none. I am proud to say that I had no interest in the matter. I act entirely from a sense of public duty..."

NOTES, COMMENTS AND HINTS

The rhythm and pace of the dialogue, punctuated as it is with mild oaths practically play themselves. Frankland "cried, with many chuckles"—a perfect clue as to how to read the lines. And punctuate vocally such phrases as "confound them!"

He is bluff and hearty as well as truculent. His character suggests that he has a deep, perhaps somewhat gruff voice. Use all the adjectives (attitudes) to inform the reading. Think of the words "to ride roughshod over someone." That is what Frankland does to everyone. On the line "Look it up in the books, sir" he challenges Dr. Watson a bit churlishly. "But I got my verdict" is triumphant. Don't change your attitude on "None, sir, none" to a rueful one. Keep that belligerent tone. After all, Frankland tells us immediately how proud he is. And your listeners will laugh.

3. Impolite, rude, sneering, cantankerous, ornery, persnickety, rambunctious (March Hare; Mad Hatter); indignant, adventurous, fun-loving (Alice); sleepy (Dormouse)

From Lewis Carroll's *Alice's Adventures in Wonderland* (1865), Chapter VII: "A Mad Tea-Party"

"Have some wine," the March Hare said in an encouraging tone.

Alice looked all round the table, but there was nothing on it but tea. "I don't see any wine," she remarked.

"There isn't any," said the March Hare.

"Then it wasn't very civil of you to offer it," said Alice angrily.

"It wasn't very civil of you to sit down without being invited," said the March Hare.

"I didn't know it was *your* table," said Alice; "it's laid for a great many more than three."

"Your hair wants cutting," said the Hatter. He had been looking at Alice for some time with great curiosity, and this was his first speech.

"You should learn not to make personal remarks," Alice said with some severity; "it's very rude."

The Hatter opened his eyes very wide on hearing this; but all he *said* was, "Why is a raven like a writing-desk?"

NOTES, COMMENTS AND HINTS

One of the answers to the riddle is "Because Poe wrote on both." I am indebted for that answer to *The Annotated Alice*, containing both the Alice books, with an Introduction and Notes by Martin Gardner (Clarkson N. Potter, Inc., 1960). W. W. Norton published a revised version, called *The Annotated Alice: The Definitive Edition* in 1999. Were you to record the Alice books, you would find it useful to consult Gardner's thoroughly researched editions.

Use the entire chapter in the book for practice. Read this scene very seriously, and its hilarious ridiculousness will be apparent. The March Hare and the Mad Hatter are both deadly serious, and they think nothing of being extremely rude with one another and with Alice, who is a bit nonplussed. As the March Hare you can be really nasty and cutting to Alice, for instance on his line "Then you should say what you mean." The end of the line could be spoken on a rising tone. a possibility for this character would be a sneering tone, with perhaps a slightly nasal voice—direct the air to the center of the upper palate while keeping the nasal passage the back of the throat open. Try curling your lip up and turning down the corners of your mouth (or only do one of those things) when reading his lines and you almost can't help sneering. Be cold and distant as well as ornery. The March Hare's very first line, said in "an encouraging tone," should be false and phony.

The Mad Hatter is kinder, and his "personal remark" about Alice's hair needing cutting is more in the nature of an observation than an insult. He should be less sarcastic, and in his own world to some extent, a world from which he returns to ours from time to time to seek answers to his questions, such as the one about the raven and the writing-desk.. Try reading his lines "as if" you were looking into the distance. He might have a slight suggestion of one of the London accents, and his general nervousness might raise his a voice to a medium high pitch.

For the Dormouse's line, you might try opening your mouth wide, almost as if you were yawning. That should give you a kind of breathy voice, perfect for this character, who seems always about to yawn.

Read Alice with a neutral voice, but play her actions and attitudes, of course. Her indignation and her enthusiasm should both come through the microphone and onto the recording.

Charles Lutwidge Dodgson, known as Lewis Carroll (1832–1898), was a noted logician and a mathematics lecturer at Christ Church, Oxford University. He befriended Christ Church's Dean Liddell's family, one of whom, Alice, was the inspiration for the Alice books. She asked him one day to write down the wonderful stories he told her and the other children. For background, see the sweetly evocative film with its dark, Freudian undertones, *DreamChild* (1985), with Ian Holm as Dodgson and Coral Browne as the aged Alice Liddell, who goes to New York to attend a reception in her honor.

4. Formidable, imposing, impressive, challenging (Queen of Hearts); timid, hesitant, conciliatory (King of Hearts)

From Lewis Carroll's *Alice's Adventures in Wonderland* (1865), Chapter VIII: "The Queen's Croquet-Ground"

"And who are *these*?" said the Queen, pointing to the three gardeners who were lying round the rose-tree; for, you see, as they were lying on their faces, and the pattern on their backs was the same as the rest of the pack, she could not tell whether they were gardeners, or soldiers, or courtiers, or three of her own children.

"How should I know?" said Alice, surprised at her own courage. "It's no business of *mine*."

The Queen turned crimson with fury, and, after glaring at her for a moment like a wild beast, screamed "Off with her head! Off with—"

"Nonsense!" said Alice, very loudly and decidedly, and the Queen was silent.

The King laid his hand upon her arm, and timidly said "Consider, my dear: she is only a child!"

The Queen turned angrily away from him, and said to the Knave "Turn them over!"

The Knave did so, very carefully, with one foot.

"Get up!" said the Queen, in a shrill, loud voice, and the three gardeners instantly jumped up, and began bowing to the King, the Queen, the royal children, and everybody else.

"Leave off that!" screamed the Queen. "You make me giddy." And then, turning to the rose-tree, she went on, "What *have* you been doing here?"

"May it please your Majesty," said Two, in a very humble tone, going down on one knee as he spoke, "we were trying—"

"I see!" said the Queen, who had meanwhile been examining the roses. "Off with their heads!" and the procession moved on, three of the soldiers remaining behind to execute the unfortunate gardeners, who ran to Alice for protection.

NOTES, COMMENTS AND HINTS

"In a shrill loud voice" is a perfect hint for the character of the Queen of Hearts. Everybody is intimidated by her—a kind of nightmare Queen Victoria, accompanied by her timid Prince Albert husband, the King of Hearts, whose temperament changes later in the book when he conducts the trial against the Knave of Hearts; see page 237.

Be careful of actually screaming into the microphone. Instead, you might snarl and almost spit out the Queen's furious lines through closed teeth. Hers is a red-hot anger, and you should find your eyes almost starting from your head as you read her lines. If you do, you will know you are on the right track. Have the mental intention of shouting, that is, think: "shouting" without actually doing so, and your voice will communicate "as if" you actually were shouting.

Substitute for the Queen's "crimson fury" at the gardeners (and at everybody around her) something in your life that made you livid with anger. But try delivering the Queen's last "Off with their heads" very firmly, and at the same time with a lofty, superior air, as if you (as the Queen) are already beyond the situation and moving on to other things.

For the King, substitute your reaction to someone who was furious with you, and whom you wanted to placate. Use a timid delivery, and either a slightly high-pitched voice, or its opposite: a deep, almost growling voice, as if he is afraid to be heard and almost swallows his words.

The gardeners who have painted the white roses red to avoid the Queen's wrath should be absolutely trembling with terror. Only Alice maintains her equilibrium and sense of outrage at the Queen's behavior. This is a child's dream of confronting her parents.

5. Moribund, feverish, desperate, despairing, miserable, wretched (Goriot)

From Honoré de Balzac's *La Comédie humaine* (*The Human Comedy*): *Le père Goriot* (*Old Goriot*) (1835), 4: "La mort du père" ("The Father's Death"); my translation.

To set the scene: Old Goriot is on his deathbed. His doctor, Bianchon (a recurring character in the monumental series of novels and short stories Balzac called The Human Comedy—meant to parallel Dante's title, The Divine Comedy) says: "The man doesn't have two days to live, perhaps not even six hours."

"Ah! If I were rich, if I had kept my fortune, if I hadn't given it to them, they would be here, they would cover my cheeks with kisses! I would live in a town house, I would have beautiful rooms, servants, a fireplace all for myself; and they would be in tears, with their husbands, their children. I would have all that. But, nothing! Money gives you everything, even daughters. Oh! my money, where is it? If I had a treasure to leave, they would dress my wounds, they would care for me; I would hear them, I would see them. Ah! my dear child, my only child, I prefer my abandonment and my misery. At least when an unfortunate person is loved, he is quite sure he is loved. No, I wish I were rich; then I would see them. My goodness, who knows? They both have hearts of stone. I loved them too much for them to have returned my love. A father must be always rich; he must hold his daughters by a bridle, like unruly horses. And I was on my knees before them. The wretches! This is the worthy culmination of their behavior towards me for the last ten years! If you knew how they took care of my every little want when they were first married! (Oh! I suffer a cruel martyrdom!) . . ."

NOTES, COMMENTS AND HINTS

One of the two great themes in Balzac's books is the corroding, corrupting influence of money on individuals and on society as a whole. The other great theme—related to the first, in Balzac's mind—is love in all its forms and all its aspects. Uniting the two themes, *Le père Goriot*, literally *The Father Goriot*, is the story of a man who sacrifices everything for the two daughters he loves, only to be abandoned by them, even on his deathbed, after they marry wealthy and influential men.

"Ah! my dear child, my only child" is addressed to Eugène de Rastignac (pronounced "ö ZHEN də ra: sti NYA:K"), who is like a son to the dying man. Rastignac is a young lawyer from the provinces—in later novels in the series he is the Minister of Justice—recently arrived in Paris, and staying at the same pension as Goriot. (The word "pension" here is pronounced in the French manner, "pa:*N* SYO*N*," meaning a boardinghouse; the English word is pronounced "PEN shən" when it means a retiree's income.) He is still an innocent in the ways of the world, is very sympathetic to the old man, and takes care of him, but the death of the abandoned father opens his eyes to the callousness of people and the crassness of their motivations.

Use a plaintive tone for this desperate, despairing, rambling and sometimes incoherent monologue, which varies from energetic to feeble. Since it goes on for about ten pages in much the same vein, you have to discover the variety—the changes of "beat"—within it. You may wish to get the novel, and use the entire monologue for practice.

From my experience in recording *Le père Goriot*, I can tell you that the deathbed monologue is not easy to read, partly because it is so long—a bit like a long aria sung by the dying heroine or hero in an opera—but it is a great acting assignment to determine and orchestrate the many changes of beat. To sustain the level of emotional involvement on the part of this moribund, feeble and at the same time almost frenetic man requires a commitment to the material, a commitment that can only be aroused and maintained by the use of substitutions for the objects of his affection and for the situation that has made him unhappy. You can't just read this: It has to mean something deeply personal to you. You must recall people who mean or meant a great deal to you, and who betrayed you, and you must also recall a time when you felt deathly ill. Use sense memory to bring back the sensations of how hard it was physically for you to express yourself, and the difficulty you had with a dry throat and cold sweats. The character's voice will be naturally what it would it be in those circumstances. A caveat: You don't want to sound declamatory, or the listener will quickly lose interest. Really talk to Rastignac, for whom you must also select a substitution.

The commas and semi-colons which separate the clauses in many of the sentences, and the briefer full sentences, give you a clue as to the pace and rhythm—alternately legato and staccato—of the monologue: Pauses in the longer sentences are not necessary, except for the dying man's difficulty in breathing; they are full of run-on thoughts and should be delivered that way. The many exclamation points are another clue: They indicate feverish energy. Goriot is almost on the point of delirium, as well as being terribly upset and desperately miserable. He adores his daughters. He lives for them, and they have betrayed him. He is in a paroxysm of grief, wracked with emotional pain, and he feels completely helpless. He alternates between bouts of energy and moments of weakness and collapse. Don't overdo the melodrama (although some people might say that in this case you couldn't overdo it enough!).

To situate this book in its social, literary and historical context, you should know that the novel was part of Balzac's project to give the world a complete picture of the life of his era and of his society. He divided *The Human Comedy* into such sections as "Scenes of Private Life," of which *Le père Goriot* is one; "Scenes of Parisian Life," "Scenes of Provincial Life," etc. and, like Charles Dickens, he created a magnificent gallery of unforgettable characters and told a series of riveting, intricately plotted stories.

Despite Balzac's astounding intelligence, his project is marred for some readers by his political reactionaryism, which obtrudes itself from time to time (like the politically more progressive Dickens, Balzac is reactive rather than prescriptive); and by his ethnocentric prejudices, such as anti-Semitism of the kind that attributes certain negative character traits (cupidity, avarice, etc.) to all Jews, although most of his villains are not Jewish, nor are all of his Jews villains; nor does he attribute all of society's woes to monolithic Jewish financial and media manipulation, as in the usual anti-Semitic conspiracy theory. In his last completed novel, *L'Envers de l'histoire contemporaine* (1847–9) (*The Underside of Contemporary History*), Balzac even has a Jewish hero: the erudite, generous Doctor Halpersohn. But like many of Balzac's other Jewish characters, he is physically caricatured, and stereotypically alien, strange, mysterious, unpleasant, and avid for gain. Among Balzac's greatest recurring characters is the emotional, somewhat coarse, brilliantly shrewd financial speculator, the Jewish banker, baron de Nucingen (complete with caricatural Germanic Jewish accent), who is married to one of Goriot's daughters.

6. Nervous, courageous, reckless (Hawkins); overconfident, stupid, sly, drunk (Israel Hands)

From Robert Louis Stevenson's *Treasure Island* (1883), Chapter 26: "Israel Hands"

. . . Then, with a pistol in either hand, I addressed him.

"One more step, Mr. Hands," said I, "and I'll blow your brains out! Dead men don't bite, you know," I added with a chuckle.

He stopped instantly. I could see by the working of his face that he was trying to think, and the process was so slow and laborious that, in my new-found security, I laughed aloud. At last, with a swallow or two, he spoke, his face still wearing the same expression of extreme perplexity. In order to speak he had to take the dagger from his mouth, but in all else he remained unmoved.

"Jim," says he, "I reckon we're fouled, you and me, and we'll have to sign articles. I'd have had you but for that there lurch, but I don't have no luck, not I; and I reckon I'll have to strike, which comes hard, you see, for a master mariner to a ship's younker like you, Jim."

I was drinking in his words and smiling away, as conceited as a cock upon a wall, when, all in a breath, back went his right hand over his shoulder. Something sang like an arrow through the air; I felt a blow and then a sharp pang, and there I was pinned by the shoulder to the mast. In the horrid pain and surprise of the moment—I scarce can say it was by my own volition, and I am sure it was without a conscious aim—both my pistols went off, and both escaped out of my hands. They did not fall alone; with a choked cry, the coxswain loosed his grasp upon the shrouds and plunged head first into the water.

NOTES, COMMENTS AND HINTS

The evening after the battle at the stockade on Treasure Island (see page 184) Jim Hawkins borrows Ben Gunn's tiny boat, and steals aboard the all but deserted *Hispaniola*, left in the guard of two drunken, feuding louts, in order to beach the ship, and render it impossible for Silver and his gang of pirates to escape from the island. Israel Hands has killed his fellow guard, and discovered what Hawkins is up to. He is not too drunk to pursue the lad, who flees into the crow's nest, and then confronts his attacker.

Jim's chuckle belies his underlying fear; although he now thinks he is safe, and is as "conceited as a cock upon a wall." His lines to Israel Hands should be delivered with great bravado, as if he thinks he has already won the day.

The sly, but not terribly clever Israel Hands, who should have rather a gruff voice and a suggestion of a lower class accent, clearly has contempt for the boy he thinks it will be easy to outwit. But his overly confident attitude is his undoing. It is said that "Pride goeth before a fall," and so it does with Israel Hands—literally.

Even though Hawkins is telling us his story long after it happened, use the sense memory of an incident in which you experienced incredible pain to help you relive the "horrid pain of the moment," the searing pain of that knife stabbing through his shoulder. You will find your voice and your feelings changing once that knife hits its mark, and if you find your face scrunching up with pain, you will know you are on the right track. The listener will hear that expression on your face, and it will allow the listener into the story. It should be very effective. Once again, Stevenson has supplied you with powerful verbs and images to emphasize so that the story comes visually alive for the listener.

7, Cogent, incisive, indignant, ruminative (Holmes)

From Sir Arthur Conan Doyle's *The Valley of Fear* (1915), Chapter Six: A Dawning Light

He sat with his mouth full of toast and his eyes sparkling with mischief, watching my intellectual entanglement. The mere sight of his excellent appetite was an assurance of success, for I had very clear recollections of days and nights without a thought of food, when his baffled mind had chafed before some problem while his thin, eager features became more attenuated with the asceticism of complete mental concentration. Finally he lit his pipe, and sitting in the inglenook of the old village inn he talked slowly and at random about his case, rather as one who thinks aloud than as one who makes a considered statement.

"A lie, Watson—a great, big, thumping, obtrusive, uncompromising lie—that's what meets us on the threshold! That is our starting point. The whole story told by Barker is a lie. But Barker's story is corroborated by Mrs. Douglas. Therefore she is lying also. They are both

> lying and in a conspiracy. So now we have the clear problem. Why are they lying, and what is the truth which they are trying so hard to conceal? Let us try, Watson, you and I, if we can get behind the lie and reconstruct the truth.
>
> "How do I know that they are lying? Because it is a clumsy fabrication which simply could not be true..."

NOTES, COMMENTS AND HINTS

Watson gives a great hint, and one that it is necessary to adopt, when he tell us that Holmes talked "slowly and at random, rather as one who thinks aloud ..." A better hint as to how to read this selection aloud could not be given.

"A lie, Watson—a great, big, thumping, obtrusive, uncompromising lie—that's what meets us on the threshold..." When I recorded this line I gave every adjective a deliberate, but not labored, stress—that was the technical aspect of the recording. And in the book itself I underlined each adjective singly, and the word "lie" doubly. The organic aspect of the recording, which the listener could hear, was Holmes thinking: There was subtext underneath the adjectives; something was going on in my (his) subconscious.

That something is the action Holmes is playing: Trying to solve the problem by reasoning it out, or, if you prefer, by analyzing it. Holmes is ruminating upon the problem. He is talking to himself as much as he is to Watson. His objective is to solve the mystery. The obstacles in his way are the many details he has to link together to form a chain. His attitude is the one described by the adjectives listed above. The delivery of his lines must be incisive, pointed, indignant (Holmes is outraged at having been lied to), and cogent, at the same time as it is ruminative. The listener must hear all this in the reader's voice.

Although superficially similar to the scene on page 207 from *The Hound of the Baskervilles*, this scene is different, even though the same adjectives listed above could apply to it. In *The Hound of the Baskervilles* Holmes has not yet been informed about any sort of murder or mayhem. He is merely examining a cane because he is interested and amused by it, perhaps feeling slightly competitive with Dr. Watson, and wishing subconsciously to assert his superiority for reasons of narcissistic self-satisfaction. In *The Valley of Fear* there has already been a murder, and the mystery must be solved. There is more at stake, much more. There is thus the kind of intensity in this little excerpt that you do not find in the scene where Holmes examines Dr. Mortimer's cane. In other words, the same actions are played differently in the two scenes because the circumstances are different.

Knowing how high the stakes are for any character is always important, because this conditions absolutely the way in which you will read the story. In *The Cask of Amontillado*, for example, the stakes are very high indeed; literally a matter of life and death (page 203).

Actions Are Verbs

Here are some examples of actions, and some examples drawn from literature to illustrate them. Actions are simply physical, or else psychological. Of course, the physical actions have a psychological component, because the physical action exists for psychological reasons. The actions aid the character in fulfilling her or his objectives, which can be expressed in terms of either verbs or nouns: the character wants "to be at peace"; the character wants "peace of mind." Don't confuse actions and objectives; you will find both for every illustrative text below; I describe the objective under Notes, Comments and Hints. To express an action, you can think of the verb infinitive: The action is "to ___."

How an action is played is central. Adverbs often modify verbs and tell you how the action is to be played, e.g. excitedly, slowly, roughly.

For examples of psychologically subtle, internalized actions see the selections from Marcel Proust's *Swann's Way* on pages 164 and 255.

1. To lie around in bed, doing as little as possible (Oblomov)

From Ivan Goncharov's *Oblomov* (1858; translated by C. J. Hogarth, 1915; translation slightly modified by me), Part One, Chapter One

Half-past ten struck, and Oblomov gave himself a shake. "What is the matter?" he said, annoyed. "In all conscience it's time that I were doing something! If I could make up my mind to—" He broke off with a shout of "Zakhar!" whereupon there entered an elderly man in a grey suit and brass buttons—a man who sported beneath a perfectly bald pate a pair of long, bushy, grizzled whiskers that would have sufficed to fit out three ordinary men with beards. His clothes, it is true, were cut according to a country pattern, but he cherished them as a faint reminder of his former livery, as the one surviving token of the dignity of the house of Oblomov. The house of Oblomov was one which had once been wealthy and distinguished, but which, of late years, had undergone impoverishment and diminution, until finally it had become lost among a crowd of noble houses of more recent creation.

For a few moments Oblomov remained too plunged in thought to notice Zakhar's presence; but at length the valet coughed.

"What do you want?" Oblomov inquired.

"You called me just now, Master?"

"I called you, you say? Well, I cannot remember why I did so. Go back to your room until I have remembered."

Zakhar retired, and Oblomov spent another quarter of an hour in thinking over the accursed letter.

"I have lain here long enough," at last he said to himself. "Really, I must rise... But suppose I were to read the letter through carefully and then to rise? Zakhar!"

Zakhar re-entered, and Oblomov straightway sank into a reverie.

NOTES, COMMENTS AND HINTS

Goncharov is pronounced "gawn cha: RAWF." Oblomov is pronounced "u BLAW məf," with the "u" in the first syllable like the "u" in *but*. Zakhar is pronounced "ZA: kha:r."

Oblomov's objective is "to expend only as much energy as I have to for my entire life," and the action he plays is as stated: "to lie around in bed."

This satirical, yet whimsically tender novel by Ivan Goncharov (1812–1891), who, to earn a living, was a government bureaucrat for thirty years, writing novels and travel books in his spare time, gave the word "oblomovism" to the Russian language. It is a pointed indictment of the do-nothing absentee aristocratic Russian landlords, who exploited the serfs who worked their land under the brutal system which kept them tied to it. They lived far away in the great cities of Moscow or St. Petersburg, receiving the income from their country estates and taking the system for granted. At the same time the book, instead of being bitter, is funny and heartwarming, in spite of the awfulness of Oblomov's oblivious behavior. See the 1980 Russian film *Oblomov* for a keenly observed adaptation with an excellent feeling for the period.

Quite aside from playing the character's actions, placing this novel in its historical and political context will allow you to enter the world of the book. Serfdom, the inhuman, exploitative system of half-slavery instituted among peasants, was only ended in Russia in 1861. It was a system dating from the medieval era, when peasants were bound to the land of their manorial lord, and had to work at their lord's bidding. Peasants could not legally leave the land and quit their master's service, but they did have certain rights, unlike slaves, who had none and were simply chattels. The peasants were paid and could keep some of the products of their labors to sell at country marketplaces, and they could buy their freedom. In western Europe the system had disappeared long before 1861, the French Revolution having swept it away along with other oppressive systems that kept people in various kinds of bondage, such as slavery in Haiti as well as in France itself (there were black members of the French Revolutionary Convention), and the laws decreeing the ghettoization and marginalization of Jews, who were not citizens until the Revolution gave them citizenship. For more about serfdom, see page 270 under Notes, Comments and Hints for Chekhov's *On the Harmfulness of Tobacco.*

Zakhar is as lazy as his master, Oblomov, and nothing ever gets done:

> "A nice way to do your cleaning!" he said. "What a lot of dust and dirt, to be sure! Look at those corners! You never exert yourself at all."
>
> "If I never exert myself," retorted Zakhar, offended, "at least I do my best, and I don't spare myself. I dust and sweep almost every day. Everything looks clean and bright enough for a wedding."
>
> "What a lie!" cried Oblomov, "Go back to your room again!"

Oblomov sends Zakhar to his room, instead of asking him to clean up the place, because he doesn't care. Oblomov is incapable of working up enough energy to care about anything. The tone of the lines here should be airily dismissive, as if you were waving him away with your hand. On the line "What a lie!" instead of being really indignant, simply be contemptuously dismissive; you might drop your pitch on the end of the line. Oblomov thinks: "Oh, he's just impossible. He's always telling lies. What a fool he is..." Try waving him away with your hand as you read "Go back to your room again!" even though you will have to sit quite still in the recording studio. By implication, neither the upper nor the lower classes care enough to solve the problem, so everything gives way before the natural entropy of the universe. However, there are those who wish to effect changes, and one of them is Oblomov's friend, Stolz.

For Oblomov you can adopt a generally lazy tone and an almost yawning kind of voice, and rather a slow rhythm and pace in reading his lines. Be what we call nowadays "laid back." On the lines "I called you, you say?..." be genuinely surprised. But even the surprise is lazy, and it might sound almost as if you were half asleep, or as if you saw everything through a gauze curtain.

2. To talk concisely, convincingly and firmly (Stolz); to avoid having to do anything; to evade; to find excuses (Oblomov)

From Ivan Goncharov's *Oblomov* (1858; translated by C. J. Hogarth, 1915), Part Four, Chapter One

To set the scene: Stolz, Oblomov's old friend, who has shown up on an unexpected, whirlwind visit, is the first to speak.

> "...Ah, Ilya, Ilya! Life passes too swiftly for it to be spent in slumber. Would, rather, it were a perpetual fire!—that one could live for hundreds and hundreds of years! Then what an immensity of work would one not do!"

"You and I are of different types," said Oblomov. "You have wings; you do not merely exist—you also fly. You have gifts and ambition; you do not grow fat; specks do not dance before your eyes; and the back of your neck does not need to be periodically scratched. In short, my organism and yours are wholly dissimilar."

"Fie, fie! Man was created to order his own being, and even to change his own nature; yet, instead, he goes and develops a paunch, and then supposes that nature has laid upon him that burden. Once upon a time you too had wings. Now you have laid them aside."

"Where are they?" asked Oblomov. "I am powerless, completely powerless."

"Rather, you are determined to be powerless. Even during your boyhood at Oblomovka, and amid the circle of your aunts and nurses and valets, you had begun to waste your intellect, and to be unable to put on your own socks, and so forth. Hence your present inability to live."

"All that may be so," said Oblomov with a sigh; "but now it is too late to turn back."

NOTES, COMMENTS AND HINTS

Ilya is pronounced "il YA:." Stolz, which means "proud" in German, is pronounced "shto:lts." "Oblomovka" is pronounced "u BLAW mof ka:."

Stolz provides quite a striking contrast with his friend Oblomov. He tries his best to get Oblomov out of his laziness and the rut he is in. His rhythm and pace are the diametrical opposite of Oblomov's slow-moving dullness. Even in love, which plays a major part in the story, Oblomov is too lazy to pursue the woman he desires, and he loses Olga to Stolz out of sheer inertia. Read Stolz's lines with a quick, excited energy, which will help you find his voice easily; he knows how to make his points. Oblomov's lines should be read more slowly and wearily. Energy and exuberance are contrasted with weakness and lethargy.

Stolz's immediate objective is to get Oblomov to change his ways by talking to him with an energy he hopes will be persuasive and inspiring almost by itself. For his own life in general, Stolz's objective is "to do everything possible, with as much energy as possible"—to travel the world, to experience everything life has to offer and to do so in the pink of health. And Stolz is concerned about his friend and wants him to enjoy life just as he himself enjoys it.

Oblomov wants only to avoid doing anything at all; his objective hasn't changed from what it was in the first excerpt. Everything he says, even when complimenting Stolz, is really an evasion. If you have that in mind, then your reading will automatically take on the tone of someone who is constantly making excuses: "Well, you're fine; you can do anything; but I'm not and I can't." It is almost as if Oblomov's real objective is to get back to sleep. Read his lines in a tired and even cosmically world-weary tone of voice. Remember a time when you were very tired and couldn't get to bed fast enough, when you just conked out from sheer exhaustion. Oblomov is always tired, because he does nothing, and doing nothing is terribly debilitating. He simply can't be bothered to make any effort whatsoever. The biggest effort he makes here is to get rid of Stolz: "Oh, leave me alone, can't you?"

3. To explain; to justify (Narrator)

From Edgar Allan Poe's *The Tell-Tale Heart* (1840)

> TRUE!—nervous—very, very dreadfully nervous I had been and am; but why *will* you say that I am mad? The disease had sharpened my senses—not destroyed—not dulled them. Above all was the sense of hearing acute. I heard all things in the heavens and in the earth. I heard many things in hell. How, then, am I mad? Hearken! and observe how healthily—how calmly I can tell you the whole story.
>
> It is impossible to say how the idea first entered my brain; but once conceived, it haunted me day and night. Object there was none. Passion there was none. I loved the old man. He had never wronged me. He had never given me insult. For his gold I had no desire. I think it was his eye! yes, it was this! One of his eyes resembled that of a vulture—a pale blue eye, with a film over it. Whenever it fell upon me, my blood ran cold; and so by degrees—very gradually—I made up my mind to take the life of the old man, and thus rid myself of the eye for ever.

NOTES, COMMENTS AND HINTS

Our unnamed first-person narrator's objective is to justify himself in the eyes of the person he is talking to (possibly a police inspector or a doctor), and to persuade that person of his sanity. The action of explaining is in pursuit of a subtler objective: "I want to convince myself that I am not insane, so that I can feel good about myself. Therefore I will convince you first, and if I succeed I will have proved my point to myself as well as to you."

The story builds to a terrifying climax. Begin the story in rather a calm, reasonable, rational tone of voice, repressed, restrained, a bit tense, but still, lucid and plausible, with a smile on your face that belies the tension within. It is more eerie and frightening to open the story that way, I think, than if you were to read it as if you were challenging the listener, although that is certainly a possible choice. But remember that the first word is a fairly loud (to judge by the capital letters and the exclamation mark), overdone, overly ingratiating "TRUE!" which is the immediate concession to the listener that what he has said is right.

The listener has said: "You are nervous and you seem quite mad," and the character has replied: "TRUE!—nervous—very, very dreadfully nervous..."

It is instructive to listen to Basil Rathbone's chilling reading of this story (see the Bibliography). He obviously enjoys himself immensely. And his enjoyment is infectious. It communicates itself instantly, and compels us to listen in a kind of horrified fascination, as he almost whispers when he describes how he stealthily looked in upon the old man; his rhythm is slow, and we relive with him his sneaking into the old man's room, as if we were looking over his shoulder. We can feel the place, and we can feel the hour as he reads. Rathbone really becomes the character, and although he describes events in this world, we almost have the impression that he is living in another world. And yet he is very calm, very objective, almost dispassionate and quite detached. As he talks of the old man's "vulture eye" he relives, audibly—one might almost say visibly—his hatred for that blue, filmed eye. And we hear it, we hear it, we hear it! And he never loses the idea that he is trying to convince his interlocutor that he is not mad, an idea that Poe reinforces periodically in lines directed to the person our narrator is talking to. It is as if Rathbone is constantly saying as subtext "This is what I said, this is what I did, and you can see that I am perfectly rational and sane." Describing the murder of the old man, Rathbone suddenly becomes very energetic, and his rhythm quickens. Then he calms down on "If still you think me mad, you will think so no longer..." He delights in telling us of his cleverness and of how he fools the police. When he says, "I smiled, for what had I to fear?" he chuckles, and his voice rises higher than usual on the word "fear." His attitude is first "They are so stupid," and then "This is all making me uncomfortable and I don't feel well." And gradually he falls apart: "I foamed, I raged, I swore..." Rathbone foams, he rages, and rushes headlong from there to the end, and collapses.

4. To maintain a point of view and a position; to keep one's dignity (all characters)

From Jane Austen's *Pride and Prejudice* (1813), Chapter 20

Note: Mrs. Bennet, Lizzy's mother, is speaking.

"But depend upon it, Mr. Collins," she added, "that Lizzy shall be brought to reason. I will speak to her about it myself directly. She is a very headstrong foolish girl, and does not know her own interest; but I will *make* her know it."

"Pardon me for interrupting you, Madam," cried Mr. Collins; "but if she is really headstrong and foolish, I know not whether she would altogether be a very desirable wife to a man in my situation, who naturally looks for happiness in the marriage state. If therefore she actually persists in rejecting my suit, perhaps it were better not to force her into accepting me, because if liable to such defects of temper, she could not contribute much to my felicity."

"Sir, you quite misunderstand me," said Mrs. Bennet, alarmed. "Lizzy is only headstrong in such matters as these. In every thing else she is as good natured a girl as ever lived. I will go directly to Mr. Bennet, and we shall very soon settle it with her, I am sure."

She would not give him time to reply, but hurrying instantly to her husband, called out as she entered the library,

"Oh! Mr. Bennet, you are wanted immediately; we are all in an uproar. You must come and make Lizzy marry Mr. Collins, for she vows she will not have him, and if you do not make haste he will change his mind and not have *her*."

Mr. Bennet raised his eyes from his book as she entered, and fixed them on her face with a calm unconcern which was not in the least altered by her communication.

"I have not the pleasure of understanding you," said he, when she had finished her speech. "Of what are you talking?"

"Of Mr. Collins and Lizzy. Lizzy declares she will not have Mr. Collins, and Mr. Collins begins to say that he will not have Lizzy."

"And what am I to do on the occasion? It seems an hopeless business."

"Speak to Lizzy about it yourself. Tell her that you insist upon her marrying him."

"Let her be called down. She shall hear my opinion."

Mrs. Bennet rang the bell, and Miss Elizabeth was summoned to the library.

"Come here, child," cried her father as she appeared. "I have sent for you on an affair of importance. I understand that Mr. Collins has made you an offer of marriage. Is it true?" Elizabeth replied that it was. "Very well—and this offer of marriage you have refused?"

"I have, Sir."

"Very well. We now come to the point. Your mother insists upon your accepting it. Is not it so, Mrs. Bennet?"

"Yes, or I will never see her again."

"An unhappy alternative is before you, Elizabeth. From this day you must be a stranger to one of your parents. Your mother will never see you again if you do *not* marry Mr. Collins, and I will never see you again if you *do*."

NOTES, COMMENTS AND HINTS

The characters each have their own objectives or, rather, sub-objectives: to maintain dignity (Mr. Collins; Mrs. Bennet); to overcome anxiety (Mrs. Bennet); to persuade (Mrs. Bennet); to calm things down, so he can get back to what he is doing as soon as possible (Mr. Bennet) to maintain her resolve (Elizabeth Bennet). They are all quite stubborn and Elizabeth's parents are at loggerheads, whereas Mr. Collins, terribly embarrassed, only wishes to get out of his appalling situation as gracefully as possible. He is horrified that he could have made such a dreadful mistake, and more than a little self-righteous. Elizabeth, while knowing she has made the right decision, is not happy that her parents are bickering, and she is sensitive enough to pity Mr. Collins's pain, even though she finds his unctuous pretense of holier-than-thou virtue disgusting. All of that should be reflected in your voice as you talk back and forth to yourself, for that is literally what you are doing, but the listener accepts the convention that different people are talking.

Keep the vocal characterizations of all the characters honest and straightforward: a neutral voice for Elizabeth; a slightly deeper voice for her father; a higher, fluttering voice (as in other scenes in the book; be consistent) for her mother; and a mellow, but nervous, self-righteous voice and delivery for Mr. Collins.

This text is a good example of why vocal characterizations should be kept fairly simple. There are four people speaking, without "he saids" and "she saids" to tell the listener who they are, although that should be obvious in your reading of the scene. But when vocal characterizations are not clear and simple, it is easy for the listener to get confused and to have difficulty in following the story. If you play all the characters' attitudes and actions, as well as their subtexts, however, the story will be clear.

For another excerpt from *Pride and Prejudice* see page 171.

5. To interrogate (Villefort); to respond honestly and to cooperate (Dantès)

From Alexandre Dumas' *The Count of Monte Cristo* (1844–1845), Chapter VII: "The Interrogation"; my translation

"Who are you and what is your name?" asked Villefort, rifling through the notes that the police agent had given to him as he entered, and that had already within an hour assumed voluminous proportions, so much does the corrupt charge of espionage stick immediately to detainees.

"My name is Edmond Dantès, monsieur," replied the young man in a calm and sonorous voice; "I am mate of the *Pharaon*, which belongs to Messrs. Morrel & Son."

"Your age?" continued Villefort.

"Nineteen," answered Dantès.

"What were you doing at the moment you were arrested?"

"I was at my betrothal banquet, monsieur," said the young man, in a somewhat moved tone of voice, so sorrowful was the contrast between those moments of joy and the lugubrious ceremony now taking place; so much did the somber face of M. de Villefort illuminate by contrast the face of Mercédès in all its radiance.

"You were at your betrothal banquet?" said the deputy, shivering in spite of himself.

"Yes, monsieur; I am on the point of marrying a woman I have loved for three years." Villefort, all impassive as he ordinarily was, was nevertheless struck with this coincidence; and the moved tone of voice of Dantès, surprised in the midst of his happiness, was about to arouse a sympathetic chord in his inmost soul: he, too, was getting married; he, too, was happy, and his happiness was interrupted so that he might contribute to the destruction of the joy of a man, who like him, was just about to touch on happiness.

"This philosophic coincidence," thought he, "will create a great effect upon my return to M. de Saint-Méran's salon"; and he arranged mentally in advance, and while Dantès awaited further questions, the antitheses with the help of which orators construct the ambitious phrases which will earn them applause, and which sometimes make people believe them eloquent.

When his little interior *speech* had been arranged, Villefort smiled at its effect, and returned to Dantès.

"Continue, monsieur" said he.

"What should I continue?"

"The enlightenment of justice."

"Let justice say on what point she would like to be enlightened, and I will tell her all I know; only," he added, smiling in turn, "I warn her that I don't know much."

"Have you served under the usurper?"

"I was about to be mustered into the Marines when he fell."

"They tell me your political opinions are extreme," said Villefort, to whom nobody had ever breathed a word of such a thing, but who was not sorry to ask this question as if it were an accusation.

"*My* political opinions? *Mine*, monsieur? Alas! It is almost a shame to say so, but I have never had what people call an opinion: I am barely nineteen, as I have had the honor to tell you; I know nothing; I am not destined to play any role. The little I am and shall be, if they give me the situation I am ambitious to have, I will owe to M. Morrel. So all my opinions—I will not say public, but private—are limited to these three sentiments: I love my father, I respect M. Morrel, and I adore Mercédès. This, sir, is all I can tell justice; you see how little of interest it holds for her."

As Dantès spoke, Villefort gazed at his face, so sweet and so open at the same time...

NOTES, COMMENTS AND HINTS

Some pronounciations: *Pharaon,* the name of the ship (far: a AW*N*; the word means "pharaoh"); Villefort (vi:l FAWR); Dantès (da:*N* TES); M. de Saint-Méran (mə syə də se*N* mé RAW*N*); Mercédes (mer sé DES); Morrel (maw REL).

Villefort's immediate objective is to handle the case before him so that he can get back to his engagement party; his objective soon becomes to save his own skin. And Dantès's immediate objective is to get himself released, so that he can return to his own betrothal banquet. He has no idea why he has been arrested in the first place.

That face, "so sweet and so open," belongs to the man whose life Villefort is about to ruin. Dantès has been entrusted with a letter, on account of which the young sailor, who knows nothing about it beyond his commission to deliver it, has been arrested on a secret denunciation by malicious, jealous enemies he thought were his friends. Villefort is about to let Dantès go—thus accomplishing both their objectives—knowing him to be innocent, when he examines the letter for the first time. It is from Napoleon himself, and meant to be given into the hands of Villefort's own father, a Bonapartist. Napoleon had been defeated and exiled to the isle of Elba, but he is on the point of returning with an army to France, to overthrow the restored Bourbon monarchy. Villefort himself is a loyal supporter of the Bourbon King Louis XVIII, and very ambitious to advance in his career. So that the secret of his father's conspiratorial politics, which might be seen as a direct reflection on Villefort himself, will never be revealed, he burns the letter and has Dantès imprisoned. In prison Dantès meets an Italian priest, who reveals to him the secret of a treasure buried on the isle of Monte Cristo. When the priest dies, Dantès wraps himself in the old man's winding sheet, and escapes when the guards throw the supposed corpse into the sea. He manages to get to the isle of Monte Cristo and discover the treasure. Now wealthy, he assumes the identity of the Count of Monte Cristo and wreaks revenge on his betrayers.

This novel is based on a true story! During the days when Napoleon was emperor a shoemaker engaged to a wealthy widow in the town of Nîmes was imprisoned as a British spy after some envious friends, playing a practical joke, had denounced him to the police. They dared not reveal to the police that they had been joking, and their friend served seven years. In prison he met an Italian priest, who told him of a buried treasure. He died, and when the former shoemaker was released his first act was to find the treasure. He then proceeded to murder all his friends, but the last one realized what was going on, turned the tables, and killed him. Only on his deathbed did the murderer tell the entire story to his priest, who told the story to the police once the man was dead. It was recounted in a very popular book, published posthumously in 1839: the six volumes of memoirs by Jacques Peuchet (1758–1830), the police archivist. Dumas read it, and said immediately that he had to turn it into a novel, which he did, completely transforming the story in the process.

Dumas uses the English word "speech," italicized in the French text, to emphasize Villefort's callousness and pretension. Villefort's tone and his attitude are cold and suspicious and extremely calculating. He is in a position of power and authority, and he asserts both. He feels superior to this naïve young man, for whom he ultimately has contempt. The shrewd, cunning Villefort is dispassionate and immovable, and never gives an inch if he can help it. All of this subtext infuses and informs the way you should read his lines.

On the other hand, the guileless, candid Dantès is frank and open and serious, but not so serious that he cannot respond in a slightly joking tone to Villefort's injunction to continue with "the enlightenment of justice." He is sweet, he is loyal, and his life is about to change forever. He is a bit worried, but, knowing that he is innocent of any wrongdoing, and being a trusting soul without artifice, he suspects nothing and cannot believe that others are not as honest as himself. Your tone of voice as Dantès should therefore be slightly subdued, but ingenuous and unassuming. He wants to get out of Villefort's office, and he knows that the best way to accomplish this it to be cooperative.

There is thus a salient contrast between these two characters, the one disingenuous scheming, complicated, worldly and sophisticated, the other simple, ingenuous, upright, parochial and naïve. It is a vocal contrast also: Villefort's smooth, cold yet almost velvety voice reflecting his attempt to be always in control of himself and others; Dantès's pleasant, at times "tremulous," voice, reflecting his frankness and nervousness. Young Dantès does not have the "deep, sonorous yet well-pitched voice" Dumas tells us he has as the Count (Chapter XXXIV: "Apparition"). Much later in the book Villefort can say, "Where have I heard that voice before?" and Dumas tells us in the excerpt above that Dantès' voice is "calm and sonorous," so there is clearly some similarity with his more mature voice. All the characters' voices change naturally as they mature over the course of the novel. To find their voices and make them organic, I had first to discover and play the characters' various actions, attitudes and objectives. I had to find all Villefort's and the Count's dark, hidden emotions and feelings of guilt, betrayal and hurt underneath their suave cultivated exteriors, and then the voices came naturally to me; I didn't have to calculate them or look for them. I was naturally impelled to use the lower end of my range for the Count's voice, just as I had used a slightly higher voice for the young, innocent Dantès. For Villefort in later chapters I automatically used a sharper tone and an even more authoritative delivery than in the scene excerpted above—the old lion, as opposed to the young cub—more set in his ways, more inflexible, more embittered, self-loathing, paranoid. Dumas often tells us about the quality of characters' voices and about the way the characters speak ("softly"; "in a choking voice," etc.); to arrive at climactic moments, for instance when a character sobs or breaks down in some way, you have to score the scenes as you would the script of a play.

To alternate characters, which requires you to switch back and forth instantaneously, you must know both the characters and the through-line of the story so well that you feel comfortable doing this. And you must know where you are in the story, so that you can read the moment correctly. The characters are at specific early stages of their development. The naïve Dantès is quite different from the sophisticated Count of Monte Cristo he will become, with his breadth of knowledge and his astonishing ability to disguise himself completely and undetectably. This last trait is drawn from a friend of Dumas, the great detective Eugène-François Vidocq (pronounced "vi: DUCK"), an ex-convict who became head of the French Sûreté (pronounced "sür TÉ"; the Security Service of the French police). An altogether extraordinary individual, this real-life Sherlock Holmes was an acquaintance of Victor Hugo, who based both Jean Valjean and Inspector Javert in *Les Misérables* on him; and a friend of Balzac, whose character Vautrin is even more closely inspired by and modeled on Vidocq. He wrote his memoirs, and gave one-man shows based on his life and career at the Cosmopolitan Theatre in London in 1846. During his extremely popular presentations he assumed various disguises, putting on costumes and makeup in front of the audience.

Alexandre Dumas (1802–1870) was not only a great and prolific writer of travel books, novels (including such lesser known works of genius as *The Mohicans of Paris*, in which the character of Inspector Jackal is based on Vidocq), and criminological studies, but also a great gourmet. His posthumous *Grand Dictionary of Cuisine* (1873) is worth delving into. It is an astonishing book, full of worldwide culinary lore, and highly amusing, delicious recipes, which you can use to practice reading nonfiction, as well as for cooking.

6. To look for something (Ahab)

From Herman Melville's *Moby-Dick; or, The Whale* (1851), Chapter CXXXV: "The Chase—Third Day"

"D'ye see him?" cried Ahab; but the whale was not yet in sight.

"In his infallible wake, though; but follow that wake, that's all. Helm there; steady, as thou goest, and hast been going. What a lovely day again; were it a new-made world, and made for a summer-house to the angels, and this morning the first of its throwing open to them, a fairer day could not dawn upon that world. Here's food for thought, had Ahab time to think; but Ahab never thinks; he only feels, feels, feels; that's tingling enough for mortal man! to think's audacity. God only has that right and privilege. Thinking is, or ought to be, a coolness and a calmness; and our poor hearts throb, and our poor brains beat too much for that. And yet, I've sometimes thought my brain was very calm—frozen calm, this old skull cracks so, like a glass in which the contents turned to ice, and shiver it. And still this hair is growing now; this moment growing, and heat must breed it; but no, it's like that sort of common grass that will grow anywhere, between the earthy clefts of Greenland ice or in Vesuvius lava. How the wild winds blow it; they whip it about me as the torn shreds of split sails lash the tossed ship they cling to. A vile wind that has no doubt blown ere this through prison corridors and cells, and wards of hospitals, and ventilated them, and now comes blowing hither as innocent as fleeces. Out upon it!—it's tainted. Were I the wind, I'd blow no more on such a wicked, miserable world. I'd crawl somewhere to a cave, and slink there. And yet, 'tis a noble and heroic thing, the wind! who ever conquered it? In every fight it has the last and bitterest blow. Run tilting at it, and you but run through it. Ha! a coward wind that strikes stark naked men, but will not stand to receive a single blow. Even Ahab is a braver thing—a nobler thing that that. Would now the wind but had a body; but all the things that most exasperate and outrage mortal man, all these things are bodiless, but only bodiless as objects, not as agents. There's a most special, a most cunning, oh, a most malicious difference! And yet, I say again, and swear it now, that there's something all glorious and gracious in the wind. These warm Trade Winds, at least, that in the clear heavens blow straight on, in strong and steadfast, vigorous mildness; and veer not from their mark, however the baser currents of the sea may turn and tack, and mightiest Mississippies of the land swift and swerve about, uncertain where to go at last. And by the eternal Poles!

these same Trades that so directly blow my good ship on; these Trades, or something like them—something so unchangeable, and full as strong, blow my keeled soul along! To it! Aloft there! What d'ye see?"

"Nothing, Sir."

"Nothing! and noon at hand! The doubloon goes a-begging! See the sun! Aye, aye, it must be so. I've oversailed him. How, got the start? Aye, he's chasing me now; not I, him—that's bad; I might have known it, too. Fool! the lines—the harpoons he's towing. Aye, aye, I have run him by last night. About! about! Come down, all of ye, but the regular look outs! Man the braces!"

NOTES, COMMENTS AND HINTS

You might say that to state the main action as "to look for something" is rather an understatement when applied to Captain Ahab, but that is only because he is so obsessive and intense in pursuing his desired objective of finding and killing the whale that took his leg. His actions include: giving orders to lower the boats; screaming questions at the lookout; ruminating on where the whale could be, etc. Each action is a change of beat, so as you go from one to the other your voice will automatically change.

Peleg, one of the owners of the *Pequod*, calls its captain, Ahab, "a grand, ungodly, god-like man." A man of great intelligence, Ahab is proof that intelligence does not mean someone cannot be deeply disturbed and compulsive. Ahab is obsessed with accomplishing his revenge on the whale to the exclusion of everything and everybody else, including his own family. He takes himself to be a god, or at least to be above the rest of humanity, and, convincing himself that his cause is noble and just and not merely one of personal vengeance, he behaves in a godlike way. And he pursues that whale for forty years, never wavering in his determination! Ahab is a fascinating, complicated character: He is fascinating because he is self-aware, and not merely in the grip of his compulsions, or, rather, he is aware that he is in their grip. He knows who he is and what he is doing, and he stubbornly insists on doing it. He will not bow, he will not bend, he insists on his freedom—and there is something to admire in that and in his courage and fortitude. He will fight the universe that caused him pain, if he die for it. He is very much like a Greek mythological hero, rushing self-destructively to the doom he seeks. Although he compares himself to God, he compares his hair, and thus himself self-deprecatingly, to common grass. But he proceeds to play God nonetheless.

When you are reading this scene, do not forget that forty years of a man's life have been spent in the ardent, passionate hope of arriving at just this day, which has finally come. Melville's heightened language is really very difficult, but Ahab's voice will come naturally to you if you just play the circumstances. Whatever substitution you use, it must be an extremely powerful one, one that will drive you ahead and propel the narrative forward, in spite of the mass of verbiage. You almost have to play against the language by playing the subtext. If you dwell on the words too much, if you make everything important, you will be lost—and so will the listener, because it will be impossible to listen to. You have to pick quite carefully, and perhaps technically, exactly what points you want to make.

Clearly, the sentence about how "glorious and gracious" the wind is, is not the point of that section of Ahab's monologue. The idea towards which everything in Ahab's passionate speech drives, and that section's main point, is at the end, in the clause I have underlined:

> "And yet, I say again, and swear it now, that there's something all glorious and gracious in the wind. These warm Trade Winds, at least, that in the clear heavens blow straight on, in strong and steadfast, vigorous mildness; and veer not from their mark, however the baser currents of the sea may turn and tack, and mightiest Mississippies of the land swift and swerve about, uncertain where to go at last. And by the eternal Poles! these same Trades that so directly blow my good ship on; these Trades, or something like them—something so unchangeable, and full as strong, blow my keeled soul along!"

Everything in this speech about the elemental wind should drive like the wind to get to that point in this melodramatic passage. Ahab, who sometimes speaks of himself in the third person, as if he were looking at himself from without, sees himself as elemental and in the grip of elemental forces. I do not mean that you should rush the tempo, but Ahab clearly does not speak slowly. The subtext might be in part his vast realization of the cosmic point he is making, and it surprises even him.

The biblical Ahab, king of Israel, whose story is told in the First Book of Kings, Chapters 16–22, is punished for his wickedness and for his idolatry. Egged on by his wife, Jezebel, he has rejected God, worshiped only Baal, and covetously pursued the things of this world. King Ahab reigned twenty-two years, and was confronted with drought in his kingdom. He lived in the desert as Melville's Ahab lives on the ocean. The biblical Ahab is obsessed by his power and his desires, which overwhelm him. Ahab in *Moby-Dick*, overwhelmed like his biblical counterpart by his obsession, follows no law but his own, and after forty years of pursuing his desire at the expense of everyone and everything else, is also punished.

For another excerpt and more information about this book see page 179.

7. To scold (Aunt Polly); to escape retribution (Tom Sawyer)

From Mark Twain's *The Adventures of Tom Sawyer* (1876), Chapter I: "Tom Plays, Fights, and Hides"

There was a slight noise behind her and she turned just in time to seize a small boy by the slack of his roundabout and arrest his flight.

"There! I might 'a' thought of that closet. What you been doing in there?"

"Nothing."

"Nothing! Look at your hands. And look at your mouth. What *is* that truck?"

"*I* don't know, aunt."

"Well, *I* know. It's jam—that's what it is. Forty times I've said if you didn't let that jam alone I'd skin you. Hand me that switch."

The switch hovered in the air—the peril was desperate—

"My! Look behind you, aunt!"

The old lady whirled round, and snatched her skirts out of danger. The lad fled on the instant, scrambled up the high board-fence, and disappeared over it.

His aunt Polly stood surprised a moment, and then broke into a gentle laugh.

"Hang the boy, can't I never learn anything? Ain't he played me tricks enough like that for me to be looking out for him by this time? But old fools is the biggest fools there is. Can't learn an old dog new tricks, as the saying is. But my goodness, he never plays them alike, two days, and how is a body to know what's coming? He 'pears to know just how long he can torment me before I get my dander up, and he knows if he can make out to put me off for a minute or make me laugh, it's all down again and I can't hit him a lick. I ain't doing my duty by that boy, and that's the Lord's truth, goodness knows. Spare the rod and spile the child, as the Good Book says. I'm a laying up sin and suffering for us both, *I* know. He's full of the Old Scratch, but laws-a-me! He's my own dead sister's boy, poor thing, and I ain't got the heart to lash him, some-how. Every time I let him off, my conscience does hurt me so, and every time I hit him my old heart most breaks. Well-a-well, man that is born of woman is of few days and full of trouble, as the Scripture says, and I reckon it's so. He'll play hookey this evening, and I'll just be obleeged to make him work, to-morrow, to punish him. It's mighty hard to make him work

Saturdays, when all the boys is having holiday, but he hates work more than he hates anything else, and I've *got* to do some of my duty by him, or I'll be the ruination of the child."

NOTES, COMMENTS AND HINTS

By the word "evening" Aunt Polly means what we would call "afternoon."

Aunt Polly's objective in scolding Tom is to bring him up right, to do her duty, to give him tough love. Underneath her starchy, rigid, strait-laced surface is a heart of gold, as her breaking into a "gentle laugh" shows. She is really a very kind and loving woman, confronted with an unruly, wonderfully energetic, intelligent boy, full of the joy of life, whom she loves and wants to do the right thing by. She isn't really sure how to deal with him, and all this is reflected in her monologue.

The first action in this scene, "to scold," changes to a new beat, and a new action takes the place of the first one: "to ruminate" about Tom Sawyer and the situation she is in with him. This change will automatically be reflected in the tone of your voice as you play the actions.

Tom, of course, plays innocent. You know he will grow up to be an upright, good, moral and ethical man.

A slight southern U.S. accent (there are many, of course) is written into the well-observed colloquial dialogue of this character. The reality of the way people speak, not at all in a literary way and with nonstandard grammar, makes it easy to relax your jaw and get into the character's mind and heart. Jist drawl them lines away, and, laws a mercy, have fun with 'em! This is delightful stuff, and if you have fun with it, the listeners will, too. For another excerpt and more information about this book see page 175.

8. To talk firmly and authoritatively (King of Hearts); to respond without collapsing (Mad Hatter)

From Lewis Carroll's *Alice's Adventures in Wonderland* (1865), Chapter XII: "Who Stole the Tarts?"

"Give your evidence," the King repeated angrily, "or I'll have you executed, whether you're nervous or not."

"I'm a poor man, your Majesty," the Hatter began, in a trembling voice, "—and I hadn't begun my tea—not above a week or so—and what with the bread-and-butter getting so thin—and the twinkling of the tea—"

"The twinkling of *what*?" said the King.

"It *began* with the tea," the Hatter replied.

"Of course twinkling begins with a T!" said the King sharply. "Do you take me for a dunce? Go on!"

"I'm a poor man," the Hatter went on, "and most things twinkled after that—only the March Hare said—"

"I didn't!" the March Hare interrupted in a great hurry.

"You did!" said the Hatter.

"I deny it!" said the March Hare.

"He denies it," said the King: "leave out that part."

"Well, at any rate, the Dormouse said—" the Hatter went on, looking anxiously round to see if he would deny it too: but the Dormouse denied nothing, being fast asleep.

"After that," continued the Hatter, "I cut some more bread-and-butter—"

"But what did the Dormouse say?" one of the jury asked.

"That I can't remember," said the Hatter.

"You *must* remember," remarked the King, "or I'll have you executed."

The miserable Hatter dropped his teacup and bread-and-butter, and went down on one knee. "I'm a poor man, your Majesty," he began.

"You're a *very* poor *speaker*," said the King.

NOTES, COMMENTS AND HINTS

The King's objective is to intimidate and to impose his will, if not to terrify his victim outright. He now assumes the position his wife, the Queen of Hearts, had previously assumed, in "The Queen's Croquet-Ground"; see page 214. Having been intimidated, he now becomes the intimidator. The Mad Hatter speaks in a "trembling voice," showing how terrified he is; so the King has almost gained his objective already.

For the Mad Hatter find a good substitution using a situation in which you have been terrified, and you may then find some unexpectedly comic results in your reading of the Mad Hatter's already comic dialogue. Use your sense memory of how it feels to breathe quickly, almost hyperventilating. The experience of stage fright might be a serviceable substitution, or the fear you may have experienced before a job interview.

Try reading the Mad Hatter's last line as if you were almost about to faint, which should give you a weak, feeble tone of voice. Think of a time when you felt quite ill. Or perhaps you have experienced vertigo, acrophobia or claustrophobia. Use any of the sensations you felt as substitutions.

On the King's last line—"You're a *very* poor *speaker*"—try, as a technical exercise, delivering the line:

1. Almost flat and very drily, stressing the words "very" and "speaker" (but not the word "poor," as Lewis Carroll has suggested with his italics);
2. Stressing the words "poor" and "speaker" (but not the word "very");
3. Stressing the word "very" (but not the words "poor" or "speaker"); lengthening the first syllable "ve-" while speaking it on an upward inflection, letting the tone fall quite low on the second syllable "-ry";
4. Stressing only the word "speaker."

You will find other variations as well, but in recording the line you should observe Carroll's italics, I think.

Compare and contrast this with the Pickwick trial on page 112 and with the interrogation of Dantès by Villefort, above. For another excerpt from *Alice in Wonderland* see page 212.

Using Accents

Note: See also Pages 30–34.

There are many characters, native speakers of English and people for whom English was originally a foreign language, that require the use of accents, from the London shopkeeper to the New York deli counterman to the French or German diplomat. The Irish accents in James Joyce's novels and stories, the South African accents in Alan Paton's *Cry, the Beloved Country* (1948) and in Anthony Sher's *Middlepost* (1989), which requires Scottish, Yiddish and various English accents as well; the southern US accents in William Faulkner's works and in Pat Conroy's *Beach Music* (1995), which also requires Italian accents, represent only the tip of the iceberg. It is generally a good idea to keep the accent fairly light, unless the character is supposed to have a heavy accent, such as the "thick Italian accent" assumed by the Count of Monte Cristo when disguised as the Abbé Busoni, or the distinct Aberdonian accent of Inspector MacDonald of Scotland Yard in *The Valley of Fear,* which Dr. Watson makes a point of telling us gets thicker the more excited the Inspector gets. The Sherlock Holmes canon is full of characters who have accents: upper-class British English, Cockney, general London, English Provincial accents, Irish, Scottish, Australian, American, Canadian, French, German, Italian, Spanish, Russian—and I am sure I must have left a few out. Look, as well, at the excerpts from Stoker's *Dracula* on page 121 and Captain Meadows Taylor's *Confessions of a Thug* on page 127.

James Mason's intense reading of an abridged version of Mary Shelley's *Frankenstein* on the Caedmon CD album *Spine Chilling Tales of Horror* is an object lesson in the use of accents; see the Bibliography. The first line of Chapter One in the novel, a first-person narrative by Dr. Frankenstein, is "I am by birth a Genevan." Taking his cue from that line, Mason reads the text with a very slight accent, and pronounces all the French and German names perfectly. I say he "reads," but I almost hesitate to use the word, because, really, he plays Frankenstein with such incredible reality, artfulness and variety, ringing every change in the text. And he also becomes the other characters very subtly: Dr. Waldman, the young Frankenstein's professor, for instance. There is nothing overdone in Mason's reading: His is the kind of performance we all aspire to achieve. He almost makes a completely new beginning to the story—in technical terms he starts a completely new beat—when, as Frankenstein, thinking of what he will do, of how he will create life, he is inspired and thrilled, and he is uncannily real when he then tells us that he "revolved the circumstances in my mind." He stresses such words as "decay" and "corruption," drawing out the vowels slightly, when talking of the corpses he is using to create his creature, but that is a technical analysis of his reading, which does not appear in the least technical or calculated. His change of beat as he tells us of the night he created the creature is also remarkable, as he builds the story, but not in an ordinary, expected way, with breathless climaxes; rather he is so excited internally that his excitement communicates itself without any pyrotechnics or vocal effects. Mason's suave phrasing and his breath control are perfect. And all this while he is playing Frankenstein with that slight accent, which he never forgets!

A useful sound substitution for foreign accents in general is the intermediate vowel "i:" for both the "i" sound in *bit* and the "ee" sound in *machine*. This intermediate vowel is so called because the tongue, in shaping the vowel, is in between the position it assumes in shaping the short "i" sound in *bit* and the longer "ee" sound in *machine*. You can easily pronounce this sound by starting with either "i," then saying "ee," going back and forth between the two a few times, then keeping your tongue in an intermediate position while uttering the vowel "i:."

For more on accents see my book *Accents: A Manual for Actors*.

Here are some examples of often-encountered foreign accents:

1. French

From Henry James's *The American* (1877), Chapter One

"Oh, I mean to buy a great many pictures—beaucoup, beaucoup," said Christopher Newman.

"The honor is not less for me," the young lady answered, "for I am sure monsieur has a great deal of taste."

"But you must give me your card," Newman said; "your card, you know."

The young lady looked severe for an instant, and then said, "My father will wait upon you."

But this time Mr. Newman's powers of divination were at fault. "Your card, your address," he simply repeated.

"My address?" said mademoiselle. Then with a little shrug, "Happily for you, you are an American! It is the first time I ever gave my card to a gentleman." And, taking from her pocket a rather greasy porte-monnaie, she extracted from it a small glazed visiting card, and presented the latter to her patron. It was neatly inscribed in pencil, with a great many flourishes, "Mlle. Noemie Nioche." But Mr. Newman, unlike his companion, read the name with perfect gravity; all French names to him were equally droll.

"And precisely, here is my father, who has come to escort me home," said Mademoiselle Noemie. "He speaks English. He will arrange with you." And she turned to welcome a little old gentleman who came shuffling up, peering over his spectacles at Newman.

• • •

"Monsieur has bought my picture," said Mademoiselle Noemie. "When it's finished you'll carry it to him in a cab."

"In a cab!" cried M. Nioche; and he stared, in a bewildered way, as if he had seen the sun rising at midnight.

"Are you the young lady's father?" said Newman. "I think she said you speak English."

"Speak English—yes," said the old man slowly rubbing his hands. "I will bring it in a cab."

NOTES, COMMENTS AND HINTS

French accent: The first thing to remember in doing a French accent is its salient rhythm, in which the stress, or emphasis, is on the last syllable of a group of words forming a natural entity, such as a noun with its adjectives or a subject and verb, except when that syllable contains a schwa. Such a group is called variously a rhythmic group, a stress group, or a breath group. The tendency of French people speaking English is to stress the ends of phrases even in English. Stress multi-syllable words evenly, or incorrectly in a heavy French accent. Because any French person learning English knows that the emphatic end-syllable stressing is not correct there is usually an attempt to compensate for the incorrect stressing by making both syllables fairly even, as if there were a slight confusion as to which syllable should be stressed

In a heavy accent do a French uvular "r." See Chapter Two, page 33 for how to do it. Another important sound is the French "l," which is articulated with the tongue raised; the tip of the tongue is just behind where it is in articulating an American "l."

Initial consonants are generally "softer," while final consonants are often "harder" than in English. You can, for a fairly heavy accent, drop the initial "h," and you may want to substitute "z" and "s" or "d" and "t" for voiced and voiceless "th" (as in "this" and "think," respectively).

The name "Nioche" is pronounced "nee O:SH." "Noemie" is pronounced "no: é MEE."

Henry James (1843–1916), who tells intriguing stories, is known for his complicated, verbose style, and many consider him very difficult to read. James's biographer, the literary scholar Leon Edel, said "he was exquisitely baroque" and "not to everyone's taste." He can certainly be difficult to read aloud, as I can tell you, after the experience of recording two of his abstrusely written travel books. But here he has written a very accessible, easy to play scene.

The objectives and obstacles of the characters are quite clear, and, consequently the actions they must play, as well as their attitudes, are easy to realize vocally. The young artist copying a painting in the Louvre is even more eager to sell her painting (her objective), than the American, obviously attracted to her, is to buy it (his objective). The American's simultaneous additional objective is "to get to know her." (Characters can have more than one objective at a time.) Mlle. Nioche's father is supportive, but puzzled, and amazed at the American's profligacy in hiring a cab, but hoping that he and his daughter will earn some money, is eager to please and to be of service (his objective).

The language barrier is one of the obstacles all three have to overcome, so a certain hesitancy in reading the dialogue, as they try to communicate, is in order. The sub-objective is "to overcome the language difficulties." In this passage you have an opportunity to do two different French accents (three, if you count the few words of French the American speaks in an American accent). The young lady's should be lighter than her father's, for although she says he speaks English, judging from his grammar, he clearly understands and speaks it less well than she.

Reading *The American* is good practice, because it has a great many French characters. It is the story of the naïve, well-meaning American millionaire, Christopher Newman, who wishes to find a wife in Paris, and submerges himself in European culture, only to find himself rejected by the Bellegardes, an old French family with whose daughter he has fallen in love. He has the opportunity to blackmail them into allowing him to marry her, but he refuses to do so, thus showing the true nobility of his character.

2. German

From Sir Arthur Conan Doyle's *A Scandal in Bohemia* (1892)

"You had my note?" he asked with a deep harsh voice and a strongly marked German accent. "I told you that I would call." He looked from one to the other of us, as if uncertain which to address.

"Pray take a seat," said Holmes. "This is my friend and colleague, Dr. Watson, who is occasionally good enough to help me in my cases. Whom have I the honour to address?"

"You may address me as the Count von Kramm, a Bohemian nobleman. I understand that this gentleman, your friend, is a man of honour and discretion, whom I may trust with a matter of the most extreme importance. If not, I should much prefer to communicate with you alone.

I rose to go, but Holmes caught me by the wrist and pushed me back down into my chair. "It is both, or none," said he. "You may say before this gentleman anything you may say to me."

The Count shrugged his broad shoulders. "Then I must begin," said he, "by binding you both to absolute secrecy for two years; at the end of that time the matter will be of no importance. At present it is not too much to say that it is of such weight it may have an influence upon European history."

"I promise," said Holmes.

"And I."

"You will excuse this mask," continued our strange visitor. "The august person who employs me wishes his agent to be unknown to you, and I may confess at once that the title by which I have just called myself is not exactly my own."

"I was aware of it," said Holmes drily.

NOTES, COMMENTS AND HINTS

German accent: In all German accents drop the post-vocalic "r" in final position and/or before another consonant, exactly as in British English. For North German accents use a uvular "r," similar to the one in French; for South German/Austrian accents use a trilled "r" with one tap. See Chapter Two, page 33, for how to pronounce these sounds.

Final voiced consonants ("b," "d," "g," "v," "z") shift to voiceless ("p," "t," "k," "f," "s"). Initial "w" shifts to a light "v" sound, and initial "s" sometimes shifts to "z." For voiced and unvoiced "th" sounds substitute, respectively, "z" and "s" for North German; "d" and "t" for South German.

When it comes to vowels, substitute the lengthened pure vowel "o:" for the diphthong "oh" (as in *home*); and substitute "e" for "æ" (as in *cat* and *that*).

The Count, we are told by Dr. Watson, has "a strongly marked German accent." Therefore we will assume that his initial "w" sounds are "v" sounds in the following words: would, with, will, weight, wishes, once [vunts], which. On the other hand, I would avoid pronouncing too many initial "s" sounds as "z," because it is a bit too "muddy" and difficult to understand.

The substitutions for "th" sounds would be your choice of either "z" and "s" or "d" and "t," for voiced and unvoiced, respectively.

Final consonants are also important: "You had my note?" would be pronounced "yoo het" my note. The "z" sound at the end of the word *years* would be pronounced as an "s."

What "r" to use is up to you: trilled or guttural. But in a heavy accent you should probably not use the standard retroflex "r" heard at the beginnings of words in both British English and General American.

The word *august* should be pronounced as it is in German: OU goost. The voiced "g" [dg] sound in *agent* should be devoiced, so the word is pronounced "AY chent." If you wish to do what some speakers do and compensate for what they know is an error in devoicing consonants, you might overcompensate by pronouncing the word *excuses* as "eg SGYOO zes" and the word *discretion* as "diz GRE shun," although that may be a bit too much.

The first thing you notice about this text is that it switches back and forth between the Count speaking, Holmes talking, and Dr. Watson telling us the story. In order to be able to switch back and forth in a seemingly effortless manner among the three characters, you must rehearse assiduously.

Watson tell us the Count has a "deep, harsh voice," and that is a perfect hint. He takes an authoritarian tone, and his autocratic, dictatorial attitude is "I command and you obey."

For Watson himself you should adopt the same neutral, pleasant voice you used in the other selections from the Sherlock Holmes canon.

Holmes says what he has to say in a direct, forthright manner, and puts things simply in this scene. He comes to the point and expects other people to do the same, without shilly-shallying.

3. Russian

From Sir Arthur Conan Doyle's *The Adventure of the Golden Pince-Nez* (1905)

"I have only a little time here," she said, "but I would have you to know the whole truth. I am this man's wife. He is not an Englishman. He is a Russian. His name I will not tell."

For the first time the old man stirred. "God bless you, Anna!" he cried. "God bless you!"

She cast a look of the deepest disdain in his direction. "Why should you cling so hard to that wretched life of yours, Sergius?" said she. "It has done harm to many and good to none—not even to yourself. However, it is not for me to cause the frail thread to be snapped before God's time. I have enough already upon my soul since I crossed the threshold of this cursed house. But I must speak or I shall be too late. "I have said, gentlemen, that I am this man's wife. He was fifty and I a foolish girl of twenty when we married. It was in a city of Russia, a university—I will not name the place."

"God bless you, Anna!" murmured the old man again.

"We were reformers—revolutionists—Nihilists, you understand. He and I and many more. Then there came a time of trouble, a police officer was killed, many were arrested, evidence was wanted, and in order to save his own life and to earn a great reward, my husband betrayed his own wife and his companions. Yes, we were all arrested upon his confession. Some of us found our way to the gallows, and some to Siberia. I was among these last, but my term was not for life. My husband came to England with his ill-gotten gains and has lived in quiet ever since, knowing well that if the Brotherhood knew where he was not a week would pass before justice would be done."

NOTES, COMMENTS AND HINTS

Russian accent: For consonants, to do a heavy Russian accent, palatalize "d," "l," "n," and "t," especially before the vowels "i" and "e" (as in the Russian word for "no": *nyet*). To palatalize a consonant means to raise the tongue to the roof of the mouth (the palate), so that just after you say the consonant you hear a "y" sound inserted before the vowel; the word *article* would sound like "AR tyi kəl," or even "AR chi kəl." See Chapter Two, page 32 for how to do a Russian "l."

Substitute a soft "kh" as in Scottish *loch* for an initial "h," and substitute "v" for initial "w," or pronounce "w" correctly, as many Russians do. For voiced and voiceless "th," respectively, substitute "d" and "t" or "v" and "f." Substitute the pure vowel "aw" for the diphthong "oh," so the word *home* is pronounced "khawm," or "hawm."

The old man does not have a Russian accent, and is clearly always taken for English, or it would not be necessary for Anna to mention the fact that he is not English, aside from the plot of the story making it necessary for her to specify that he is a Russian. Her accent, on the other hand, is clearly quite pronounced, and Dr. Watson remarks on it in his narrative when he tells us that she speaks "in a strange foreign voice." However, the accent should still not be a very heavy one, for, as always, clarity is very important. When you cannot see someone's lips move, but can only hear him or her, diction becomes even more important for comprehension.

One of the circumstances that conditions how Anna speaks is that, unknown to the other participants in the scene, she has taken poison, and is going to die, but the poison has not yet begun to take effect, although its growing effects will cause her to have increasingly slurred speech as the scene goes on. Nevertheless, Anna's anticipation that it is about to take effect is an important part of the subtext which underlies everything she says. That subtext also conditions the pace and rhythm of the scene. This is a good lesson in two things: 1) the necessity to prepare so that you as a reader/actor are not taken by surprise by a revelation (Anna's having taken poison) or an event (in this case, Anna's collapse); and 2) the nature of unspoken, unexpressed circumstances which condition how a scene is played because they constitute a character's secret knowledge.

4. Scottish

From Robert Louis Stevenson's *The Master of Ballantrae* (1889), Summary of Events During the Master's Wanderings

To set the scene: This selection is from the opening chapter. The old steward and faithful family retainer, Ephraim MacKellar, is the narrator. "These four" are the old Lord Durrisdeer; his elder son, James Durie, called the "Master of Ballantrae"; his younger, Henry Durie; and the Laird's niece and ward, Alison, with whom both brothers are in love.

To these four came the news of Prince Charlie's landing, and set them presently by the ears. My lord, like the chimney-keeper that he was, was all for temporising. Miss Alison held the other side, because it appeared romantical; and the Master (though I have heard they did not agree often) was for this once of her opinion. The adventure tempted him, as I conceive; he was tempted by the opportunity to raise the fortunes of the house, and not less by the hope of paying off his private liabilities, which were heavy beyond all opinion. As for Mr. Henry, it appears he said little enough at first; his part came later on. It took the three a whole day's disputation, before they agreed to steer a middle course, one son going forth to strike a blow for King James, my lord and the other staying at home to keep in favour with King George. Doubtless this was my lord's decision; and, as is well known, it was the part played by many considerable families. But the one dispute settled, another opened. For my lord, Miss Alison, and Mr. Henry all held the one view: that it was the cadet's part to go out; and the Master, what with restlessness and vanity, would at no rate consent to stay at home. My lord pleaded, Miss Alison wept, Mr. Henry was very plain spoken: all was of no avail.

"It is the direct heir of Durrisdeer that should ride by his King's bridle," says the Master.

"If we were playing a manly part," says Mr. Henry, "there might be sense in such talk. But what are we doing? Cheating at cards!"

"We are saving the house of Durrisdeer, Henry," his father said.

"And see, James," said Mr. Henry, "if I go, and the Prince has the upper hand, it will be easy to make your peace with King James. But if you go, and the expedition fails, we divide the right and the title. And what shall I be then?"

"You will be Lord Durrisdeer," said the Master. "I put all I have upon the table."

"I play at no such game," cries Mr. Henry. "I shall be left in such a situation as no man of sense and honour could endure. I shall be neither fish nor flesh!" he cried. And a little after he had another expression, plainer perhaps than he intended. "It is your duty to be here with my father," said he. "You know well enough you are the favourite."

"Ay?" said the Master. "And there spoke Envy! Would you trip up my heels—Jacob?" said he, and dwelled upon the name maliciously.

NOTES, COMMENTS AND HINTS

Scottish accents: Get a copy of the book and use the entire scene for practice. You are playing four characters in this scene (five, when Alison comes in later), all of whom have Scottish accents, which should be clear and not heavy. All the "R" sounds should be pronounced and often given one very slight tap or trill; see page 33 for information on how to pronounce that sound. Lengthen vowels slightly before "R," "m," and "n." The diphthong "oh" in such words as *know* and *hope* is lengthened slightly, and almost becomes the pure vowel "aw" in *law*. Pronounce the word *your* as "yoor," with the "oo" in *boot*. In such words as *duty* and *endure* do a "liquid u": DYOO tee, en DYOOR. MacKellar should sound almost English, with a very clear Lowlands accent. The old Laird should have a heavier accent, and his two sons lighter accents. Later chapters are narrated by the Chevalier Burke, who befriends the Master and travels with him in the New World. Burke should have a lovely, clear southern Irish accent.

Stevenson's tale revolves around the armed rebellion mounted in 1745 by Prince Charles Edward Stuart (1720–1788), popularly known as Bonnie Prince Charlie, and also called the Young Pretender (the word means "claimant"), who landed in Scotland and unsuccessfully attempted to regain for his father the throne lost to their family in 1688, when his grandfather, the autocratic and unpopular King James II (1633–1701), was forced into exile with his family during the "Glorious Revolution," partly because of their adherence to Roman Catholicism. The Stuart line was then excluded from succession to the British monarchy by the "Act of Settlement."

Bonnie Prince Charlie's father, the self-styled James III (1688–1766), also called the Auld (Old) Pretender, had raised an army in Scotland in 1715 in an enterprise as unsuccessful as his son's would prove to be. The Young Pretender met his final defeat at the hands of the British army on Scotland's Culloden Moor and escaped back to exile in France, where he was joined by many of the rebellious Scottish lairds and their faithful retainers. Jamie and Henry's father, the old lord, had participated in the 1715 rebellion.

Robert Louis Stevenson's *Kidnapped* (1886) and its sequel *David Balfour* (1893) deal with the tragic aftermath of the 1745 rebellion, including the terrible reprisals and repression visited on the Highlands. Later, due in part to the influential and extraordinarily popular historical novels of Sir Walter Scott, including his tale of the 1745 rebellion, *Waverley*, the wearing of the kilt and the playing of the bagpipes (so beloved of Queen Victoria), both forbidden after 1745, came back into fashion.

Our first-person narrator, MacKellar, is an intelligent, deeply loyal servant, full of compassion, and a great observer of events and people. He can only shake his head in sorrow and frustration, because he is powerless to change events, which are dictated in this sad tale of love and sibling rivalry by the characters of its protagonists. As you read this selection aloud, you might also shake your head symbolically (not literally), as an internal attitude. Although he has his feelings about what happened, his tone of voice as he tells the tale should be neutral and simple.

This tragic scene of the rivalry between two brothers is the origin and fount of all the subsequent events of the novel. Act the dialogue and play the attitudes and actions of the other characters, following the previously mentioned convention for recording fiction, because MacKellar would undoubtedly not assume the voices and play the actions of the different characters, but as a reader you will be doing just that all the way through.

There are plenty of clues in the text as to the attitudes of the characters and their manners of speaking. James, the Master, "dwelled upon the name [Jacob] maliciously," and so forth. "Jacob" refers to the story of Esau and Jacob in Genesis, Chapter 25. Jacob, the younger brother of Isaac's first-born son Esau, buys the ravenously hungry Esau's birthright from him for "a mess of pottage"—an unjust bargain amounting to theft. James, willfully and unfairly misusing the Bible story, means that Henry, profiting by the mere toss of a coin, has every intention of stealing his birthright, as Jacob stole Esau's.

All the characters reach a fever pitch of emotional excitement, as they each play their actions against each other. You have to be able, as usual, to switch back and forth from character to character, from objective to objective, from attitude to attitude and from action to action, and all in a clear manner, keeping the story moving forward at a good clip. This is not a scene of slow, leisurely conversation, but a heated argument. Switching characters requires a good deal of preparation and rehearsal, so that they can be sustained over the course of the recording. And, once again, by doing different voices as simply as possible, you will confuse neither yourself nor your listeners.

More Practice Texts

From James Weldon Johnson's *The Autobiography of an Ex-Colored Man* (1912), Chapter IX

Note: The text of this excerpt is taken from the original edition, published anonymously in Boston by Sherman, French & Company, and not from the copyrighted 1927 edition published by Vintage. The introductory material by Carl van Vechten, and the New Introduction by Henry Louis Gates, Jr., in the readily available Vintage paperback, make that edition well worth reading.

After the first few weeks spent in sight-seeing, I had a great deal of time left to myself, my friend was often I did not know where. When not with him I spent the day nosing about all the curious nooks and corners of Paris; of this I never grew tired. At night I usually went to some theater, but always ended up at the big café on the Grand Boulevards. I wish the reader to know that it was not alone the gayety which drew me there; aside from that I had a laudable purpose. I had purchased an English-French conversational dictionary, and I went there every night to take a language lesson. I used to get three or four of the young women who frequented the place at a table and buy beer and cigarettes for them. In return I received my lesson. I got more than my money's worth; for they actually compelled me to speak the language. This, together with reading the papers every day, enabled me within a few months to express myself fairly well, and, before I left Paris, to have more than an ordinary command of French. Of course, every person who goes to Paris could not dare to learn French in this manner, but I can think of no easier or quicker way of doing it. The acquiring of another foreign language awoke me to the fact that with a little effort I could secure an added accomplishment as fine and as valuable as music; so I determined to make myself as much of a linguist as possible. I bought a Spanish newspaper every day in order to freshen my memory on that language, and, for French, devised what was, so far as I knew, an original system of study. I compiled a list which I termed "Three hundred necessary words." These I thoroughly committed to memory, also the conjugation of the verbs which were included in the list. I studied these words over and over, much like children of a couple of generations ago studied the alphabet. I also practiced a set of phrases like the following: "How?" "What did you say?" "What does the word ____ mean?" "I understand all you say except ____." "Please repeat." "What do you call ____?" "How do you say ____?" These I called my working sentences. In an astonishingly short time I reached the point where the language taught itself,—where I learned to speak merely by speaking. This point is the place which students taught foreign languages in our schools and colleges find great difficulty in reaching. I think the main trouble is that they learn too much of a language at a time. A French child with a vocabulary of two hundred words can express more spoken ideas than a student of French can with a knowledge of two thousand. A small vocabulary, the smaller the better, which embraces the common, everyday-used ideas, thoroughly mastered, is the key to a language. When that much is acquired the vocabulary can be increased simply by talking. And it is easy. Who cannot commit three hundred words to memory? Later I tried my method, if I may so term it, with German, and found that it worked in the same way.

I spent a good many evenings at the Grand Opera. The music there made me strangely reminiscent of my life in Connecticut, it was an atmosphere in which I caught a fresh breath of my boyhood days and early youth. Generally, in the morning, after I had attended a performance, I would sit at the piano and for a couple of hours play the music which I used to play in my mother's little parlor.

One night I went to hear *Faust*. I got into my seat just as the lights went down for the first act. At the end of the act I noticed that my neighbor on the left was a young girl. I cannot describe her either as to feature, color of her hair, or of her eyes; she was so young, so fair, so ethereal, that I felt to stare at her would be a violation; yet I was distinctly conscious of her beauty. During the intermission she spoke English in a low voice to a gentleman and a lady who sat in the seats to her left, addressing them as father and mother. I held my programme as though studying it, but listened to catch every sound of her voice. Her observations on the performance and the audience were so fresh and naïve as to be almost amusing. I gathered that she was just out of school, and that this was her first trip to Paris. I occasionally stole a glance at her, and each time I did so my heart leaped into my throat. Once I glanced beyond to the gentleman who sat next to her. My glance immediately turned into a stare. Yes, there he was, unmistakably, my father! looking hardly a day older than when I had seen him some ten years before. What a strange coincidence! What should I say to him? What would he say to me? Before I had recovered from my first surprise there came another shock in the realization that the beautiful, tender girl at my side was my sister. Then all the springs of affection in my heart, stopped since my mother's death, burst out in fresh and terrible torrents, and I could have fallen at her feet and worshiped her. They were singing the second act, but I did not hear the music. Slowly the desolate loneliness of my position became clear to me. I knew that I could not speak, but I would have given a part of my life to touch her hand with mine and call her sister. I sat through the opera until I could stand it no longer. I felt that I was suffocating. Valentine's love seemed like mockery, and I felt an almost uncontrollable impulse to rise up and scream to the audience, "Here, here in your very midst, is a tragedy, a real tragedy!" This impulse grew so strong that I became afraid of myself, and in the darkness of one of the scenes I stumbled out of the theater. I walked aimlessly about for an hour or so, my feelings divided between a desire to weep and a desire to curse.

NOTES, COMMENTS AND HINTS

From the vantage point of a much older man, our unnamed first-person narrator tells us his story, which begins at the time when he was a little boy discovering from the cruel, negative way he was treated the down side of what it meant to be black. The son of a wealthy white Southern father, he grows up in Connecticut under the tender care of his loving mother, a black seamstress. His father never married his mother, but married instead a rich white girl. The narrator is a very musical boy, and his father, who has kept sporadically in touch with his mother, sends the boy a piano after meeting him for the first time, when he is already a young boy. He continues to study music with great pleasure. After many adventures in the North and in the South, during which he meets all classes of African-American society, and goes deeply into the questions of race and racism as it affects not only himself but everyone around him, he befriends a white millionaire in New York, and goes to France with him as his companion and ostensibly as his valet. Our narrator loves Paris, but he breaks off relations with his millionaire friend over the prospect of going on a long trip to Japan. Although disappointed, his millionaire friend gives him money to return to the US to become a composer. He enters a new phase of his life, but you must read the book for the rest of our narrator's profoundly moving story.

James Weldon Johnson (1871–1938) was a diplomat, poet, songwriter (with many Broadway hits, on which he and his brother J. Rosamond Johnson and a friend, Bob Cole, collaborated), professor of literature, civil rights activist with the NAACP, and Renaissance man. He was a literary precursor of Richard White and James Baldwin. He also compiled poetry anthologies, and was part of the Harlem Renaissance. Johnson grew up in a very artistic, intellectual and musical family; it was while he was ambassador to Venezuela that he wrote his masterpiece, *Autobiography of an Ex-Colored Man*, which he felt compelled to publish anonymously.

In this excerpt follow the through-line from the pleasure of our narrator's seeing Paris and learning French and going to the Opéra, which should give a joyous tone to the narration, until that one night when he goes to see *Faust*. He refers to the second act of the opera, in which Marguerite's soldier brother, Valentin (pronounced "væ la:*N* TÆ:*N*"; "Valentine" in English) leaves for the wars and sings a tender farewell aria commending his sister to divine care: *Avant de quitter ces lieux* (pronounced "a: va:*N* də ki: TÉ sé LYÖ"; translation: "Before I leave this place").

The tone of the narration should gradually become less jocular and more serious, but do not for one second play any kind of self-pity, which would be a facile and wrong choice. This character does not pity himself, even though he talks of his feeling of desolation, and experiences his isolation and alienation all the time—as do all human beings to a greater or lesser extent, no matter what their background: That is one of Johnson's great themes. Our narrator is very clear-eyed and objective when viewing himself and his situation, but, as he says, his feelings are "divided between a desire to weep and a desire to curse," which is a great thing for an actor to have to play: a conflict between two potential actions. Feel that conflict when you read this excerpt aloud. Feel it viscerally, in your body, even though you have to sit quite still when recording, and it will come through in your voice. You do not want the listener to pity the narrator, but to empathize with him, and to realize the tragedy (his word) obtaining in the circumstances. Think of this as a tragedy of the ancient Greek kind, in which the hero is powerless against the gods who have decreed his fate, with the difference that it is not the gods but other human beings who have attempted to decree the fate of our hero. But in the end he will not allow them to do so.

Personalize the incident of seeing his father and sister in Paris. Utilize the pain from something in your own life, perhaps when you unexpectedly saw someone you loved and still love, and from whom you had parted a long time before. You have to bare your soul and open your heart when you record this kind of description of emotional life, and experience again the same searing pain you felt, just as you do when preparing a part for the stage, only the audience, of course, will never see you.

From Wilkie Collins's *The Law and the Lady* (1875), Chapter IX: "The Defeat of the Major"

The servant returned to us, bringing with him a tiny bottle of champagne and a plateful of delicate little sugared biscuits.

'I have had this wine bottled expressly for the ladies,' said the Major. 'The biscuits came to me direct from Paris. As a favor to *me*, you must take some refreshment. And then—' He stopped and looked at me very attentively. 'And then,' he resumed, 'shall I go to my young prima donna upstairs and leave you here alone?'

It was impossible to hint more delicately at the one request which I now had it in my mind to make to him. I took his hand and pressed it gratefully.

'The tranquillity of my whole life to come is at stake,' I said. 'When I am left here by myself, does your generous sympathy permit me to examine everything in the room?'

He signed to me to drink the champagne and eat a biscuit before he gave his answer.

'This is serious,' he said. 'I wish you to be in perfect possession of yourself. Restore your strength—and then I will speak to you.'

I did as he bade me. In a minute from the time when I drank it the delicious sparkling wine had begun to revive me.

'Is it your express wish,' he resumed, 'that I should leave you here by yourself to search the room?'

'It is my express wish,' I answered.

'I take a heavy responsibility on myself in granting your request. But I grant it for all that, because I sincerely believe—as you believe—that the tranquillity of your life to come depends on your discovering the truth.' Saying those words, he took two keys from his pocket, 'You will naturally feel a suspicion,' he went on, 'of any locked doors that you may find here. The only locked places in the room are the doors of the cupboards under the long book-case, and the door of the Italian cabinet in that corner. The small key opens the book-case cupboards; the long key opens the cabinet door.'

With that explanation, he laid the keys before me on the table.

> 'Thus far,' he said, 'I have rigidly respected the promise which I made to your husband. I shall continue to be faithful to my promise, whatever may be the result of your examination of the room. I am bound in honor not to assist you by word or deed. I am not even at liberty to offer you the slightest hint. Is that understood?'
>
> 'Certainly!'
>
> 'Very good. I have now a last word of warning to give you—and then I have done. If you do by any chance succeed in laying your hand on the clew, remember this—*the discovery which follows will be a terrible one . . .*'

NOTES, COMMENTS AND HINTS

"Clew" is, of course, the old English spelling for the word "clue." The Major's "prima donna" is an aspiring opera singer in whom he has taken an amorous interest; she is taking her singing lesson upstairs in his house while the above scene takes place.

Valeria Brinton, the narrator, has married Eustace Woodville, a man her family disapproved of because he was a stranger for whom they could not secure proper references—the one friendly reference being a curt reply from Major Fitz-David. Nevertheless, Valeria's family attended the wedding ceremony and wished the couple well, while Eustace Woodville's own family chose to disapprove of his marriage, and his mother refused to attend the wedding. Valeria is ecstatically happy and deeply in love with Eustace Woodville as they leave for their honeymoon at Ramsgate. There, while walking on the beach, she meets his mother by accident—or perhaps by his mother's design—and discovers that her husband has married her under an assumed name, and that he is really called Macallan. He refuses to enlighten her, and begs her to trust him. They remain together after she learns on consulting her lawyers that the marriage is indeed a legal one, but they are naturally very unhappy with one another. In the scene you have just read Valeria has gone clandestinely to visit Major Fitz-David at his London home, in order to find out more about her husband's background. What she discovers is, indeed, terrible.

Wilkie Collins (1824–1889) is best known for being the father of the English mystery novel. *The Moonstone* and *The Woman in White* are both still exciting to read. Less well known today, except among aficionados, are his novels of social commentary. Wilkie Collins was ahead of his time in demanding absolute equality for women, and in understanding how the restrictive, repressive social system of Victorian England was completely unjust to half the population. The narrator in *The Law and the Lady* is the first woman detective in English fiction—most unusual for the times when this book was written. See p. 188 for an interesting incident connected with its publication.

From an actor's point of view, the contrast between the phlegmatic Major, with his underlying tone of lechery—he never saw a woman he wasn't attracted to—and the nervous terror of Valeria, which she controls admirably, makes this scene very enjoyable.

It is always a pleasure and a great acting assignment to have to play two conflicting opposites in one character at the same time. Here we have Valeria's calm exterior and her underlying fear of what she might find out, both informed by her love for her husband, even though he has become a mystery to her, and treats her with a coldness she could not have anticipated. In other words, her character is complex, and this is a life and death issue. Her stakes are very much higher than the major's. You have simply to play her actions vocally from moment to moment.

The major, too, is conflicted: On the one hand he wishes to behave gallantly towards a woman, and on the other he is fearful of betraying her husband, who is his friend; this fear is an "obstacle." So he, too, experiences a certain underlying dread and nervousness, which he controls.

We have two nervous, polite people with conflicting objectives sitting opposite one another and conversing in a civilized drawing room, and they are playing a kind of cat and mouse game with each other. They are in the Major Fitz-David's drawing room, so immediately he is at home and more comfortable than Valeria, who has never been there before—an example of how the circumstance of place conditions the playing of a scene.

Think of substitutions for the situations in which the two characters find themselves. For Valeria, think of a room in which you were very uncomfortable and felt strange, and for the major think of a place in which you are really at home, and are only uncomfortable because of the visit of a stranger, perhaps a proselytizer or a salesperson. Think, as an image, that the circumstances require you to behave "as if" you (Valeria and the major) were looking searchingly into each other's eyes. To find how this feels, stare into your own eyes in a mirror while reading this text aloud for practice.

From Marcel Proust's *Remembrance of Things Past,* Part Two: "A Love of Swann's" (*Un amour de Swann,* usually translated as *Swann in Love*); (1913); my translation

To set the scene: The wealthy friend of highly-placed aristocrats, Charles Swann is in love with the courtesan, Odette de Crécy (his love for her does not prevent him from having a little affair on the side with a seamstress), and they see each other all the time at the salon of the Verdurins, a rich social-climbing bourgeois couple with artistic pretensions. Swann usually accompanies Odette home, and nothing ever happens. He simply drops her at her door and departs.

But one time, when, having thought glumly of this inevitable return home together, he took his little working girl as far as the Bois, in order to delay the moment of going to the Verdurins, he arrived there so late that Odette, thinking he would not come, had left. Seeing that she was no longer in the salon, Swann felt an ache in his heart; he trembled at being deprived of a pleasure which he measured for the first time, having had until then the certainty of finding it when he wished, which, for all pleasures, diminishes for us, or even prevents us from perceiving their greatness in any way.

"Did you see the face he made when he saw she wasn't there?" said M. Verdurin to his wife, "I think one may say that we've caught him!"

"The face he made?" asked Dr. Cottard with violence; he had been to see a patient for an instant and was coming back to get his wife and didn't know whom they were talking about.

"What? You didn't meet the handsomest of Swanns at the door..."

"No. M. Swann was here?"

"Oh! Only for an instant. We had a very agitated, a very nervous Swann. You see, Odette had left."

"You mean he's 'on the best of terms' with her, that she has 'given him a scenic tour of the countryside'," said the doctor, trying out with prudence the meaning of these expressions.

"Well, no, there's absolutely nothing to it, and, just between us, I think she's very wrong and that she's behaving like a first-class jug head, which she is anyway."

"Ta, ta, ta," said M. Verdurin," how do you know there's nothing to it? We haven't been over there to see, have we?"

"She would have told *me* about it," replied Mme. Verdurin proudly. "I tell you, she tells me all about her little affairs! As she no longer has anyone at the moment, I told her she should sleep with him. She claims she can't, that she had a real crush on him, but that he's timid with her, that that intimidates her in turn, and then that she doesn't like him 'like that,' that he's an ideal being, that she's afraid of destroying the feeling she has for him, do *I* know? It would, however, be absolutely what she needs."

"You will allow me not to share your opinion," said M. Verdurin, "I don't like this gentleman that much; I think he's a poseur."

Mme. Verdurin became immobile, assumed an inert expression as if she had become a statue, a fiction that allowed her to pretend she had not heard that unbearable word "poseur," which seemed to imply that someone could "pose" with them, that therefore someone was "better than they."

"Well, if there's nothing to it, I don't think it's because this gentleman thinks her *virtuous*," said M. Verdurin ironically. "And after all, one can't say anything, as he seems to think her intelligent. I don't know if you heard what he was reeling off to her the other evening about the Vinteuil sonata; I love Odette with all my heart, but to expound theories of aesthetics to her, one has to be a notorious ass!"

"Now, now, speak no evil of Odette," said Mme. Verdurin, in a child's voice. "She is charming."

"But that doesn't stop her from being charming; we are 'speaking no evil' of her, we're saying that she's neither virtuous nor intelligent. At bottom," he said to the painter, "do you really care as much as all that if she's virtuous? Perhaps she would be less charming, who knows?"

On the staircase Swann had been joined by the butler, who had not been there when he arrived and had been charged by Odette to tell him—but this was a good hour before—in case he should still show up, that she would probably go take some chocolate at Prévost's before going home. Swann left for Prévost's, but at every step his carriage was stopped by others or by people crossing the street, odious obstacles which he would have been happy to run over if the policeman's interrogation would not have delayed him even more than the crossing of a pedestrian. He counted the time it took, adding several seconds to each minute in order to be sure not to make them too short, which might allow him to believe his chance of arriving soon enough and still finding Odette greater than it was in reality. And in one moment, like someone with a fever who has just slept and who becomes conscious of the absurdity of the musings which he has been ruminating on without detaching himself from them, Swann perceived all of a sudden the strangeness of the thoughts he had been rolling around since the moment they had told him at the Verdurins' that Odette had already left, the newness of the heartache from which he suffered, but which he observed as if he had only just awakened. What? All this agitation because he would not see Odette until tomorrow, which was precisely what he had wished an hour before when he went to Madame Verdurin's! He was obliged to notice that in this same carriage which was taking him to Prévost's, he was no longer the same, and that he was no longer alone, that a new being was there with him, adhering to, amalgamated with him, which he could perhaps not rid himself of, with which he would be obliged to use precautions as with a master or a malady. And yet since the moment when he felt that a new person had been thus added to himself, his life appeared more interesting to him. He thought hardly at all that this possible meeting at Prévost's (the expectation of which played havoc with, stripped naked, the moments which preceded it, to the point that he no longer found one idea, one memory behind which he could make his spirit repose), would probably, if it took place, be like the others: nothing much. As on every evening, as soon as he was with Odette, looking furtively at her changing visage and immediately turning away for fear lest she see the beginning of desire and no longer believe in his lack of interest, he would cease to be able to think of her, too occupied in finding pretexts which would allow him not to leave her immediately, to assure himself without appearing to be too concerned about it, that he would find her again the next evening at the Verdurins': that is, that he would prolong the instant and renew for another day the disappointment and the torture brought to him by the vain presence of this woman whom he pursued without daring to embrace her.

She was not at Prévost's....

[Swann continues to search for Odette, and ends by finding her. She is startled, but gets into his carriage. After this the Narrator tells us the following, perhaps echoing the sentiments of Proust himself, but this is by no means Proust's, or his narrator's (the Narrator's), last word on the subject of love, of course. Nor is it to be taken, as it often is by people who read no more than this first volume of the novel, as his final view of the nature of the psychology of love. Remember: We are in the first volume of a very long book, even if the sequence is out of Time. And this is the character, the Narrator, speaking:]

Of all the methods by which love is produced, of all the disseminating agents of the sacred evil, one of the most efficacious is that great breath of agitation which passes over us. Then the die is cast, the person we are amusing ourselves with at the moment is the person we will love. There is not even any need for that person to have pleased us up till then more than or even as much as others. What is necessary is that our taste for that person become exclusive. And that condition is realized when—at the moment when that person is not there—in search of the pleasures which we enjoyed with that person, an anxious need is brusquely substituted in us, which has as its object that person exactly, an absurd need, which the laws of this world render impossible to satisfy and difficult to cure—the senseless and sorrowful need of possession.

NOTES, COMMENTS AND HINTS

Prévost's is pronounced "pré VOHZ."

The astonishing Part Two of Proust's first volume, *Du côté de chez Swann* (*Swann's Way*) is, first of all, a third-person narrative in a book that is everywhere else a first-person narrative. In telling the story of Charles Swann's unhappy love for Odette de Crécy, the Narrator gives us a brilliant paradigmatic analysis of the psychology of someone in love. (Does he express Proust's ideas, or his own? At any rate, those ideas speak to us very profoundly.) Swann is a friend of the Narrator's family, and he has known Swann ever since he was a young boy. The story he relates was told to him years afterwards. The Narrator, however, tells us things he could not possibly have known, and thus assumes the posture of the omniscient third-person narrators in so many novels, yet without his insights seeming intrusive or unnatural; quite the contrary, in fact. His illumination of the story fills us with profound compassion.

The Verdurins (pronounced "ve:r dü RÆNz") are the epitome of nouveau riche parvenus, with shallow and superficial values, and they are sometimes heartless. Mme. Verdurin is pretentious, but artistic, and devoted to the members of her salon, to which she aspires to invite aristocrats. At the same time, any perceived defection, however slight, such as the mere mention that one has attended another salon, is considered treason, and there is no punishment too great for the traitor, who is promptly ostracized. Swann, who really does have friends among the highest aristocrats and is invited everywhere, but conceals that fact from the Verdurins as much as he can, sees through them, but his adoration of Odette brings him to the Verdurins anyway. Among other things, this book is a great comic masterpiece, and the hilarious scenes in the Verdurins' salon are reminiscent of Dickensian satire.

This is very much the world before the First World War and the Russian Revolution changed it forever in certain ways, although anti-Semitism, with which Swann, a third-generation Catholic, his grandfather having converted from Judaism, has to put up, and which follows him everywhere, has never disappeared. The exposé of the snobbery and viciousness of the Verdurins is extraordinary, the more so because these characters emerge as very real people, and because, in spite of their awfulness, we have a certain sympathy for them, thanks to Proust's artistry in portraying their insecurity. Proust was a master psychologist, a brilliant observer of humanity and human motivations, and he was writing at the same time as Sigmund Freud, whose books, apparently he never read. He had possibly heard them discussed, however, by his father and brother, both of them physicians and professors of medicine, and both of them fascinated by the ideas of the Viennese pioneer of psychology.

Now the question before us is: How do we read this section of the book aloud? The Narrator is sophisticated and philosophical. He is wise in the ways of the world and he understands what it means to have one's heart broken. Is this the same person who began the book by telling us about his experiences tossing and turning in bed at night? It is. But he is obviously older now, and wiser. We will have to wait until much later in the book to find out how he gained wisdom, if indeed he can really be said to have done so.

One of the first things to notice about this excerpt is that there is a change of scene and attitude after the dialogue ends, when we become silent witnesses to Swann's pursuit of Odette.

To make the listener live through what Swann goes through, even as the Narrator tells us his thoughts, one choice is to read the scene as if you were Swann talking to himself, and not simply the Narrator narrating. Swann is surprised to find painful thoughts of love suddenly flooding over him, and his realizations cause him to pause, as it were, and to say, "What is happening to me? I can't believe it!" Thus his attitude is one of "incredulity," and his actions are "taking stock of the situation" and "trying to regain equilibrium." We have to hear Swann ruminating and being upset, even if you make the perfectly valid choice simply to read this as the third-person narration it actually is.

Proust's long sentences, with their numerous subordinate clauses, in which every thought is qualified and analyzed and added to, flow expansively when read aloud. They make such exquisite sense, and they lead us on an on. This is one of Proust's methods of plunging us into his world: He catches us up in his sentences and holds us aloft, as it were. There is no real trick to reading this material: A tempo determined and decided by the prose itself should simply take you with it. Don't just decide that you have to read slowly; you will automatically read slowly enough, without being too slow, to make every thought and every event clear. And there is so much emotion in the writing that you will find yourself getting emotional as you read, especially once you have personalized the text.

As to the dialogue in the first half of this excerpt, it should also flow and sparkle, and it must be very real. It is very arch dialogue, and the tone of the Verdurin couple with each other should reflect the fact that he is clearly subordinate to her, which will be apparent in the way you read their lines to each other. Read the dialogue very really and simply, because the subtext revealing these characters' unconscious minds should remain below the surface. In that way the listener will be able to have a sense of the unconscious rage, jealousy, and antagonism which is hidden from the characters themselves, but comes through the surface expression of their words. These characters think they are merely joking around, but they are deeply envious, insecure people, and they haven't an inkling of why.

There are some gorgeous technical, descriptive clues in what Proust tells us: At one point Madame Verdurin speaks "proudly"; at another she speaks in "a child's voice." Dr. Cottard (pronounced "ko: TA:R")—an excellent diagnostician, but a bit of a boor and a bit of an ignoramus in other areas—speaks "with violence," which means loudly and boorishly, like someone who interrupts someone else's conversation in a rude way. Monsieur Verdurin speaks "ironically" at one point. In their egotism, these characters think they are the center of the universe. These few indications are all you need to read the dialogue aloud.

Of course, it helps to know who these characters are as well, so that you know their objectives. In the case of Dr. Cottard, one may say that in this scene his objective is "to ingratiate" himself with the host and hostess he admires, and whom he thus gives power over him. In the case of the Verdurins, their objective is "to maintain their sense of their own power and superiority." They find the love of Swann and Odette threatening (this love is an "obstacle"), and they are jealous of it, because it means they, the Verdurins, will no longer have power over them, that is, will no longer be the arbiters of taste and fashion they take themselves to be, or, rather whom they wish others to take them to be. Swann threatens them because he really is an art critic, and very knowledgeable and erudite. As the story develops, the Verdurins will find ways to engineer a rupture between Swann and Odette.

The thoughts about the way in which love is awakened and steals over us are expressed in such poetic, terrible and enthralling language that I think one has to take a simple, uncomplicated narrative tone, perhaps with an element of reminiscence in it, in order to let the words speak for themselves. Here, select a substitution your own less happy experiences, so that the passage will be informed and surrounded by it. This disquisition is sad and apprehensive: Love is characterized as a "sacred evil." Love is a god against whom we are powerless. We must succumb to it, will we or no. And love as described here is neither more nor less than the impossible "senseless and sorrowful need of possession."

CHAPTER 7

Recording Plays

If you record a play of which you have done a production, you will probably be standing, rather than sitting, as you do when you record a play from a book. I have recorded plays by Anton Chekhov, Victor Hugo and Clifford Odets, among others, and I used all of the acting methods and techniques for analyzing a character's motivations and actions that I would have used in performing the play on stage, except that I played all the characters, and had to analyze each one.

If you are recording the unabridged text of a play, when you read the characters' names before their speeches, as well as the stage directions, you will have to make your voice sound parenthetical by lowering its pitch and adopting a neutral tone. One of the difficulties in recording plays is the necessity of switching from saying a character's name to reading/acting his or her speech, then going on to the next character's name and speech, and so forth. At times you will have to sound as if one character is interrupting another (you will actually be interrupting yourself) after reading the character's name. You have to have worked out the characters' objectives, obstacles, actions, and circumstances so thoroughly that you can switch back and forth at will, as you do when recording prose fiction. Practice using any play and any scenes with two or more characters.

You will benefit greatly by listening to such original-cast recordings as Dylan Thomas's *Under Milk Wood*, with Dylan Thomas himself; or Edward Albee's *Who's Afraid of Virginia Woolf*, with performances by Uta Hagen and

Arthur Hill (although they sound more "stagy" than they did in the theater, where I saw the original production); or the 1960 Chichester Festival production of Anton Chekhov's *Uncle Vanya*, with Laurence Olivier as Astrov, Michael Redgrave as Vanya, Rosemary Harris as Yelena, and Joan Plowright as Sonya. There are many available recordings of plays from every period; every play by Shakespeare has been recorded many times.

As in other forms of literature, styles in theater differ from period to period. Written in free verse or prose, the Romantic dramas of Victor Hugo, such as *Hernani* or *Ruy Blas*, differ in tone and use of language from the Classic plays of Corneille or Racine, with their verses in the required twelve-syllable alexandrines, and generally strictly followed rules of Aristotelian poetics.

Different types of English make a great deal of difference in the style of a play translated from another language. Michael Frayn's excellent translations of Chekhov's plays are so English in their use of British colloquialisms that they are impossible for American actors to perform. (When I was recording, in my normal General American accent, an English translation of Gustave Flaubert's *A Sentimental Education* I had some difficulty reading the dialogue of a French workman, having to say things like "Arf a mo, guv' " A *French* workman?! I ended up saying that line with a light suggestion of a London Cockney accent; there wasn't too much of a choice.)

As with recording prose fiction written in different periods, so with plays: no matter what the period of the play, you have to make the grammar your own, so that it feels natural, and is simply the character's habitual, unconscious way of expressing her or himself. Shakespeare's Early Modern English grammar presents fewer problems than people generally imagine; it is his vocabulary and the verse that present the greater difficulties—more for audience comprehension than for the actor's understanding.

For practice, prepare the script of any play and record it without stopping. Here are two further exercises that you might enjoy.

Notes, Comments and Hints on Lady Macbeth's Monologue

In your copy of William Shakespeare's *Macbeth* (1605/06; first published 1623) turn to Act I, Scene V.—*Inverness. Macbeth's Castle./ Enter* LADY MACBETH *reading a letter*. Practice using the entire monologue from "*They met me in the day of success: and I have learned by the perfectest report . . .*" through to the end: "Come, thick night,/ And pall thee in the dunnest smoke of hell,/

That my keen knife see not the wound it makes,/ Nor heaven peep through the blanket of the dark,/ To cry, "Hold, hold!" "

Macbeth, Thane of Glamis, one of King Duncan's generals, is hailed by three witches who prophesy that he will be first Thane of Cawdor, then King of Scotland, as his letter tells Lady Macbeth. And he believes them. So does Lady Macbeth: "The raven himself is hoarse/That croaks the fatal entrance of Duncan/Under my battlements." She immediately thinks of murdering Duncan. One of the significant things about that line is that she says "my" battlements. After all, that castle doesn't belong only to her. By using that one word Shakespeare has let us see quite clearly the egocentricity of Lady Macbeth. This is the key to her character: Only she counts, as far as she is concerned.

Here is William Hazlitt on *Macbeth* in his 1817 classic *Characters of Shakespear's Plays*, another text you can use as a practice exercise:

> ...Macbeth himself appears driven along by the violence of his fate like a vessel drifting before a storm; he reels to and fro like a drunken man; he staggers under the weight of his own purposes and the suggestions of others; he stands at bay with his situation; and from the superstitious awe and breathless suspense into which the communications of the Weïrd Sisters throw him, is hurried on with daring impatience to verify their predictions, and with impious and bloody hand to tear aside the veil which hides the uncertainty of the future. He is not equal to the struggle with fate and conscience... His speeches and soliloquies are dark riddles on human life, baffling solution, and entangling him in their labyrinths. In thought he is absent and perplexed, sudden and desperate in act, from a distrust of his own resolution. His energy springs from the anxiety and agitation of his mind. His blindly rushing forward on the objects of his ambition and revenge, or his recoiling from them, equally betrays the harassed state of his feelings.—This part of his character is admirably set off by being brought in connection with that of Lady Macbeth, whose obdurate strength of will and masculine firmness give her the ascendancy over her husband's faultering virtue. She at once seizes on the opportunity that offers for the accomplishment of all their wished-for greatness, and never flinches from her object till all is over. The magnitude of her resolution almost covers the magnitude of her guilt. She is a great bad woman, whom we hate, but whom we fear more than we hate... Her fault seems to have been an excess of that strong principle of self-interest and family aggrandizement, not amenable to the common feelings of compassion and justice...
>
> In speaking of the character of Lady Macbeth, we ought not to pass over Mrs. Siddons's manner of acting that part. We can conceive of

> nothing grander. It was something above nature. It seemed almost as if a being of a superior order had dropped from a higher sphere to awe the world with the majesty of her appearance. Power was seated on her brow, passion emanated from her breast as from a shrine; she was tragedy personified. In coming on in the sleeping scene, her eyes were open, but their sense was shut. She was like a person bewildered and unconscious of what she did. Her lips moved involuntarily—all her gestures were involuntary and mechanical. She glided on and off the stage like an apparition. To have seen her in that character was an event in every one's life, not to be forgotten.

Sarah Siddons (1755–1851) is still considered one of the very greatest tragedians of the English theater. She was apparently prudish, dignified, unapproachable and difficult to work with, but her accomplishments and ability were unquestioned. In 1812 she made her farewell appearance in the part of Lady Macbeth.

To speak this speech, follow Hamlet's advice to the players, of which you will find excerpts on pages 88 and 144. You should not ignore the rhythm of the verses, but do not allow it to take over at the expense of the content and subtext of what Lady Macbeth is saying or of how she is behaving. The following example will demonstrate how the run-on lines and caesuras work to help you sound real and natural, even though you are speaking verse that is written in heightened, poetic language. (See page 274 in Chapter Eight, on poetry, for more information about meter and rhythm.)

> Stop up the access and passage to remorse,
> That no compunctious visitings of nature
> Shake my fell purpose, nor keep peace between
> The effect and it! Come to my woman's breasts,

The second and third lines are called "run-on lines," because the thought and the sentence are continued from one to the next. In the last line, where the thought is broken and a new sentence with a new thought begins in the same line, the pause between the thoughts is called a "caesura."

Even though the verse is important, it is Lady Macbeth's psychological objectives and her actions that are paramount. But you can still enjoy the way in which Lady Macbeth plays with language and dwells lovingly on the words. In fact, she loves language more than she loves human beings, whom she is incapable of loving anyway. If the good Duncan must die so that she may be queen, so be it! She is thrilled that she will be able to kill him with her own hands, and astounded at what she perceives as his incredible stupidity in coming to spend the night at her castle.

Everything that follows is grist for your subtextual mill, and represents one way of approaching the character of Lady Macbeth from a psychological point of view:

Lady Macbeth is what we would today call a psychopath, which is what William Hazlitt implies when he says that she is "not amenable to the common feelings of compassion and justice." Lady Macbeth wouldn't know what compassion meant if it hit her over the head with a hockey stick. She might be able to use the word in a sentence, and she might think she knows what it means, but she is incapable of feeling it, any more than she is capable of feeling love.

One of the other attitudes and feelings that epitomize psychopathy is that psychopaths do not see people as terribly real, with their own fears and desires, which is just how Lady Macbeth feels. To her, people are only pawns in the vast game of chess she plays. In fact, she thinks life is a game.

Everything must be sacrificed to her ambition. Everyone in her life is there to be manipulated to her ends, including her weak-willed, miserable, puny, small-hearted husband—another psychopath. The one thing that redeems her—if she can be said to be redeemed at all, or even redeemable—is that somewhere deep down, where she doesn't even know it exists, is a lurking ability to feel guilt and remorse for her evil deeds. It is this deep guilt, this ultimate sense of right and wrong that will drive her mad. The fact that Lady Macbeth can ultimately feel guilt is implied—and will be borne out later in the play—by the lines:

> . . . Come, thick night,
> And pall thee in the dunnest smoke of hell,
> That my keen knife see not the wound it makes,
> Nor heaven peep through the blanket of the dark,
> To cry, "Hold, hold!"

Of course, it is also true that she just doesn't want to get caught.

Another of the characteristics of psychopathy is the general inability to take responsibility for one's actions. If something goes wrong, it is always someone else's fault. The underlying, fundamental attitude is, "I am surrounded by idiots." That, indeed, is basically what Lady Macbeth thinks in the short term, until her underlying guilt takes over and drives her mad.

A further characteristic of psychopaths is that they can often be very charming and disarming. In other words, they put on a good act. They don't really feel charming inside; they just think that the people they have charmed in order to control and manipulate them are stupid. Lady Macbeth is a charming hostess, and Duncan (that dope, from Lady Macbeth's point of view), falls for it.

Macbeth and Lady Macbeth believe the prophecies concerning his future give them a right to act as they do. Psychopaths tend to love and be comfortable with anything in the way of easy, facile categorization, and superstition and pseudo-science appeal greatly to the psychopathic mind. It is also true that Macbeth and Lady Macbeth lived in a pre-scientific age, when people seeking explanations for natural phenomena were much given to explaining them by resorting to the supernatural.

For a really excellent discussion of this play, and, indeed, of all Shakespeare's plays, see Harold Bloom's magisterial *Shakespeare: The Invention of the Human* (Penguin Putnam, Inc., 1998). On page 524 there is a very instructive comparison of Macbeth and Captain Ahab in Melville's *Moby-Dick* (see pages 179 and 233 in this book for excerpts from *Moby-Dick*). Harold Bloom calls Ahab a "visionary maniac."

Anton Chekhov's *On the Harmfulness of Tobacco*, Scene-Monologue in One Act; my translation

Dramatis Personae:

Ivan Ivanovich Nyoukhin: The husband of his wife, who is the director of a woman's music and boarding school.

The action takes place on the lecture platform of a provincial club.

NYOUKHIN (*With huge sideburns, no mustache, in an old, worn out frock coat; HE enters magnificently, bows and adjusts his waistcoat.*): Ladies and, as it were, Gentlemen. (*Playing with his sideburns*) A proposition was made to my wife that I should give some sort of popular lecture here for charitable purposes. So what? If I lecture, I lecture. It makes absolutely no difference whatsoever to me. To make a long story short, I'm not a professor and I have avoided getting academic degrees, but, nevertheless, despite all that, I have already, for thirty-five years, without stopping, I may say, and to the detriment of my health and so forth, been working on questions of a purely scientific kind; thinking and writing articles—some of them have even been published—on purely scientific subjects—well, not exactly purely scientific, but if you will excuse the expression, rather, virtually scientific. By the way, a few days ago, I wrote a huge article entitled "On the Harmfulness of Certain Insects." My daughters went into raptures over it, especially the part about bedbugs, but I just read it through and tore it up. You know, it doesn't matter if you write about things like that; you still have to use insecticide. At our house

> we have bedbugs even in the grand piano... As the topic of my lecture this evening I have chosen, so to speak, the harmfulness which is done to the human race by the consumption of tobacco. I myself smoke, but my wife wanted me to lecture this evening on the harmfulness of tobacco, and, to make a long story short, you don't argue with her. On tobacco. Very well, then. On tobacco—it really makes no difference to me, but as for you, ladies and gentlemen, I must beg you to pay the strictest attention to my lecture, or I won't answer for the consequences, which could be pretty drastic. But if you can't stand the idea of a dry, boring lecture, if you are not absolutely delighted at the prospect, then you don't have to listen. You can leave. (*Adjusts his waistcoat*) I particularly wish to have the attention of any distinguished doctors who may be present. They may be able to get a good deal of scientific information from my lecture, such as the fact that tobacco, aside from its harmful effects, is also used in medicine. So, to begin with, if a fly lands in a snuffbox, it drops dead—this is true—from a nervous breakdown. Tobacco, strictly speaking, is a plant... When I lecture I have developed the habit of blinking my right eye, but don't worry about it. It's only nerves. I am a very nervous person, generally speaking, and my eye began to blink on the 13th of September, 1889, to be exact, on the very day when my wife gave birth, so to speak, to our fourth daughter...

NOTES, COMMENTS AND HINTS

The lecturer's name is pronounced "ee VA:N ee VA:N vich NYOO khi:n"). All Russians have three names: a first name; a patronymic, which is the name of the father (it is always stressed as the original first name is stressed, as is the case here; the syllable "ov" in the patronymic is generally not stressed, except in "Petrovich," based on the name "Pyotr" [Peter]); and a last name. Nyoukhin's last name suggests the words "sniveler" and "sniffles" in Russian, and, with the "kh" pronounced like the Scots word *loch*, is onomatopoetic in English as well.

The audience reaction to *On the Harmfulness of Tobacco* should be complicated: We laugh, sometimes uproariously, at the ridiculous things Nyoukhin says, but, as the play goes on, we want to cry, too, because he is so sad. What you want to avoid is playing him as self-pitying, because one of his objectives is to maintain his dignity, and this he does so well, that by the end of the play we empathize with him, and perhaps we have a tear in our eye, even as we laugh.

Then how do you play Nyoukhin, who is just a little drunk (later on he surreptitiously takes a sip out of a flask), and who has no idea what to say, as he hems and haws his way through the first part of his lecture, and, except near the beginning, talks about everything but tobacco? Is he perhaps quivering with stage fright? You must first think of the specific circumstances of the character's life, both as it is actually taking place in the present moment, and as it took place in the past. For Nyoukhin's deep unhappiness, select the proper emotional substitution from your own life to infuse into the character. You have to make it apparent that he is a miserable, henpecked husband and an unhappy father, whose daughters laugh at him. When he says that they went into raptures over his article on the harmfulness of certain insects, or at least over the part about bedbugs, your reading should make us suspect that what really happened was probably that they went into gales of laughter. One also has to get the impression that his wife suggested the topic of the lecture, on the harmfulness of tobacco, after she, too, had seen his article; that she probably screamed at him something like, "You idiot! Why don't you give a lecture on the harmfulness of *tobacco*?! And stop stinking up the house! Put out that cigarette!" You must gradually reveal just how miserable and upset he is, and how much a failure he feels. His only desire, he tells us, is to run away and forget everything. The monologue ends on an ironic note when his wife shows up at the back of the lecture hall, and, terrified, he reverts to the subject he hasn't actually talked about, and ends the lecture.

What is it like in the lecture hall? Is it too hot? Is it stuffy? What has he just been doing before he walks on stage? He has probably been taking a wee drop, maybe to stave off that stage fright, and certainly having a smoke.

What would be the first thing Nyoukhin wants when he steps out onto the lecture platform (aside from running away to the ends of the earth the moment he sees the audience)? Perhaps he wants a glass of water? But there is none available. Alcohol is dehydrating, and only alcohol allows him to confide in the group of strangers before him, as the lecture goes on. Of course, he would never confide in anyone he knew personally. But then, whom does he know? He has no friends. He feels completely alone and alienated. He has no one to talk to. No one understands or appreciates him, let alone loves him. He started life with dreams, but they have all been shattered, and his life has become a disappointment. As he comes out onto the lecture platform his discomfort, indeed his terror, is compounded by his thirst. He is probably shaking from sheer nervousness. His eye will soon begin to blink...

At the beginning, it is almost as if Nyoukhin is talking to himself at the same time as he is addressing the audience, so your first action, once you are past the introduction of yourself to the audience might be, "I am talking to myself." And your subconscious train of thought could run on like this: "I am trying to make sense of the things in my life that make no sense, and because I feel incompetent and unworthy I am trying to convince the audience that I am, indeed, a competent lecturer and worthy to appear before them. Of course, they see right through me."

Once you have discovered how the character enters and what he does first, you can launch yourself hesitatingly and self-protectively into the lecture and take it from there. All the physical life of the character, and all the circumstances, past and present will inform the character's voice and delivery and be reflected vocally, and organically, as you use this piece for recording practice.

Anton Pavlovich Chekhov (1860–1904) wrote the first version of this one-act play in 1886 and revised it several times, the last version being that of 1903, which I have translated, and performed in several different venues.

Chekhov was born into a family that had been serfs until his grandfather, Yegor Mikhailovich, by saving his money for the purpose no matter what the deprivations and suffering, purchased freedom for himself and his wife and children. (For more about the system of serfdom see page 222 under Ivan Goncharov's *Oblomov*.) Yegor Mikhailovich thus entered the next highest social class in Russia, the lower middle class. Chekhov's mother's family had come from the same roots and done the same thing. The ambitious Yegor Mikhailovich forced his sons into a higher class still. So Chekhov's father became a merchant, and the family moved eventually to Moscow, where they did not do well. As a young man with a great sense of responsibility, Anton Pavlovich felt he had to help support them, so he became a doctor. He first started writing simply in order to earn extra money. You can learn more about him from one of the biographies listed in the Bibliography.

He knew from the firsthand experience of his own and his family's struggles all about the intolerance, bigotry, inhumanity and brutality of the economic system, which is why his writing is so full of love and compassion. As a compassionate, empathetic observer of humanity with a great understanding of human psychology, and as a concise writer with a sense of the essential, he was also able to portray human beings with an uncanny reality in his amazing short stories and realistic plays.

It is often said that Chekhov productions are too serious, that they take no account of the comedy in the plays he wrote, which should be very funny to audiences. But this is to misunderstand Chekhov, in my opinion. His farces are indeed out and out hilarious comedies, even providing belly laughs. But the full-length plays, called comedies, and even this farcical monologue, are comedies of irony. The comedy arises from the fact that the people in the plays are so involved in their personal situations and problems, and in their egotism; that they don't see that the solution to their problems lies right in front of them.

Try to get hold of Michael Redgrave's recording of this piece, alas, no longer available; the LP was published by Spoken Arts, SA 828, 1962. It was my first acquaintance with the play, and the very first line almost had me on the floor. In a tense, high-pitched, slightly hoarse voice he said, "Ladies and Gentlemen . . . so to speak." He was extremely funny, pathetic and very real, all at the same time, and one had the impression of constant tension, of a man on the edge of a nervous breakdown, like the fly in the snuffbox. In addition, his voice suggests perfectly the tobacco smoker, the alcoholic, and the pedant, with his constant insertion of meaningless little phrases ("so to speak"; "as it were"). What makes those phrases so hilarious is that they qualify things that don't ordinarily need to be qualified, such as "Ladies and Gentlemen," and "my wife gave birth." Redgrave did not read the stage directions or character description (which you might be called on to do in a noncommercial book recording), only the monologue itself.

An imaginative exercise of the sort Michael Chekhov, the writer's nephew, might have suggested is to tell yourself: "I am standing here in front of the audience completely naked, and I want to hide, so I am looking around for a hiding place." Another: "I desperately want to run away, but there is a ball and chain attached to my ankle and tied to a post right there on stage in front of me."

If you think these procedures apply only to a performance onstage, think again. Even if nobody sees you, all of these kinds of questions and answers inform the entire reading.

CHAPTER 8

Recording Poetry

About Poetry

Poetry was originally meant to be heard. Its recitation was an art practiced by the ancient bards and later by minstrels, and poetry's affinity with music made it easy to unite the two arts in song. Poets use what is called "heightened" language—language that is distilled, crystallized, concentrated, carefully chosen, often metaphorical, and always imagistic—to tell their stories. And when you tell the stories in the poems, whether lyric or narrative, you have to make that language real. You have to deal with rhythm and often with rhyme. You have to sing, but only figuratively.

Two of the principal forms of poetry are lyric poetry and narrative poetry. Among the latter are the ancient Icelandic sagas; classical epics, including Homer's *Iliad* and *Odyssey* and Virgil's *Aeneid* (all three often translated into prose); medieval sagas, such as *Beowulf* and epics such as *La Chanson de Roland* (*The Song of Roland*); Dante's *Divine Comedy;* and in the Elizabethan era Shakespeare's *The Rape of Lucrece.* The seventeenth century saw Milton's *Paradise Lost;* the eighteenth, Alexander Pope's comic *Dunciad;* the nineteenth, Samuel Taylor Coleridge's *The Rime of the Ancient Mariner;* Sir Walter Scott's *Marmion* and *The Lady of the Lake;* Alfred Lord Tennyson's *Idylls of the King;* Lewis Carroll's nonsense epic *The Hunting of the Snark: An Agony in Eight Fits;* and Robert Browning's verse novel *The Ring and the Book* and his dramatic monologues, of which one of the most famous is *My Last Duchess.*

A great deal of poetry, from Elizabethan days to the present, is "lyric." Lyric poems often consist of several short verses, written in different forms and styles, and are frequently the expression of a feeling or an action. An "ode" is a longer lyric poem, quite complex in structure, and meditative or descriptive, a tribute to someone or something. In a way, forms don't particularly matter when you are reading poetry aloud. You have to convey meaning, whether you are dealing with the formal sonnet or with free verse; whether you are reading a love lyric or an apostrophe to a Grecian urn. What counts, and what you have to look for in analyzing a poem from the point of view of making its contents clear to listeners, is how the poet breaks up lines, with caesuras, for instance, and how the poet uses grammar and vocabulary, metaphor and symbol, to convey meaning. Narrative poetry does not, of course, exclude lyricism or symbolism.

Often, in a lyric poem that appears to be only a description, you are conveying an image as part of a story. In the evocative Japanese form Haiku, for example, the readers, or listeners, supply their own stories in their reactions to the images. Something in the listener will be awakened, and he or she will respond in a very personal way to the poem. Perhaps the listener's sensibilities will be expanded, or educated, to some degree.

Poetry works partly by metaphor, which is also very important in prose. Theories of metaphor are quite complicated, and metaphor is a vast, much debated and much explored subject. Briefly, to take the simplest definition, a metaphor is an implied comparison and/or an association of one thing with another; the words "like" or "as" are not used, and do not have to be. If they are used, you have what is called a simile. When Poe says, "Helen, thy beauty is to me/Like those Nicean barks of yore..." he has written a simile, as has Coleridge, when he writes in *The Rime of the Ancient Mariner* "As idle as a painted ship/Upon a painted ocean."

A metaphor, ideally, should appear to be inevitable. Marcel Proust criticized Paul Morand in a preface Proust wrote for a book of Morand's short stories because he felt that Morand's metaphors were contrived, that they were too calculated, too recherché, that they were not inevitable.

Here are some examples of metaphors, underlined:

1. From Matthew Arnold's *Dover Beach*: "the turbid ebb and flow of human misery"

2. From A. E. Housman's *A Shropshire Lad*:

   Loveliest of trees, the cherry now
   Is hung with bloom along the bough,
   And stands about the woodland ride
   Wearing white for Eastertide.

3. From William Shakespeare's *Sonnet XXX*: "For precious friends hid in death's dateless night."

Rhyme schemes and rhythms are very important to consider in reading poetry aloud. Do you make the rhyme apparent by stressing it? Or do you bury it, so that it is not obvious? In other words, do you emphasize simply the meaning of the words, or do you emphasize the rhyme and/or the rhythm. The answer is: Sometimes the first, sometimes the second, depending on the poem. In limericks, for instance, the rhyme is of paramount importance and has to be emphasized; it's part of the joke, if not the joke itself. See the limericks on page 56. Rhymes will be apparent to the listener whether you stress them or not, if only subconsciously, because the rhyme is there, after all.

Reading poetry requires you to deal with specific rhythms, and often, particularly in poetry written before the twentieth century, with rhythms that are also classical meters. Meters alternate strong and weak stresses in a predetermined, recurring pattern, called a "foot." A metric line of poetry is named after the number of feet it contains: a tetrameter contains four feet; a pentameter five; a hexameter six; a heptameter seven, and so on. (Stress the second syllables of all four nouns.)

One of the most commonly used meters is "iambic pentameter." An "iamb" (pronounced "I am"; but "iambic" is pronounced "eye AM bik") is a foot containing one weakly stressed syllable followed by one more strongly stressed syllable; there are five iambs (or iambic feet) in a line of iambic pentameter, in the following rhythm: te TUM / te TUM / te TUM / te TUM / te TUM. An example: "The paths/of glo/ry lead/but to/the grave," from Thomas Gray's *Elegy Written in a Country Churchyard*. Shakespeare's verse in his plays is usually iambic pentameter.

Three other standard feet that you should be familiar with are: 1) the anapest, consisting of two weak syllables followed by one strong syllable; 2) the trochee, consisting of one strong syllable, followed by one weak syllable (the opposite of the iamb); and 3) the dactyl, consisting of one strong syllable followed by two weak syllables.

To help you in reading poems aloud, you should know that iambs and anapests are said to be written on a rising rhythm, because the strong syllables are at the end; and trochees and dactyls are referred to as being written on a falling rhythm, because the weak syllables are at the end. This means that although the pitch on which those syllables are spoken may also be higher or lower, you should not drop your voice on the ends of lines, unless it is absolutely necessary to do so. In most cases it is best not to reinforce the meter, but to leave it alone or even to obscure it; like rhyme, it will be heard anyway.

Here are some examples of different meters:

1. iambic tetrameter: "Alone,/alone,/all all/alone" (Coleridge's *The Rime of the Ancient Mariner*; see below). When read slowly, with each repetition on exactly the same tone, this is very effective in conveying the aloneness of the speaker. Another choice would be to raise the pitch of the second "alone," as if this line is a dawning realization; and then to drop, or raise, the pitch on "all, all alone," in growing despair. The simpler the better, though. It would be too easy and too facile to reflect the melodrama of the situation vocally, and not as effective as a quiet internal sense of the speaker's condition, which you should personalize by finding substitutions.

2. trochaic tetrameter: "Fill the/cup, and/fill the/can" (Alfred, Lord Tennyson's *The Vision of Sin: Song at the Ruin'd Inn, of a grey and gap-toothed man*). Trochees are often missing the final weak syllable. You can emphasize either the word "fill" or the words "cup" and "can"; or you can give this a strong rhythmic pattern, since this is a drinking song.

3. trochaic pentameter: "Blow, bugle; answer, echoes, dying, dying, dying" (Alfred, Lord Tennyson's *The Princess: Songs*). The trochee begins on the word "answer," preceded by a "spondee" on the words "Blow, bugle" (a "spondee" is a foot consisting of two syllables with equal stress on both). Try lowering the pitch successively on the last three words. Don't be afraid of the rhythm here, but don't stress it too much either; for instance, stress the opening spondee, then stress "echoes" more strongly than "answer," take a slight pause, and then say the final three words in a slow and stately rhythm, or, if you prefer, a slightly faster tempo.

Poets can vary or alternate meters throughout a poem, or, writing in "free verse," use no uniform metric pattern at all. They can also use run-on lines, meaning that a thought is continued into the next line, as Matthew Arnold does, for instance, in *Dover Beach*. And poets regularly employ caesuras, which are the end of one thought and the beginning of another somewhere in a line, such that a pause is necessitated in the reading of it, as you will see in Robert Browning's *My Last Duchess* below. The use of run-on lines and caesuras facilitates enormously the task, and the pleasure, of reading poetry aloud.

See the cogent entry "Meter" in M. H. Abrams' *A Glossary of Literary Terms* (Heinle & Heinle, 1999), one of the most useful, thorough reference books I know.

One of the first things to do with any poem is to figure out how to deal with its rhythm. Don't read in a singsong fashion, and don't be a slave to the rhythm; use it to help convey meaning. Nothing would be worse than pounding away at iambic pentameter. Nobody could listen for long to that. As one possibility, speak the line from Thomas Gray's poem, previously cited, as if it were a prose line, stressing the underlined words: "The paths of glory lead but to the grave." On the other hand, it is certainly possible, and could be quite effective, to read with just a bit—a slight bit—more emphasis on the rhythm: "The paths of glory lead but to the grave."

Many poets have recorded their own works, some far more successfully than others, although it is always fascinating to hear the poet's voice and interpretations, and it is always most instructive to listen to them. Edna St. Vincent Millay (1892–1950), for instance, is a charming reader, with beautiful diction, who reads with great vitality and variety; in some poems she emphasizes the rhythms and rhymes, in others she buries them and reads simply to clarify the meaning of the words. Another fine reader of her own poems is Dorothy Parker (1893–1967), whose sense of the irony of her own words is quite apparent; she is very funny and reads for meaning, sometimes emphasizing rhymes, and always with the dry wit with which she wrote. W. H. Auden (1907–1973) also reads his poetry with a sense of the meaning, and buries the rhymes, which we hear anyway; he is occasionally somewhat declamatory. Langston Hughes (1902–1967) reads with a fine sense of realism and reality, and, when his poems are about music, emphasizes rhythm and rhyme; but, when they are not, he buries the rhymes and the rhythms, and reads for meaning. In your own reading avoid being declamatory, as E. E. Cummings (1894–1962) is, because it can be rather boring to listeners; he seems very artificial, although his writing usually doesn't. On the other hand, you might want to emulate Ogden Nash (1902–1975) who is hilarious, and emphasizes the rhymes, which are frequently the jokes in his poems. He sounds quite natural, and makes sure we hear the meaning. He speaks, incidentally, with a delightful old-fashioned upper-class accent, reminiscent of Franklin D. Roosevelt. Dylan Thomas (1914–1953) also read his own poetry magnificently, and he had a naturally resonant voice, albeit a rather declamatory style of reading, as you can hear in recordings of *Under Milk Wood* and *A Child's Christmas in Wales*. See the Bibliography for a list of recordings. For more poetry to practice reading aloud, see the exercises at the end of Chapter Two.

To summarize, there is no necessary hard and fast rule about when to emphasize rhyme and rhythm, but you never want to do so at the expense of meaning. Rhymes can be delicious to hear, and rhythm to experience. Just be careful how and when you use them.

Some Poems

Matthew Arnold (1822–1888), *"Dover Beach"* (published in 1867)

The sea is calm to-night.
The tide is full, the moon lies fair
Upon the straits;—on the French coast the light
Gleams and is gone; the cliffs of England stand,
Glimmering and vast, out in the tranquil bay.
Come to the window, sweet is the night-air!
Only, from the long line of spray
Where the sea meets the moon-blanch'd land,
Listen! you hear the grating roar
Of pebbles which the waves draw back, and fling,
At their return, up the high strand,
Begin, and cease, and then again begin,
With tremulous cadence slow, and bring
The eternal note of sadness in.

Sophocles long ago
Heard it on the Ægean, and it brought
Into his mind the turbid ebb and flow
Of human misery; we
Find also in the sound a thought,
Hearing it by this distant northern sea.

The Sea of Faith
Was once, too, at the full, and round earth's shore
Lay like the folds of a bright girdle furl'd.
But now I only hear
Its melancholy, long, withdrawing roar,
Retreating, to the breath
Of the night-wind, down the vast edges drear
And naked shingles of the world.

Ah, love, let us be true
To one another! for the world, which seems
To lie before us like a land of dreams,
So various, so beautiful, so new,

Hath really neither joy, nor love, nor light,
Nor certitude, nor peace, nor help for pain;
And we are here as on a darkling plain
Swept with confused alarms of struggle and flight,
Where ignorant armies clash by night.

NOTES, COMMENTS AND HINTS

"The sea is calm to-night"—the image is simple and clear. By stressing the word "calm," you convey the idea that the sea is not calm on every night, and you prefigure the rest of the poem. If you choose to stress the word "tonight," you convey the same idea. However, those are only two possible choices, and it would be just as effective, and perhaps even better, to read the words evenly and thus allow the reader to form his or her own idea of the image and its meaning.

Some technical points: The second line of the poem is a run-on with the third line, so connect them in one sentence, then take a pause at the caesura. The third and fourth lines are also run-ons, so connect them to each other as well.

Read the words simply and naturally, and envision the sea, as if you were standing at the window overlooking it, as the person in the poem does, while she or he is talking to the other person in the room with her or him. This poem has a speaker addressing a listener, so substitute someone for the person the poet (you) is talking to.

Arnold wrote this poem in 1851–1852, when he had just been married, but did not publish it until 1867. Therefore, the speaker is undoubtedly meant to be Arnold, and the listener his wife; that is very specific and concrete. But since the poem is actually abstracted, and the genders of the speaker and the listener are not specified, it could be any two people who are in a loving relationship, whether a new one or one of long duration. I think this ambiguity and universality account for the poem's enduring popularity. Personalizing the poem by choosing substitutions will allow you to attain to the general through the specific, thus permitting the listener to enter the poem and make his or her own substitutions as he or she listens.

As you read the poem aloud, enjoy the beauty of its images and language. The poem's sounds and the beauty of its language are of paramount importance, always, which is why diction and pronunciation are so important. The rhythm and the rhyme scheme vary here, which helps you in reading it aloud, because you don't have to worry about them. Stress lightly such lines as "The Sea of Faith," in order to make Arnold's points. There should be a kind of serene, quiescent, intimate feeling to your reading, and almost a whispered quality to your communication to your imagined interlocutor.

Sophocles, who wrote *Oedipus* and *Antigone* was the great tragedian of Ancient Greece. The lines "here as on a darkling plain . . . Where ignorant armies clash by night" is an allusion to Thucydides' account of a nighttime battle during the Peloponnesian War at Epipolae, where the soldiers had difficulty distinguishing friend from enemy, but the lines could refer to any battle, and certainly to life.

There is an evident contrast between the beauty of the starry night and the calm sea, and the confusion and unhappiness of the human condition, metaphorical at first, then explicit at the conclusion of the poem. The sea is changeable, as human fate and life are changeable, and the vastness of the universe can be frightening and make us feel how small we are, and how powerless. This is a poem with a humanist philosophy, from which God has disappeared. The "Sea of Faith" once provided consolation for human unhappiness and security in the face of the chaotic universe, but we can no longer believe in what has turned out to be an illusion. The only thing we really have, we human beings, is each other, so "let us be true to one another." Therein, and not in some religious myth, lies our salvation, if that is even a word we can find valid. At any rate, the solution to our problem is: to love. Analogy and metaphor: What do the words stand for, as signs or symbols, and what do the images evoke? The "grating roar" is the "turbid ebb and flow/Of human misery." The sea and the Sea of Faith are explicitly compared.

Matthew Arnold was the epitome of a Victorian gentleman, refined and genteel and a great classicist and educator. He was Inspector of Schools from 1851 to 1886, and chair of poetry at Oxford University for ten years. He believed in universality and humanism, and in the classical virtues of the unity of images, time and place, and in clean, elegant, simple expression and strong construction. His lifelong debate with religion, which he basically believed in, despite the apparent irreligion of *Dover Beach,* ended in his acceptance of religious faith.

Aphra Behn (1640–1689), "Song" from *Abdelazer* (1676)

Love in fantastic triumph sat,
   Whilst bleeding hearts around him flow'd,
For whom fresh pains he did create,
   And strange tyrannic power he shew'd;
From thy bright eyes he took his fire,
   Which round about in sport he hurl'd;
But 'twas from mine he took desire
   Enough to undo the amorous world.

From me he took his sighs and tears,
   From thee his pride and cruelty;

From me his languishments and fears,
And every killing dart from thee;
Thus thou and I the God have arm'd,
And set him up a Deity;
But my poor heart alone is harm'd,
Whilst thine the victor is, and free.

NOTES, COMMENTS AND HINTS

Aphra Behn led a very interesting life. She was not only a great poet, but also a prolific and very popular playwright, as well as the author of several novels. She was born Aphra Johnson in England, but at the age of twenty-three or so she went to live in Surinam, where she met and married Mr. Behn, a wealthy merchant, who died a year or so after their marriage. She then returned to England, having first been a spy in Antwerp for King Charles II. She was never paid, and in 1668, unable to pay the debts she had incurred largely because of her services to the king, she was sent to debtor's prison, but she was soon released. It was then that she began to write her successful plays, some of which starred the well-known actress Nell Gwyn, famous also as the mistress of Charles II. Aphra Behn is buried in Poets' Corner in Westminster Abbey, and that is an honor reserved for only the most revered poets.

Abdelazer, or The Moor's Revenge, Aphra Behn's only tragedy, was a great success when it was produced in 1676. There are echoes in it of Shakespeare's *Hamlet, Macbeth* and *Othello*, and of Jacobean revenge tragedies. Thomas Betterton, the great actor of the Restoration stage, much acclaimed for both his Hamlet and his Othello, created the title role of the Moor. The plot is extremely complicated:

The General of the Army of Spain, Abdelazer the Moor, is a wealthy Christian convert in love with the Queen of Spain, who loves him passionately in return. When the King dies, the jealous Cardinal Mendozo, who is also in love with the Queen, uses Abdelazer's love affair with her to deprive the Moor of his high offices and to banish him from the court. Despite the protestations of the Cardinal and of the new young King Ferdinand's brother Philip, and because Ferdinand loves Abdelazer's wife, Florella, he rescinds the banishment, after Florella pleads with him to do so. For all the insults he has received, and because he knows the new King loves his wife, the jealous Abdelazer vows revenge, as do Philip and the Cardinal. After a great banquet of only feigned reconciliation, the Cardinal and Philip flee in order to escape Abdelazer's assassins. Abdelazer forces Florella to attempt to murder Ferdinand, but the Queen prevents her from doing so, and Florella then kills herself with the dagger she had intended to use on Ferdinand. Abdelazer rushes in and kills Ferdinand. Philip claims the crown, and the Queen joins Abdelazer in making war on her son, who loses the battle and is arrested and imprisoned. The plot complications grow apace, until the end, when Abdelazer is killed.

After Behn's death a revival of *Abdelazer* with music by Henry Purcell was highly successful, but he did not set the poem which appears above, and which opens the play. The song displeases Abdelazer, who orders the music stopped—the opposite of Orsino at the opening of Shakespeare's *Twelfth Night*: "If music be the food of love, play on..."

The rhythm of the poem is iambic tetrameter, with occasional variations, as in the first line. The rhyme scheme for each verse is "a, b, a, b, c, d, c, d," but the poet has buried the rhymes by not repeating the construction of the sentences, so the first three lines have almost the same construction, but the third line is a variation, enabling you to read it aloud in a way which imparts the meaning and the contrast of the opposites without sounding singsong:

From me he took his sighs and tears,
From thee his pride and cruelty;
From me his languishments and fears,
And every killing dart from thee;

As we have seen, the subject of the poem is unrequited love. What the god of love took from you and gave to me is your cruel rejection of me, and what he took from me and gave to you is my love for you. Once again, you must personalize this poem, and use substitutions from a time in your life when you were unhappy in love, when you loved and were not loved in return. Aphra Behn tells us that the only person hurt in such a situation is the one who loves. There is no self-pity in this poem, and taking a tone of self-pity would simply ruin it. It is her elegant expression of the thoughts about unrequited love that makes this poem so lovely and so moving, even though it is full of precious conceits.

Robert Browning (1812–1889), *My Last Duchess* (1842 in a volume called *Dramatic Lyrics*; given its title in 1849 in *Dramatic Romances and Lyrics*)

FERRARA
That's my last Duchess painted on the wall,
Looking as if she were alive. I call
That piece a wonder, now: Frà Pandolf's hands
Worked busily a day, and there she stands.
Will 't please you sit and look at her? I said

"Frà Pandolf" by design, for never read
Strangers like you that pictured countenance,
The depth and passion of its earnest glance,
But to myself they turned (since none puts by
The curtain I have drawn for you, but I)
And seemed as they would ask me, if they durst,
How such a glance came there; so, not the first
Are you to turn and ask thus. Sir, 'twas not
Her husband's presence only, called that spot
Of joy into the Duchess' cheek: perhaps
Frà Pandolf chanced to say, "Her mantle laps
Over my Lady's wrist too much," or "Paint
Must never hope to reproduce the faint
Half-flush that dies along her throat"; such stuff
Was courtesy, she thought, and cause enough
For calling up that spot of joy. She had
A heart—how shall I say?—too soon made glad,
Too easily impressed; she liked whate'er
She looked on, and her looks went everywhere.
Sir, 'twas all one! My favour at her breast,
The dropping of the daylight in the West,
The bough of cherries some officious fool
Broke in the orchard for her, the white mule
She rode with round the terrace—all and each
Would draw from her alike the approving speech,
Or blush, at least. She thanked men,—good; but thanked
Somehow—I know not how—as if she ranked
My gift of a nine-hundred-years-old name
With anybody's gift. Who'd stoop to blame
This sort of trifling? Even had you skill
In speech—(which I have not)—to make your will
Quite clear to such an one, and say, "Just this
Or that in you disgusts me; here you miss,
Or there exceed the mark"—and if she let
Herself be lessoned so, nor plainly set
Her wits to yours, forsooth, and made excuse,
—E'en then would be some stooping; and I chuse
Never to stoop. Oh, sir, she smiled, no doubt,
Whene'er I passed her; but who passed without
Much the same smile? This grew; I gave commands;
Then all smiles stopped together. There she stands
As if alive. Will 't please you rise? We'll meet

The company below, then. I repeat,
The Count your Master's known munificence
Is ample warrant that no just pretence
Of mine for dowry will be disallowed;
Though his fair daughter's self, as I avowed
At starting, is my object. Nay, we'll go
Together down, Sir! Notice Neptune, though,
Taming a sea-horse, thought a rarity,
Which Claus of Innsbruck cast in bronze for me.

NOTES, COMMENTS AND HINTS

This dramatic monologue is a play in miniature, and you are playing the part of the Duke of Ferrara.

The Duke is talking to the envoy of his prospective father-in-law, the Count (we are not told what he is Count of), and showing him some of the treasures of his palace so as to convince him that he would be a good match (actions and objective). They have stopped before a portrait of his first wife, which is covered by a curtain that the Duke has drawn aside in order to show the picture to his visitor, whom he invites to sit down before it. The Duke calls it "a wonder," and expatiates upon it, revealing a good deal about himself and the Duchess, and their relationship, in the process. She did not love him as he wished to be loved. She loved life and looked in the same curious, interested, intrigued manner at everything and everyone. The portrait painter was obviously very attracted to her, and she to him, although she thought him merely kind at first, but still, his attentions brought a flush to her cheek—all of which made the Duke insanely jealous. She would not stop her flirting, he declined to be put in the position of always having to lecture her on her conduct, and, eventually, the implication is that he had her murdered: "I gave commands;/Then all smiles stopped together." The Duke then suggests they go downstairs, and as they descend he discusses the dowry and points out a statue he particularly prizes to the envoy.

Browning has created a character, so you must approach this narrative poem exactly as you would a play or a piece of prose fiction, using substitutions, and playing actions. You can read this poem without worrying that the rhythm will be too apparent. Use the run-on lines to help you read as if you were really talking to someone. As a substitution for the envoy you are talking to, you might select someone you once wished to impress, and whose feelings you weren't sure about, particularly when it came to how that person felt about you.

Place is important: We are in a grand palace, filled with art treasures; you might picture the Metropolitan Museum of Art in New York, or an Italian palazzo you have visited. Select a particular portrait to substitute for the abstract one you can't see. The portrait in the poem doesn't actually exist. In fact, Browning had no specific painting in mind, but there are many Renaissance portraits you might choose from. For Browning, as for Ferrara, it is not so much the portrait itself that is important as what happened while it was being painted, as well as the feelings the portrait awakens in the Duke.

Time is important to Ferrara as an immediate circumstance. Time presses, and he must deal with that pressure: The monologue takes place just before a great banquet, given to impress the envoy, as the line "We'll meet the company below" implies. The Duke is apprehensive. Has he said too much? Has he impressed the Count's envoy sufficiently?

A technical suggestion: Stress the word "last" in the poem's first line—the word here means "most recent," although there is of course the ironic connotation of "ultimate"—and you will make the meaning of the word clear, and also be in the middle of the story, a fact which the listener will hear.

On the line "looking as if she were alive" there might be a twinge of nostalgia and the return of those pangs of jealousy, which the listener learns later in the poem that the Duke has felt—but which you know already, because you have learned it when you prepared the text.

When we begin to hear the poem, we, the listeners, don't know who these people are. By the end of this brief dramatic monologue we have learned everything we need to know about the autocratic, reserved, mysterious Ferrara, whose charm as a host is superficial. He is charming because he has something to gain from the envoy: the Count's daughter in marriage.

This is a murder mystery. Why was the Duchess killed, if she was? Was she really in love with the painter, or was this a figment of the Duke's jealous imagination? And why does the Duke feel free to admit to murder, if indeed that line about giving commands is an admission of murder? The Duke's self-contempt and anger at having his happiness destroyed are very clear, and he feels deeply humiliated and profoundly jealous because his wife smiled at other people. She was too naïve to notice how deeply hurt he felt—would she have cared if she did? Was she even capable of loving him? She was undoubtedly much younger than her husband. And he assumed she was merely hiding things from him. Ferrara is nervous, because he doesn't know what his visitor will think, or what he will tell the Count.

Both Frà Pandolf, the portrait painter of whom the Duke is jealous, and Claus of Innsbruck, one of the Duke's favorite sculptors, are characters, not real artists. Neptune is the Roman god of the sea.

Was there a Ferrara historically on whom Browning based this character? Possibly he had in mind Alfonso II (1533–1598), fifth Duke of Ferrara. He was the last surviving member of the Este family, which could trace its lineage back for 650 years. He married twice, his first wife being a Medici, from a family 900 years old, and very aware of the prestige of its own lineage. And it was rumored that Ferrara might have murdered his first wife. Whatever the historical background, this is a compelling miniature narrative.

Russell O'Neal Clay, "The Sculptor Becomes His Work," from *From Ghost Through Bone to Man* (New and Selected Poems, 1994–1996)

The man is becoming stone—
Cells harden, thickened blood cannot flow
And he leans on a cane.

The back is bowed beneath years
Like a pine glazed to earth
By ice in January.

The stone grows cold—
Machines quarry pieces of the soul
Memories come to light

In the hands of the archaeologists
Who ponder shards of dream.
Did this man love? Did he weep

When the night was filled with stars
And the warm ghost of his breath ascended?

NOTES, COMMENTS AND HINTS

Russell Clay's work has appeared in numerous periodicals and anthologies, including *The Sow's Ear Poetry Review*, *Poetry Atlanta*, and *Confluence*. He teaches poetry workshops in writers' conferences around the country and serves as a mentor to a number of poets. In 1997 he created West End Poetry Press to support the publication of rising voices in poetry. Russell lives in New York City with his wife Stephanie Cowell, some of whose historical novels you will find excerpted on pages 195 and 200.

Mr. Clay wrote to me that, " 'The Sculptor Becomes His Work' seeks to explore the relationship between art and artist. When a work of art is created, something of the artist goes into the work. This poem asks, 'What if the artist informs the work to the extent that artist and work become one?' In the narrative of the poem the artist, a sculptor, literally turns to stone as a result of his artistic passion, thus subjugating all other aspects of life for art and, in the process, finding an ironic spiritual ascension."

When reading this poem, see the clear images in it in your imagination, right in front of you. Select a substitution from someone you know or have seen, who is growing older. If as you read you wonder internally about that person and what he was like, your wonder will be externally reflected, in your voice. Or you might use your own experience of growing older. The poem is unrhymed and the verse is free, so it is easy to make it sound like real speech, and to allow the poetic images and metaphors to emerge starkly. And the images are stark: "shards of dream" is a metaphor in which the shattered pieces of pottery an archaeologist might find is compared to the destroyed fragments of a dream, not simply a dream one has at night, but an aspiration, a desire. Was the dream an ancient one? Was it lifelong?

And then there is perhaps—only perhaps—a warmth in the images that succeed "shards of dream"; they are in the form of a question: "Did this man love? Did he weep...?" And the words "the warm ghost of his breath," reversed, give us immediately a sense of the future: "the warm breath of his ghost." That future does not appear to be happy, but this is not a pessimistic poem, because when the artist and the work become one, "Memories come to light." And they are happy memories, as well as sad ones. Creation is itself a pleasure, especially when the artist is one with the work—both the work itself, as process and occupation; and the specific work of art, which satisfies the creator that he has said what he wanted to say.

Samuel Taylor Coleridge (1772–1834), *The Rime of the Ancient Mariner, in Seven Parts* (first published in *Lyrical Ballads* in 1798; 1834 version); some excerpts.

The poem begins:

It is an ancient Mariner,
And he stoppeth one of three.
"By thy long grey beard and glittering eye,
Now wherefore stopp'st thou me?

The Bridegroom's doors are opened wide,
And I am next of kin;
The guests are met, the feast is set:
May'st hear the merry din."

He holds him with his skinny hand,
"There was a ship," quoth he.

"Hold off! unhand me, grey-beard loon!"
Eftsoons his hand dropt he.

In the middle of the poem we have the famous verses:

All in a hot and copper sky,
The bloody Sun, at noon,
Right up above the mast did stand,
No bigger than the Moon.

Day after day, day after day,
We stuck, nor breath nor motion;
As idle as a painted ship
Upon a painted ocean.
And the Albatross begins to be avenged.

Water, water, every where,
And all the boards did shrink;
Water, water, every where,
Nor any drop to drink.

And the poem ends in "Part the Seventh" as follows:

The Mariner, whose eye is bright,
Whose beard with age is hoar,
Is gone: and now the Wedding-Guest
Turned from the bridegroom's door.

He went like one that hath been stunned,
And is of sense forlorn:
A sadder and a wiser man,
He rose the morrow morn.

NOTES, COMMENTS AND HINTS

Coleridge continually revised his poems, even after they were published. This poem, of which he wrote several versions, was inspired by a strange dream about a skeleton ship that a friend of Coleridge's told him. The incident of the shooting of the albatross came from Wordsworth, so he claims, based on accounts of voyages he had been reading.

Coleridge and William Wordsworth (1770–1850), friends, neighbors and fellow poets, discussed the different kinds of poetry one day (a conversation recorded by each of them in autobiographical memoirs), and concluded that there were "poems of nature," meant to invoke nature in a real way, by describing moonlight, and so on; and poems dealing with the imagination and the supernatural that required a suspension of disbelief, as this one does.

You can't ignore the rhythm, but play against it a bit, for meaning, especially when one line carries over into the next to make a complete thought, as in the lines: "The Mariner, whose eye is bright, / Whose beard with age is hoar, / Is gone." As a possible way of reading these lines: Stress the underlined words, and immediately after "hoar," with no pause, read the word "Is," making a complete sentence, and a startling break in the rhythm.

The delightful rhythm in this poem carries you along with it, and intrudes itself into the reading in a most enjoyable way. The point is to try not to read the poem constantly and heavy-handedly in the rhythm in which it is written, because the rhythm will automatically assert itself, and to most pleasing effect. Because the rhymes can also be very pleasing to the ear, you should occasionally make them stand out. They can be quite delicious.

A verse not cited above contains the lines: "We were the first that ever burst/Into that silent sea." The first line contains an internal rhyme, and the first and second lines are run-on lines, so that you can link them and make them sound naturally like the one thought they represent. You need not emphasize the internal rhyme, because we will hear it anyway.

The opening gives you an opportunity to do character voices, but do them very lightly, if you choose to do them at all. It would be better, perhaps, just to let us hear the characters' attitudes: the haughtiness and haste of the wedding guest; and the intransigence of the mariner, desperate to tell his tale. His "skinny hand" might suggest a thin, reedy voice to you.

The rhythm alternates lines of iambic tetrameter with lines of iambic trimeter (three feet). The rhyme scheme varies from a simple "a, b, a, b" in some verses to "a, b, c, a" in others, to "a, b, c" then "b, d, e, f, d" in the final two verses presented here.

William Shakespeare (1564–1616) *Sonnet XXX*: "When to the Sessions of Sweet Silent Thought"

When to the sessions of sweet silent thought
I summon up remembrance of things past,
And sigh the lack of many a thing I sought,
And with old woes new wail my dear time's waste:
Then can I drown an eye, unus'd to flow,
For precious friends hid in death's dateless night,

And weep afresh love's long since cancell'd woe,
And moan th' expense of many a vanish'd sight;
Then can I grieve at grievances foregone,
And heavily from woe to woe tell o'er
The sad account of fore-bemoaned moan,
Which I new pay as if not paid before.
    But if the while I think on thee, dear friend,
    All losses are restor'd, and sorrows end.

NOTES, COMMENTS AND HINTS

See the excerpts from Stephanie Cowell's *The Players* on page 195, with its Notes on the Dark Lady of the Sonnets. C. K. Scott Moncrieff, Marcel Proust's first translator, chose the end of the second line of this sonnet, "... remembrance of things past," as the overall title of Proust's book.

This sonnet consists of the usual fourteen lines of iambic pentameter that the form, consisting of three quatrains and a couplet, demands, and its rhyme scheme is Shakespeare's usual: a, b, a, b c, d, c, d, e, f, e, f, g, g. Each quatrain is connected in part by the repetition of thematic words dealing with mourning and grieving for the past: In the first quatrain we have the words "sigh," and "wail"; in the second, "drown an eye," "weep," "moan"; and in the third we have "grieve," "woe" and "moan." The many memories of past losses, both of love and of people now gone, which the poet grieves for, are offset in the final couplet, which always brings a sonnet to a conclusion or resolution of the situation described in it, when the poet thinks of the present and his "dear friend," who ends his sorrows.

That, then, is the "story" or at least the evocation of feelings around a story (of which we are not told the details) of this sonnet. It has a shape, with its beginning, middle and conclusion, and you should read it with that shape in mind, so that you have somewhere to go with it. Do not read it all on one note, in other words. And do not overplay the past grief, which for a long time the poet refused to acknowledge, or at least to give in to ("an eye, unus'd to flow").

As usual, my advice is to read the poem simply, and not to play the rhythm. If anything, play against it, so that the meaning of the words becomes clear. Make the poem mean something to you, as always, by personalizing it with relevant substitutions from your own life. You cannot read this sonnet, or any piece of material, as something abstract and apart from yourself. You must go to those places in yourself that respond to a poem, and use them to inform your reading of it.

An excellent book, if you wish to explore the Sonnets further, is Helen Vendler's *The Art of Shakespeare's Sonnets* (*The Belknap Press* of Harvard University Press, 1997). A CD of all the sonnets comes bound with the book.

Two Poems by Tom Smith, from *Waiting on Pentecost* (1999)

THE SENTENCE

Let my sentence
come forth
from thy presence.
—Psalms 17:2

A mute and blinding presence
swells my tongue and my sentence
spills on a fat shore. I come

with a dry mouth. I have come
with wounds seeking the presence
that broods behind each sentence.

I wait upon the sentence.
It is a garden and comes
Forth greening from the presence.

HARPING DARKNESS/I

I will open
my dark saying
upon the harp.
—Psalms 49:4

The rivers have borne the harp
seaward. It strings the open
plain. Heaven sows its saying
among the stars growing dark.

A blackbird lifts off the dark.
My spine and ribs make a harp
and we hang on our saying,
watching what wind will open.

We spell the earth to open
and urge us up from the dark,
me and the blackbird, saying
we will be trees and a harp.

NOTES, COMMENTS AND HINTS

Surrounded by rolling, wooded hills and serene villages and gardens, including his own beautiful flower garden, professor emeritus of English at Castleton State Teachers' College Tom Smith lives and writes in Vermont. He has published a brilliant, innovative novel, called *A Well-Behaved Little Boy* (STARbooks Press, 1993), as well as several volumes of his poetry, a great deal of which has also been published in dozens of literary magazines. A gifted actor, as is his wife Virginia De Angelis Smith, Tom Smith is often invited to do readings of his poetry.

When you read these poems aloud, see the images. Feel the images. Savor the words. If you do all that, the listener will do all that, too. Use the run-on lines and caesuras to give these poems their natural rhythm.

Both these poems are lyrically musical in their cadences and rhythms, and symbolic in their images. They are at once soothing and disturbing, stark and lush.

The surreal landscapes and surrealistic images present themselves to our view, almost as if we were standing in the middle of a Dalí landscape, surrounded by unfamiliar, familiar objects which have some connection with us and with each other, but which also remain somehow mysterious, perhaps vaguely frightening, and seem beyond our ken, but then draw close and seem comforting. The tree and the blackbird seem to exist by themselves, disembodied, away from a landscape where they could anchor and take root. Yet we will unite ourselves with them. The harp floating, being borne to the sea, is the opposite of our arrival on the "fat shore" in the first poem.

What is the mute and blinding presence in "The Sentence?" Psalm 17, which inspired the poem, takes place merely in "the presence," but it is not described, yet it must be mute, for "the presence" says nothing. And it may be blinding; at least we cannot see it. The psalm is about being delivered from wicked enemies that surround the psalmist. It recalls, indeed, the later story of Christ, and the poem reflects that possible allusion to the future. Where did we get the wounds (again an allusion to Christ) that we come into this landscape with, and where did we come from?

The place we are delivered to in the poem, wounded as we are by our wicked enemies (or perhaps by ourselves, if we are our own worst enemy), is a desolate shore. The wounded poet waits for a "sentence," a word that means both a series of phrases (perhaps the poet waits for the words to come), and a judicial sentence (or sentencing). And the shore becomes a garden, through the sentence, which arrives, meting out not punishment, but redemption, as a poem arrives after a period of feeling uncreative.

We arrived on the shore with a sentence spilling out, seeking the "presence" behind each sentence: "Presence" rhymes with "presents," suggesting both gifts and immediate time. And we wait for the sentence that will redeem us.

"The Sentence" is also a highly erotic poem—"... my sentence spills on a fat shore./I come/with a dry mouth"—as is so much in the Bible itself. The metaphor is clearly sexual: The sentence spilling reminds one of masturbation, since the poet is alone on the shore. And the relation between sex and creativity is also clear.

In Psalm 49, the psalmist has just said in the previous line that he will "open mine ear to a parable," and the poem is a parable. Everyone must die, the wicked and the good, the poor and the rich, but God will redeem everyone's soul. How is this to be accomplished? What transformation must take place for this to happen? Smith's poem "Harping Darkness/I" (which suggests also that we harp on darkness, a symbol which stands for despair and death, among other things; cf. Shakespeare in Sonnet XXX: "hid in death's dateless night") is based on Psalm 49. The psalm suggests the oneness, the unity of nature, which the poem also suggests: Tree, bird, and man, and the harp (man-made) providing the transforming, uplifting art that is music, are all ultimately one. We should not, therefore, harp on darkness, but rather listen to the promising music of the harp playing in the darkness.

These superbly beautiful, very powerful poems both evoke landscapes, but "The Sentence" does it with a starkly frightening, almost nightmarish quality: The landscape is a forbidding shore, but it turns into a garden, so that the end of the poem is reassuring, whereas the strange, dreamlike landscape in "Harping Darkness/I" is almost reassuring even at the outset.

Both these poems read aloud well, and this is hardly surprising, because when Tom Smith composes a poem, he almost always reads it aloud as part of his process of composition. He thinks of a poem as something musical, and both the poem and the process of composition are very physical for him. "You must," he says, "have a poem in the mouth as well as in the ear. There is something about eating one's words that is delicious."

I have told you something about the cosmic and human symbolism of these poems, and what the images suggest to me. But the images are very personal for each reader. Just go with them, let yourself be carried away, and see what they suggest to you. Then read the poems simply, and allow the listener to have his or her own images.

Alfred Lord Tennyson, "Break, break, break" (1842)

Break, break, break,
  On thy cold grey stones, O Sea!
And I would that my tongue could utter
  The thoughts that arise in me.

O, well for the fisherman's boy,
   That he shouts with his sister at play!
O, well for the sailor lad,
   That he sings in his boat on the bay!

And the stately ships go on
   To their haven under the hill;
But O for the touch of a vanish'd hand,
   And the sound of a voice that is still!

Break, break, break
   At the foot of thy crags, O Sea!
But the tender grace of a day that is dead
   Will never come back to me.

NOTES, COMMENTS AND HINTS

Alfred, Lord Tennyson (1809–1892) wrote this poem in 1833 to commemorate the death of his friend Arthur Hallam, but it was published first in his two-volume *Poems* in 1842. Tennyson wrote: "Made in a Lincolnshire lane at five o'clock in the morning between blossoming hedges."

The rhyme scheme is "a, b, c, b." This is one poem in which you should observe the rhythm in certain places, and make it even, for instance on "Break, break, break." It is not only the waves, but also the heart, for which the metaphor, that is breaking, so in personalizing this text go to a place where your own heart has been broken, and remember "the tender grace of a day that is dead." Think about what the other metaphors in the poem stand for ("cold grey stones," "stately ships," "crags," etc.), and what they might mean to you.

Observe also, in reading aloud, the breaks between lines. In the first verse connect the first line "Break, break, break" to the second line "On thy cold grey stones, O Sea!" You might stress every word in the phrase "cold grey stones." Similarly, in the last verse, connect "Break, break, break" to "At the foot of thy crags, O Sea!" so that it is one sentence, and stress the words "foot," "crags," and "Sea."

Recording the first verse of a poem from *The Princess*, "The Splendour Falls on Castle Walls," on wax cylinder in 1889, Lord Tennyson does everything I have told you not to do: He declaims; he says every line and almost every word on one note, an upper pitch; he lets his voice fall off in volume at the ends of some of the lines; and he pounds away at the rhythm very strongly. It is simply fascinating to hear him do it, in his rather sonorously deep, but still sometimes tremulous voice. He reminds me of some nineteenth-century Shakespearean actors whose voices I have heard, declamatory and almost stentorian. It is possible that he shouted a bit because he felt he had to scream into the acoustic horn, but the impression is nevertheless one of an oratorical style we associate with the Victorian era. While it is an extraordinary thing just to hear him, I think this poem sounds better and is more evocative if delivered in a somewhat less declamatory style. But who am I to criticize Alfred, Lord Tennyson?

The splendour falls on castle walls
  And snowy summits old in story:
The long light shakes across the lakes,
  And the wild cataract leaps in glory.
Blow, bugle, blow, set the wild echoes flying,
Blow, bugle; answer, echoes, dying, dying, dying.

Phillis Wheatley (1753?-1784), "On Virtue" (1766)

ON VIRTUE

Thou bright jewel in my aim I strive
To comprehend thee. Thine own words declare
Wisdom is higher than a fool can reach.
Cease to wonder, and no more attempt
Thine height t'explore, or fathom thy profound.
But, O my soul, sink not into despair,
Virtue is near thee, and with gentle hand
Would now embrace thee, hovers o'er thine head.
Fain would the heav'n-born soul with her converse,
Then seek, then court her for her promis'd bliss.

Auspicious queen, thine heav'nly pinions spread,
And lead celestial *Chastity* along;
Lo! now her sacred retinue descends,
Array'd in glory from the orbs above.
Attend me, *Virtue*, thro' my youthful years!
O leave me not to the false joys of time!
But guide my steps to endless life and bliss.
Greatness, or *Goodness*, say what I shall call thee,
To give an higher appellation still,
Teach me a better strain, a nobler lay,
O thou, enthron'd with Cherubs in the realms of day!

NOTES, COMMENTS AND HINTS

Phillis Wheatley took her first name from that of the slave ship on which she was brought to America from West Africa. She was purchased (hideous term when applied to a human being!) by Susannah Wheatley, the wife of a Boston merchant, John Wheatley, whose daughter Mary taught Phillis to read and write, which she began to do in 1765. The Wheatleys remarked her genius and her great gifts as a poet immediately, and when she was about fourteen she had a poem published in a Boston newspaper. By 1772 she had composed enough poems to make a volume, which she submitted to an incredulous publisher, Mr. Bell, who had her examined by a jury of eighteen men, to make sure she really was the author. Mary's brother took Phillis to England, where, through the good offices of the Countess of Huntingdon, to whom she dedicated the volume, her poems were published. Susannah Wheatley died shortly after Phillis's return to Boston, and John Wheatley set Phillis free. She married and had three children, who predeceased her, and, having tried and failed to have another volume of her poetry published, died in poverty at the age of thirty-one, after working as a servant. Two years later her poems were published in the United States.

On Virtue was first published in *Poems on Various Subjects, Religious and Moral* in 1773, but it was composed in 1766. The poem is unrhymed.

English was not Phillis Wheatley's first language, which was probably a West African language, but nothing is known for certain. Yet she learned to write it superbly, and she had been at the Wheatley's only a little over a year when she had already learned to read from the Bible, as well as studying Greek and Latin. Her classical education is reflected in the poem. She also studied history, English literature, and the sciences of astronomy and geography.

This formally classical poem brings to my mind the painted ceilings of certain Baroque or Rococo churches I have seen, with great billowing clouds and cherubim floating in the air, and the great Baroque paintings in the Louvre, where they hover in the clouds next to chariots driven by goddesses and gods, or rather by earthly rulers represented as deities. You might take a look at such works to help give you a visceral feeling for a long vanished mode of art and of the tradition of personifying human attributes and feelings, in which this poem participates.

Wisdom and virtue go hand in hand, and wisdom helps us to find virtue, which is allied with chastity. By living virtuously we will be happy and free from all pangs of conscience. This moral point is the lesson of the poem. And the story of the poem is the poet's search for Virtue, which is near at hand and waiting to embrace the poet, who is in doubt at the beginning of the poem, and who ends, after Virtue descends to attend her, by striving to be even nobler. Virtue, with its link to chastity, is implicitly connected to Mary, Mother of God, and thus to the virtues she embodies, including that of motherly compassion and pure love. Phillis Wheatley was, in fact, a religious person, and other poems of hers are more explicitly religious. This poem might almost be written, except for the images of Cherubim, which come to Christianity from the Judaic tradition, by an ancient Roman or Greek, so classical does the context of Virtue's existence seem.

Read the poem simply and unaffectedly, and allow the images to speak for themselves. If you try to read in a flowery way, embellishing the phrases with your voice, you will not only obscure what the poem is saying, but render it difficult to listen to. You can use the run-on lines to help clarify the meaning, and to make the reading of something that is written in an essentially artificial Rococo style sound natural; cf. Aphra Behn's poem on page 279.

CHAPTER 9

Recording Nonfiction: Making the Text Come Alive

When you record nonfiction, whether it is history, biography, a mathematics, chemistry, biology or physics text, a cookbook, a philosophical treatise, a travel book, a collection of essays, or a work meant for the general public about one of the natural sciences or about religion, you cannot *interpret* the text, as if you were dealing with a work of fiction. With nonfiction you are reading as if *you* were the author of the book, and in that sense only you are playing a part. Do not think of the author as a character; think of the author as a person very much like you. The author is not there to be analyzed the way you analyze a fictitious character. You are simply the author's voice, and your objective is to make clearly the points the author wishes to make. This should keep the reading fairly simple and straightforward, as well as lively and interesting. And you certainly want to avoid being too academic or pedantic in your approach. You want to sound relaxed. You are simply talking.

If the material is very abstruse, as in, say, a book on modern physics; or very stylistically difficult, as in, say a translation of Kant's *Critique of Pure Reason* or Hegel's *Phenomenology*, you want to play against the way in which the material is written, by being as informal as you can, so that the listener may listen with as much ease as possible. The formality is inevitably there, since it is in the writing.

In recording history, autobiography, memoir or biography you are telling a story, which, with its "cast of characters," is similar to fiction, but you should not do "characters' " voices, character voices or accents. For instance, if you are doing a book about Winston Churchill or President Franklin Delano Roosevelt or reading their letters or memoirs, you must not imitate them, whereas if they were characters in a novel you would be free to do so.

There are exceptions to the rule. When I recorded a biography of Natalie Wood by Gavin Lambert for BBC Audiobooks, I was surprised to be asked to do Russian accents for her immigrant parents and a British RP accent for her English husband. (I did not do imitations of any well-known public figures.) Doing accents is most unusual in nonfiction recording.

The four basic types of popular nonfiction are:

1. Cliché-ridden, badly written pulp, in which almost no attention is paid to grammar, with the result that its style is both facile and execrable;

2. Scholarly and academic works (biographies, histories, literary criticism, philosophy, psychology, etc.) that are well and even beautifully written, and meant for a literate general public, which it respects, whether they are familiar with the subject or not;

3. Scholarly publications for a limited audience of academics, scientists, experts or technicians in a particular field (medicine, computers, etc.), whom the author can expect to be almost the only people to read it, and recorded by people familiar with the field;

4. Writing devoted to popular subjects such as cooking, gardening, pets, computers, travel, and how-to guides on everything you can think of from carpentry and construction to learning languages.

Pulp nonfiction is usually written in what is often called, perhaps unfairly, a journalistic style: Like newspaper articles, such books seem to be written quickly, as if the writer were under the constraint and pressure of a deadline. Big words, abstruse vocabulary, and careful grammar, are avoided. These books are apt to patronize and talk down to the public that reads them.

Pick up almost any self-help book and you will see what I mean. There is something vulgar and untrustworthy about the expression of the author's often platitudinous, commonplace thoughts and facile solutions to people's problems. And there is always something a bit suspect and unconvincing about the trite, banal ready-made anecdotes meant to elucidate the author's points. Books of this sort have as much relationship to psychology as instant coffee has to coffee freshly brewed from beans: They resemble the real thing, but they aren't quite it. And the author usually appears to assume that the reader is an illiterate, depressive dodo. Many of the so-called self-help books are a far less than respectable substitute for real therapy, even though there are people who swear by the efficacy of such tripe, which has been foisted onto a gullible and unhappy public. The only persons really helped by self-help books are their authors, who sometimes earn, I am sure, substantial royalties.

Of course there are pulp books on many subjects other than that of pop self-help psychology. There are religious books full of phony spiritualism and mysticism, meant, apparently, for idiots, if one may judge by their style, not to mention their contents. There's a lot of political pulp out there, completely topical in nature, such as campaign biographies of people running for office; books that, like their subjects, are ephemeral (fortunately, in the case of some of the politicians, and in the case of all of the books).

If you have to record such a book, it is your job and your responsibility not to comment on the material by showing in your tone of voice your contempt for it. Read it with all the seriousness it may not deserve, and make it live. Make it as interesting to listen to as possible, even if you think the book is written in an execrable, overburdened style.

Academically oriented, commercially published nonfiction meant for a literate audience, on the other hand, can be read with pleasure by both an audience familiar with the field (think of Graham Robb's biographies of Victor Hugo, Honoré de Balzac, and Arthur Rimbaud, for example; William Carter's books about Marcel Proust, including his magisterial biography; or Mark Kurlansky's books about the Basque people and their history, and the world history of salt; and any books by Antonia Fraser, Simon Winchester or Alain de Botton), as well as by a public perhaps unfamiliar with the subject, and learning about it for the first time. Such an author does not talk down to her or his public, but assumes she or he is writing for a knowledgeable audience with a genuine interest in the subject of the book. It is a pleasure to record and to learn at the same time from such books, because they are well planned, written in a lively manner, well paced, and have a good eye for the main events.

Although you may have the enjoyment of recording such books, you will also meet deadly dull academic tomes that manage to kill their subjects, because some authors manage to make even the most fascinating subject so soporific that you could fall asleep as they drone on. It requires quite an effort on your part to make them come alive. But, as my dear father said, in his admirably concise and pithy way, when I told him once that I was recording a very boring book, "What do you care? It's work." He was right. Besides, what I found boring, some listener might really enjoy.

As for the fourth type of nonfiction, it can be lots of fun to record. Books on cooking and travel may vary in quality, but they can be well written and put together. Recipes can make your mouth water and travel guides can take you to faraway places. If your record a cookbook right before lunch, you may develop quite an appetite!

For practice use any of the nonfiction books mentioned above.

How to Read Biography, Autobiography and Memoirs, and History

Biography, autobiography and memoirs are forms of historical writing that focus on individual lives, whereas histories deal with a larger picture of events, such as the American Revolution; with a specific event, such as the battle of Waterloo, or with a vast overview covering centuries of history, such as Will and Ariel Durant's multi-volume *The Story of Civilization*.

Whatever the form, historians tell stories. In a way, history, biography, and autobiography are often forms of fiction, because they are selective narratives told with their author's particular point of view about the stories they relate.

Biographers and autobiographers have a keen interest in their subject, and present it as they wish the world to see it. The writer's point of view is therefore of supreme importance in understanding the subject, however objective the writer wishes to appear, and some appear to be quite objective. Others appear entirely subjective, especially autobiographers, although the facts they give us are often not in dispute. Still, no autobiographer wishes to present himself or herself in a bad light. People want to justify themselves and their actions. If you read, for instance, the memoirs of the war criminal Albert Speer, one of the top Nazis and, as it turns out, a notorious liar and distorter of the truth, who appeared to be abjectly contrite and sincere in confessing his crimes (but only those already known), you will not get an objective view of events in World War Two. On the other hand, you can certainly trust the truthfulness of diaries like that of Anne Frank, whose perspective is individual, rather than generally historical, or autobiographies like that of Frederick Douglass. Born a slave in 1818, he escaped in 1838 and went North, and his account of the horrors he lived through and of the brutally inhuman treatment of slaves in the old South is heartbreaking, and true beyond doubt. We also know from many other primary sources what went on in the antebellum South, just as we do about what happened during the Holocaust in World War Two, for example.

In preparing a work of history or biography for recording, you might want to do research, so you can put the book into a context. Historians speak of primary and secondary sources. Primary sources are original documentary evidence, such as the proceedings of the Constitutional Convention in 1788, or firsthand accounts of events in state papers, diaries and autobiographies. Another primary source is the public utterances of well-known people. Lincoln's Gettysburg Address, for instance, is a piece of history in itself. When we recite it we often stress the prepositions in the famous phrase "government of the people, by the people, for the people," but if you were to record it as part of biography, you might want to know that accounts of Lincoln's delivery report that he continually stressed the word "people," which makes a difference in his emphasis on what is important.

Trial transcripts are another kind of primary source, but the evidence is not always trustworthy as a true picture of historical events. For example, decades after the 1951 trial of Ethel and Julius Rosenberg, set against the background of the 1950s Red Scare, David Greenglass, Ethel's brother, admitted that much of his testimony was false and self-serving. But, partly on the strength of that testimony, the Rosenbergs were convicted of passing the secret of the atomic bomb to the USSR, and executed. Although their guilt or innocence is hotly debated to this day, there is no clear, convincing, incontrovertible evidence for their guilt, and the charges against them were in many ways preposterous. And the transcripts in general show a very peculiar, upsetting and bizarre trial, with many irregularities in the proceedings. Yet what trial witnesses tell us is history in itself, even if it is a history of lies. Sifting through a trial transcript and determining its value is one of the historian's jobs.

Secondary sources draw on primary sources to tell their stories. See, for example the selection from George Dolby's *Charles Dickens as I Knew Him* on page 99, recounting Dickens's audience with Queen Victoria. Dolby wasn't there, but there is no reason to doubt the veracity of his account of what Dickens told him. He is a secondary source talking to a primary source.

Some secondary sources, on the other hand, could be classified as "hearsay evidence" of the sort that would not, or should not, be admitted in a court of law. For example, the journalist Frank Harris knew Oscar Wilde quite well and was on occasion a good and supportive friend (we have corroborative evidence for this from other sources, such as George Bernard Shaw, who knew them both; and Wilde dedicated *An Ideal Husband* to Harris on its publication in 1899), and is therefore a primary source for information on the part of Wilde's life he knew firsthand. He would also be a secondary source when he recounts Wilde's version of events as the Irish poet and esthete supposedly told them to him, except that he probably made most of their conversations up. See the excerpts below for a further account.

Historiography is the study of how history is written, using scholarly methods of criticism and research. The historian is obliged to be selective, while evaluating the facts in a critical manner. But historiographic analysis shows that she or he selects the facts to be evaluated, as well as the interpretation of them, on the basis of her or his political point of view. Read a history of the French Revolution written by a Monarchist and one written by a Marxist, and you have two very different French Revolutions. (See the excerpt from Thomas Carlyle's *The French Revolution* below.) The same can be said of official histories and authorized biographies, which present the point of view of whoever commissioned the work.

It is your obligation as a reader to bear all this in mind and to assume the point of view of the writer while you are reading, and, as I said earlier, not to comment on the material, but to bring it to life as it is.

A technical point: Very often the innumerable obscure vocabulary words, such as the ones in some of the selections below, will have been looked up in dictionaries for the readers of commercial recordings. It is always a good idea to check them for yourself anyway.

Illustrative Texts

Biography

Two excerpts from James Boswell's *The Life of Samuel Johnson, LL.D.* (1791)

May, 1776

"Mr. Dilly, Sir, sends his respectful compliments to you, and would be happy if you would do him the honour to dine with him on Wednesday next along with me, as I must soon go to Scotland." JOHNSON. "Sir, I am obliged to Mr. Dilly. I will wait upon him—" BOSWELL. "Provided, Sir, I suppose, that the company which he is to have, is agreeable to you." JOHNSON. "What do you mean, Sir? What do you take me for? Do you think I am so ignorant of the world as to imagine that I am to prescribe to a gentleman what company he is to have at his table?" BOSWELL. "I beg your pardon, Sir, for wishing to prevent you from meeting people whom you might not like. Perhaps he may have some of what he calls his patriotick friends with him." JOHNSON. "Well, Sir, and what then? What care *I* for his *patriotick friends*? Poh!" BOSWELL. "I should not be surprized to find Jack Wilkes there." JOHNSON. "And if Jack Wilkes *should* be there, what is that to *me*, Sir? My dear friend, let us have no more of this. I am sorry to be angry with you; but really it is treating me strangely to talk to me as if I could not meet any company whatever, occasionally." BOSWELL. "Pray forgive me, Sir: I meant well. But you shall meet whoever comes, for me." Thus I secured him, and told Dilly that he would find him very well pleased to be one of his guests on the day appointed.

Upon the much-expected Wednesday, I called on him about half an hour before dinner, as I often did when we were to dine out together, to see that he was ready in time, and to accompany him. I found him buffeting his books, as upon a former occasion, covered with dust, and making no preparation for going abroad. "How is this, Sir? (said I.) Don't you recollect that you are to dine at Mr. Dilly's?" JOHNSON. "Sir, I did not think of going to Dilly's: it went out of my head. I have ordered dinner at home with Mrs. Williams." BOSWELL. "But, my dear Sir, you know you were engaged to Mr. Dilly, and I told him so. He will expect you, and will be much disappointed if you don't come." JOHNSON. "You must talk to Mrs. Williams about this."

• • •

Sunday 1 April, 1781

On Sunday, April 1, I dined with him at Mr. Thrale's, with Sir Philip Jennings Clerk and Mr. Perkins, who had the superintendence of Mr. Thrale's brewery, with a salary of five hundred pounds a year. Sir Philip had the appearance of a gentleman of ancient family, well advanced in life. He wore his own white hair in a bag of goodly size, a black velvet coat, with an embroidered waistcoat, and very rich laced ruffles; which Mrs. Thrale said were old fashioned, but which, for that reason, I thought the more respectable, more like a Tory; yet Sir Philip was then in Opposition in Parliament. "Ah, Sir, (said Johnson,) ancient ruffles and modern principles do not agree." Sir Philip defended the Opposition to the American war ably and with temper, and I joined him. He said, the majority of the nation was against the ministry. JOHNSON. "*I*, Sir, am against the ministry; but it is for having too little of that, of which Opposition thinks they have too much. Were I minister, if any man wagged his finger against me, he should be turned out; for that which it is in the power of Government to give at pleasure to one or to another, should be given to the supporters of Government. If you will not oppose at the expense of losing your place, your opposition will not be honest, you will feel no serious grievance; and the present opposition is only a contest to get what others have. Sir Robert Walpole acted as I should do. As to the American war, the *sense* of the nation is *with* the ministry. The majority of those who can *understand* is with it; the majority of those who can only *hear* is against it; and as those who can only hear are more numerous than those who can understand, and Opposition is always loudest, a majority of the rabble will be for Opposition."

This boisterous vivacity entertained us; but the truth in my opinion was, that those who could understand the best were against the American war, as almost every man now is, when the question has been coolly considered.

NOTES, COMMENTS AND HINTS

The conversation in the first excerpt takes place only a few months before the promulgation of the Declaration of Independence on July 4, 1776. The war had hardly started, and the outcome of the conflict was still too far in the future to predict, but whether Britain should fight the war at all was a hotly debated issue.

On October 19, 1781 Cornwallis surrendered to Washington at Yorktown, thus effectively ending the "American war," as Boswell calls it. In 1783 the Treaty of Paris was signed, and the United States of America became an independent nation.

The name James Boswell (1740–1795) has become almost a synonym for the word "biographer," and we say, "So-and-so is his Boswell," as Sherlock Holmes did of Dr. Watson.

In 1763 the Scottish law student and would-be officer in the foot guards met Samuel Johnson (1709–1784), the phenomenal, if eccentric lexicographer (his famous *A Dictionary of the English Language* was published in 1755), biographer, essayist, critic, journalist and witty conversationalist, and the two became great friends. Boswell admired the older man, and determined to write his biography, and to that end, wherever he went with Johnson, Boswell took copious notes and kept extensive journals, which are in themselves fascinating reading.

Boswell's "Advertisement to the First Edition" tells us: "The labour and anxious attention with which I have collected and arranged the materials of which these volumes are composed, will hardly be conceived by those who read them with careless facility." His Introduction to his famous labor of love opens with what has become a very famous sentence: "To write the Life of him who excelled all mankind in writing the lives of others, and who, whether we consider his extraordinary endowments, or his various works, has been equalled by few in any age, is an arduous, and may be reckoned in me a presumptuous task." In which, one may add, he succeeded very well. You will have noticed the clear syntax of that celebrated sentence, typical of Boswell's elegant, precise manner of expression. He was a master at really saying what he meant.

This material often reads like fiction. The conversations resemble those in a play, but you should not read them as if you were doing a play. Do not change your voice or do character voices when reading Boswell and Johnson's words. If this were fiction you might do a deep, growling sort of voice for Johnson, and a slightly higher voice and an Edinburgh accent for Boswell, but here you should avoid such vocal changes, unless the director or publisher wishes you to do them, which would not usually be the case. Also, while you should decide what each person's intentions are, you do not need to bother with substitutions for them, and you do not want to play them very strongly.

Do not be too belligerent as Johnson or too annoyed as Boswell, for instance. They may be at loggerheads, but don't play the conflict in any kind of heavy way. And make your voice parenthetical when you tell us who is speaking.

Jack Wilkes is John Wilkes (1727–1797), the controversial political reformer and champion of America during the Revolution. He was known for his profligate life, was involved in several libel trials, and was elected to and expelled from parliament several times. Johnson detested his political views.

As Johnson in the second excerpt, do not read the lines of dialogue in an opinionated, sarcastic, insulting or challenging tone; all those qualities will be there, because they are in the writing. You need not be furiously sincere when reading Johnson's political remarks, for instance, but do make his intentions clear. Stress the words in italics, as Boswell has indicated, and expressive intonation patterns should arise naturally and organically as you read, but—I repeat—you cannot be committed to the material as if you were acting a part in a play. Boswell tells us that the political conversation in the second excerpt was "boisterous," "vivacious" and "entertaining," but you can entertain the listener quite well without being boisterous or vivacious.

Two excerpts from Frank Harris's *Oscar Wilde: His Life and Confessions* (Brentano's, 1916)

FROM CHAPTER X

Years later Oscar told me that from the first he dreaded Alfred Douglas' aristocratic, insolent boldness:

"He frightened me, Frank, as much as he attracted me, and I held away from him. But he wouldn't have it; he sought me out again and again and I couldn't resist him. That is my only fault. That's what ruined me. He increased my expenses so that I could not meet them. Over and over again I tried to free myself from him; but he came back and I yielded—alas!"

Though this is Oscar's later gloss on what actually happened, it is fairly accurate. He was never able to realize how his meeting with Lord Alfred Douglas had changed the world to him and him to the world. The effect on the harder fibre of the boy was chiefly mental: to Alfred Douglas, Oscar was merely a quickening, inspiring, intellectual influence; but the boy's effect on Oscar was of character and induced imitation. Lord Alfred Douglas' boldness gave Oscar *outrecuidance*, an insolent arrogance: artist-like he tried to outdo his model in aristocratic disdain. Without knowing the cause the change in Oscar astonished me again and again, and in the course of this narrative I shall have to notice many instances of it.

• • •

FROM CHAPTER XXV

"I shall never write again, Frank," he said. "I can't, I simply can't face my thoughts. Don't ask me!" Then suddenly: "Why don't you buy the scenario and write the play yourself?"

"I don't care for the stage," I replied; "it's a sort of rude encaustic work I don't like; its effects are theatrical!"

"A play pays far better than a book, you know—"

But I was not interested. That evening thinking over what he had said, I realized all at once that a story I had in mind to write would suit "the screen scene" of Oscar's scenario; why shouldn't I write a play instead of a story? When we met next day I broached the idea to Oscar:

"I have a story in my head," I said, "which would fit into that scenario of yours, so far as you have sketched it to me. I could write it as a play and do the second, third and fourth acts very quickly, as all the personages are alive to me. Could you do the first act?"

"Of course I could, Frank."

"But," I said, "will you?"

"What would be the good, you could not sell it, Frank."

"In any case," I went on, "I could try; but I would infinitely prefer you to write the whole play if you would; then it would sell fast enough."

"Oh, Frank, don't ask me."

NOTES, COMMENTS AND HINTS

The French word "outrecuidance" is pronounced "oo trə küi: DA*N*S."

If Boswell's *Life of Johnson* often reads as entertainingly as fiction, and is nevertheless fact, Frank Harris's book on Wilde often reads as entertainingly as fiction, and is in large measure... fiction.

Frank Harris (1856–1931) journalist, editor, and author of specious autobiographical memoirs, wrote his book as a purportedly objective biography of Oscar Wilde (1854–1900). He tells us what Wilde, Lord Alfred Douglas (Wilde's lover, and his downfall, some would say), and others said in their own words, or rather in Frank Harris's own words. The problem is that Harris was a notorious liar, who was always being sued for libel, and he gave his book plausibility by mixing real, well-known events in with his invented bogus ones, and he was actually a friend of Wilde's.

At one point in the book Harris even goes so far as to have Wilde discoursing on and justifying his homosexuality in a speech clearly rewritten from the published trial transcripts (in fact, Harris mentions that very speech elsewhere in the book), a speech Wilde could not possibly have made during a train journey with Harris, a journey undoubtedly invented by Harris in the first place. And Wilde's speech in the trial transcripts is much better and more moving than Harris's rewritten version. Harris counted, probably, on few people having read the original trial transcripts printed in the newspapers in 1895, and not republished until 1920 in a version used as source material by H. Montgomery Hyde in 1948, when he edited *The Three Trials of Oscar Wilde* for publication (University Books, first United States printing, 1956).

The account Harris gives us is also suspect because the book is clearly meant to serve Harris's interests and to exaggerate and inflate the connection he had with the famous writer. In fact, in many ways Wilde couldn't stand the pretentious Harris, even though Harris was often loyal and supportive. When the two were traveling together on the continent after Wilde's release from prison, Wilde wrote to a friend: "Frank Harris is exhausting. After our literary talk in the evening I stagger to my room..." He thought Harris was basically insensitive, obnoxious and dishonest; he was right.

Yet when Frank Harris wrote his book, which he couldn't get published in England, he was being courageous and standing on real moral principle in even daring to write the biography of a man who was stupidly held in unjustified opprobrium at the time, and who had been so brutally and unjustly condemned under an inhuman law simply because he was homosexual, and because he took a rebellious stance against Victorian conservatism.

Were you to record this or any other book about Wilde it would be a good idea to research the subject by reading real biographies of Wilde: Richard Ellmann's *Oscar Wilde* (Alfred A. Knopf, 1988) and Oscar Wilde's grandson, Merlin Holland's *Irish Peacock and Scarlet Marquis: The Real Trial of Oscar Wilde* (Fourth Estate, 2003), as well as any of the many books by the admirable H. Montgomery Hyde. For Wilde's own account, certainly filled with self-justification and less than objective, read his long letter *De Profundis* published in *The Complete Letters of Oscar Wilde* (Henry Holt, 2000).

In the first excerpt above Oscar Wilde is talking in a most uncharacteristic way to Frank Harris, and the conversation reads like the invention it undoubtedly is. Harris was not a good enough observer to be able to imitate accurately the manner or style of his subject's expression. It is very doubtful that "Years later Oscar told me" anything of the sort. Wilde's speech in the book is simply watered-down *De Profundis*. Lord Alfred Douglas was, indeed, eminently dislikeable in many ways, and after Wilde's death the ambivalent, self-loathing Douglas denounced Wilde, and claimed, in a most notorious lie, that he and Wilde had never had homosexual relations.

The conversation in the second excerpt is supposed to have taken place on the French Riviera, where Wilde was in exile after he got out of prison, having served two years at hard labor after his conviction for "gross indecency." Probably, like the first excerpt, it is not a conversation that actually took place, but something like it could possibly have taken place, and it is based on what we know of Wilde's thinking.

By "the screen scene" Harris presumably means something like the screen scene in Richard Brinsley Sheridan's *The School for Scandal* (1777).

The way to read this material aloud is simply to treat it as if it were truthful. You can read it like a novel, because this notoriously faked biography is fictitious. I think you can feel freer to act the characters than you would in a more authentic biography, such as Boswell's.

One of the other problems with the book is that Harris is a bad writer. His book is the equivalent of pulp fiction, with his mastery of the inaccurate word, almost to the point of malapropism, as in the sentence "Though this is Oscar's later gloss on what actually happened, it is fairly accurate." In the first place, he means "version of," not "gloss on." In the second place, one meaning of the word "gloss" is an inaccurate or deliberately misleading interpretation of an event. (The noun also means "a marginal note explaining the meaning of some obscure term or expression in a text" or, when used as a verb, "to treat something in a dismissive manner," as in the expression "to gloss over.") Isn't Harris's sentence unnecessary, and even silly, since it implies that Wilde is simultaneously accurate and inaccurate? And how can something be "fairly accurate"? It is accurate, or it isn't!

And what on earth is a recording artist or anyone else to make of Harris's "The effect on the harder fibre of the boy was chiefly mental" and "but the boy's effect on Oscar was one of character and induced imitation?" I cannot even dimly guess the answer, although I imagine Harris knew what he meant. And what of "... the change in Oscar astonished me again and again, and in the course of this narrative I shall have to notice many instances of it?" One simply has to read the words and imagine they will make as much sense to the listener as they do to the reader.

Autobiography and Memoirs

Two excerpts from Benjamin Franklin's *Autobiography* (1788)

Then I walked up the street, gazing about till near the market-house I met a boy with bread. I had made many a meal on bread, and, inquiring where he got it, I went immediately to the baker's he directed me to, in Second-street, and ask'd for bisket, intending such as we had in Boston; but they, it seems, were not made in Philadelphia. Then I asked for a three-penny loaf, and was told they had none such. So not considering or knowing the difference of money, and the greater cheapness nor the names of his bread, I made him give me three-penny worth of any sort. He gave me, accordingly, three great puffy rolls. I was surpriz'd at the quantity, but took it, and, having no room in my pockets, walk'd off with a roll under each arm, and eating the other. Thus I went up Market-street as far as Fourth-street, passing by the door of Mr. Read, my future wife's father; when she, standing at the door, saw me, and thought I made, as I certainly did, a most awkward, ridiculous appearance. Then I turned and went down Chestnut-street and part of Walnut-street, eating my roll all the way, and, coming round, found myself again at Market-street wharf, near the boat I came in, to which I went for a draught of the river water; and, being filled with one of my rolls, gave the other two to a woman and her child that came down the river in the boat with us, and were waiting to go farther.

• • •

In 1754, war with France being again apprehended, a congress of commissioners from the different colonies was, by an order of the Lords of Trade, to be assembled at Albany, there to confer with the chiefs of the Six Nations concerning the means of defending both their country and ours. Governor Hamilton, having receiv'd this order, acquainted the House with it, requesting they would furnish proper presents for the Indians, to be given on this occasion; and naming the speaker (Mr. Norris) and myself to join Mr. Thomas Penn and Mr. Secretary Peters as commissioners to act for Pennsylvania. The House approv'd the nomination, and provided the goods for the present, tho' they did not much like treating out of the province, and we met the other commissioners at Albany about the middle of June.

In our way thither, I projected and drew a plan for the union of all the colonies under one government, so far as might be necessary for defense, and other important general purposes. As we pass'd thro' New York, I had there shown my project to Mr. James Alexander and Mr. Kennedy, two gentlemen of great knowledge in public affairs, and, being fortified by their approbation, I ventur'd to lay it before the Congress. It then appeared that several of the commissioners had form'd plans of the same kind. A previous question was first taken, whether a union should be established, which pass'd in the affirmative unanimously. A committee was then appointed, one member from each colony, to consider the several plans and report. Mine happen'd to be preferr'd, and, with a few amendments, was accordingly reported.

By this plan the general government was to be administered by a president-general, appointed and supported by the crown, and a grand council was to be chosen by the representatives of the people of the several colonies, met in their respective assemblies. The debates upon it in Congress went on daily, hand in hand with the Indian business. Many objections and difficulties were started, but at length they were all overcome, and the plan was unanimously agreed to, and copies ordered to be transmitted to the Board of Trade and to the assemblies of the several provinces. Its fate was singular: the assemblies did not adopt it, as they all thought there was too much *prerogative* in it, and in England it was judg'd to have too much of the *democratic*.

NOTES, COMMENTS AND HINTS

The great writer, statesman and diplomat Benjamin Franklin (1706–1790) began writing his autobiography in England in 1771, wrote five chapters, and then stopped. He did not pick it up again until 1784, after the American Revolution and the formation of the United States, in both of which he played such an instrumental part. Then he dropped it again until 1788. By the time he stopped writing it, he had only brought the account of his life as far as 1757. This is a shame, because it is after that time that his life really gets interesting. One would love to have had his account of the American Revolution, especially because he writes not simply as an autobiographer, but as a historian recounting the events of his time. He wrote his book as a benefit to posterity, to whom he wanted to be a role model of sobriety, humanitarianism and purposefulness, and he does emerge as a very remarkable self-made man.

The *Autobiography* was published posthumously by Buisson in Paris in 1791 in a French translation; but nobody knows where or how the French publisher got a copy of the manuscript. Benjamin Franklin had sent a copy of it to a Parisian friend of his, Monsieur Le Veillard, but he claimed to know nothing about its publication.

The original manuscript had been left to Franklin's grandson, William Temple Franklin, Benjamin's literary executor, who proceeded to publish his grandfather's papers in 1817. The manuscript itself went on an absolutely extraordinary odyssey. Thinking that Le Veillard's copy might be in a better state than the manuscript, and thus more easily edited for publication, Temple Franklin contacted Monsieur Le Veillard's daughter, and asked her to send her father's copy to him, which she did. In exchange he sent them his grandfather's original. John Bigelow, United States Ambassador to France, eventually purchased it from the Le Veillard family in 1867, later selling it to E. Dwight Church of New York, who left it, along with the rest of his library, to Henry F. Huntington. Through the early part of the twentieth century it remained in a vault in Church's house at Fifth Avenue and 57th Street, before winding up in the Huntington Library in San Marino, California.

Back in 1868, Bigelow published an authentic version of the *Life of Benjamin*

Franklin by Himself, based on a scrupulous reading of the original manuscript. Bigelow had been astonished to find that the version Franklin's grandson had published was highly inaccurate, nobody quite knows why.

These excerpts are from two different phases of Franklin's life, so the first has a kind of naïve quality and tone, the second that of a more seasoned statesman.

Governor James Hamilton (1710–1783), son of Andrew Hamilton, Pennsylvania's first colonial governor, was the lieutenant governor of Pennsylvania from 1748 to1754. Thomas Penn and the other sons of William Penn, founder of the proprietary colony, had appointed him to the post. Having been imprisoned three times for religious and political nonconformity, William Penn had left England in 1680 for the new world in order to be free to worship as a member of the Protestant religious sect that believed in pacifism, the Society of Friends, also called the Quakers.

Hamilton was lieutenant governor during the first phase of the French and Indian War (1754–1760), the last of a series of colonial wars between Britain and France, which in 1759 saw the loss of Quebec to the British. In 1754 the British colonies were threatened with invasion by the French and some of their Native American allies.

The "Six Nations," also known as the "Iroquois Confederacy," consisting of the Mohawks, Oneidas, Onandagas, Cayugas, Senecas, and Tuscaroras, all from what is now upstate New York and parts of Canada, still exists and calls itself "the oldest *participatory* democracy in the world." During the American Revolution, they sent representatives to discuss their rights with the Continental Congress. Franklin and Thomas Jefferson were inspired by their democratic practices.

Franklin goes to a meeting "to confer with the chiefs of the Six Nations concerning the means of defending both their country and ours"—a remarkable statement, considering the general attitude towards and the treatment of Native Americans by European colonists, and even more remarkable to us today considering the nearly genocidal treatment meted out to Native Americans after the colonial period. It is surprising to realize that in 1754 the idea that the Native Americans had national rights, and were to be respected and treated as having such rights to "their country," which is also "ours," was accepted as truth and as reality—at least on the surface; one must also consider the hypocrisy involved in using Native Americans to serve the ends of the European colonists. This background information will help inform your reading, and you can point up such phrases as "to confer with the chiefs of the Six Nations" and "both their country and ours" by taking slight pauses after them.

Franklin writes quite clearly and colloquially, so we really see what eighteenth-century American English was like. On occasion he can wax oratorical, but usually he just tells us his story with truth and simplicity, and in a very authoritative manner at the same time. Reflect all of that, in the tone of your reading.

Two excerpts from Grace Dalrymple Elliott's *Journal of My Life During the French Revolution* (published in 1859 in London by Richard Bentley, New Burlington Street), Chapter IV.

It was on a Thursday, the 17th of January, 1793, that they both [the Duke of Orleans and the Duc de Biron] came. I had seen little of the Duke of Orleans for some time before. On my asking him what he now thought of the wicked trial going on [the trial of Louis XVI], and saying "that I hoped he did not go near such vile miscreants?" He replied that "he was obliged to go, as he was a deputy." I said, "How can you sit and see your King and cousin brought before a set of blackguards, and that they should dare to insult him by asking him questions?" adding that "I wished I had been at the Convention; for I should have pulled off both my shoes, and have thrown them at the head of the President and of Santerre, for daring to insult their King and master."

I was very warm on the subject. The Duke of Orleans seemed out of humour. The Duc de Biron then asked him some questions about the trial. I could not help saying, "I hope, Monseigneur, that you will vote for the King's deliverance?" "Certainly," he answered, "and for my own death."

I saw that he was angry, and the Duc de Biron said, "The Duke will not vote. The King has used him very ill all his life; but he is his cousin, therefore he will feign illness and stay at home on Saturday, the day of the *Appel Nominal* [the role call], which is to decide the King's fate."

I said, "Then, Monseigneur, I am sure you will not go to the Convention on Saturday. Pray don't."

He said that he certainly would not go; that he never had intended to go; and he gave me his sacred word of honour that he would not go; that "though he thought the King had been guilty by forfeiting his word to the nation, yet nothing should induce him, being his relation, to vote against him." This I thought a poor consolation, but I could do no more, and the two Dukes left me.

• • •

[The Duke of Orleans did vote for his cousin's death after all. Grace Elliott protested, "But you promised you would not vote."]

On this he got up, observing, "This is an unpleasant subject. You cannot—must not judge for me. I know my own situation. I could not avoid doing what I have done. I am perhaps more to be pitied than you can form an idea of. I am more a slave of faction than anybody in France; but from this instant let us drop the subject. Things are at their worst. I wish you were safe in England, but how to get you out of France is what I cannot contrive. If money can procure you a passport I will give five hundred pounds. This is my last resource for you. The rulers like money, and I have hopes for you. I will do what I can with some of the leaders, but Robespierre, to whom I never speak, is all powerful."

NOTES, COMMENTS AND HINTS

Louis XVI was guillotined on January 21, 1793, in what is now the place de la Concorde, then called the place Louis XV, and renamed the place de la Révolution. It was later in 1793 that the lawyer and deputy from Arras, the firebrand orator and precursor of socialism, Maximilien de Robespierre (1758–1794), and the Committee of Public Safety, of which he was the Chairman, instituted what has come to be known as the Reign of Terror, in the course of which Louis Philippe Joseph d'Orléans (1747–1793), duke of Orleans, known as Philippe Égalité (pronounced "é ga: li: TÉ") because of his support for the Revolution, met his own death on the scaffold (see the excerpt from Carlyle's *French Revolution* below), where, in due course, Robespierre himself was executed. Eventually Grace Elliott did escape from Paris and made her way back home.

Grace Elliott (1757–1823), a Scotswoman, was one of the great courtesans of the age. She was the youngest daughter of an attorney, Hew Dalrymple, of Edinburgh. As a girl she was sent to be educated in a convent in France, but in 1771 she returned to Edinburgh, where she turned all heads on her debut in society. She married a physician, Dr. John Elliott, twenty years older than she, from whom she was divorced—the divorce settlement left her quite wealthy—after running away with Lord Valentia, the latest of several extramarital liaisons. Her brother followed her to France, and imprisoned her in a convent, from which she was rescued by one of her admirers and taken to London, to be presented at court. Eventually she became a mistress of the Prince of Wales and various high-ranking aristocrats. In 1786 she returned to France, becoming the mistress of the Duke of Orleans, whom she had met two years earlier in England, and conducting affairs with several other French aristocrats, such as Armand Louis de Gontaut, duc de Biron, also known as the duc de Lauzun (1747–1793); pronunciations: gawn TOH; bi: RON; loh ZUN. He had fought in the American Revolution and was a representative of the nobility in the Estates-General in 1789; he was guillotined during the Reign of

Terror. After the defeat of Napoleon, Grace Elliott returned to Paris. She died at Ville-d'Avray, where she had become the mistress of the mayor.

Once again we have a piece of nonfiction that reads like fiction, in which the conversations, while reflecting the well-known sentiments of the Duke of Orleans and of Mrs. Elliott, are probably not in their actual words; although purporting to be a journal, the book was actually written long after the events it describes. Read the dialogue with the underlying intentions, but do not act the scenes fully. And select as your imaginary audience to tell this story to someone in whom you usually confide; this should give you the intimate, real tone necessary for reading this text.

You might like to compare the kind of work in the performances in Sax Rohmer's film *L'Anglaise et le duc* (*The Lady and the Duke*) (2002), based on Elliott's *Journal*, where the characters are fully brought to life and acted, with the necessary task of not acting them fully when recording *The Journal of My Life*.

Two excerpts from Frederick Douglass's *Narrative of the Life of Frederick Douglass, an American Slave* (1845)

CHAPTER VII

My mistress was, as I have said, a kind and tender-hearted woman; and in the simplicity of her soul she commenced, when I first went to live with her, to treat me as she supposed one human being ought to treat another. In entering upon the duties of a slaveholder, she did not seem to perceive that I sustained to her the relation of a mere chattel, and that for her to treat me as a human being was not only wrong, but dangerously so. Slavery proved as injurious to her as it did to me. When I went there, she was a pious, warm, and tender-hearted woman. There was no sorrow or suffering for which she had not a tear. She had bread for the hungry, clothes for the naked, and comfort for every mourner that came within her reach. Slavery soon proved its ability to divest her of these heavenly qualities. Under its influence, the tender heart became stone, and the lamblike disposition gave way to one of tiger-like fierceness. The first step in her downward course was in her ceasing to instruct me. She now commenced to practise her husband's precepts. She finally became even more violent in her opposition than her husband himself. She was not satisfied with simply doing as well as he had commanded; she seemed anxious to do better. Nothing seemed to make her more angry than to see me with a newspaper. She seemed to think that here lay the danger. I have had her rush at me with a face made all up of fury, and snatch from me a newspaper, in a manner that fully revealed her apprehension. She was an apt woman; and a little experience soon demonstrated, to her satisfaction, that education and slavery were incompatible with each other.

From this time I was most narrowly watched. If I was in a separate room any considerable length of time, I was sure to be suspected of having a book, and was at once called to give an account of myself. All this, however, was too late. The first step had been taken. Mistress, in teaching me the alphabet, had given me the ~inch,~ and no precaution could prevent me from taking the ~ell.~

The plan which I adopted, and the one by which I was most successful, was that of making friends of all the little white boys whom I met in the street. As many of these as I could, I converted into teachers. With their kindly aid, obtained at different times and in different places, I finally succeeded in learning to read.

• • •

CHAPTER XI

Things went on without very smoothly indeed, but within there was trouble. It is impossible for me to describe my feelings as the time of my contemplated start drew near. I had a number of warm-hearted friends in Baltimore,—friends that I loved almost as I did my life,—and the thought of being separated from them forever was painful beyond expression. It is my opinion that thousands would escape from slavery, who now remain, but for the strong cords of affection that bind them to their friends. The thought of leaving my friends was decidedly the most painful thought with which I had to contend. The love of them was my tender point, and shook my decision more than all things else. Besides the pain of separation, the dread and apprehension of a failure exceeded what I had experienced at my first attempt. The appalling defeat I then sustained returned to torment me. I felt assured that, if I failed in this attempt, my case would be a hopeless one—it would seal my fate as a slave forever. I could not hope to get off with any thing less than the severest punishment, and being placed beyond the means of escape. It required no very vivid imagination to depict the most frightful scenes through which I should have to pass, in case I failed. The wretchedness of slavery, and the blessedness of freedom, were perpetually before me. It was life and death with me. But I remained firm, and, according to my resolution, on the third day of September, 1838, I left my chains, and succeeded in reaching New York without the slightest interruption of any kind. How I did so,—what means I adopted,—what direction I travelled, and by what mode of conveyance,—I must leave unexplained, for the reasons before mentioned.

I have been frequently asked how I felt when I found myself in a free State. I have never been able to answer the question with any satisfaction to myself. It was a moment of the highest excitement I ever experienced. I suppose I felt as one may imagine the unarmed mariner to feel when he is rescued by a friendly man-of-war from the pursuit of a pirate. In writing to a dear friend, immediately after my arrival at New York, I said I felt like one who had escaped a den of hungry lions. This state of mind, however, very soon subsided; and I was again seized with a feeling of great insecurity and loneliness. I was yet liable to be taken back, and subjected to all the tortures of slavery. This in itself was enough to damp the ardor of my enthusiasm. But the loneliness overcame me. There I was in the midst of thousands, and yet a perfect stranger; without home and without friends, in the midst of thousands of my own brethren—children of a common Father, and yet I dared not to unfold to any one of them my sad condition. I was afraid to speak to any one for fear of speaking to the wrong one, and thereby falling into the hands of money-loving kidnappers, whose business it was to lie in wait for the panting fugitive, as the ferocious beasts of the forest lie in wait for their prey.

NOTES, COMMENTS AND HINTS

Frederick Douglass was a slave in a household in Baltimore, Md. at the time of the events he describes in the first excerpt.

This narrative begins with a chilling, horrifying account of what slavery was like, and of Frederick Douglass's early sufferings—he was born into slavery in Talbot, Maryland. It goes on to describe his escape from slavery, and his subsequent life. The book was first "Published at the Anti-Slavery Office" in Boston. For more on the absolutely nightmarish horror and brutality of life under the criminal system that was slavery read Chapters Fifteen and Sixteen in Mark Kurlansky's book *Salt: A World History* (Penguin USA paperback, 2003); and read especially Hugh Thomas's *The Slave Trade: The Story of the Atlantic Slave Trade: 1440–1870* (Simon & Schuster, 1997).

In his Preface to the *Autobiography*, the ardent abolitionist William Lloyd Garrison wrote the following, after hearing Frederick Douglass speak at an anti-slavery convention in Nantucket in 1841:

> I shall never forget his first speech at the convention—the extraordinary emotion it excited in my own mind—the powerful impression it

> created upon a crowded auditory, completely taken by surprise—the applause which followed from the beginning to the end of his felicitous remarks. I think I never hated slavery so intensely as at that moment; certainly, my perception of the enormous outrage which is inflicted by it, on the godlike nature of its victims, was rendered far more clear than ever. There stood one, in physical proportion and stature commanding and exact—in intellect richly endowed—in natural eloquence a prodigy—in soul manifestly "created but a little lower than the angels"—yet a slave, ay, a fugitive slave,—trembling for his safety, hardly daring to believe that on the American soil, a single white person could be found who would befriend him at all hazards, for the love of God and humanity!

Garrison is referring to the fact that Douglass, as a fugitive slave, was not absolutely safe, even in northern states where slavery had been abolished, from being kidnapped by bounty hunters and sent back to the south.

It was a shameful and hypocritical travesty that the Constitution of the United States, a nation supposedly founded on the principle that all people have equal rights, had not done away with slavery, which existed in the North (it was abolished over time in the northern states, and had disappeared there well before the Civil War), as well as in the South, or with other abuses of human rights, such as the oppression of women. Despite its crude and transparent ignoring of the actual facts of life, the document did at least have the virtue of promulgating high ideals for the future. But even a century after the bloody conflict known as the Civil War and even after Emancipation, those ideals were not being lived up to, so that there was in the 1960s and through the rest of the twentieth century, as there is in the twenty-first, the necessity of continuing the fight to advance the cause of civil rights for everyone, in which progress, despite lingering inequities and abuses, is being made.

Douglass terrified to speak to anyone for fear of being turned in to the authorities as a fugitive slave is reminiscent of more recent history: the harrowing stories of what happened to some of those Jews in Europe during World War Two who had managed to escape from the ghettos where they had been confined, and attempted to find hiding places on the other side of the wall, only to fall prey to blackmailers and worse.

While nobody can have a visceral understanding of what Douglass went through who has not been through something similar her or himself, his narrative is so powerfully evocative that we can empathize with him, and we can enter his mind and his heart, as it were. If you are recording this autobiography you can allow us to do this by reading it sincerely and with clear meaning, and without adding your own emotions, based on substitutions, to it. We need to hear how Douglass felt about what happened to him, but we don't need to hear about how you felt.

Douglass's narrative is poignant, touching, elegant and clearly and forthrightly written, so that it flows very nicely when read aloud. Read it simply and lucidly, and your listeners will find it very moving.

In 1983 I performed in George Steiner's *The Portage to San Cristóbal of A. H.* at the Hartford Stage Company in Connecticut. In the play Israeli commandos are bringing Hitler, who has been discovered alive in a jungle in South America, back to Israel to stand trial. The commandos are pursued by the forces of other countries, who also wish to capture Hitler, and, as time is running out, the Israelis hold a trial right there in a clearing. Sitting still at the side of the stage at a reading desk with a single lit lamp (much as when recording a book), I played the part of Lieber, an Israeli official broadcasting to the commandos in the jungle, in order to embolden them and to remind them why they were doing their task.

When I began rehearsing the play I was very emotional, and I had all I could do not to weep during my long speeches about the Holocaust: "In Maidanek 10,000 a day..." and so forth. My obstacle, I told myself, was that I needed to control myself and found it difficult because of the horror of the events. But Mark Lamos, the director, quickly put me on the right path. "If you cry, or even show us that you are trying not to cry," he said, "the audience won't." And he directed me to deliver the material dispassionately, almost coldly, simply building the speeches to their climaxes, but without any affect or emotional involvement. My objective and the action I played were to remind them, to remind them, and to remind them again, not by pounding away, but by simply telling them the story, by simply making points: "At Maidanek 10,000 a day..." This allowed the audience to absorb the images and to imagine events for themselves.

I was doing a play, a work of fiction, but Frederick Douglass's autobiography is, of course, not a work of fiction. The advice about how to read it aloud applies also to the excerpts below from Sojourner Truth's narrative: The more calmly, unemotionally and dispassionately you read, the more detached and objective you appear, and the more moving and effective will your reading be. Telling us the story is all you have to do, and that is quite sufficient to allow us to empathize completely with it, and to enter into it with our hearts and our love. You will arouse in your listeners the same kind of "extraordinary emotion" Garrison had when he heard Douglass speak, and you will create, as Douglass does, a most "powerful impression." (The same advice applies to recording first-person memoirs and autobiographies by survivors of the Holocaust, South African apartheid, Soviet gulags, and the more recent genocidal horrors perpetrated in Cambodia, Rwanda, the former Yugoslavia, and elsewhere.)

From Sojourner Truth's *The Narrative of Sojourner Truth* (1850), dictated by Sojourner Truth (ca.1797–1883); edited by Olive Gilbert, "Commencement of Isabella's Trials in Life"

Having seen the sad end of her parents, so far as it relates to *this* earthly life, we will return with Isabella to that memorable auction which threatened to separate her father and mother. A slave auction is a terrible affair to its victims, and its incidents and consequences are graven on their hearts as with a pen of burning steel.

At this memorable time, Isabella was struck off, for the sum of one hundred dollars, to one John Nealy, of Ulster County, New York; and she has an impression that in this sale she was connected with a lot of sheep. She was now nine years of age, and her trials in life may be dated from this period. She says, with emphasis, *"Now the war begun."* She could only talk Dutch—and the Nealys could only talk English. Mr. Nealy could *understand* Dutch, but Isabel and her mistress could neither of them understand the language of the other—and this, of itself, was a formidable obstacle in the way of a *good* understanding between them, and for some time was a fruitful source of dissatisfaction to the mistress, and of punishment and suffering to Isabella. She says, "If they sent me for a frying-pan, not knowing what they meant, perhaps I carried them pot-hooks and trammels. Then, oh! how angry mistress would be with me!" Then she suffered *"terribly—terribly,"* with the cold. During the winter her feet were badly frozen, for want of proper covering. They gave her a plenty to eat, and also a plenty of whippings. One Sunday morning, in particular, she was told to go to the barn; on going there, she found her master with a bundle of rods, prepared in the embers, and bound together with cords. When he had tied her hands together before her, he gave her the most cruel whipping she was ever tortured with. He whipped her till the flesh was deeply lacerated, and the blood streamed from her wounds—and the scars remain to the present day, to testify to the fact. "And now," she says, "when I hear 'em tell of whipping women on the bare flesh, it makes *my* flesh crawl, and my very hair rise on my head! Oh! my God!" she continues, "what a way is this of treating human beings?" In those hours of her extremity, she did not forget the instructions of her mother, to go to God in all her trials, and every affliction; and she not only remembered, but obeyed: going to him, "and telling him all–and asking Him if He thought it was right," and begging him to protect and shield her from her persecutors. She always asked with an unwavering faith that she should receive just what she pleaded

> for—"And now," she says, "though it seems *curious*, I do not remember ever asking for any thing but what I got it. And I always received it as an answer to my prayers. When I got beaten, I never knew it long enough to go beforehand to pray; and I always thought that if I only had *had* time to pray to God for help, I should have escaped the beating." She had no idea God had any knowledge of her thoughts, save what she told him; or heard her prayers, unless they were spoken audibly. And consequently, she could not pray unless she had time and opportunity to go by herself, where she could talk to God without being overheard.

NOTES, COMMENTS AND HINTS

At the time Sojourner Truth wrote her book slavery was still legal in the south and many other parts of the United States.

In 1827 New York passed an Emancipation Act ending slavery in that state forever. Sojourner Truth, who had been born into slavery under the name Isabella, was now free. Having taken the name of her former owners, Van Wagener, she moved to New York City and worked there as a household servant. She discovered religion in earnest and became an evangelist, taking the name Sojourner Truth. She soon became an ardent abolitionist and an advocate of women's rights, and often appeared with Frederick Douglass on the public speaking platform. She was known as a compelling, even a hypnotic speaker, which is even more remarkable when you consider that, born into slavery in New York, her native language was Dutch, her owner's language, and that she only learned English later on. She was also illiterate, so this narrative was dictated to a friend, Olive Gilbert.

During the Civil War she was active in gathering supplies for black regiments. Abraham Lincoln received her at the White House, and appointed her to the National Freedmen's Relief Association, where she was an adviser and counselor to former slaves. All her life this brilliant woman continued to speak publicly against injustice and for women's rights.

I repeat what I said above about reading from Frederick Douglass's autobiography: Read this heart-wrenching and harrowing excerpt from her narrative without emotional affect. If you tell us the story simply we will experience the horror and the dignity of Sojourner Truth in her suffering. If you try to add your own feelings to it you will lose the listener, who will perceive an unreality in your reading, without quite knowing why. It would be a mistake to pretend that you do have a visceral memory of the kind of experience you have not lived through, no matter how much you empathize. But the power and deep feeling of Sojourner Truth's narrative will come through if you read it as a kind of discovery for yourself, by which I do not mean that you should have a tone of voice that sounds to us like you are discovering something. That *feeling* of discovery, with its concomitant growing sense of outrage, should be there as you read, but the horror, the anger and the hurt themselves are right there in the words, and you don't need to add those emotions to them. Allow the listeners into the experience, so they can feel the experience as much as possible. You have lines like " '...Oh! my God!' she continues, 'what a way is this of treating human beings?' " Just making that statement makes the statement. All you have to do is mean it, which you cannot help doing.

History

From Edward Gibbon (1737–1794), *The Decline and Fall of the Roman Empire*

TWO EXCERPTS FROM CHAPTER I: THE EXTENT AND MILITARY FORCE OF THE EMPIRE IN THE AGE OF THE ANTONINES

...it was reserved for Augustus to relinquish the ambitious design of subduing the whole earth, and to introduce a spirit of moderation into the public councils...

The only accession which the Roman empire received, during the first century of the Christian era, was the province of Britain. In this single instance the successors of Caesar and Augustus were persuaded to follow the example of the former, rather than the precept of the latter. The proximity of its situation to the coast of Gaul seemed to invite their arms; the pleasing though doubtful intelligence, of a pearl fishery, attracted their avarice; and as Britain was viewed in the light of a distinct and insulated world, the conquest scarcely formed any exception to the general system of continental measures. After a war of about forty years, undertaken by the most stupid, maintained by the most dissolute, and terminated by the most timid of all the emperors, the far greater part of the island submitted to the Roman yoke. The various tribes of Britons possessed valour without conduct, and the love of freedom without the spirit of union. They took up arms with savage fierceness; they laid them down, or turned them against each other with savage inconstancy; and while they fought singly, they were successively subdued. Neither the fortitude of Caractacus, nor the despair of Boadicea, nor the fanaticism of the Druids, could avert the slavery of their country, or resist the steady progress of the Imperial generals, who maintained the national glory, when the throne was disgraced by the weakest, or the most vicious of mankind.

• • •

Trajan was ambitious of fame; and as long as mankind shall continue to bestow more liberal applause on their destroyers than on their benefactors, the thirst of military glory will ever be the vice of the most exalted characters. The praises of Alexander, transmitted by a succession of poets and historians, had kindled a dangerous emulation in the mind of Trajan. Like him the Roman emperor undertook an expedition against the nations of the east, but he lamented with a sigh, that his advanced age scarcely left him any hopes of equaling the renown of the son of Philip. Yet the success of Trajan, however transient, was rapid and specious. The degenerate Parthians, broken by intestine discord, fled before his arms. He descended the river Tigris in triumph, from the mountains of Armenia to the Persian gulf. He enjoyed the honor of being the first, as he was the last, of the Roman generals, who ever navigated that remote sea. His fleets ravaged the coasts of Arabia; and Trajan vainly flattered himself that he was approaching towards the confines of India. Every day the astonished senate received the intelligence of new names and new nations, that acknowledged his sway. They were informed that the kings of Bosphorus, Colchos, Iberia, Albania, Osrhoene, and even the Parthian monarch himself, had accepted their diadems from the hands of the emperor; that the independent tribes of the Median and Carduchian hills had implored his protection; and that the rich countries of Armenia, Mesopotamia, and Assyria, were reduced into the state of provinces. But the death of Trajan soon clouded the splendid prospect; and it was justly to be dreaded, that so many distant nations would throw off the unaccustomed yoke, when they were no longer restrained by the powerful hand which had imposed it.

NOTES, COMMENTS AND HINTS

I omit the voluminous footnotes from these selections. Gibbon's footnotes are often about the veracity and reliability of his sources, or they are comments on the events he describes, or they are direct quotations in Latin from his source material. If you have to record footnotes, there are a number of ways of proceeding, and you will be informed by the people in charge of the recording as to exactly what procedure they wish you to use: You can interrupt the main text, lower your voice parenthetically and say either the number of the footnote ("Footnote One") or just "Footnote" or "Note," then read it, and say "End of Footnote," or "End of Note," and go back to the main text; or you may be asked to read them all at the end of the book, or at the end of the chapter in which they occur. In books with notes that are all in a section near the end of the book, or in sections immediately following chapters, you may be asked to read them when and as they occur in the text (which will, of course, necessitate the turning back and forth of pages, this slowing down the recording process), using a formula similar to the ones mentioned above: either "Note... End of Note," or "Note One... End of Note One," etc. In commercial recordings notes and footnotes are often omitted altogether.

The Decline and Fall of the Roman Empire is one of the great histories in the English language, and certainly one of the finest from the point of view of the writing. Edward Gibbon (1737–1794) worked on it for twenty years, polishing each sentence until it shone like a piece of rare silver or gold. Gibbon's grammar is perfect and admirably precise.

Your reading of such a stylishly crafted, elegantly written text should reflect your delight in its robust, yet refined language. The reading should flow like the Tiber River under the bridges of Rome. The commas in Gibbon's sentences give you a wonderful hint as to where to take pauses, and are thus useful for practicing breath control and phrasing. There is no need to embellish with vocal pyrotechnics texts that are already sufficiently embellished with elegant turns of phrase. You have only to let their urbanity, refinement and sinuosity stand out for themselves, which they will do when you stress the important words and observe the natural rhythm of the texts. Eat them up as you would rich homemade peach ice cream on a hot August day! Not too fast—or you might lose the flavor!

The ancient Britons' names in the first excerpt are pronounced "kə RÆK tə kəs" and "boh æ di SEE ə." (Do you remember the Major General's claim in Gilbert and Sullivan's *The Pirates of Penzance* that he could "tell you every detail of Caractacus's uniform"?) The Roman emperor's name is pronounced "TRAY dgən." Born in Spain, Trajan (52/3–117) reigned from 98 to 117, and was known for his military prowess and his numerous bridge- and road-building projects throughout the empire.

Here are a few pronunciations of the more obscure geographical names: the name of the ancient semi-Hellenistic state of Osrhoene (which, if it still existed, would be east of the Euphrates River in present-day southeastern Turkey) is pronounced "o:s roh EE nee"; Colchos (known as Colchis today, is in western Georgia on the Black Sea) is pronounced "KO:L ko:s"; Carduchian (the Carduchian Hills are on what is now the Iranian plateau) is pronounced "ka:r DOO kee ən." Look up anything else you don't know.

From Thomas Carlyle's The French Revolution

BOOK VII: TERROR THE ORDER OF THE DAY, CHAPTER II: "DEATH."

...For, be the month named Brumaire year 2 of Liberty, or November year 1793 of Slavery, the Guillotine goes always, Guillotine va toujours.

Enough, Philippe's indictment is soon drawn, his jury soon convinced. He finds himself made guilty of Royalism, Conspiracy and much else; nay, it is a guilt in him that he voted Louis's Death, though he answers, "I voted in my soul and conscience." The doom he finds is death forthwith; this present sixth dim day of November is the last day that Philippe is to see. Philippe, says Montgaillard, thereupon called for breakfast: sufficiency of "oysters, two cutlets, best part of an excellent bottle of claret"; and consumed the same with apparent relish. A Revolutionary Judge, or some official Convention Emissary, then arrived, to signify that he might still do the State some service by revealing the truth about a plot or two. Philippe answered that, on him, in the pass things had come to, the State had, he thought, small claim; that nevertheless, in the interest of Liberty, he, having still some leisure on his hands, was willing, were a reasonable question asked him, to give reasonable answer. And so, says Montgaillard, he lent his elbow on the mantel-piece, and conversed in an under-tone, with great seeming composure; till the leisure was done, or the Emissary went his ways.

At the door of the Conciergerie, Philippe's attitude was erect and easy, almost commanding. It is five years, all but a few days, since Philippe, within these same stone walls, stood up with an air of graciosity, and asked King Louis, "Whether it was a Royal Session, then, or a Bed of Justice?" O Heaven! Three poor blackguards were to ride and die with him: some say, they objected to such company, and had to be flung in, neck and heels; but it seems not true. Objecting or not objecting, the gallows-vehicle gets under way. Philippe's dress is remarked for its elegance; green frock, waistcoat of white piqué, yellow buckskins, boots clear as Warren: his air, as before, entirely composed, impassive, not to say easy and Brummellean-polite. Through street after street; slowly, amid execrations; past the Palais Égalité, whilom Palais-Royal! The cruel Populace stopped him there, some minutes: Dame de Buffon, it is said, looked out on him, in Jezebel head-tire; along the ashlar Wall, there ran these words in huge tricolor print, REPUBLIC ONE AND INDIVISIBLE; LIBERTY, EQUALITY, FRATERNITY OR DEATH: *National Property*. Philippe's eyes flashed hellfire, one instant; but the next instant it was gone, and he sat impassive, Brummellean-polite. On the scaffold, Sanson was for drawing of his boots: "Tush," said Philippe, "they will come better off after; let us have done, *dépêchons-nous*!"

So Philippe was not without virtue, then? God forbid that there should be any living man without it! He had the virtue to keep living for five-and-forty years; other virtues perhaps more than we know of. Probably no mortal ever had such things recorded of him: such facts, and also such lies. For he was a *Jacobin Prince of the Blood*; consider what a combination! Also, unlike any Nero, any Borgia, he lived in the Age of Pamphlets. Enough for us: Chaos *has* reabsorbed him; may it late or never bear his like again! Brave young Orleans Égalité, deprived of all, only not deprived of himself, is gone to Coire in the Grisons, under the name of Corby, to teach Mathematics. The Égalité Family is at the darkest depths of the Nadir.

NOTES, COMMENTS AND HINTS

One gets the impression that the proto-fascistic Carlyle got carried away with himself and his rather purple prose, which is less purple here than elsewhere in the book. Carlyle clearly deplores the Revolution in all its aspects.

There has been an almost uncountable number of books about the revolution, from the magisterial, monumental, controversial, multi-volume work *Histoire de la Révolution Française* (1847–1853) by the French historian Jules Michelet (1798–1874), to Marxist histories such as those by the eminent twentieth-century historians Albert Mathiez and François Furet. Michelet attempted to recreate events from the point of view of the participants, and his descriptions and style influenced Carlyle's writing. The Marxists, whose analyses are profound and far-reaching, emphasize the economic causes of the Revolution and see the entire socio-economic system in France as a cause of it. Along with extensive other research, they consult documents that other historians have not bothered with, such as the election returns and the lists of members of the Convention, as well as the provincial registers of voters.

This approach has its antecedents in fiction: Victor Hugo's extraordinary achievement in bringing the Convention vividly to life in Part Two, Book Three of *Quatrevingt-Treize* (*Ninety-Three*), his 1874 novel about the counter-revolutionary insurrection in the Vendée, by naming and briefly describing the appearance and political point of view of every member of it. Hugo is by no means against the Revolution's progressivism, but he admires the heroism and gallantry of those misguided adventurers who fought on the royalist side.

For Carlyle, as at times for Michelet, the whole momentous event seems to have been more a stage play or a novel than an event involving real people and a real society in which the deluge predicted by Louis XV drenched the earth, and the misery and poverty of the populace overflowed into sometimes almost uncontrollable chaos.

As he does in the excerpt above, Carlyle puts people on stage, and he finds Philippe—we have already met him in the excerpts from Grace Elliott's *Journal*—who sincerely supported the democratic ideals of the Revolution, a despicable traitor to his class, deeming his motives personal and not altruistic.

When the Revolution and its gains were threatened by internal conspiracies and external defeats and betrayals, the result was the Terror, to which nobody was immune; the majority of the people executed were not aristocrats, but economic criminals, many of whom had committed petty offenses. The Terror was embarked on reluctantly by the Committee of Public Safety and its presiding officer, Robespierre, a dedicated man of strong egalitarian principles who had at one point opposed capital punishment and who had been much admired in some quarters and decried in others for his attempts at social and economic reform, but whose power had gone to his head, although it had not absolutely corrupted him, and the sobriquet which was applied to him—L'Incorruptible (pronounced "læ*N* ko: rüp TI: blə"; the Incorruptible)—appears to have been entirely justified. Stern, stubborn and high-minded, he could not be bribed, and he could not be moved or swayed, when he thought he was right.

Unfortunately, it is always the Terror most people think of when they think of the Revolution, and not what the Revolution accomplished for the advancement of humanity. The Revolution not only promulgated the Declaration of the Rights of Man, but also saw the first abolition of slavery in the west (in the French Caribbean colonies), and the first emancipation of Jews, as well as attempts to institute democratic socialism. Efforts were made to control the chaotic economy, and to pass laws regulating wages and prices. Unfortunately, much of it backfired, and the enemies of the reforms gained the day. Then came Napoleon, the Revolutionary general who declared himself emperor.

Here is a necessarily brief outline of the causes of the conflagration that is the background to this excerpt from Carlyle:

1. Famine resulting from crop failures in the several years preceding the Revolution, the resultant poverty, and the seething unrest of the peasantry;

2. The emptying of the treasury to finance the American war to fight the British;

3. A rigid caste system, in which it was almost impossible to rise above the social class one was born into, and which entailed an incredible gulf between the astonishingly wealthy, highly privileged aristocratic class and the incredibly wretched poorer class, between which the growing middle class of merchants and the professional classes who were, in effect, servants of the aristocracy, were interposing themselves and demanding their own rights and an end to the endless corruption;

4. The sale by the king of every office in the kingdom, from usher to court judge to admiral to general to tax collector, resulting in a system rife with corruption, as those who bought their offices, paid for annually, tried to make their money back;

5. The gulf between the great urban centers, such as Paris, with its sprawling slums, and the poverty-stricken countryside;

6. A totally arbitrary and inconsistent system of justice and taxation, including the infamous salt tax;

7. The spread of Enlightenment ideas of democracy and egalitarianism.

Philippe Égalité, a member of the cadet branch of the Bourbon family, was intensely disliked by the king and queen because he had opposed them and come down so strongly on the side of the people's Revolution, and against all of the abuses. But he was still a member of a class hated and despised by the people, and as such he was suspect, so in the paranoia of the day his estates were confiscated, and he was brought to trial and condemned to death. In 1830 his son became King Louis-Philippe after another revolution (the one in Victor Hugo's *Les Misérables*), which overthrew the restored Bourbon monarchy that had replaced Napoleon in 1815 after Waterloo.

The Montgaillard (pronounced "mo:*N* ga· YA·R") Carlyle mentions is Jean Baptiste de Ferouil de Montgaillard (1760-ca. 1820), deputy of the Estates-General from Béziers, from an old noble family, with many descendants, lasting through the twentieth century.

Dame du Buffon (pronounced "da:m dü bü FO:*N*") is the "light wife of a great Naturalist much too old for her," Georges-Louis Leclerc, comte de Buffon (1707–1788), who died one year before the Revolution started, and was a typical Enlightenment philosopher, an amateur scientist and popularizer of scientific theories, and a precursor of Darwin. Buffon also challenged the received ideas of religion, and believed humanity should be studied in all its variety. He is considered the Father of anthropology.

Brumaire (pronounced "brü ME:R"), which comes from the French word for fog, is the name of the revolutionary month that replaced November. The Revolutionists started their own calendar to replace the old one, which for them symbolized an oppressive system, and to signify that they were beginning a new world. The calendar was redivided, and months were named for seasonal characteristics.

The Conciergerie (pronounced "ko:*N* sye:r zhə REE") was one of the prisons in Paris. It is still the building that houses the law courts, and at its back is a museum where you can see the cells as they were during the Revolution, including the one where Marie-Antoinette spent her last days.

Nero is, of course, the corrupt decadent emperor who "fiddled while Rome burned." Actually, according to Suetonius, Nero had Rome set on fire so he could sing his opera, *The Fall of Troy*, against a background of real flames. He accompanied himself on the lyre, and afterwards he forced the citizenry to pay for the damage and to help pay the costs of a new palace by making them subscribe to the first fire insurance company in history.

The Borgias were the vicious, ruthless ruling family of central Italy during the Renaissance, famous for being infamous and for poisoning each other to secure their power.

A Jacobin was a member of the leftist revolutionary Jacobin Club, or, by extension, anyone who espouses their principles. The club was named after its meeting place, the monastery of the Jacobins, which was the Parisian name for the Dominicans. Beginning as moderates in 1789, the Jacobins soon turned to more radical political philosophies. Robespierre was one of their leaders.

The adjective Brummellean (sometimes spelled Brummellian) derives from George Bryan "Beau" Brummel (1778–1840), a great British dandy, arbiter of fashion, and a close friend of the Prince of Wales, the future King George IV.

Charles-Henri Sanson (1739–1806; pronounced " sa:*N* SO:*N*") was the executioner of the Revolution. He came from a long line of executioners, and wrote his memoirs, which, as you can imagine, make rather grisly and bizarre reading. Although a Royalist, he nevertheless executed Marie-Antoinette and Louis XVI, and he showed as much compassion and commiseration as he could to those whom he felt obliged to execute. *Dépêchons-nous* (pronounced "dé pe sho:*N* NOO") means "Let's hurry [it] up!" A related English word is "to dispatch"; "to do something with dispatch." "Guillotine va toujours" means "The guillotine goes always, or still"; the phrase is pronounced "gee o: TI:N va: too ZHOOR."

The Palais-Royal (pronounced "pa: lé rwa: YA:L"), present home of various government organizations and ministries and of the Comédie Française, was once the home of various members of the royal family, such as Louis XIV's younger brother. Its beautiful garden is now lined with shops and restaurants under the arcades, and is open to the public.

The Duke's question to King Louis, "Whether it was a Royal Session, then, or a Bed of Justice?" refers to the absolutist custom of the *lit de justice* (pronounced "lee də jüs TI:S"), literally "bed of justice," which is akin to the English phrase "laying down the law." The King of France, in a special royal session would summon his ministers and court and declare: "The King wills it!" And a law or some extraordinary measure would be passed. In other words, the Duke sarcastically asks the King whether the King's trial is a special royal session, willed by the King himself.

When reading this text, be confident and even perhaps a bit authoritarian in tone. Enjoy Carlyle's colorful language, and his descriptions of the Duke's costume. Carlyle describes the ride through the streets to the guillotine vividly, and you must make the listener see it, almost to the point of hearing the crowd shout and jeer. Think of a time when you were at a parade or a crowded July 4 fireworks celebration, or even when you saw such an event on television. Madame de Buffon leering is also a vivid image, which you can allow us to see. Throughout, the Duke is always in the forefront: Make us feel his reactions. You can afford to be very sarcastic in the last paragraph, where Carlyle excoriates the Duke. The text is quite histrionic, almost to the point of being melodramatic, and this is one of the few times when I would recommend that you read nonfiction theatrically, almost as if it were a work of fiction. You can play up the declamatory language in a way that you should not indulge in when reading Gibbon, for instance. Whereas Gibbon is unfailingly elegant, Carlyle is often somewhat vulgar, and his prose lends itself to being just a bit bombastic.

To help you get a feeling for the life of French Revolutionary period and for its epochal events, take a look at the many engravings and drawings from the era, including portraits of all the people mentioned in the book. And listen to some of the many recordings of French Revolutionary music. The most well known-song of the period is, of course, the French national anthem, the "Marseillaise."

Essays and Philosophy

An essay is a short, informal prose composition, serious or humorous, in which the writer deals with one subject (usually) in a succinct way. It does not attempt to be a complete summary of its subject, and can be analytical, didactic, interpretive or persuasive, or simply discursive. While it can be on any subject, music, philosophy, science, medicine, travel, cooking, literature, politics, history, sociology, and psychology are usual. Many essays give the reader an overview, or are a summary discussion, of subjects often dealt with in a more extended way in history, science and philosophy books. Articles in such magazines as *The New Yorker*, *Scientific American*, *Foreign Affairs*, *The New England Journal of Medicine*, and *The New York Review of Books* are often essays.

Theatrical reviews are often excellent essays, at least when written by interesting, knowledgeable critics, such as the playwright George Bernard Shaw, or the dapper, witty Max Beerbohm (his review of Sarah Bernhardt's production of Shakespeare's *Hamlet*, in which she played the title role, is called "Hamlet, Princess of Denmark"), or those for the show business paper *Variety*, among them Matt Wolf and Charles Isherwood.

Michel de Montaigne in France was one of the first great essayists, whose book of *Essays*, first published in 1580, is a classic that is still much read and admired today. Among others are Sir Francis Bacon, William Hazlitt and Charles Lamb in Great Britain; and Ralph Waldo Emerson and Henry David Thoreau in the United States. You can use any of the works of the foregoing authors for practice, and you will learn a good deal in the process.

From Sir Francis Bacon's *The Essayes or Counsels Civill and Morall* (first published 1597; revised editions 1601 and 1625)

10. OF LOVE

The stage is more beholding to love, than the life of man. For as to the stage, love is ever matter of comedies, and now and then of tragedies; but in life it doth much mischief; sometimes like a siren, sometimes like a fury. You may observe, that amongst all the great and worthy persons (whereof the memory remaineth, either ancient or recent) there is not one, that hath been transported to the mad degree of love: which shows that great spirits, and great business, do keep out this weak passion. You must except, nevertheless, Marcus Antonius, the half partner of the empire of Rome, and Appius Claudius, the decemvir and lawgiver; whereof the former was indeed a voluptuous man, and inordinate; but the latter was an austere and wise man: and therefore it seems (though rarely) that love can find entrance, not only into an open heart, but also into a heart well fortified, if watch be not well kept. It is a poor saying of Epicurus, *Satis magnum alter alteri theatrum sumus:* as if man, made for the contemplation of heaven, and all noble objects, should do nothing but kneel before a little idol and make himself a subject, though not of the mouth (as beasts are), yet of the eye; which was given him for higher purposes. It is a strange thing, to note the excess of this passion, and how it braves the nature, and value of things, by this; that the speaking in a perpetual hyperbole, is comely in nothing but in love. Neither is it merely in the phrase; for whereas it hath been well said, that the arch-flatterer, with whom all the petty flatterers have intelligence, is a man's self; certainly the lover is more. For there was never proud man thought so absurdly well of himself, as the lover doth of the person loved; and therefore it was well said, *That it is impossible to love and to be wise.* Neither doth this weakness appear to others only, and not to the party loved; but to the loved most of all, except the love be reciproque. For it is a true rule, that love is ever rewarded, either with the reciproque, or with an inward and secret contempt. By how much the more, men ought to be-

> ware of this passion, which loseth not only other things, but itself! As for the other losses, the poet's relation doth well figure them: that he that preferred Helena, quitted the gifts of Juno and Pallas. For whosoever esteemeth too much of amorous affection, quitteth both riches and wisdom. This passion hath his floods, in very times of weakness; which are great prosperity, and great adversity; though this latter hath been less observed: both which times kindle love, and make it more fervent, and therefore show it to be the child of folly. They do best, who if they cannot but admit love, yet make it keep quarters; and sever it wholly from their serious affairs, and actions, of life; for if it check once with business, it troubleth men's fortunes, and maketh men, that they can no ways be true to their own ends. I know not how, but martial men are given to love: I think, it is but as they are given to wine; for perils commonly ask to be paid in pleasures. There is in man's nature, a secret inclination and motion, towards love of others, which if it be not spent upon some one or a few, doth naturally spread itself towards many, and maketh men become humane and charitable; as it is seen sometime in friars. Nuptial love maketh mankind; friendly love perfecteth it; but wanton love corrupteth, and embaseth it.

NOTES, COMMENTS AND HINTS

This is the complete essay.

The Elizabethan philosopher and moralist, Sir Francis Bacon (1561–1626), was much given to pessimism in his ideas about human relationships, and this essay is typical of his somewhat florid expression of them. Compare Bacon's ideas on love to Proust's; see pages 164 and 255.

Bacon is simply opposed to love: It's great as the underpinning of a plot in a comedy or a tragedy, but in real life the emotion of love is a weakness leading to disaster. His conclusion, on the eve of Puritanism, is that love in marriage is worthy, and that the love of friends for each other is perfection, but that love in the sense of sexual love outside marriage is base and corrupt. You can't help falling in love, says Bacon, but, for heaven's sake (literally), do try to control yourself, and do not let love control you.

The word "reciproque" (pronounced "ree si PROHK") means, of course, reciprocal; it is close to the French *réciproque* (pronounced "ré si: PRO:CK").

All of the references to antiquity are absolutely typical, not only of Elizabethans, but of educated people up through the early part of the twentieth century, when it was still considered *de rigueur* to have a classical education that involved learning Greek and Latin.

"Marcus Antonius" is the Mark Anthony who was madly in love with Cleopatra.

"Appius Claudius" (there are several ancient Romans of that name) is the

Roman consul who instituted a reign of terror, and awarded Virginia, with whom he was in love, as a slave to a friend of his, in order to procure her for himself. Her father, Virginius, stabbed his daughter to death, rather than let her be disgraced by falling into the tyrant's hands. Appius Claudius was forced to resign, and died in prison.

"Helena" is Helen of Troy, reputedly the most beautiful woman of the ancient world, on whose account the Trojan War was fought.

"Juno," queen of the gods, is the wife of Jupiter, king of the Roman gods (their respective Greek names are Hera and Zeus). "Pallas" is the goddess of wisdom, Pallas Athena, daughter of Zeus; she sprang full-grown out of his forehead. The "he" referred to in the line "...he that preferred Helena, quitted the gifts of Juno and Pallas" is Paris, who abducted Helen. Bacon means that Paris preferred the love of Helen to the gifts of a stable marriage (Paris was not married at the time when he eloped with Helen, but she was) and of mature wisdom. Bacon is, perhaps, being obscurely ironic, since Juno's stormy marriage to the constantly unfaithful Jupiter was hardly a model of conjugal felicity.

Satis magnum alter alteri theatrum sumus means, literally, "Enough great other to-other theater we-are," or "We are each a great enough theater to the other." Here is the phrase using the three different systems of Latin pronunciation. (See Chapter Two, page 53, for more on these systems.) Bacon would have used either the second or the third, the first, based on the presumed actual ancient Roman pronunciation, not having been devised until much later. You will see that the first and second are not very different from each other here, but there are many cases in which the two systems differ widely. The orthography "oo" represents the sound in the word "book":

1. (Ancient Roman) SA: ti:s MA:G noom A:L te:r a:l TE: ree tay A: troom SOO moos.

2. (Church/Medieval) SA: ti:s MA nyoom A:L te:r a:l TE: ree tay A: troom SOO moos.

3. (Old Oxford system of Anglicization) SAY tis MÆG noom ÆL teer æl TEER ee thee AY troom SOO moos.

Bacon's essay is good practice for accustoming yourself to Elizabethan grammar, and for making it your own. Nowadays we say "beholden," instead of "beholding." The third person singular verb ending, "-eth", is present tense ("corrupteth"), and it should be pretty easy to get used to. "Doth" means "does," of course; and "hath" means "has." If you ever record or perform Shakespeare, practicing this essay may come in handy.

Read the essay pretty straightforwardly, perhaps even with a slight tone of disdain. It is actually quite funny in its sour, mean-spirited, crabby condemnation of love. One almost wants to say to him: "A bit past it, are we, Sir Francis? Feeling unloved, perhaps?" This is the sort of nonfiction that permits you to do some acting, without which it might actually be deadly. Play the moralizer and the knowledgeable, but dry-as-dust, opinionated, pontificating scholar of antiquity. The pedantic, snotty subtext might be: "You know whom I mean when I mention Appius Claudius, of course." (Actually, everybody who could read back then did know; they were all familiar with the legend.) Think of a time when you were disappointed in love, and developed a jaundiced view of the whole idea of love as a result, temporary as that development may have been.

Two excerpts from Michel de Montaigne's *Essays*; Chapter XIII: "Of Experience," (written in 1580) translated by Charles Cotton (1685), revised by William Carew Hazlitt (1877).

Never did two men make the same judgment of the same thing; and 'tis impossible to find two opinions exactly alike, not only in several men, but in the same man, at diverse hours. I often find matter of doubt in things of which the commentary has disdained to take notice; I am most apt to stumble in an even country, like some horses that I have known, that make most trips in the smoothest way.

Who will not say that glosses augment doubts and ignorance, since there's no book to be found, either human or divine, which the world busies itself about, whereof the difficulties are cleared by interpretation. The hundredth commentator passes it on to the next, still more knotty and perplexed than he found it. When were we ever agreed amongst ourselves: "This book has enough; there is now no more to be said about it?" This is most apparent in the law; we give the authority of law to infinite doctors, infinite decrees, and as many interpretations; yet do we find any end of the need of interpretating? Is there, for all that, any progress or advancement towards peace, or do we stand in need of any fewer advocates and judges than when this great mass of law was yet in its first infancy? On the contrary, we darken and bury intelligence; we can no longer discover it, but at the mercy of so many fences and barriers.

• • •

How many innocent people have we known that have been punished, and this without the judge's fault; and how many that have

> not arrived at our knowledge? This happened in my time: certain men were condemned to die for a murder committed; their sentence, if not pronounced, at least determined and concluded on. The judges, just in the nick, are informed by the officers of an inferior court hard by, that they have some men in custody, who have directly confessed the murder, and made an indubitable discovery of all the particulars of the fact. Yet it was gravely deliberated whether or not they ought to suspend the execution of the sentence already passed upon the first accused: they considered the novelty of the example judicially, and the consequence of reversing judgments; that the sentence was passed, and the judges deprived of repentance; and in the result, these poor devils were sacrificed by the forms of justice. Philip, or some other, provided against a like inconvenience after this manner. He had condemned a man in a great fine towards another by an absolute judgment. The truth some time after being discovered, he found that he had passed an unjust sentence. On one side was the reason of the cause; on the other side, the reason of the judicial forms: he in some sort satisfied both, leaving the sentence in the state it was, and out of his own purse recompensing the condemned party. But he had to do with a reparable affair; my men were irreparably hanged. How many condemnations have I seen more criminal than the crimes themselves?

NOTES, COMMENTS AND HINTS

A lawyer and a classicist by training, Michel de Montaigne (1533–1592), former courtier of the unfortunate French king Charles IX (read Alexandre Dumas' novel *Queen Margot*, or see the 1994 film based on it), planned to spend his retirement after 1571 writing his essays, but interrupted his leisure to accept the post of Lord Mayor of Bordeaux, and to mediate, as a moderate Roman Catholic, for the Huguenot Henri de Bourbon of Navarre (the future King Henri IV) with the royal party in Paris. He was known as an advocate of toleration towards the Protestant Huguenots, his attitude arising perhaps from his background, since his mother was a Jewish convert.

You can reflect on how contemporary this essay seems today, in light of the ongoing debate in the United States about capital punishment, which is no longer a penalty in the European Union! Montaigne saw that the death of innocent people was totally unjustifiable. It is, in fact, a good and sufficient reason (and there are many others) to do away with capital punishment. As he says, "How many condemnations have I seen more criminal than the crimes themselves?"

Montaigne is indignant and even outraged by miscarriages of justice, and you can feel free to act the role of Montaigne himself. But since this is nonfiction, do not play all of his anger too strongly, even though you can adopt his attitude of outrage, and his dignified, saddened feeling. Montaigne appears to have been quite an urbane man, and an urbane tone of disapproval might not be inappropriate. I don't imagine you will need any substitution other than your own outrage at a miscarriage of justice.

The following two excerpts, which you may use as practice exercises, are from William Carew Hazlitt's Preface to an 1877 edition of the *Essays*, which he edited and revised; they are an excellent summary of what Montaigne's essays are all about:

> Above all, the essayist uncased himself, and made his intellectual and physical organism public property. He took the world into his confidence on all subjects. His essays were a sort of literary anatomy, where we get a diagnosis of the writer's mind, made by himself at different levels and under a large variety of operating influences.
>
> Of all egotists, Montaigne, if not the greatest, was the most fascinating, because, perhaps, he was the least affected and most truthful. What he did, and what he had professed to do, was to dissect his mind, and show us, as best he could, how it was made, and what relation it bore to external objects. He investigated his mental structure as a schoolboy pulls his watch to pieces, to examine the mechanism of the works; and the result, accompanied by illustrations abounding with originality and force, he delivered to his fellow men in a book.
>
> • • •
>
> He did not write from necessity, scarcely perhaps for fame. But he desired to leave France, nay, and the world, something to be remembered by, something which should tell what kind of a man he was—what he felt, thought, suffered—and he succeeded immeasurably, I apprehend, beyond his expectations.
>
> It was reasonable enough that Montaigne should expect for his work a certain share of celebrity in Gascony, and even, as time went on, throughout France; but it is scarcely probable that he foresaw how his renown was to become world-wide; how he was to occupy an almost unique position as a man of letters and a moralist; how the Essays would be read, in all the principal languages of Europe, by millions of intelligent human beings, who never heard of Perigord or the League, and who are in doubt, if they are questioned, whether the author lived in the sixteenth or the eighteenth century. This is true fame. A man of genius belongs to no period and no country. He speaks the language of nature, which is always everywhere the same.

William Carew Hazlitt (1834–1913), a noted bibliographer, author and editor, was the grandson of the famous and prolific essayist William Hazlitt. You will find an excerpt from the latter author's essay, *On Prejudice,* on page 340.

To read the straightforward excerpts from the seventeenth-century-style translation of the essays, despite Carew Hazlitt's revisions, and the excerpts from the Victorian-style Preface, you have to make two different styles of grammar your own, and then to read both simply in order to make points, as usual. Carew Hazlitt's admiration for Montaigne, which is evident in his assessment of the *Essays,* should not be overdone.

From George Berkeley's A Treatise Concerning the Principles of Human Knowledge, Wherein the Chief Causes of Error and Difficulty in the Sciences with the Grounds of Scepticism, Atheism and Irreligion are Inquired Into (1710), Part I.

1. It is evident to any one who takes a survey of the objects of human knowledge, that they are either ideas actually imprinted on the senses; or else such as are perceived by attending to the passions and operations of the mind; or lastly, ideas formed by help of memory and imagination—either compounding, dividing, or barely representing those originally perceived in the aforesaid ways. By sight I have the ideas of light and colours, with their several degrees and variations. By touch I perceive hard and soft, heat and cold, motion and resistance, and of all these more and less either as to quantity or degree. Smelling furnishes me with odours; the palate with tastes; and hearing conveys sounds to the mind in all their variety of tone and composition. And as several of these are observed to accompany each other, they come to be marked by one name, and so to be reputed as one thing. Thus, for example a certain colour, taste, smell, figure and consistence having been observed to go together, are accounted one distinct thing, signified by the name apple; other collections of ideas constitute a stone, a tree, a book, and the like sensible things—which as they are pleasing or disagreeable excite the passions of love, hatred, joy, grief, and so forth.

2. But, besides all that endless variety of ideas or objects of knowledge, there is likewise something which knows or perceives them, and exercises divers operations, as willing, imagining, remembering, about them. This perceiving, active being is what I call mind, spirit, soul, or myself. By which words I do not denote any one of my ideas,

but a thing entirely distinct from them, wherein, they exist, or, which is the same thing, whereby they are perceived—for the existence of an idea consists in being perceived.

3. That neither our thoughts, nor passions, nor ideas formed by the imagination, exist without the mind, is what everybody will allow. And it seems no less evident that the various sensations or ideas imprinted on the sense, however blended or combined together (that is, whatever objects they compose), cannot exist otherwise than in a mind perceiving them.—I think an intuitive knowledge may be obtained of this by any one that shall attend to what is meant by the term exists, when applied to sensible things. The table I write on I say exists, that is, I see and feel it; and if I were out of my study I should say it existed—meaning thereby that if I was in my study I might perceive it, or that some other spirit actually does perceive it. There was an odour, that is, it was smelt; there was a sound, that is, it was heard; a colour or figure, and it was perceived by sight or touch. This is all that I can understand by these and the like expressions. For as to what is said of the absolute existence of unthinking things without any relation to their being perceived, that seems perfectly unintelligible. Their esse is percepi, nor is it possible they should have any existence out of the minds or thinking things which perceive them.

NOTES, COMMENTS AND HINTS

Bishop George Berkeley (1685–1753) was a friend of Jonathan Swift's, and yet Swift's satire of the Royal Academy in *Gulliver's Travels* might well apply to his friend, whose philosophy was not particularly congenial to Swift's own very practical and political thinking. Berkeley, who lived for a time in America and held many important positions in the Anglican Church in his native Ireland, is known for his philosophy of "subjective idealism," which holds that the essence of everything is in how we perceive it, and that nothing has any real existence outside the mind. He was thus a precursor of Mary Baker Eddy's Christian Science, but he was ridiculed by some of his contemporaries, and refuted by later rationalists like the Scottish philosopher David Hume.

"Their esse is percepi" (Latin; "esse" is pronounced "EH say" [use Ancient Roman and Church/Medieval] or "EH see" [old English system]; and "percepi" is either "pair CHEH pee" [Church/Medieval] or "pair KEH pee" [Ancient Roman] or "pər SEE pie" [old English system]) means "their 'being' is the 'perceiving' or 'perception' of them"; in other words, they only exist when we perceive—or think of—them, and they don't exist unless we perceive—or think of—them.

Samuel Johnson did not appreciate Berkeley's pre-Enlightenment philosophy. There is a famous anecdote, which takes place on "Saturday, 6 August, 1763," recounted in Boswell's biography:

> After we came out of the church, we stood talking for some time together of Bishop Berkeley's ingenious sophistry to prove the non-existence of matter, and that every thing in the universe is merely ideal. I observed, that though we are satisfied his doctrine is not true, it is impossible to refute it. I shall never forget the alacrity with which Johnson answered, striking his foot with mighty force against a large stone, till he rebounded from it, "I refute it *thus*."

Berkeley's abstruse, complicated prose is not easy to read aloud. Essentially, however, he makes simple points, couched in florid language. You have to decide what those points are and stress the words that make them clear, while de-emphasizing the words around the important nuclear phrases. For instance, after reading the initial generalizations without too much emphasis on anything in particular, stress the words "sight," "touch," and so forth in the following sentences, to make clear that these are specific explanations and examples of Berkeley's general point.

When you finish section one, emphasize the word "But," that begins section two, and explain ("to explain" is your actor's action) that, despite all the foregoing about the senses and what the senses perceive, the important point to bear in mind is that "there is likewise something which knows or perceives them," and which you will proceed to expound upon.

Here is a suggestion on how to stress words in this text to make its meaning clear. Make your voice parenthetical when you read the number "2":

> 2. But, [Pause] besides all that endless variety of ideas or objects of knowledge, there is likewise something which knows or perceives them, and exercises divers operations, as willing, imagining, remembering, about them. This perceiving, active being is what I call mind, spirit, soul, or myself.

In section three you will carefully lay out the main point of your philosophy. Do try to avoid sounding as though you were talking to an idiot. Instead, read this "as if" you were talking to yourself, in order to make your ideas clear to yourself (your actor's objective), which is one of the things Uta Hagen tells us we do when we talk to ourselves. ". . . that seems perfectly unintelligible" is your point proved to yourself and to everybody else, and you can take some satisfaction in having reached your conclusion, but don't overdo it, or you will merely sound fatuous.

From Mary Wollstonecraft's *A Vindication of the Rights of Woman: with Strictures on Political and Moral Subjects* (1792)

CHAP. IX.

OF THE PERNICIOUS EFFECTS WHICH ARISE FROM THE UNNATURAL DISTINCTIONS ESTABLISHED IN SOCIETY.

From the respect paid to property flow, as from a poisoned fountain, most of the evils and vices which render this world such a dreary scene to the contemplative mind. For it is in the most polished society that noisome reptiles and venomous serpents lurk under the rank herbage; and there is voluptuousness pampered by the still sultry air, which relaxes every good disposition before it ripens into virtue.

One class presses on another; for all are aiming to procure respect on account of their property: and property, once gained, will procure the respect due only to talents and virtue. Men neglect the duties incumbent on man, yet are treated like demi-gods; religion is also separated from morality by a ceremonial veil, yet men wonder that the world is almost, literally speaking, a den of sharpers or oppressors.

There is a homely proverb, which speaks a shrewd truth, that whoever the devil finds idle he will employ. And what but habitual idleness can hereditary wealth and titles produce? For man is so constituted that he can only attain a proper use of his faculties by exercising them, and will not exercise them unless necessity, of some kind, first set the wheels in motion. Virtue likewise can only be acquired by the discharge of relative duties; but the importance of these sacred duties will scarcely be felt by the being who is cajoled out of his humanity by the flattery of sycophants. There must be more equality established in society, or morality will never gain ground, and this virtuous equality will not rest firmly even when founded on a rock, if one half of mankind be chained to its bottom by fate, for they will be continually undermining it through ignorance or pride.

NOTES, COMMENTS AND HINTS

Among the many social issues that the French Revolution was instrumental in bringing to the fore, women's rights and place in society was one of the most enduring, because the problems of women's hard-won, hard-fought struggle for rights are not yet resolved centuries later, although progress has been made. French revolutionary women wrote about women's rights, and in England, while the Revolution was raging across the Channel, Mary Wollstonecraft (1759–1797) awakened to the condition of women in her own country. She was one of the first to write on the subject, and she wrote a long and deeply thought out pioneering book. She was a precursor of the later nineteenth-century fighters for women's rights, such as Susan B. Anthony; see page 117. See also the excerpt from *Jane Eyre* on page 174.

Mary Wollstonecraft married William Godwin in 1797, after the end of an unhappy relationship with Gilbert Imlay, by whom she had a daughter, Fanny. Mary died in childbirth, having given birth to Godwin's daughter, also named Mary (1797–1851), who became the second wife of the poet Percy Bysshe Shelley. Mary Wollstonecraft Godwin Shelley is famous as the author of *Frankenstein* (1818).

Wollstonecraft was a progressive thinker, and an advocate of the absolute equality of the sexes, and an impassioned believer in the necessity of equal rights for both sexes. She was a very independent person, yet she managed to get herself involved in unhappy love affairs. She was harshly criticized for her opinions, her irreverence and her progressive ideas about reforming society. Her advocacy of women's rights provoked such a terrible and bitter response, that she left England to go to Paris, and stayed there during the Reign of Terror. And one can perceive precursive shades of Karl Marx in the social analysis in this excerpt.

You may read this as a deeply impassioned polemic about social injustice, convinced of its truth, and therefore convincing to your listeners. Use as a substitution, if indeed you need one for this, anything you really feel passionate about. After all, a statement like "There must be more equality established in society, or morality will never gain ground" remains as true today as when it was written, and requires no substitutions.

When you come to "How grossly do they insult us who thus advise us only to render ourselves gentle, domestic brutes!" you might try reading this line in a cold, hard, steely voice. This is a simple, but heartfelt, statement of fact, and the writer is very angry, indeed.

Let yourself go with this material. Unlike autobiography or memoirs or history, this is political writing which attempts directly to be persuasive, and that is your actor's objective: to persuade, to convince.

From William Hazlitt's *On Prejudice* (1821)

> Prejudice, in its ordinary and literal sense, is prejudging any question without having sufficiently examined it, and adhering to our opinion upon it through ignorance, malice, or perversity, in spite of every evidence to the contrary. The little that we know has a strong alloy of misgivings and uncertainty in it; the mass of things of which we have no means of judging, but of which we form a blind and confident opinion, as if we were thoroughly acquainted with them, is monstrous. Preju-

dice is the child of ignorance: for as our actual knowledge falls short of our desire to know, or curiosity and interest in the world about us, so must we be tempted to decide upon a greater number of things at a venture; and having no check from reason or inquiry, we shall grow more obstinate and bigoted in our conclusions, according as we have been rash and presumptuous. The absence of proof, instead of suspending our judgment, only gives us an opportunity of making things out according to our wishes and fancies; mere ignorance is a blank canvas, on which we lay what colours we please, and paint objects black or white, as angels or devils, magnify or diminish them at our option; and in the *vacuum* either of facts or arguments, the weight of prejudice and passion falls with double force, and bears down everything before it.

NOTES, COMMENTS AND HINTS

William Hazlitt (1778–1830) was the son of an Irish Unitarian minister, forced to return from England to Ireland because of his outspoken support for Irish independence and for the American side during the American War of Independence. He was a friend of Wordsworth and Coleridge and other Romantic poets. But he quarreled with most of his friends, and felt that he was despised for his leftist political opinions, and two failed marriages made this progressive thinker even more miserable.

Hazlitt's grammar and syntax are somewhat complicated, by present-day standards. However, his insights are profound, and his essay, often quoted, is still relevant today. Make his points clearly, feelingly and logically, as he does. Take a somewhat conversational tone and you will avoid sounding academic or pedantic, which this old-fashioned style might lead you to do; play against the style. Treat the subject of the essay as if you were involved in a passionate attempt to convince a listener of your point of view. If you need a substitution, think that you are talking to someone to whose political views you are absolutely opposed.

Compare this piece to Hazlitt's grandson's preface to Montaigne's *Essays*, excerpted on page 335. The prose style of essay writing in the Romantic era is not that different from the later Victorian essayist's style. Both authors value clear expression and good grammar. You won't find a dangling participle between them!

Other Genres

There are a great many books written on all kinds of subjects, from mathematics and the various sciences to cooking, taking care of your pets, riding horses, playing polo or cricket or baseball, instructional books about putting down a linoleum floor, using Microsoft Word, or playing the piano. There are books to suit every interest. There are encyclopedias of baseball, science fiction, music, art, birds, dinosaurs, trees and roses; and coffee-table books with gorgeous illustrations of famous paintings, castles and stately homes, the scenery of various countries, and the architecture of various cities. There are travel writings penned by enthusiastic voyagers, such as Richard Burton, Lawrence of Arabia and Mary McCarthy (read her *Venice Observed*, Harcourt, Brace Jovanovich, 1963, and you will want to go there); how-to books on plumbing, gardening, painting in watercolors or oils, and any other hobby you care to name. You may be called on to record any of these nonfiction works, and the idea is basically the same for all of them: You are the author's voice and you have to make clearly the points the author makes. Your listeners really want to visualize that charming chateau in the Loire Valley, or to understand step by step how to bake that chocolate cake so that it comes out perfectly.

If you are asked to record a cookbook, take proper, brief pauses between the ingredients on the list at the beginning of a recipe, and then state all the points of procedure very clearly. For the text that precedes and describes the recipes, follow the usual advice and stress the important words that make your points, without sounding pedantic or labored. If you like food, you will love recording cookbooks! For practice try anything by Roy Andries de Groot, especially *The Auberge of the Flowering Hearth* (Bobbs-Merrill, 1973); you will savor the taste and smell the perfume and hear the sizzling sounds of French mountain cookery, so vividly does he describe everything.

To give you an idea about how to approach one genre that is sometimes recorded, and that is a little different from the travel guide genre mentioned above, use these brief excerpts from my unpublished *Short Guide to Paris Restaurants* (2003). Try to read the entire selection all the way through without stopping, as a practice exercise in sustaining a nonfiction text.

SOME TERMS

A *bistro* is a small restaurant, usually a neighborhood place, that serves much the same kind of food as a *brasserie*. By French law, brasseries serve continuously from their opening to their closing times, usually from about 12 noon to about 2 a.m. *Restaurants*, on the other hand, including bistros, are permitted by law to have specific hours for lunch and dinner (usually 12–3 p.m. and 8–11 p.m., respectively); some serve only lunch or only dinner; closing days and hours vary.

At a *café* you can get coffee (*café* is the French word for coffee), tea, hot chocolate, soda, wine, beer, whiskey and other beverages. You can also get light food, such as omelettes and sandwiches. Cafés that used to be wonderful for breakfasts of coffee and croissants are still good, but with the advent of the euro have gotten quite expensive. If you want fresh orange juice, don't ask for a *jus d'orange* (which comes in a bottle), but for *une orange pressée*: It comes freshly squeezed and served with water and sugar on the side, so you can make your own orangeade; *un citron pressé* is the same deal with a lemon. Most cafés are open from about 8 or 9 a.m. to about 1 or 2 a.m.

At any brasserie you can get great platters of fresh and cooked shellfish, Alsatian sauerkraut and sausages (*choucroute garnie*), and classic standbys of French cuisine such as roast chicken, *cassoulet* (a bean stew with lamb, sausage and goose; there are umpteen recipes), beef stews, roast veal with creamed spinach, roast leg of lamb and green beans, filet of sole, steak with French fries, and chocolate mousse, fresh fruit tarts, and ice creams or sorbets for dessert. If you've never had green apple or cassis (blackcurrant) sorbet you are in for a treat!

Restaurants themselves vary tremendously, from those "gastronomic" establishments devoted to the cooking of specific chefs, to those devoted to a particular provincial or foreign cuisine. At first-class restaurants expect surprise *amuse-bouches* (appetizers; hors-d'oeuvres) at the beginning of a meal, and a little tray of *friandises* (miniature pastries, candies, chocolate truffles, etc.) at the end as an accompaniment to your coffee; every restaurant has its own scrumptious versions of both courses. Reservations are generally required at restaurants, and at some brasseries (especially if you wish to be seated in nonsmoking sections or rooms), but certainly not at cafes or at most brasseries.

• • •

SOME EXPENSIVE RESTAURANTS

You must make reservations at all the following places. If you are a nonsmoker, be sure to inform the person taking the reservation. They will try to accommodate you. I have seldom encountered a problem in any of the restaurants listed below.

L'Espadon, the restaurant at the Ritz Hotel, on the Place Vendôme, 1st arrondissement, phone: 01 43 16 30 30. Jacket and tie required for the men. Open every day, including Sunday.

All I can say is that the Ritz lives up to its name. Wow! Great atmosphere and classic cuisine. Courtly service. A glass of Jurançon or Sauternes with your foie gras; roast duck or lobster; a small salad, and a little pot de chocolat—all make for a heavenly meal, especially when served on a sunny day in the utterly charming enclosed garden terrace restaurant, off the sumptuous main dining room.

Pierre Gagnaire, 6, rue Balzac, in the Hotel Balzac, 8th arrondissement, just off the Champs-Élysées, up a steep hill, near the Arc de Triomphe; phone: 01 58 36 12 50.

Not to be missed; amazing, innovative, occasionally slightly weird contemporary cuisine from genius chef Pierre Gagnaire. Sometimes the food is more interesting than delicious. One rather wonders what the point is of a luscious melting chocolate cake surmounted by a chocolate crackling biscuit with a spoonful of lentils on top of it—seems to me rather redundant and unnecessary, but, oh, that chocolate cake! Wow! Sometimes Gagnaire combines Asian and French cuisines with marvelous results, such as the way he does a kind of Peking-style duck with fresh figs. Recently I had, as a starter, a wonderful terrine of chicken and foie gras with artichoke purée and a puff pastry filled with sautéed onions on the side, followed by a main course of miniature lamb steaks with celery purée and (get this!) snails in watercress purée—the snails were underdone and a bit off-putting, but the lamb was superb. Dessert consisted of seven small courses, which varied from sublime to ridiculous—wild strawberries and red-bell-pepper whipped cream were quite good, actually, and the stewed figs with pistachio jelly were marvelous. The meal is poetry on a plate, superbly presented.

Taillevent, 15 rue Lammenais, 8th arrondissement, phone: 01 44 95 15 01. Jacket and tie required for the men. Closed Saturday and Sunday.

Truly the cream of the cream, this is the greatest classic French restaurant in existence today, the temple of gastronomy, the management handed down from father to son. Monsieur Vrinat is old-world charm and warmth personified. The service is a positive ballet. Classic, exquisite, light cuisine is prepared with the best and freshest ingredients. Don't miss the asparagus with truffles, roast duck (with almost no fat) prepared with two different sauces, or the creative, incredibly delicious desserts, among them a melting, rich individual chocolate cake accompanied by ambrosial thyme-flavored ice cream. And wait until you see the magnificent, comprehensive wine list! A recent meal: freshly made hot cheese puffs with the house cocktail (champagne with raspberry purée); ravioli of girolles and cèpe mushrooms with a foamy, frothy light butter sauce; cold foie gras with chutney and toast; a spit-roasted chicken stuffed with truffles, with a truffle sauce for the breast and, as a "second service," the thigh in cream sauce, with a light green salad and potato pancake on the side; all washed down with a mellow 1994 Château Pape Clément (a red Bordeaux); for dessert: wild strawberries and whipped cream, and a small slice of rich chocolate mousse cake floating in a purée of pistachio cream sauce. Coffee so good I had two cups. Always astoundingly flavorful, subtle, delicate food. Charlie Chaplin's favorite restaurant, too. Taillevent is located near the Champs-Élysées in a gorgeous, tasteful mansion which used to belong to the duc de Morny, Napoleon III's half-brother, who also wrote libretti for Offenbach. There are two large rooms, one of which is usually reserved for nonsmokers.

• • •

SOME EXCELLENT, LESS EXPENSIVE RESTAURANTS

Chez Jean, 8 rue St. Lazare; 9th arrondissement; closed Sunday and Monday; reservations a must; telephone: 01 48 78 62 73.

Monsieur Frédéric Guidoni was a *maître d'hôtel* at Taillevent for twenty years, and he and his charming wife, Madame Delphine Guidoni, an artist who designed the beautiful menus, decided to open their own restaurant, to which he has brought his expertise and exquisite politeness. The service is very charming and assiduous, and, most importantly, the food prepared by chef Benoît Bordier is just excellent. Some examples: a succulent risotto with girolles mushrooms as a first course; a casserole of snails and artichoke hearts, another flavorsome starter; and for main courses roast chicken supremes, done to perfection; or succulent roast pork, crusty on the outside, tasty and tender on the inside, served with carrots and onions and a flavorful, mouthwatering pan-juice sauce; or meltingly tender pan-roasted foie gras with rhubarb puree; followed by desserts that bring tears to the eyes (liquored dark cherries with vanilla ice cream on the side, for instance; or a very fine, delicate apple tart). The coffee is also excellent. Prices are reasonable, and the wine list is terrific.

NOTES, COMMENTS AND HINTS

Here are most of the French pronunciations, as clearly as I can give them to you, in the order in which they appear in the excerpts: Use the guttural "r"; if you don't know how to pronounce it, see page 33. It will be neat trick to switch from language to language, and you can develop that skill with practice. Practice the French separately, until you are confident you can pronounce it correctly, then incorporate it slowly into the excerpts, sentence by sentence, and then read the whole text.

jus d'orange: zhü do: RA:*N*ZH

une orange pressée: ün o: ra:*N*zh pre SÉ

un citron pressé: u*N* si: tro:*N* pre SÉ

choucroute garnie: shoo kroot ga:r NEE

amuse-bouches: a: müz BOOSH

friandises: fri: ya:*N* DEEZ

cassoulet: ka: soo LÉ

L'Espadon: les pa: DO:*N*; *Place Vendôme*: pla:s va:*N* DOHM; *Jurançon*: zhoo ra:*N* SO:*N*

Gagnaire: ga: NYE:R

Taillevent: teye VA:*N*; *Lammenais*: la: mə NÉ; *Vrinat*: vri: NA:

Chez Jean: shé ZHA:*N*; *St. Lazare*: se:*N* la: ZA:R; *Guidoni*: gee do: NEE; *Benoît Bordier*: be NWA bawr DYAY

If you enjoy reading this as much as I enjoyed writing it (and eating those fabulous meals), you will be able to communicate your pleasure to the listener. That is all you really have to do. Visualize that food on the plate and think of any meal and of any restaurant you have enjoyed. Such adjectives as "succulent" and "mouth-watering" speak for themselves, and you don't have to add anything to them by dwelling on them, although drawing out the vowels slightly is appropriate. You can keep your reading simple, and let the listener into the restaurant by doing so. Making too many things important vitiates the importance of any one of them, and makes it difficult for the listener to get involved, or even to hear what is being described. So for a list of dishes, for instance, rather than acting out vocally how delicious they are, just read them with a visualization of them in your mind's eye, and taste them in your imagination. That should be sufficient to make the images clear to the listener.

Humorous Nonfiction

There is a great deal of extremely funny humorous nonfiction in the form of essays or of entire books. Of the well-known practitioners of the art of the humorous essay, which sends up everything from travel literature to memoirs to what have you, I recommend especially Robert Benchley, Stephen Leacock, S. J. Perelman, and James Thurber. Use their essays for practice and for relaxing laughter.

Humorous nonfiction includes fake histories, such as Will Cuppy's highly amusing *The Decline and Fall of Practically Everybody* (Dell Publishing Co., 1950); *1066 and All That* (E. P. Dutton & Co., Inc., 1931) by W. C. Sellar and R. J. Yeatman, who spoof English history uproariously; Richard Armour's *It All Started with Columbus* (McGraw-Hill, 1961), a spoof of American history, and the first of a whole series of *It All Started with* books, among them *It All Started with Eve* (McGraw-Hill, 1963) and *It All Started with Europa* (McGraw-Hill, 1971). The Roman writer Suetonius's serious biography, *The Twelve Caesars* (read it in a superb translation by Robert Graves; Penguin Books, 1957; often reprinted), is so scurrilous and scandalous in its portraits of such emperors as Tiberius and Nero that it reads like humorous nonfiction—and is perhaps less than truthful, but it is hilarious and appalling at the same time. Richard Armour's *Twisted Tales from Shakespeare* (McGraw-Hill, 1983) is an amusing guying of literary criticism.

Two excerpts from Mark Twain's *Fenimore Cooper's Literary Offenses* (1895).

Note: As with the excerpts from my Short Guide to Paris Restaurants try to read this all the way through without stopping, for practice in sustaining a text.

Cooper's gift in the way of invention was not a rich endowment; but such as it was he liked to work it, he was pleased with the effects, and indeed he did some quite sweet things with it. In his little box of stage-properties he kept six or eight cunning devices, tricks, artifices for his savages and woodsmen to deceive and circumvent each other with, and he was never so happy as when he was working these innocent things and seeing them go. A favorite one was to make a moccasined person tread in the tracks of a moccasined enemy, and thus hide his own trail. Cooper wore out barrels and barrels of moccasins in working that trick. Another stage-property that he pulled out of his box pretty frequently was the broken twig. He prized his broken twig above all the rest of his effects, and worked it the hardest. It is a restful chapter in any book of his when somebody doesn't step on a dry twig and alarm all the reds and whites for two hundred yards around. Every time a Cooper person is in peril, and absolute silence is worth four dollars a minute, he is sure to step on a dry twig. There may be a hundred other handier things to step on, but that wouldn't satisfy Cooper. Cooper requires him to turn out and find a dry twig; and if he can't do it, go and borrow one. In fact, the Leatherstocking Series ought to have been called the Broken Twig Series.

I am sorry that there is not room to put in a few dozen instances of the delicate art of the forest, as practiced by Natty Bumppo and some of the other Cooperian experts. Perhaps we may venture two or three samples. Cooper was a sailor—a naval officer; yet he gravely tells us how a vessel, driving toward a lee shore in a gale, is steered for a particular spot by her skipper because he knows of an *undertow* there which will hold her back against the gale and save her. For just pure woodcraft, or sailorcraft, or whatever it is, isn't that neat? For several years, Cooper was daily in the society of artillery, and he ought to have noticed that when a cannon-ball strikes the ground it either buries itself or skips a hundred feet or so; skips again a hundred feet or so—and so on, till finally it gets tired and rolls. Now in one place he loses some "females"—as he always calls women—in the edge of a wood near a plain at night in a fog, on purpose to give Bumppo a chance to show off the delicate art of the forest before the reader. These mislaid people are hunting for a fort. They hear a cannon-blast, and a cannon-ball presently comes rolling into the wood and stops at their feet. To the females this suggests nothing. The case is very different with the admirable Bumppo. I wish I may never know peace again if he doesn't strike out promptly and *follow the track* of that cannon-ball across the plain in the dense fog and find the fort. Isn't it a daisy? If Cooper had any real knowledge of Nature's ways of doing things, he had a most delicate art in concealing the fact. For instance: one of his acute Indian experts, Chingachgook (pronounced Chicago, I think), has lost the trail of a person he is tracking through the forest. Apparently that trail is hopelessly lost. Neither you nor I could ever have guessed the way to find it. It was very different with Chicago. Chicago was not stumped for long. He turned a running stream out of its course, and there, in the slush in its old bed, were that person's moccasin tracks. The current did not wash them away, as it would have done in all other like cases—no, even the eternal laws of Nature have to vacate when Cooper wants to put up a delicate job of woodcraft on the reader.

• • •

Pathfinder showed off handsomely that day before the ladies. His very first feat a thing which no Wild West show can touch. He was standing with the group of marksmen, observing—a hundred yards from the target, mind; one Jasper raised his rifle and drove the center of the bull's-eye. Then the Quartermaster fired. The target exhibited no result this time. There was a laugh. "It's a dead miss," said Major Lundie. Pathfinder waited an impressive moment or two; then said, in that calm, indifferent, know-it-all way of his, "No, Major, he has covered Jasper's bullet, as will be seen if any one will take the trouble to examine the target."

Wasn't it remarkable! How *could* he see that little pellet fly through the air and enter that distant bullet-hole? Yet that is what he did; for nothing is impossible to a Cooper person. Did any of those people have any deep-seated doubts about this thing? No; for that would imply sanity, and these were all Cooper people.

The respect for Pathfinder's skill and for his quickness and accuracy of sight *[the emphasis is mine] was so profound and general, that the instant he made this declaration the spectators began to distrust their own opinions, and a dozen rushed to the target in order to ascertain the fact. There, sure enough, it was found that the Quartermaster's bullet had gone through the hole made by Jasper's, and that, too, so accurately as to require a minute examination to be certain of the circumstance, which, however, was soon clearly established by discovering one bullet over the other in the stump against which the target was placed.*

They made a "minute" examination; but never mind, how could they know that there were two bullets in that hole without digging the latest one out? for neither probe nor eyesight could prove the presence of any more than one bullet. Did they dig? No; as we shall see. It is the Pathfinder's turn now; he steps out before the ladies, takes aim, and fires.

But, alas! here is a disappointment; in incredible, an unimaginable disappointment—for the target's aspect is unchanged; there is nothing there but that same old bullet hole!

"If one dared to hint at such a thing," cried Major Duncan, "I should say that the Pathfinder has also missed the target."

As nobody had missed it yet, the "also" was not necessary; but never mind about that, for the Pathfinder is going to speak.

"No, no, Major," said he, confidently, "that would be a risky declaration. I didn't load the piece, and can't say what was in it; but if it was lead, you will find the bullet driving down those of the Quartermaster and Jasper, else is not my name Pathfinder." A shout from the target announced the truth of this assertion.

Is the miracle sufficient as it stands? Not for Cooper. The Pathfinder speaks again, as he "now slowly advances toward the stage occupied by the females":

"That's not all, boys, that's not all; if you find the target touched at all, I'll own to a miss. The Quartermaster cut the wood, but you'll find no wood cut by that last messenger."

> The miracle is at last complete. He knew—doubtless *saw*—at the distance of a hundred yards—this his bullet had passed into the hole *without fraying the edges.* There were now three bullets in that one hole—three bullets embedded processionally in the body of the stump back of the target. Everybody knew this—somehow or other—and yet nobody had dug any of them out to make sure. Cooper is not a close observer, but he is interesting. He is certainly always that, no matter what happens. And he is more interesting when he is not noticing what he is about than when he is. This is a considerable merit.

NOTES, COMMENTS AND HINTS

James Fenimore Cooper (1789–1851), the American Sir Walter Scott, was prolific and hugely popular, but many modern readers find his books difficult to read, clumsy in style, and heavy-handed in general. Cooper's books earned him a lasting place nevertheless in America's literary hall of fame: Along with Washington Irving, he was one of America's first internationally acclaimed authors. And his stories can be stirring and even compelling. Cooper's first big success was his novel about the American revolutionary war, *The Spy* (1821), and it is still interesting and entertaining; he was known for his sea epics as well. In his most famous series of novels, The Leatherstocking Tales, about life among the Native Americans and European colonists on the New York and Western frontiers in the eighteenth century, Cooper created the memorable character of the crafty and humane woodsman Natty Bumppo, known as Leatherstocking (and also as Deerslayer and Pathfinder), hence the title of the series. In the order in which the novels recount Natty Bumppo's life from youth to old age, they are: *The Deerslayer* (1841), *The Last of the Mohicans* (1826), *The Pathfinder* (1840), *The Pioneers* (1823), and *The Prairie* (1827).

Among Cooper's detractors was Mark Twain, and what a caustic detractor he was! Hilariously severe and sarcastic to the last degree, he tears Cooper's writing apart with ridicule, not only for its style and grammar and content, but from every point of view. Twain lists the "large rules" of style, and continues:

> In addition to these large rules, there are some little ones. These require that the author shall:

12. Say what he is proposing to say, not merely come near it.

13. Use the right word, not its second cousin.

14. Eschew surplusage.

15. Not omit necessary details.

16. Avoid slovenliness of form.

17. Use good grammar.
18. Employ a simple and straightforward style.

Cooper, he says, violates all of the rules. Twain also tears apart the professors of literature and the writers who held Cooper's books up as models and shining examples of what good books should be, and who admired and extolled his writing: "It seems to me that it was far from right for the Professor of English Literature at Yale, the Professor of English Literature in Columbia, and Wilkie Collins to deliver opinions on Cooper's literature without having read some of it. It would have been much more decorous to keep silent and let persons talk who have read Cooper."

When Twain had an opinion, he expressed it in the most extravagant terms; he hated Cooper's ponderous style and what he saw as Cooper's ludicrous characters, as well as Cooper's patronizing racist attitudes to Native Americans, who had suffered and continued to suffer so horribly, as Twain well knew, at the hands of the eastern seaboard settlers, the pioneers, and the oppressive United States government, which consistently broke its treaties with the Native American nations. Twain was simply disgusted by Cooper's obliviousness and obtuseness, and it is his disgust with Cooper's political attitudes, rather than just with his writing, that is really at the heart of this essay. Twain goes right after Fenimore Cooper. He pulls no punches. He destroys Cooper with laughter.

The cumulative effect of this essay, as Twain piles on point after point and quotation after quotation, is to bring tears of laughter to the eyes of even those readers who have not read Cooper. In fact, even if you haven't, you will feel as if you have. But you won't elicit those tears of mirth and merriment from a listener unless you read this piece as if it were as serious a bit of literary criticism—which it is—as any written by the most serious critic for *The New York Review of Books*. Make point after point with the absolute sense that you know how droll this material is, but only in the back of your mind, without showing us how funny you think it is. Again: If you laugh, we won't! Twain's sarcasm comes through so adequately in the writing, that it will be there no matter how neutrally you read the text. The drier and more understated (without being flat and uninteresting) your reading is, the more hysterically funny will be the result. You can practically see Mark Twain, cigar in hand, tongue in cheek, a twinkle in his eye, as he read this aloud in his drollest and most deadpan manner.

Here are some purely technical hints:

1. You might try drawing out the word "no" in the last sentence of the first excerpt, after you have read the rest of it in the flattest way possible. Try it again, being more sarcastic this time. See which you like better, and then try it your own way.

2. In the penultimate sentence of the second excerpt—"And he is more interesting when he is not noticing what he is about than when he is"—stress the words "not" and the last "is"; it is always important to make contrasts clear, and stressing the words that give you the contrast is, of course, the way to do it. But there are other ways of reading that sentence: Try, for instance, stressing "more" and "interesting," and "not" and "noticing," and the last two appearances of "is" for a slightly different intonation pattern. That reading, however, might give you too much variety, and not enough dryness.

3. You might also want to try the experiment of saying "a Cooper person" or "Cooper people" with exactly the same intonation pattern every time, with a slightly smart-alecky delivery; those terms occur a lot in the full essay. If that seems like a contradiction to the idea of not commenting on the material, bear in mind that if you mean the words seriously you will be commenting on Cooper in the way Twain does, not commenting on Twain's idea that what he is saying is funny. And nobody has ever been funnier than Mark Twain, the great humanist and humanitarian, whose laughter is always informed by love.

A kind of slightly drawling, dry, relaxed, folksy delivery would be excellent for this selection, since the piece is written in a colloquial style. I heartily recommend the sort of deadpan delivery Hal Holbrook cultivated for Twain's sly asides and quips in his wonderful show *Mark Twain Tonight*, available both as an audio CD from Sony and on VHS and DVD from Kultur Video. Hal Holbrook knows how to make a point in an offhand way, throw away a devastatingly funny line to maximum effect, and deliver a punch line without telegraphing it to the audience. He was hilarious in person. I have rarely laughed so hard in my life as I did the night my parents and brothers and I saw his show at the McCarter Theater in Princeton, New Jersey. I had tears in my eyes and laughter in my heart. Now that's entertainment!

I will conclude by telling you that if you decide to go into the book-recording business, you will bring tears and laughter and entertainment to many appreciative listeners. You will learn a great deal, while enjoying yourself immensely. I hope you find the experience immeasurably enriching and fulfilling. And I hope you sometimes have occasion to laugh as heartily as I did in the theater on that memorable evening forty-five years ago!

Selected Bibliography

1) Books About Books, Authors and Literature; Anthologies

There are a great many *Oxford Companions* to music, history, literature, and other subjects; and a large number of *Norton Anthologies* of literature, history, music, and other areas of interest. A few of them are listed below. I dare say the entire series of both are worth looking into, as is the extensive series of *Cambridge Companions*, many of them devoted to individual authors.

Abrams, M. H. *A Glossary of Literary Terms*. (7th Ed.) United States: Heinle & Heinle, 1999.

Ackroyd, Peter. *Dickens*. New York: HarperCollins, 1990.

Auerbach, Erich. *Mimesis*. Translated by Willard R. Trask. Princeton: Princeton University Press, 1968.

Basbanes, Nicholas A. *A Gentle Madness: Bibliophiles, Bibliomanes, and the Eternal Passion for Books*. New York: Henry Holt, 1995.

Bloom, Harold. *Shakespeare: The Invention of the Human*. New York, Penguin Putnam, Inc., 1998.

Bulfinch, Thomas. *Mythology: The Age of Fable; The Age of Chivalry; The Age of Charlemagne*. New York: The Modern Library, n.d.

Carter, William. *Marcel Proust: A Life*. New Haven: Yale University Press, 2000.

Carter, William. *The Proustian Quest*. New York: New York University Press, 1992.

Chametzky, Jules et al., eds. *Jewish American Literature: A Norton Anthology*. New York: W. W. Norton, 2000.

Dickens, Charles. *Sikes and Nancy and Other Public Readings*. Edited and with an Introduction by Philip Collins. New York: Oxford University Press, 1983.

Dolby, George. *Charles Dickens as I Knew Him: The Story of the Reading Tours in Great Britain and America (1866–1870)*. London: T. Fisher Unwin, 1887.

Drabble, Margaret, ed. *The Oxford Companion to English Literature*. New York: Oxford University Press, 2000.

Ellmann, Richard. *Oscar Wilde*. New York: Alfred A. Knopf, 1988.

Field, Kate. *Pen Photographs of Charles Dickens's Readings, Taken from Life*. Boston: James R. Osgood & Co., 1871.

Fitzsimmons, Raymund. *Garish Lights: The Public Reading Tours of Charles Dickens*. Philadelphia: J. B. Lippincott, 1970.

Forster, E. M. *Aspects of the Novel*. New York: Harcourt, Brace & World, 1927.

Fussell, Paul, gen. ed. *The Norton Book of Travel*. New York: W. W. Norton, 1987.

Gates, Henry Louis, Jr., and Nellie Y. McKay, eds. *The Norton Anthology of African American Literature*. New York: W. W. Norton, 1996.

Hart, James David, and Phillip Leininger, eds. *The Oxford Companion to American Literature*. 6th ed. New York: Oxford University Press, 1995.

Holland, Merlin. *Irish Peacock and Scarlet Marquis: The Real Trial of Oscar Wilde*. Foreword by Sir John Mortimer. London: Fourth Estate, 2003.

Kent, Charles. *Charles Dickens as a Reader*. London: Chapman & Hall, 1872.

Koch, Stephen. *The Modern Library Writer's Workshop*. New York: The Modern Library, 2003.

Leitch, Vincent B., gen. ed. *The Norton Anthology of Theory and Criticism*. New York, London: W. W. Norton & Company, 2001.

Macdonald, Dwight, ed. *Parodies: An Anthology from Chaucer to Beerbohm—and After*. New York: Random House, 1960.

Merriam-Webster's Encyclopedia of Literature. Springfield, Mass.: Merriam-Webster, Inc., 1995.

O'Brien, Geoffrey. *The Browser's Ecstasy: A Meditation on Reading*. Washington, D.C.: Counterpoint, 2000.

Plimpton, George E. *The Writer's Chapbook: A Compendium of Fact, Opinion, Wit, and Advice from the 20th Century's Preeminent Writers*. Edited from the *Paris Review* interviews and with an Introduction by George E. Plimpton. New York: Penguin Books, 1989.

The Portable Chekhov. Edited, and with an Introduction, by Avrahm Yarmolimsky. New York: Penguin Books, 1947.
An anthology of short stories, plays and letters.

Rayfield, Donald. *Anton Chekhov: A Life*. New York: Henry Holt, 1997.

Robb, Graham. *Balzac: A Biography*. New York: W. W. Norton, 1994.

Robb, Graham. *Victor Hugo: A Biography*. New York: W. W. Norton, 1997.

Robb, Graham. *Rimbaud: A Biography*. New York: W. W. Norton, 2000.

Shattuck, Roger. *Proust's Way: A Field Guide to In Search of Lost Time*. New York,: W. W. Norton, 2000.

Simmons, Ernest J. *Chekhov: A Biography*. Boston: *An Atlantic Monthly Book*, Little, Brown & Co., 1962.

Vendler, Helen. *The Art of Shakespeare's Sonnets*. With a CD. Cambridge, Mass.: *The Belknap Press* of Harvard University Press, 1997.

Wharton, Edith. *The Writing of Fiction*. New York: A Touchstone Book, Simon and Schuster, (reprint ed.), 1997.

Winchester, Simon. *The Professor and the Madman: A Tale of Murder, Insanity, and the Making of the Oxford English Dictionary*. New York: HarperCollins, 1998.

Winchester, Simon. *The Meaning of Everything: The Story of the Oxford English Dictionary*. New York: Oxford University Press, 2003.

2) Books about English and Phonetics

Crystal, David. *The Cambridge Encyclopedia of the English Language*. Cambridge: Cambridge University Press, 1987.

Gimson's *Pronunciation of English*. 5th ed., Revised by Alan Cruttenden. London: Edward Arnold, 1994.

Cramley, Stephan, and Kurt-Michael Pätzold. *A Survey of Modern English*. London: Routledge, 1992.

Jones, Daniel. *The Pronunciation of English*. Cambridge: Cambridge University Press, 1992.

Ladefoged, Peter, and Ian Maddieson. *The Sounds of the World's Languages*. Oxford, England: Blackwell Publishers, 1996.

Laver, John. *Principles of Phonetics*. Cambridge: Cambridge University Press, 1994.

McArthur, Tom, ed. *The Oxford Companion to the English Language*. New York: Oxford University Press, 1992.

McCrum, Robert, William Cran, and Robert MacNeil. *The Story of English: A Companion to the PBS Television Series*. New York: Viking, 1986

Schur, Norman W. *British English A to Zed*. Revised by Eugene Ehrlich. New York: Checkmark Books, 2001.

3) Some Dictionaries

There are many pronouncing dictionaries for English and for other languages, all useful: Larousse for French and Duden for German, for example. The Webster's and Random House dictionaries also have many biographical and geographical pronunciations, and Webster's *New International Dictionary* (first and second editions, but not the third edition) is especially useful for everything from the correct anglicized Latin pronunciations of scientific nomenclature, to mythological, biographical and geographical names. The unabridged *Oxford English Dictionary* is in a class by itself, a superlative work which makes you want to read the dictionary. Every dictionary has its own phonetic system for indicating pronunciation; some use the International Phonetic Alphabet (IPA).

Barnhart, Clarence L., ed. *New Century Cyclopedia of Names*, in three volumes. Englewood Cliffs, NJ: Prentice-Hall, Inc., 1954.

Collins Pocket Scots Dictionary. Glasgow: HarperCollins, 1996.

Graham, William. *The Scots Word Book*, 3rd rev. ed. Edinburgh: The Ramsay Head Press, 1980.

Greet, W. Cabell. *World Words: Recommended Pronunciations*, 2nd ed. New York: Columbia University Press, by arrangement with the Columbia Broadcasting System, 1948.

Irvine, Theodora Ursula. *How to Pronounce the Names in Shakespeare*. New York: Hines, Hayden and Eldredge, Inc., 1919.

Jones, Daniel. *Cambridge Pronouncing Dictionary*, 16th ed., Cambridge: Cambridge University Press, 2003.

Kökeritz, Helge. *Shakespeare's Names: A Pronouncing Dictionary*. New Haven: Yale University Press, 1977.

Merriam-Webster's Biographical Dictionary. Springfield, Mass.: Merriam-Webster. Inc., 1995

Merriam-Webster's Geographical Dictionary, 3rd ed. Springfield, Mass.: Merriam-Webster, Inc., 1997.

Merriam-Webster's Medical Desk Dictionary. Springfield, Mass.: Merriam-Webster, Inc., 1996.

Moss, Norman. *British/American Language Dictionary*. Lincolnwood, Ill.: Passport Books, 1984.

Pointon, G.E., ed. *BBC Pronouncing Dictionary of British Names*. Oxford: Oxford University Press, 1990.

Seltzer, Leon E., ed. *The Columbia Lippincott Gazetteer of the World*, with 1961 supplement. New York: Columbia University Press, by arrangement with J.B. Lippincott Company, 1962.

Wells, J. C. *Longman Pronouncing Dictionary* London: Pearson ESL, 2000.

Zimmerman, J. E. *Dictionary of Classical Mythology*. New York: Bantam Books, 1985.

4) Books about Voice and Vocal Technique

Blumenfeld, Robert. *Accents: A Manual for Actors*. New York: Limelight Editions, Revised and Expanded Edition, with 2 CDs, 2002.

Lessac, Arthur. *The Use and Training of the Human Voice: A Practical Approach to Voice and Speech Dynamics*. New York: DBS Publications, 1967.

Skinner, Edith. *Speak with Distinction*. Revised and edited by Lilene Mansell, Timothy Monich. New York: Applause Theatre Book Publishers, 1990.

Turner, J. Clifford. *Voice and Speech in the Theatre*. 5th ed., edited by Malcolm Morrison. New York: Routledge Theatre Arts Books, 2000.

5) Books about Acting and Theatre

Adler, Stella. *The Technique of Acting*. Foreword by Marlon Brando. New York: Bantam Books, 1988.

Boleslavsky, Richard. *Acting: The First Six Lessons*. New York: Theatre Arts Books, 1962.

Brook, Peter. *The Empty Space*. New York: Avon Discus Books, 1968.

Burton, Hal, ed. *Great Acting*. New York: Bonanza Books, 1967.
Interviews with Laurence Olivier, Sybil Thorndike, Ralph Richardson, Peggy Ashcroft, Michael Redgrave, Edith Evans, John Gielgud, Noël Coward.

Caine, Michael. *Acting in Film: An Actor's Take on Movie Making*. New York: Applause Theatre Books, 1990.

Carnovsky, Morris, with Peter Sander. *The Actor's Eye*. Foreword by John Houseman. New York: Performing Arts Journal Publications, 1984.

Chaikin, Joseph. *The Presence of the Actor: Notes on the Open Theater, disguises, acting and repression*. New York: Atheneum, 1974.

Chekhov, Michael. *Lessons for the Professional Actor*. New York: Performing Arts Journal Publications, 1985.

Chekhov, Michael. *To the Actor on the Technique of Acting*. Preface by Yul Brynner. New York: Harper & Row, 1953.

Cole, Toby, ed. *Acting: A Handbook of the Stanislavsky Method*. Introduction by Lee Strasberg. New York: Crown Publishers, Inc., 1955.
A collection of essays by Stanislavsky, Vakhtangov, et al.

Funke, Lewis, and John E. Booth. *Actors Talk about Acting* (two volumes). New York: Avon Books, 1961.
Interviews with John Gielgud, Helen Hayes, Vivien Leigh, Morris Carnovsky, Shelley Winters, Bert Lahr, Sidney Poitier, Alfred Lunt, Lynn Fontanne, José Ferrer, Maureen Stapleton, Katherine Cornell, Paul Muni, Anne Bancroft.

Garfield, David. *The Actors Studio: A Player's Place*. Preface by Ellen Burstyn. New York:, Macmillan Collier Books, 1984.

Gorchakov, Nicolai. *Stanislavsky Directs*. Translated by Miriam Goldina; Foreword by Norris Houghton. New York: Limelight Editions, 1991.

Grotowski, Jerzy. *Towards a Poor Theater*. Preface by Peter Brook. Holstebro, Denmark: Odin Teatrets Forlag, 1968.

Hagen, Uta. *A Challenge for the Actor*. New York: Charles Scribner's Sons, 1991.

Hagen, Uta, with Haskell Frankel. *Respect for Acting*. New York: Macmillan, 1973.

Houghton, Norris. *Moscow Rehearsals: The Golden Age of the Soviet Theatre*. New York: Grove Press, Inc., 1962.

Joseph, B. L. *Elizabethan Acting*. 2nd ed. London: Oxford University Press, 1964.

Meisner, Sanford, and Dennis Longwell. *On Acting*. New York: Random House Vintage Books, 1987.

Moore, Sonia. *Training an Actor: The Stanislavsky System in Class*. New York: Penguin Books, 1979.

Potter, Helen. *Helen Potter's Impersonations*. New York: Edgar S. Werner, 1891.

Stanislavsky, Constantin. *An Actor Prepares*. Translated by Elizabeth Reynolds Hapgood. New York: Theatre Arts Books (23rd printing), 1969.

Stanislavsky, Constantin. *Building a Character*. Translated by Elizabeth Reynolds Hapgood. New York: Theatre Arts Books (14th printing), 1976.

Stanislavsky, Constantin. *Creating a Role*. Translated by Elizabeth Reynolds Hapgood. New York: Theatre Arts Books, (6th printing), 1976.

Stanislavsky, Constantin. *My Life in Art*. Translated by J. J. Robbins. New York: The World Publishing Co. Meridian Books (6th printing), 1966.

Stebbins, Genevieve. *Delsarte System of Expression*. New York: Edgar S. Werner Publishing & Supply Co., 1902.

Strasberg, Lee. *A Dream of Passion*. New York: Penguin Plume Books, 1987.

Strasberg at the Actors Studio: Tape-Recorded Sessions. Edited and with an Introduction by Robert H. Hethmon; Preface by Burgess Meredith. New York: Theatre Communications Group, 1991; (5th Printing), 2000.

6) Some Recordings

Recordings on Caedmon

For more information on the recordings listed below, which are widely available in bookstores, go to Caedmon's web address: www.harpercollins.com. Caedmon is now owned by HarperAudio.

The Caedmon Collection of English Poetry. William Shakespeare, John Milton, Thomas Hardy, et al. Read by John Gielgud, Dylan Thomas, James Mason, et al. Audiocassette ISBN 0694519111, 1998.

The Caedmon Poetry Collection. W. B. Yeats, T.S. Eliot, Gertrude Stein, et al. Read by William Butler Yeats, T.S. Eliot, Gertrude Stein, et al. CD 2895(3), 2000.

The Caedmon Short Story Collection. Ambrose Bierce, Guy de Maupassant, Saki, et al. Read by David McCallum, Claire Bloom, Keith Baxter, et al. CD 4154(6), 2000.

Dylan Thomas: The Caedmon Collection. Includes *Under Milk Wood* and *A Child's Christmas in Wales* read by the author. Introduced by Billy Collins. UACD 95(11), 2002. Eleven CDs.
A truly astounding collection of all his recordings.

The Edgar Allan Poe Audio Collection. Stories and poems read by Vincent Price and Basil Rathbone, Unabridged. CD 4148(5), 2000.

The Ernest Hemingway Audio Collection, Stories read by Ernest Hemingway and Charlton Heston. CD, ISBN 0694524980, 2001.

The James Joyce Audio Collection, Read by James Joyce, Cyril Cusack, Siobhan McKenna, et al., Abridged. Audio Cassette, ISBN 0060501790, 2002.

J.R.R. Tolkien Audio Collection, Read by the author and Christopher Tolkien. Abridged. CD, ISBN 0694525707, 2001.

Kurt Vonnegut, Jr. Audio Collection, Read by the author. Abridged. Audiocassette, ISBN 0694515361, 1995.

Lorraine Hansberry Audio Collection. Original Caedmon recordings of *Raisin in the Sun* and *To Be Young, Gifted, and Black.* Read by Ossie Davis, Ruby Dee, James Earl Jones, et al. HarperAudio, Audiocassette ISBN 0694525065, 2001.

The Mark Twain Audio Collection. Read by Ed Begley, Walter Brennan, et al., Unabridged. ACCD 144(6), 2001.

Robert Frost Poetry Collection, Poems read by the author, Unabridged. Audiocassette ISBN 0694522775, 2000.

Spine Chilling Tales of Horror. Excerpts from *Dracula,* performed by David McCallum and Carole Shelley; *Frankenstein,* performed by James Mason; *Dr. Jekyll and Mr. Hyde,* performed by Anthony Quayle, etc. CD 4253(6), 2002.

Recordings on Other Labels

About a Hundred Years: The History of Sound Recording. Voices of Arthur Conan Doyle, Sarah Bernhardt, Thomas Alva Edison, Johannes Brahms, Mahatma Gandhi, von Hindenburg, Neville Chamberlain, Winston Churchill, Leo Tolstoy, etc. Symposium CD 1222, 1997.

Great Actors of the Past. Compiled by Richard Bebb. Voices of Ellen Terry, Henry Irving, Sarah Bernhardt, Herbert Beerbohm Tree, Edwin Booth, Lewis Waller, Alexander Moissi, Julia Neilson and Fred Terry, Constant Coquelin, Joseph Jefferson, Tomasso Salvini, Cyril Maude. Argo Records, LP SW 510.

Great Historical Shakespeare Recordings and a Miscellany. Henry Irving, Ellen Terry, John Barrymore, Sarah Bernhardt, et al.; John Gielgud and Edith Evans in excerpts from *The Importance of Being Earnest;* Noël Coward and Gertrude Lawrence in excerpts from *Private Lives,* and much more. Naxos AudioBook 220012, 2000.

Great Shakespeareans. Voices of Edwin Booth, Herbert Beerbohm Tree, Arthur Bourchier, Lewis Waller, Ben Greet, John Barrymore, Sir Johnston Forbes-Robertson, Sir John Gielgud, Henry Ainley, Maurice Evans. Pearl, Gemm CD 9465, 1990.

In Their Own Voices: The U.S. Presidential Elections of 1908 and 1912. Voices of William Jennings Bryan, William H. Taft, Woodrow Wilson, and Theodore Roosevelt. Marston Records 52028-2 CD, 2000.

Othello, with excerpts from *Sanders of the River*. Voices of Paul Robeson, Uta Hagen, Jose Ferrer, Alexander Scourby, et al. Recorded in 1944. Pearl, Gemm CD 0037, 1998.

Poetry Speaks: Hear Great Poets Read Their Work from Tennyson to Plath. Book and 3 CDs. Narrated by Charles Osgood. Includes voices of Alfred, Lord Tennyson, Robert Browning, Walt Whitman, W. B. Yeats, Gertrude Stein, T. S. Eliot, Ezra Pound, Dorothy Parker, Edna St. Vincent Millay, Langston Hughes, Ogden Nash, Dylan Thomas, et al. Sourcebooks MediaFusion, 2001.

Proust, Marcel. *A la recherche du temps perdu: Du côté de chez Swann*. Texte intégrale recorded by André Dusollier. Éditions Thélème, CDs 654 and 655, n d.

Ruth Draper and Her Company of Characters: Selected Monologues. Includes *The Italian Lesson, The Actress, Doctors and Diets, A German Governess with a Class of Children, A Class in Greek Poise, On the Porch in a Maine Coast Village*, and *Three Women and Mr. Clifford*. BMG Special Products: DRC22685, 2000. 2 CDs.

Ruth Draper and Her Company of Characters: More Selected Monologues. Includes *A Children's Party in Philadelphia, A Scottish Immigrant at Ellis Island, Showing the Garden, At an Art Exhibition in Boston, In a Railway Station on the Western Plains, Opening a Bazaar, Three Generations in a Court of Domestic Relations, In a Church in Italy, Three Imaginary Folk-Songs*, and *A Debutante at a Dance*. BMG Special Products: DRC23805, 2001. 2 CDs.

Note: Both CD albums are available exclusively at the Ruth Draper web site: www.drapermonologues.com; e-mail: mail@drapermonologues.com.

The World of Ruth Draper. Performed by Patricia Norcia. Original Cast Records, CD OC-9900,1999.

Sir Michael Redgrave reads "On the Harmfulness of Tobacco"; "A Transgression"; "The First-Class Passenger" by Anton Chekhov. Directed by Arthur Luce Klein. Spoken Arts, SA 828, 1962. LP record.

Le Théâtre Parisien de Sarah Bernhardt à Sacha Guitry. Includes rare recordings of Sarah Bernhardt, Cocquelin Ainé (the original Cyrano de Bergerac), Yvette Guilbert, Sacha Guitry and Jean Cocteau. EMI France, CZS 7675392. 1992. 6 CDs.

About the Author

ROBERT BLUMENFELD, author of *Accents: A Manual for Actors,* lives and works as an actor, dialect coach and writer in New York City. Mr. Blumenfeld has been on the faculties of both the Stella Adler and National Shakespeare Conservatories. He has recorded more than 280 Talking Books for the American Foundation for the Blind. Among his favorites are *The Complete Sherlock Holmes* (four novels and fifty-six short stories) by Sir Arthur Conan Doyle; *Old Goriot* by Honoré de Balzac; *Balzac: A Biography* by Graham Robb; *The Hunchback of Notre Dame* by Victor Hugo; *The Count of Monte Cristo* by Alexandre Dumas; *Cromwell the Lord Protector* by Antonia Fraser; and *Jewish American Literature: A Norton Anthology*. As an actor he has worked in numerous regional and New York theaters. He created the roles of the Marquis of Queensberry and two prosecuting attorneys in the Off-Broadway hit play *Gross Indecency: The Three Trials of Oscar Wilde,* written and directed by Moisés Kaufman, and was also the production's dialect coach. On Broadway he was dialect coach for the musicals *Saturday Night Fever* and *The Scarlet Pimpernel* (the third version and national tour). Mr. Blumenfeld received the 1997 Canadian National Institute for the Blind's Torgi Award for the Talking Book of the Year in the Fiction category, for his recording of Pat Conroy's *Beach Music;* and the 1999 Alexander Scourby Talking Book Narrator of the Year Award in the Fiction category. He holds a B.A. in French from Rutgers University and an M.A. from Columbia University in French Language and Literature. At Rutgers University he completed his Ph.D. courses in Comparative Literature. He also speaks Italian and German, and has a smattering of Yiddish, Spanish and Russian.